PAUSANIAS

Travel Writing in Ancient Greece

Classical Literature and Society

Series Editor: David Taylor

CLASSICAL LITERATURE AND SOCIETY

Pausanias

Travel Writing in Ancient Greece

Maria Pretzler

Duckworth

First published in 2007 by
Gerald Duckworth & Co. Ltd.
90-93 Cowcross Street, London EC1M 6BF
Tel: 020 7490 7300
Fax: 020 7490 0080
inquiries@duckworth-publishers.co.uk
www.ducknet.co.uk

A catalogue record for this book is available
from the British Library

ISBN 978 0 7156 3496 7

Typeset by Ray Davies
Printed and bound in Great Britain by
MPG Books Ltd, Bodmin, Cornwall

Contents

Editor's Foreword

The aim of this series is to consider Greek and Roman literature primarily in relation to genre and theme. Its authors hope to break new ground in doing so but with no intention of dismissing current interpretation where this is sound; they will be more concerned to engage closely with text, subtext and context. The series therefore adopts a homologous approach in looking at classical writers, one of whose major achievements was the fashioning of distinct modes of thought and utterance in poetry and prose. This led them to create a number of literary genres evolving their own particular forms, conventions and rules – genres which live on today in contemporary culture.

Although studied within a literary tradition, these writers are also considered within their social and historical context, and the themes they explore are often both highly specific to that context and yet universal and everlasting. The ideas they conceive and formulate and the issues they debate find expression in a particular language, Latin or Greek, and belong to their particular era in the classical past. But they are also fully translatable into a form that is accessible as well as intelligible to those living in later centuries, in their own vernacular. Hence all quoted passages are rendered into clear, modern English.

These are books, then, which are equally for readers with or without knowledge of the Greek and Latin languages and with or without an acquaintance with the civilisation of the ancient world. They have plenty to offer the classical scholar, and are ideally suited to students reading for a degree in classical subjects. Yet they will interest too those studying European and contemporary literature, history and culture who wish to discover the roots and springs of our classical inheritance.

The series owes a special indebtedness and thanks to Pat Easterling, who from the start was a constant source of advice and encouragement. Others whose help has been invaluable are Robin Osborne who, if ever we were at a loss to think of an author for a particular topic, almost always came up with a suitable name or two and was never stinting of his time or opinion, and Tony Woodman, now at Virginia. The unfailing assistance of the late John W. Roberts, editor of the *Oxford Dictionary of the Classical World*, is also gratefully acknowledged. Deborah Blake, Duckworth's indefatigable Editorial Director, has throughout offered full support, boundless enthusiasm and wise advice.

Finally, I pay tribute to the inspirational genius which Michael Gunningham, *fons et origo* of the series and an editor of consummate skill and phenomenal energy, brought to the enterprise. His imprint is everywhere: *sine quo, non.*

David Taylor

Preface

'And what do you do?' 'I am working on Pausanias: he wrote a kind of travel book about Greece in the second century AD'. Over the years I have often found myself in the position of having to introduce Pausanias in one sentence, and the one thing I have learned above all else in the process is that one simply cannot do him justice in a few words. This is mainly because his work is unique: it does not fit into any generally known genre, and even among ancient texts there is nothing quite like it. Pausanias' *Periegesis* defies simple definitions, and it is highly relevant to many different areas of study within the fields of classical archaeology, ancient history and classics; beyond classical scholarship the *Periegesis* also has the potential to become a crucial source for the study of reception, art history, comparative literature (particularly travel literature) and the history of modern Greece.

This book is aimed at readers at all levels in these different disciplines, and indeed anyone who is interested in finding out more about the history of Greece and its historical landscape. I have aimed to make the subject as widely accessible as possible. All ancient texts are translated (translations are mine) and Greek phrases which are relevant to the argument are transliterated. I have, however, also included the original texts in the notes to allow those with Greek to form their own judgement. Transliterating Greek into English is an inexact science, and any overly zealous attempt to achieve consistency would produce awkward idiosyncrasies. My main principle is to make accessibility a priority over consistency. Ultimately, every author's transliterations will be an individual compromise based on common sense and personal taste. I prefer what might be called a 'moderately Greek' transliteration (Chaironeia, Lykourgos, Schoinous) to either the traditional Latinised version (Chaeronea, Lycurgus, Schoenus) or what might be called a 'purist' Greek form of transliteration which can make even familiar names look rather unusual (Khaironeia, Lukourgos, Skhoinous). Common English names such as Athens (Athenai) or Corinth (Korinthos) have been retained, and I have been more inclined to use a Latinised form where the Greek spelling suggests a pronunciation that differs from established practice (Thucydides, Mycenae rather than Thukydides, Mykenai). Modern Greek proves even more difficult to transliterate, because one needs to strike a balance between contemporary pronunciation and the spelling which is often much closer to ancient Greek equivalents and therefore looks more familiar. I generally prefer a transliteration that reflects pronunciation, but where I am dealing with ancient names that are again in use today I have opted for an 'archaising' transliteration which makes the similarity between ancient and modern names immediately apparent (e.g. Nauplia instead of Nafplio, Heraion instead of Ireo).

It has been more than ten years since I started to give serious thought to Pausanias' *Periegesis*: these years led me from my undergraduate days to postgraduate studies and through the early stages of an academic career. Many debts are incurred on such a route, beginning with academic staff and fellow students at the Department of Ancient History in Graz, particularly Klaus Tausend, Günter Stangl and Kaja Harter-Uibopuu, who first taught me to interpret and appreciate the Greek landscape and its historical significance. Once I was ready to explore Greece on my own, Christiane Reinhard patiently accompanied me on my travels in the footsteps of Pausanias. Thanks are also due to the Norwegian Arkadia Survey team at Tegea, particularly Knut Ødegård and Erik Østby. My postgraduate work at Oxford was supervised by Simon Hornblower, Ewen Bowie and Robin Osborne, whose support and rigorous questioning allowed me to explore many new aspects of Pausanias' work. Over the years many colleagues at Merton College, St John's College, Somerville College and at Swansea offered stimulating discussion, support and helpful criticism which led to further lines of enquiry; without them my work would certainly have been much less fruitful and enjoyable. I would particularly like to thank Nicholas Purcell, Tobias Reinhardt, Karen Ní Mheallaigh and John Morgan. Heartfelt thanks are also due to my colleagues at Swansea for their patience and encouragement in the last frantic months of 'writing up'. Research that ultimately fed into this book was at various stages funded by Merton College, the Oxford Craven Fund and a Kings College London Library Fellowship. Many satisfying hours of discovery were spent in the Bodleian and Sackler Libraries at Oxford, at the British School at Athens and in the special collections department of KCL library. I would also like to thank the editors at Duckworth: Michael Gunningham devised this series and commissioned this book, Deborah Blake has been extremely supportive during the various stages of writing and revision, and David Taylor read the first typescript and made many useful suggestions.

One of the most pleasant aspects of my work on Pausanias has been to make the acquaintance of fellow-Pausaniacs and scholars in related fields who have generally shown great generosity in providing ideas and discussion. I am especially grateful to Jas Elsner for his many encouraging suggestions, particularly concerning the study of Pausanias reception. Colin Adams, William Hutton, John Morgan, Karen Ní Mheallaigh, Knut Ødegård, Robert Porod and Yannis Tzifopoulos gave me access to unpublished material. Special thanks are due to those who read a draft of this book: Jas Elsner, Kate Heard, William Hutton, Karen Ní Mheallaigh,

Preface

Robert Porod, Barbara Porod and Alan Renwick. They all offered invaluable encouragement and advice – all errors that remain are of course solely mine.

Last but not least, my gratitude is due to my parents without whose support I would never have been able to turn my favourite interests into an occupation.

Swansea, March 2007

List of Illustrations

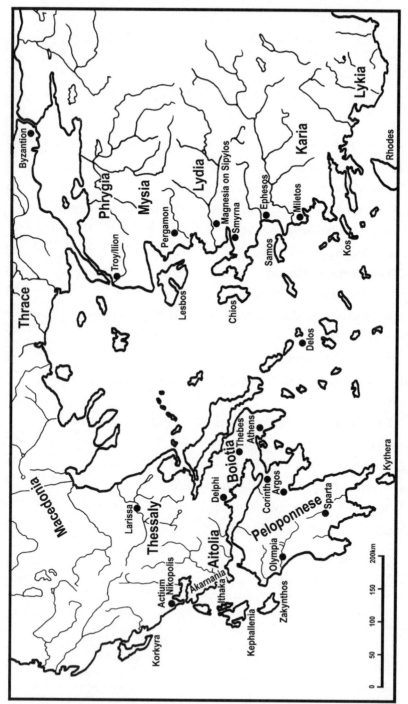

Fig. 1. Greece and the Aegean.

Approaching Pausanias' *Periegesis*

> On the Greek mainland, facing the Cyclades Islands and the Aegean Sea, Cape Sounion juts out from the mainland of Attica. When you have sailed around the cape, there is a harbour and a temple of Sounian Athena on the highest point of the promontory.[1] (Paus. 1.1.1)

Few readers approach Pausanias' *Periegesis* from the beginning, sailing round Cape Sounion and arriving in Athens, before following his convoluted routes through Greece. Not many, in fact, have read the whole work, but almost anyone with an interest in ancient Greece will have 'come across' Pausanias – usually by looking up particular passages: the *Periegesis* contains useful material for many purposes.

Pausanias took the opportunity to describe Greece at a time when most of its cities and sites were still standing, filled with art and treasures, and many were proud to remember and commemorate centuries of a great past. His work inspired thorough research into the historical topography of Greece, and guided early excavators on some of the most important ancient sites. Archaeologists working in southern and central mainland Greece today still find Pausanias invaluable, or at least unavoidable. Readers who have the chance to take the *Periegesis* to Greece might enjoy the many connections with the historical topography which seem to be intact even today, and they will appreciate its similarities to a travel guide while also realising the difficulties of following its descriptions on the ground. Pausanias covers a wide range of topics, well beyond what might be seen as directly relevant to the description of sites, and he offers a lot of information that cannot be found elsewhere. He was able to draw on much of the knowledge accumulated throughout classical antiquity, and his work offers a good sample of the interests and preoccupations of the educated élite of his time. The *Periegesis* is a unique source for many aspects of Greek religion and customs, it presents art and architecture together with myths and historical traditions in their local context, and it records a wealth of ancient place names which no other region of the ancient world can match. In recent years scholars have increasingly recognised Pausanias' value as a source for Roman Greece and, more generally, for the culture of the Greek east of the Roman empire.

Traditionally Pausanias has been considered a rather dull writer without much literary skill who was simply recording facts, which made it easy to treat his work as a mine of information without much further consideration. Recent research has, however, shown that Pausanias had ambitious literary aims which need to be taken into account in interpreting his text.[2] As an author, Pausanias almost makes a show of keeping a low profile, but he allows us to discern a man who is confident in his judgement and knowledge. In fact, the *Periegesis* leaves no doubt that its author spent many years travelling, researching and writing. Numerous cross-references and a complex geographical framework show that the whole work is carefully planned and structured. Nevertheless, individual passages can pose intricate problems, and at times it seems difficult to explain mistakes or omissions. For example, how could Pausanias at the start of his work describe sailing round Cape Sounion but not mention the temple of Poseidon which is so famous today, or identify it wrongly as a temple of Athena?[3]

Problems with Pausanias as a source arise not only from his own errors and peculiarities. In the past his work has often been mined for information without much consideration for context or chronology: a knowledge of the *Periegesis*, its background and its aims is necessary for anyone who wants to make good use of the many treasures it can offer. Tackling the *Periegesis* as a whole is not an easy task. It is difficult to gain an overview and to keep track of passages that might combine to give a more complete view of the author's opinions and approach. Studying the work in depth almost inevitably requires some elaborate method of collecting passages with common themes, just to allow the reader to appreciate the range of interests and ideas covered. While it remains crucial to gain a full overview of the range of opinions expressed in the *Periegesis*, I believe that it is impossible to understand Pausanias merely through stubborn compilation. His opinion on a subject cannot be deduced simply by collating and summarising all relevant passages, because the work is more than a sum of its many parts. Particular statements need to be interpreted within their context in the work, and with special attention to the circumstances in any given place that may have triggered a specific comment. Pausanias' errors and omissions, though highly problematic for those who use the *Periegesis* as a source for ancient Greece, can provide particularly valuable insights into his attitudes, ideas and methods. In short, it is crucial to gain an overview without losing sight of the details.

Readers of Pausanias, whether they are just interested in a specific place or piece of information, or want to get to know his work as a whole, need to be alert to the many factors that may have shaped the *Periegesis*. Apart from the author's methods and aims, we need to consider the cultural background that he shared with his informants and intended readership. Pausanias' approach to the cultural landscape of Greece should be seen as a deliberate response to already existing literary traditions. His work and his readers' expectations were shaped by travel literature (in the widest sense) and by the many texts defining the history and culture of Greece. The overarching theme of the *Periegesis* is Greece itself. Pausanias is discovering, describing and defining Greece and Greek culture for his readers, and the many details he records should be seen as integral parts of an enquiry into all things truly Greek. One crucial factor in our understanding of Pausanias has often been overlooked: since its rediscovery in the Renaissance his work has had a profound cultural impact. The *Periegesis* has not just shaped views of Greece, ancient and modern, but it has also influenced attitudes to ancient art and historical topography, and, last but not least, it has had an impact on travel writing and modern 'cultural' travel guides. It is for this reason that Pausanias' approach sometimes seems comfortably familiar.[4] For example, though experts like to object when the *Periegesis* is labelled as an 'ancient travel guide',[5] in fact modern travel guides are influenced by a long tradition of writers who travelled in Pausanias' footsteps, and some of the earliest purely archaeological guides were inspired by the close connections between the *Periegesis* and the ancient sites in Greece.[6] An understanding of Pausanias, therefore, requires not just examination of the factors that shaped his work in antiquity, but also consideration of the influence the *Periegesis* has had on our own culture and preconceptions.

Before exploring a major literary work more thoroughly, it is important to review its basic features and to survey the essential facts that are known or have been established as a consensus in the modern scholarly tradition. The text we call Pausanias' *Periegesis Hellados* ('*Tour around Greece*') is preserved in a number of manuscripts, none earlier than the fifteenth century, and all directly or indirectly based on a single copy which probably reached Italy soon after AD 1400.[7] The text itself never mentions either the title of the work or the name of its author, and it is possible that an original introduction stating name and aims of the author has been lost.[8] The author himself refers to his work as *logos* (account) or *syngraphê* (written text, account), both very general terms which do not imply a specific literary genre.[9] Some of the manuscripts provide the name of the author, although the title of the work varies.[10] The sixth-century AD geographical dictionary of Stephanos of Byzantion shows that in late antiquity the description of Greece under discussion here was already known as Pausanias' *Periegesis Hellados*: Stephanos provides specific references that allow a secure identification.[11]

The word *periêgêsis* is related to the verb *periêgeisthai*, which means 'to lead around', 'to show around'. This seems a fitting title for Pausanias' work, which seeks to take the reader on an imaginary tour, describing everything along the way that he considers worth seeing and recording.[12] There were other ancient literary works with the title *Periegesis*, but only fragments are preserved, and their form and content is often reconstructed by using Pausanias, which makes it difficult to draw conclusions about possible genre conventions, if there was indeed a *periêgêsis* genre. Some *periêgêseis* covered large regions and may have offered geographical overviews, while others were apparently very comprehensive guides to (or descriptions of) particular sites.[13] Pausanias combines features of both by

3

Fig. 2. Overview of Pausanias' 'itinerary'.

offering detailed accounts of many sites in a relatively large area and in this his work may have been unique.[14]

Pausanias' work consists of ten books in which the text follows a complex itinerary though different parts of central and southern Greece (Figs 2, 3). In Book I Pausanias approaches Attica by sea, landing at the Piraeus and exploring the city of Athens. Then he deals with parts of Attica and moves on to Megara. Book II covers Corinth and some of its neighbours as well as the Argolid, and from there Pausanias starts a clockwise tour around the Peloponnese, passing through Lakonia with Sparta as its most important city (Book III) and then moving on to

Fig. 3. Regional book divisions of the *Periegesis*.

Messenia (Book IV). The description of Elis takes two books (V, VI) because Olympia is treated in meticulous detail. Book VII, which focuses on Achaia, finishes the round trip along the coasts of the Peloponnese, after which Pausanias turns inland to describe Arkadia (Book VIII). He then returns to central Greece, describing Boiotia with a strong focus on Thebes in Book IX. The last book features Phokis, including a description of Delphi and a quick overview of Ozolian Lokris.

Pausanias was aware of the large scope of the task he had set for himself: during his description of the Acropolis he cuts short a historical comment by seemingly calling himself to task:

I have to get on with my account (*logos*), because I am dealing with all Greek matters (*panta ta Hellênika*) in the same way.[15] (Paus. 1.26.4)

Together with the title transmitted by Stephanos of Byzantion, *Periêgêsis Hellados*, this seems to suggest that the work was intended to deal with 'all of Greece', as '*panta ta Hellênika*' is often translated into English, yet it does not do so in any straightforward sense. 'Greek matters' were certainly not restricted to the area described in Pausanias' *Periegesis*. Since the archaic period the Greek world had included many areas around the coasts of the Mediterranean and the Black Sea, and with Alexander's conquests it grew considerably, expanding east into Asia. With the exception of Athens, the great cultural centres of the Greek world in the Roman period were situated outside mainland Greece, in Asia Minor and around the eastern Mediterranean. In fact, Pausanias' own use of the terms Hellas or *to Hellênikon* and *ta Hellênika* do not consistently refer to a particular region, let alone exactly the region covered in the *Periegesis*.[16] Mainland Greece could be seen as a distinct entity, but no ancient geographical definition coincides with Pausanias' selection. It is difficult to find fault with the regions that are included, but, whichever ancient definition of Greece one might choose, there are always a few areas missing without clear reason (Fig. 4).[17] Homer was recognised by many as prime geographical authority, and the places described in the Catalogue of Ships in the *Iliad* would have offered a generally acceptable framework for a *periêgêsis* of Greece.[18] Pausanias deals with issues of Homeric geography,[19] but he leaves out crucial areas, such as parts of Lokris, Thessaly and Aitolia, and one might have expected the inclusion of some of the islands as well, especially Euboia. Pausanias' Greece also does not coincide with the province of Achaia or the area of the Delphic Amphiktyony, as some have suggested.[20] One might exclude some regions on the grounds that they do not play much of a role in classical literature or, in the case of Aitolia or Akarnania, that they did not contain many ancient Greek city-states (*poleis*), but this would still make the absence of parts of central Greece difficult to explain. Is it possible that Pausanias did not finish his book or that the one manuscript which reached Renaissance Europe was incomplete? Stephanos of Byzantion, discussing Tamyna, a city in Euboia, does include one reference to 'Pausanias' Book XI', and some scholars have accepted this as good evidence for the existence of an eleventh book, while Robert went further and suggested that the original number of books was fourteen. Stephanos' reference to 'Book XI', however, may be due to a corruption of the text, as Meineke argues.[21] The best argument against the theory that a large amount of Pausanias' text might be missing is the existence of numerous cross-references, which (with one possible exception) all refer to existing passages.[22]

Pausanias probably had a plan for his whole work when he started to write, and his original outline was apparently quite close to the text as we

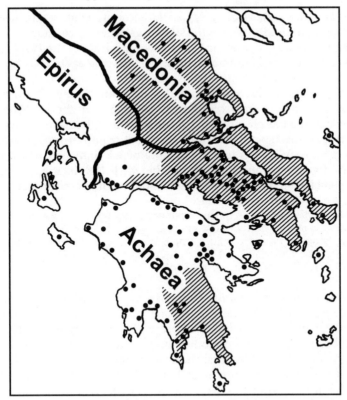

Fig. 4. Alternative geographies of Greece: Homeric sites, Roman provinces, Delphic amphiktyony. Approximate boundaries of the Roman provinces in Greece are based on Alcock (1993) 15.

Shaded area: regions included in the Delphic Amphiktyony of the classical period, based on Paus. 10.8.2 (cf. Aischines 2.116).

• = Sites mentioned in the *Iliad*, based on Allen (1921).

know it today. It has long been recognised that the ten books were written in order, and over thirty of Pausanias' cross-references refer, usually in the future tense, to passages that were yet to be written. For example, Pausanias mentions the sphinx on the helmet of Pheidias' Athena in the Parthenon, and adds: 'what is said about the Sphinx I shall write when my *logos* has reached Boiotia'. Eight books later, on the road from Thebes to Onchestos, he passes the mountain where the Sphinx was said to have lived, and he does indeed discuss various relevant traditions.[23] The regional divisions of the work were clearly devised from the beginning, because Pausanias usually refers to his books by region 'when I reach Delphi in my Phokian *logos*', 'in my *logos* about Arkadia'.[24] What is more, apparently he had a detailed plan of the sites and monuments he would describe, and the historical or mythical accounts that would need to be included in a particular passage. Pausanias' systematic adherence to his plan is remarkable, considering that the composition of the *Periegesis* took fifteen to twenty years, and perhaps more, from the early 160s at the very latest to about AD 180.[25]

Book X ends abruptly, and, although a case can be made that Pausanias may have intended it that way,[26] it is possible that the last book is not finished, or that a few chapters at its end were lost. The whole pace of Book X, however, is not as we have come to expect from Pausanias. Compared with the exhaustive treatment of Olympia which fills about one and a half books, the twenty-seven chapters dealing with Delphi seem short.[27] The description of the sanctuary starts with a statement about the victor statues:

> I will note those monuments that seemed to me most worth writing about. The athletes and participants in musical competitions which are neglected by most people I do not consider worth the effort, and those athletes who have left some fame behind I have presented in my description of Elis (*en logôi tôi ... es Êleious*).[28] (Paus. 10.9.1-2)

This is a surprising statement, coming from a man who meticulously fills eighteen chapters with the description of almost two hundred victor statues at Olympia, and who carefully reads inscriptions even on empty statue bases to record more monuments in his work. The description of Phokis is generally less detailed than we might expect on Pausanias' past record.[29] Finally, the treatment of Lokris is definitely unusual: Ozolian Lokris, the area west of Phokis, is quickly dealt with in one long chapter (10.38), while Opountian Lokris, a region northeast of Boiotia, is not included at all. It seems that while writing Book IX Pausanias still had a more lengthy treatment of Lokris in mind, because he promises to discuss a particular mythical genealogy in his Lokrian *logos*, a subject which is not raised in the one extant chapter dealing with this region.[30] This is the only cross-reference that does not match up with an appropriate passage. It seems possible, therefore, that Book X was rushed for some reason, with less time for the full consideration of even small towns and less famous monuments that we see elsewhere in his work.

The routes described in the *Periegesis* are a complex literary construct which gives the text a well-defined structure. They do not represent an account of an actual journey, although it is clear that the author has personally seen most of the places he describes.[31] The regions covered in the ten books are further divided into territories of individual cities, and, after some experimentation with the format of city descriptions in Book I, Pausanias follows a set pattern as he moves from one *polis* to the next. He usually approaches on a main route, and after crossing the boundaries he proceeds to the urban centre. At some point, usually when the town has been reached, there is a summary of the highlights of local history, including the mythical past, and then the reader is presented with the interesting monuments in the city. Pausanias deals with sites in the countryside by following major routes as far as the *polis* boundaries, discussing everything along the route he finds worth seeing. The route to the next city on his imaginary tour is tackled last, leading across another border, where Pausanias starts his description of the next city which will be organised in a similar way. This system is used throughout the *Periegesis*, but not without allowing for some variation.[32] After all, some flexibility was essential because of the great diversity of material that could be found in Greek cities, for example differences in size, the amount of interesting material to report and variations in the relative importance of local history and preserved remains. At times the structure of the text is also used to convey a particular interpretation of the historical landscape, for example when Pausanias describes most of Boiotia on routes leading out through the gates of Thebes, treating the whole region as if it were part of the Theban countryside.[33]

Pausanias was aware that he could offer only a subjective selection of the information he collected on a site. Indeed, he seems rather proud of his selective approach.

> To avoid misconceptions, I said in my account of Attica that I had not presented everything, but only a selection of what was most worth remembering. I will repeat this before my description of Sparta: from the beginning my account was intended to select the most noteworthy from the many traditions current everywhere that are not worth recording. This was a well-considered plan, and I shall not deviate from it.[34] (Paus. 3.11.1)

There are many instances where Pausanias stresses that he wants to focus on those things most worth recording, worth remembering or worth seeing,[35] but what exactly does this mean? The question of selectivity in the *Periegesis* has led to a lot of scholarly discussion, especially when conspicuous features of the archaeological record are absent from the description of a site.[36] For example, Pausanias ignores conspicuous Roman buildings, but he does not exclude all Roman structures; in fact, at times he discusses recent monuments in some detail, and some are labelled as Roman while others are mentioned without any indication of their age.[37] The site descriptions focus on places with some cultural significance, such as buildings and monuments with links to local history or myths. There is a clear preference for ancient monuments and sacred places, as well as features in the landscape that could be connected to common Greek traditions, but Pausanias takes into account later periods, particularly where this allows him to discover and present information that was not widely known.[38] It seems impossible to establish consistent criteria, and it is never made explicit what makes a story or monument 'worth recording'. Local circumstances and personal interest were probably important, but

9

literary considerations, such as the length of the description of a particular city and the chance to include particular narratives or themes may have had an influence, too. In the end, what is 'worth seeing' or 'worth recording' is a matter of the author's personal judgement, as Pausanias reminds us when he leaves Athens:

> These are in my opinion the most famous of the traditions (*logoi*) and sights (*theôrêmata*) of the Athenians, and from the beginning my account has selected from much material what is worth recording.[39] (Paus. 1.39.3)

In this passage he also addresses another conspicuous feature of his work, the combination of site descriptions with 'digressions', as the term *logoi* is often translated. The word digression suggests a certain lack of discipline or will to stick to the main subject, but for Pausanias, the *logoi* are clearly as important a part of his work as the descriptive passages. They provide information about myth or history, local customs and comparisons from the Greek world and beyond, and they offer learned comments on a variety of subjects, be they literary, cultural or in the widest sense scientific. The *logoi* vary in length from an explanatory sentence to the twenty-nine chapters on Messenian history which constitute over three-quarters of Book IV. In many cases, the reasons for including a particular *logos* are quite clear, but sometimes Pausanias seems to go off on a tangent on the flimsiest of pretexts. For example, the account of a battle at Mantinea finishes thus:

> Leokydes, who was joint commander of the Megalopolitans with Lydiades, had, as the Arkadians say, an ancestor named Arkesilaos who lived in Lykosoura nine generations earlier. There he saw the sacred deer of her who is called Despoina (Lady) suffering from old age. This deer had a collar around its neck, with an inscription: 'I was captured as a fawn when Agapenor went to Ilion'. This proves that the deer is an animal which lives even longer than the elephant.[40] (Paus. 8.10.10)

It is not always easy to understand why Pausanias is including particular comments: in this respect both site descriptions and *logoi* pose similar problems in understanding his choices in selecting his material. In spite of some surprises, however, these comments or discussions are an integral part of the text, and what the author says about his account of Athens is true for the whole book: Pausanias' Greece is evoked by the combination of those *logoi* and *theôrêmata* that are worth recording. Some modern translated editions have attempted to make the *Periegesis* look more like a modern guidebook by omitting parts of the text, usually the *logoi*. This is a misrepresentation of Pausanias' work, and it discards one of its most valuable assets, namely the unique ancient perspective on the meanings of the cultural landscape of Greece.[41]

In fact, the combination of *logoi* and *theôrêmata* lends some credence to

1. Approaching Pausanias' Periegesis

Pausanias' claim that he is dealing with 'all things Greek'. As we have already seen, his work does not coincide with any conventional geographical definition of Greece. Together with the *logoi*, however, Pausanias' description provides a thorough survey of Greek culture, focusing on history, traditions, religious customs and beliefs. The information on offer in the *logoi* is more than just a documentation of a particular region: comparative material takes into account much of the Greek world and sometimes areas beyond, and Pausanias' interpretation contributes to a picture that is much wider than just a collection of all those details he observed at particular sites in Greece. The very structure of the *Periegesis* with its insistence in moving from city to city to observe local peculiarities reflects a crucial aspect of Greek life: the importance of the *polis* with its own history and identity.

Pausanias' *Periegesis* is the most extensive text surviving from antiquity that deals with a traveller's experiences, and it can therefore be considered as travel literature.[42] There was no established genre of travel literature in ancient Greece, and I use the term 'travel literature' in the widest sense, referring to any texts that deal with the act of travelling or that record the encounter between an observer and a particular landscape. In order to understand the traditions of travel writing which may have influenced Pausanias it is necessary to investigate as wide a range of texts as possible, including examples where perhaps just a part of a text could be considered as travel literature. From the *Odyssey* and the early geographical tradition to the novels and city panegyrics of the Roman period and through to pilgrims' accounts from late antiquity, the ancients found many ways of turning travel experiences, real or imaginary, into texts. The selection of relevant examples is problematic and can perhaps never be fully satisfactory, which may explain why the general interest in travel literature is only slowly reaching the field of classics, and why the value of Pausanias' *Periegesis* for this particular field of study has attracted little scholarly attention until recently.[43] Pausanias' work can contribute to our understanding of ancient attitudes to historically significant landscapes, and it provides a detailed example of one man's attempts to make sense of his travel experience. The *Periegesis* also records the interdependence and conflict between a visitor's perspective and the self-presentation and self-image of his local informants, reminding us that travel is a form of communication, a discourse between insiders and an outside observer. At the same time, the study of other ancient approaches to writing about regions and places allows a better understanding of the choices that were open to Pausanias when he decided to write about his encounter with Greece, and the deliberate decisions about genre, structure and focus that shaped the *Periegesis*.

Since its rediscovery in the Renaissance Pausanias' work has been recognised as a valuable source for ancient Greece, a mine of antiquarian, historical and topographical information for various purposes. The history

11

of scholarly attention to the work itself, however, presents a rather mixed picture, reflecting the preferences and habits of the different disciplines concerned with the ancient world. From the seventeenth century onwards visitors to Greece found Pausanias' work an excellent resource for the reconstruction of the country's ancient topography.[44] Its usefulness for this purpose was easy to recognise, and by the early nineteenth century, when the movement for the liberation of Greece inspired many travellers from western Europe to visit Greece, Pausanias' *Periegesis* not only served as a travel guide but it was also used systematically to discover and identify ancient remains.[45] After the foundation of the Greek state in 1821 more detailed studies of routes and sites only increased the trust in Pausanias' accuracy, especially once the excavations of major sites such as Olympia, Delphi or Mycenae were under way.[46] Numismatics, epigraphy and the study of ancient art were also developing rapidly and provided further independent ancient evidence that could confirm Pausanias' account, sometimes even in cases where it seems difficult to believe him.[47] For scholars who used the *Periegesis* in the field, the value of his work was rarely in question, and discrepancies between the ancient report and the results of modern research were often just seen as a matter of discovering the correct interpretation of the relevant passages.[48] By the end of the nineteenth century research had progressed so far that an overview was needed, and two multi-volume commentaries appeared within a few years of each other: Frazer's in English, and Hitzig and Blümner's in German.[49]

Literary scholars were less willing to acknowledge the quality of the *Periegesis*. The work belonged to a group of texts that were seen as the output of a decadent Greek world under Roman rule which were not on a par with the great works of the heyday of classical Athens. Even among those late 'inferior' texts Pausanias was seen as second-rate, because he uses a style that is widely perceived as awkward. The *Periegesis* also failed to gain the respect of historians, because it contains much problematic historical information that seems to contradict the respected classical historiographers.[50] At the same time, however, the work was an invaluable source for Greek mythology and religion that could hardly be discarded. The extreme response to this dilemma was pioneered by Wilamowitz and elaborated by some of his pupils, who suggested that Pausanias had not, in fact, recorded his own observations, but that he had compiled his work from earlier literary sources.[51] This idea was never universally accepted, and prompted contradiction even among contemporaries. Ultimately, the prevailing opinion on Pausanias was that of a reliable reporter without literary aspirations, or an author with literary aspirations but no talent to match. These views were compatible with the low opinion of literary scholars while at the same time allowing the assumption that the information in the *Periegesis* could be used without much attention to its author's objectives and methods.[52] Even Frazer, a fervent advocate of the *Periegesis* with a special interest in religious and mythological details, often evinces this attitude by focusing on the site descriptions, while paying little attention to Pausanias' *logoi*, except where connections to other ancient sources needed to be pointed out, and where contradictions or discrepancies demanded discussion.[53]

For a long time after the end of the 'Pausanias boom' around 1900, attitudes apparently changed little. The *Periegesis* remained crucial for archaeological work in Greece. Further efforts to identify sites led to a more scholarly approach to topographical studies, inspiring scholars to investigate the Greek landscape beyond the great sanctuaries and cities and to look at smaller towns and settlements, rural sites or ancient roads, while excavations at the large sites were also still in progress.[54] Papachatzis's five-volume archaeological commentary of the 1960s demonstrates the ongoing dialogue between archaeology and Pausanias' text. At the same time, classicists paid little attention to Pausanias for decades; Regenbogen's article in Pauly and Wissowa's *Realencyclopädie* offered many new perspectives, but did not inspire further debate.[55] Habicht's seminal Sather lectures, published in 1985, demonstrate that Pausanias studies had suffered from the continuing division between archaeology and classics. Habicht presents numerous examples to demonstrate how archaeology or epigraphy can confirm Pausanias' text as an eye-witness account, and finally lays to rest Wilamowitz' old idea that the *Periegesis* was compiled from earlier texts and therefore unreliable. Few with experience of using Pausanias in the field in Greece would have subscribed to this idea in the first place, but it was still necessary to remind classicists of the reliability of Pausanias as a guide, and the quality of the information he offers. Habicht shows little admiration for Pausanias' literary efforts, which he presents as a failure, but he established the *Periegesis* as a subject worthy of classicists' attention. The book proved a turning point, perhaps in concert with increased interest in the Greek east of the Roman empire and the phenomenon of the Second Sophistic.

In the preface to Alcock, Cherry and Elsner's 2001 collection of articles on Pausanias, the editors proclaim a new turn-of-the century boom, mirroring the scholarly activities around 1900.[56] Two series of multi-volume text editions with translation and commentary are in progress, one in Italian (Valla) and one in French (Budé).[57] Pausanias' literary efforts have also received more attention, for example in a volume dealing with the historiographical aspects of his work,[58] and Hutton's *Describing Greece* focuses on the structure, language and literary aspirations of the *Periegesis*.[59] Both classics and archaeology have abandoned an almost exclusive focus on the archaic and classical periods and the last three decades have seen an increasing interest in Roman Greece and the Greek literature of the Roman east.[60] This sheds new light on the world Pausanias describes, and on the cultural background that he shared with his informants as well as with his intended readership. Archaeologists, however, are becoming more sceptical about the *Periegesis* as new methodologies and research questions reveal aspects of ancient Greece about which Pausanias has nothing to say. Targeted topographical studies have been replaced by systematic field-surveys which have led to the discovery of many sites that Pausanias did not mention at all, for example farms or small settlements, and excavators are no longer exclusively interested in grand architecture and works of art. In fact, there is a growing apprehension among field archaeologists about using the *Periegesis*, as the re-evaluation of past research shows just how profoundly his description has influenced researchers' aims and interests in the past, sometimes to the exclusion of alternative lines of enquiry.[61] Pausanias remains a crucial source for all fields of classical study, but as the respect for his literary efforts grows, and as he is more firmly placed in his immediate historical context, it is no longer possible to accept the *Periegesis* as an unproblematic source of information. The increased interest in Pausanias has a profound impact on how we understand and use his work.[62]

In the light of the rapid development of Pausanias studies in recent years a new general assessment of the *Periegesis* is long overdue, not just for those with a special interest in the subject, but for anyone who uses Pausanias as a source. This book aims to provide a rounded picture of the *Periegesis*, considering its cultural and literary context, the process of its composition, and its impact. I begin by looking at the author and his background: Chapter 2 investigates Pausanias' aims and attitudes, and what he reveals about himself, as well as his historical context and the cultural influences that shaped his work. This is followed by a discussion of the realities of ancient travel in Chapter 3 which also looks at travelling as an aspect of ancient élite culture, and offers an opportunity to consider Pausanias' activities as a traveller and researcher in Greece. The central part of the book focuses on specific aspects of the *Periegesis*. Chapter 4 is a survey of ancient travel literature and the variety of ancient literary responses to the experience of travel. This includes an assessment of Pausanias' literary options when he decided to write about Greece, and of the specific choices he made in composing his work. The treatment of space in ancient travel literature is the subject of Chapter 5. How does an author convey the geographical layout of an area he is describing? How does he describe the landscape and the setting of particular sites? What meanings does he attach to specific features in the landscape? I pay special attention to ancient conventions and preferences in describing mainland Greece. Chapter 6 deals with the role of time and chronology in Pausanias' work, and with his efforts as a historian. Pausanias' way of combining history and topography is the main theme of Chapter 7, which uses the description of the Arkadian city Tegea to illustrate how historical and memorial landscapes are represented in the *Periegesis*. In Chapter 8 I investigate the role of public art in Pausanias' Greece and analyse his approach to works of art in comparison with ancient art theory and other Greek texts which contain descriptions of paintings or statues. The final two chapters deal with the long-term impact of the *Periegesis*. Since its re-discovery six hundred years ago, Pausanias' description has shaped the basic methods and assumptions of classical archaeologists, art historians and cultural historians, and it had an influence of the discipline of classical studies as a whole. Last but not least, I discuss the impact of the *Periegesis* on attitudes to Greece in Western Europe, and its role in Greek self-presentation after the foundation of the modern Greek state in 1821.

Pausanias' *Periegesis* is a complex work, a collection of innumerable observations, stories and opinions, which is best understood with an intimate knowledge of the places it describes, the historical background and the literary tradition. The five extant large commentaries of Pausanias show that there are always more details and interpretations that can be added to particular passages of the text. It is, however, important to gain an impression of the whole work, and to see it as part of a larger cultural phenomenon. At the beginning of this study it seems a good idea to remember the principles that also shaped the *Periegesis*. In order to describe a landscape – or to discuss an ancient book – the author needs to survey everything carefully, and then select what is worth recording. These details need to be combined with comparative material or information from the experts one meets on the way. Then the material is arranged, combined with relevant information and interpreted to allow the reader to gain an impression. Such an account of a literary work, as of a landscape, is always personal: my tour through Pausanias' *Periegesis* includes places from which I gained a particular overview, and others which I found surprising when I saw them for the first time. Some routes will be well trodden, others will be less well-known, some may even be new. I am not so bold as to claim that I am going to deal with 'all things Pausanian', but I hope that, like a good travel guide, this book will enable readers to find their way around Pausanias and to make new discoveries of their own.

2

Pausanias: the Man and his Time

> In those days men were guests of the gods and shared a table with them because of their righteousness and piety; the gods openly honoured the good and their wrath reached those who had done wrong. Indeed, in those days [some] men became gods who are still worshipped today. ... But in my time, when evil has grown so much and has spread over every land and city, men are no longer turned into gods, except in words and flattery addressed to the powerful, and the wrath of the gods is reserved for later when they have gone hence.[1] (Paus. 8.2.4-5)

It is usually taken for granted that Pausanias keeps a low personal profile in his text, but sometimes he does step forward to voice his opinions – rarely more forcefully than in the passage quoted above. In it he expresses earnest religious views, and he criticises the circumstances of his own time in a tone that suggests strong feelings. This rare outburst is an important reminder that the man behind the mild-mannered commentary offered in the *Periegesis* might not be as disinterested a reporter as he is often assumed to be. Pausanias is notoriously elusive: he does not provide much information about himself, and little can be said about him for certain, at least if we are merely looking for hard facts about the man behind the book. What we know about his personality also has to be pieced together from sometimes contradictory statements in the *Periegesis*, combined with conjecture based on an assessment of the cultural context. It is a standard procedure in any study of an ancient author to assemble and discuss such details, and I shall return to these issues later.

Rather than asking 'who is the man behind the text?' we first need to consider what Pausanias wanted his readers to think about him as an author. It is important to remember that the text represents only what he intended to say about himself, the literary persona he wanted his readers to see. For example, the almost conspicuous silence about his own travel experience is in itself a conscious pose which needs further investigation. It is a standard procedure in literary studies to investigate how an author presents himself, and how the writer's personality relates to the narrator who emerges from the text. Since Pausanias has hardly been taken seriously as an author, such a narratological approach had not even been attempted until very recently,[2] and much remains to be done in this field. My discussion focuses on Pausanias' efforts to present himself as a trustworthy, detached reporter and knowledgeable commentator, aims that readers today have to bear in mind when they attempt to interpret

16

particular passages or to peel apart the layers of observation, commentary and interpretation in the *Periegesis*.

Most of Pausanias' descriptions of routes and sites are presented in third-person narrative, either as plain fact, for example when monuments are described, or reporting information heard from local people or discovered in the literary sources. Sometimes, usually when he is on the move from one place to another, Pausanias addresses his audience directly, using the second person.[3] Such remarks might suggest the stance of a personal guide taking his audience by the hand to show them the way, but they are mainly used to give short directions without creating the impression of a real conversation, and they may simply be designed to offer some variety of expression.

> In their market-place the Messenians have a statue of Zeus Soter [the Saviour] and a fountain Arsinoe which is named after the daughter of Leukippos, and its water flows from a spring called Klepsydra. There are sanctuaries of Poseidon and Aphrodite, and, most memorable, a statue of the Mother of the Gods of Parian marble, a work of Damophon, who also repaired the Zeus at Olympia with extreme accuracy when the ivory had come apart.[4] (Paus. 4.31.6)

This is a typical example of Pausanias' description of a site. The detached tone makes it easy to forget how much influence the author has on his description: even a relatively simple passage as this extract from the description of Messene is a carefully shaped blend of report and commentary. The market-places of most Greek cities of the Roman imperial period were full of monuments, especially statues,[5] and the description represents Pausanias' selection, as he reminds us when he points out the statue most worth mentioning. The information about Damophon is connected to the later description of the statue of Zeus in Olympia, and may be the author's own addition, based on what he knew from a visit to Elis.[6] The author's opinion or his own interpretation of a particular detail is often presented without abandoning the objective tone of factual report, and readers have to deduce for themselves how opinions were combined with observations and literary sources to shape a particular passage.

> If one goes from Corinth not towards the interior but following the road to Sikyon, there is a burned temple on the left, not far from the city. Many wars have been fought around Corinth, and houses and sanctuaries outside the walls were likely to be destroyed by fire. But they [the Corinthians] say that this temple, once dedicated to Apollo, was burned down by Pyrrhos, the son of Achilles.[7] (Paus. 2.5.5)

Pausanias is subtly undermining Corinthian tradition by pointing out that the presence of a ruined temple might not necessarily have anything to do with a very ancient mythical tradition. This is particularly poignant in

Corinth, which was sacked by the Romans in 146 BC and re-founded as a Roman colony only about a century later. In this passage Pausanias has reached the end of his description of Corinth, and there are earlier hints at scepticism towards local traditions current in the Roman city of his own time.[8] He has already discussed the violent interruption in its history, and there is no need to be explicit about problematic traditions of the Roman colony: readers are expected to take a hint.[9] Such low-key comments often juxtapose local stories with alternative versions from other places, the literary tradition, or Pausanias' own findings.[10] The use of third-person narrative allows the author to stay in the background without giving up the opportunity to express his opinion.[11] This means that even when Pausanias sounds like a detached reporter it is necessary to investigate whether a particular passage was shaped by his opinion, or the attempt to suggest a particular viewpoint.

From time to time Pausanias steps onto the scene to speak in his own voice.[12] Statements in the first person make up a small proportion of the whole text, but they establish the author's presence, allowing him to define his persona and his roles within the work. Pausanias often speaks as a writer, commenting on the composition and structure of his work. The cross-references belong to this category, as well as comments pointing out the beginning or end of a *logos*, or occasional remarks explaining why he has, or has not, decided to discuss a certain issue in detail.[13] Pausanias seems quite willing to talk about the intentions and principles which guide the composition of the *Periegesis*, and he likes to demonstrate that his text follows a well-established plan.[14]

First-person statements are also used to state opinions: Pausanias is not always satisfied with just slipping a subtle comment into his description, and sometimes he engages in a more extensive argument. Explicit statements of opinion make it easier to understand how the author's views and knowledge are displayed elsewhere in the text, even where he ostensibly keeps a low profile. Pausanias engages in discussions that demonstrate his expertise in various fields of learning. The complexity of such arguments, even where small details are concerned, is best demonstrated by an example. In the following passage Pausanias deals with a problem that is very common in the *Periegesis*: he assesses contradictory stories, using his knowledge of Greek literature and local tradition.[15]

> They [the Tegeans] also say that Kydon, Archedios and Gortys, the surviving sons of Tegeates, voluntarily settled in Crete, and that the cities of Kydonia, Gortyna and Katreus were named after them. The Cretans do not agree with the account of the Tegeans: according to them Kydon was a son of Hermes and Akakallis, the daughter of Minos, while Katreus was a son of Minos and Gortys a son of Rhadamanthys. As far as Rhadamanthys himself is concerned, Homer says in Proteus' speech to Menelaos [Hom. *Od.* 4.564] that Menelaos would go to the Elysian plain, but that Rhadamanthys had already gone before him. Kinaithon in his poem represents Rhadamanthys as a son

of Hephaistos, son of Talos, son of Kres. The myths of the Greeks differ from each other on most points, but particularly with regard to genealogical details.[16] (Paus. 8.53.4-5)

Pausanias draws on Tegean and Cretan tradition without revealing his sources, and he refers to two archaic poets, namely Homer and Kinaithon, just to discuss a minor aspect of his original material. In the end, the Cretan and the Tegean versions of the foundation stories are presented without preference,[17] and the learned genealogical discussion almost distracts the reader from the original issue. Nevertheless, Pausanias shows his skill in comparing and criticising differing accounts, before extricating himself by pointing out that Greek traditions are generally contradictory.[18] The Greek past, mythical or historical, is not the only field in which he presents himself as an expert. He also engages in debates concerning art and art history, chronology, history, literature, and a number of subjects that might be classified as part of the natural sciences. References to visits in many parts of the ancient world suggest that the author is a seasoned traveller whose assessment of what he saw in Greece is based on a wide range of comparative material and experience.

Readers are also given some information about the research that shaped Pausanias' work, especially when he draws on personal experience to support his arguments.[19] He stresses how much effort he was willing to make to collect material for his work, even if this means admitting that his enquiries were not always successful. The *Periegesis* includes dozens of references to questions that could not be resolved on site, and Pausanias confesses that, even while he was writing, he still discovered details he should have asked about when he visited a place.[20] This is not an admission of defeat or incompetence; on the contrary, it illustrates how Pausanias went about his enquiries, and in which topics he was particularly interested. These statements also suggest honesty and integrity: the author would rather admit to gaps in his research than gloss over such problems or simply invent appropriate answers. In short, many of the passages where Pausanias engages in a debate are concerned with establishing his credibility as researcher and author. Readers are given the impression that they are in the hands of a well-educated guide with extensive knowledge and experience, a man who can be trusted to assess his material carefully and to present a truthful report. The widespread idea of Pausanias as reliable, but rather dull, is at least in part an image of his own making.

In the passage that opens this chapter Pausanias frankly states his opinion about men who became gods, long ago and in his own time. Comments on moral or religious matters are almost as common in the *Periegesis* as references to the author's pursuits as a researcher and writer. It is crucial to understand how important the divine and supernatural are to Pausanias' project, but, at the same time, I find it impossible to separate this issue from his general approach to the landscape and history of Greece. For Pausanias the religious sphere is part of the physical world, and therefore his enquiries about gods, rites and sacred places are an integral part of the *Periegesis*. Discussions of religious or moral matters complement the analysis of monuments or stories: just as it was often impossible to separate sacred and historical monuments, history is influenced by fate and the gods.[21] Pausanias leaves no doubt that he takes religion very seriously. Several times he points out that he is keeping silent about a particular ritual or tradition because it has to remain a secret. Pausanias wants to be seen as an insider to many cults, especially the Eleusinian mysteries. He also comments on his involvement in some festivals and rituals in places he has visited, suggesting that for him a sacrifice may have been a fairly standard part of a visit to a sanctuary.[22]

The Greek gods were a part of the mythical tradition that for the Greeks merged into history without clear boundaries. Sanctuaries and festivals were often closely connected with local history which gave them a vital importance for an ancient community and its identity. For this reason alone an interest in traditional religion was crucial for Pausanias' research in Greece. As cultural phenomenon, traditional religion was accepted by most educated people, both as a figure of speech and as an important part of Greek culture, but personal belief was another matter.[23] Lucian often makes clever fun of the Greek gods and of later foreign additions to the pantheon, but in the *Dea Syria*, a description of the sanctuary of Hierapolis close to his home, he adopts an attitude of due reverence. Local pride, antiquarian interest and a wish to imitate Herodotos could all entice a sophist to resort to (merely verbal) piety.[24] There is no need, however, to see Pausanias' respect of the gods as mere posture. In fact, he is not the only example of a highly educated man of his period whose devotion seems to be sincere. For example, Aristeides' *Sacred Tales* are a detailed account of his reverence for Asklepios: his actions were often guided by the god who appeared to him in dreams.[25]

Although an apparently devout man, Pausanias does not believe everything he is told, and some traditions he came across require some earnest discussion, especially where they clash with his beliefs.[26]

Morpho is an epithet of Aphrodite, and she is seated wearing a veil and with fetters on her feet. They say that Tyndareos put the fetters on her, as a symbol of women's faithfulness in marriage. There is another story that Tyndareos punished the goddess with fetters because he thought that she had brought his daughters to shame, but I will not accept this for a moment: it would surely be silly to expect that one could punish the goddess by making an image of cedar wood and naming it Aphrodite.[27] (Paus. 3.15.11)

Pausanias believes in the gods, but he sees them in more abstract terms than some Greek stories would permit,[28] and therefore putting fetters on the image of Aphrodite can have only a symbolic significance. Unbelievable traditions can be dismissed, rationalised or re-interpreted to find a deeper meaning, and this way of dealing with problematic material is reminiscent of Herodotos.[29] The evaluation of such information depends on the author's personal judgement, and Pausanias sometimes feels prompted to reveal something about his own views, although such comments remain the exception rather than the rule. Nevertheless, he leaves no doubt that an encounter with Greece is not just an enquiry into history and culture: it also encourages travellers or readers to revisit their attitudes to ancestral myths, rituals and gods.

The *Periegesis* may offer a lot of material to piece together a profile of Pausanias' literary persona, but it does not provide much concrete historical information about the man behind the book. There is little that can be said for certain: everyone has to cite the same few relevant passages, and much is left to conjecture. Pausanias does not mention his own name, and small hints have to suffice to identify his native city.

> Even today there remain signs that Pelops and Tantalos once lived in our [my] region: there is a lake called after Tantalos and a conspicuous grave; moreover, there is a throne of Pelops on a peak of Mount Sipylos, beyond the sanctuary of Meter Plastene, and across the river Hermon, at Temnos, is an image of Aphrodite which is made of a living myrtle-tree. We have a tradition that it was dedicated by Pelops to propitiate the goddess and to pray that Hippodameia might become his bride.[30] (Paus. 5.13.7)

This is the only time in the *Periegesis* when Pausanias identifies with a particular place, namely Magnesia on Sipylos, a city on the river Hermos in western Asia Minor (Fig. 5, cf. Fig. 1).[31] Pausanias knows a number of notable sites on Mount Sipylos and he is well acquainted with the region and its local traditions. A thorough knowledge of a particular area might not say much in the context of Pausanias' meticulous descriptions of so many sites, but he has seen swarms of locusts destroyed on Mount Sipylos three times. This is a rare event, unlikely to be witnessed repeatedly by someone who has not actually lived in the region for some time.[32] Other places of origin have been suggested, but all such theories rely on an identification with roughly contemporary namesakes known from ancient sources.[33] None of these individuals, however, fits the profile of Pausanias the *Periegete*: as far as we can tell, the only trace he left in the ancient record is his own literary work.

Magnesia on Sipylos lies in Lydia, a part of the Roman province of Asia which was one of the most prosperous parts of the Roman empire. Smyrna, Ephesos and Pergamon were all not very far away, three of the most splendid cities of the Roman empire and centres of intellectual activities with the best possible facilities. Pausanias knew all three cities well, and they are often used as examples that come to mind easily. He refers to the history of Pergamon and knows various details about the sanctuary of Asklepios there, in Smyrna the recently constructed Asklepieion seems to

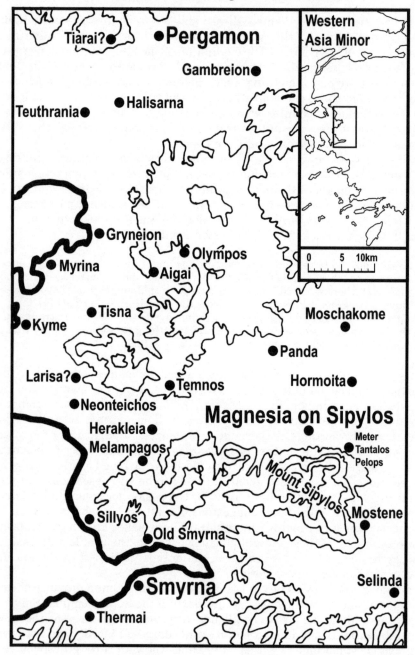

Fig. 5. Magnesia on Sipylos and its surroundings.
Based on the Barrington Atlas: Foss, Mitchell & Reger (2000).

have impressed him most, and he mentions a number of sights in Ephesos, most notably the famous Artemision.[34] A long excursus on Ionia in the Achaian book leaves no doubt that Pausanias was proud of his native western Asia Minor. For him Ionia has the best possible climate, unique sanctuaries and various other noteworthy sights that are second only to the marvels of mainland Greece.[35]

The date of the *Periegesis* is relatively uncontroversial, and there is enough evidence to determine Pausanias' approximate lifetime.[36] References to his own time, as far as they can be dated, seem to refer to a period between AD 120 and 180, and he may have been born around AD 115.[37] A number of clues in the *Periegesis* provide dates for specific passages. Book V begins with an overview of all the peoples in the Peloponnese, from the autochthonous Arkadians to the most recent additions:

> The Corinthians of today are the most recent settlers in the Peloponnese, and from the time when they received their land from the emperor it is two hundred and seventeen years to my own day.[38] (Paus. 5.1.2)

Assuming that the *Periegesis* was intended to be more than mere contemporary reportage, it seems scarcely useful to date a relatively well-known event, namely the re-foundation of Corinth by Caesar in 44 BC, by relating it to a point in time that a later reader would find impossible to determine independently. This information, however, allows us to encounter Pausanias at a specific point in time, namely in AD 174. He must have been aware that he was allowing the reader to put a firm date to the *Periegesis*, or rather to a particular point in the lengthy process of research and writing. The reader is almost invited to imagine the author at work, presumably in the process of composing the beginning of Book V, and approaching the halfway point of the *Periegesis*. The link between the beginnings of the Roman colony at Corinth and Pausanias' own time emphasises just how recently these 'new' Corinthians had become part of the ancient Peloponnesian landscape, and, perhaps more significantly, it firmly turns Pausanias' activities into a chronological reference point at the end of the long history of the Peloponnese.

By AD 174 Pausanias had already been working on the *Periegesis* for some time; in fact, after some years of writing he found it necessary to comment on one exceptional monument which had been built while his work was in progress:

> The Odeion [of Patrai] is in every way the most noteworthy in Greece, except, of course, the one at Athens. It is superior in size and style, and was built by Herodes, an Athenian, in memory of his dead wife. This Odeion is not mentioned in my account of Attica because my Athenian book was finished before Herodes began the building.[39] (Paus. 7.20.6)

'Herodes, an Athenian' seems a striking understatement for one of the most eminent and wealthy men in the empire, an ex-consul as well as a famous intellectual and orator, who left a lasting mark on the Greek monumental landscape. His wife Regilla died probably in AD 160 or 161, and it is not clear how long it took him to start with the building of the Odeion in her memory.[40] Bowie suggests that Book I could have been finished as late as AD 165, but this should be seen as the latest possible date; most other scholars prefer the early 160s or late 150s as a date for Book I, although it has been suggested that Book I may have been published as early as in the 130s, in the last years of Hadrian.[41] Such an early publication date seems improbable, but it should not come as a surprise that there is no clear indication when work on the *Periegesis* began,[42] because even the planning stage required a detailed knowledge of Greece that went beyond a mere tourist's acquaintance with the major sites. By the time Pausanias started to plan his work, and when he started writing his first book, he must already have spent a lot of time travelling in Greece, and more research was to follow once he had embarked on his project.[43]

The reference to the Odeion of Herodes Atticus also suggests that Pausanias did not intend to edit his work once a book was completed, because there is no practical reason why he should not just have added a few words to Book I. In fact, this reference has been seen as an indication that the first book was published separately, before the rest of the *Periegesis*, but this suggestion is inconclusive. Surely, late corrections to the master copy of a book were possible in a world where 'publication' meant the circulation of individually produced copies, perhaps accompanied by readings of selected passages in public or amongst interested friends.[44] By the time he composed Book VII Pausanias must have decided not to go back to add corrections to earlier books.

Passages that provide chronological evidence for Pausanias' activities after the completion of Book I all point to the later 160s and 170s. The description of Epidauros includes new buildings constructed on the site in Pausanias' own time, which, according to inscriptions, were finished in the 160s.[45] The latest reference that can be dated with confidence occurs in Book VIII. Pausanias provides a short overview of the achievements of Antoninus Pius and Marcus Aurelius, which include a victory over the Germans and Sarmatians, probably in AD 175.[46] Marcus Aurelius is the latest emperor mentioned in the *Periegesis*, and the absence of Commodus from this short overview of recent emperors may suggest that this part of Book VIII was composed before he was made joint emperor in AD 177. It seems likely that the *Periegesis* was finished before the death of Marcus Aurelius in AD 180.[47] The composition of the ten books therefore took about twenty years and Pausanias was perhaps in his fifties and sixties at the time. It is not necessary to assume that during these twenty years Pausanias was exclusively working on the *Periegesis*. For example, he may well have continued travelling outside Greece while his work was in progress; in fact, he seems to have made enquiries in Rome about the location of art works which were taken from Greece, which suggests a visit there when the project was well under way.[48] Pausanias' extensive travel in the Roman empire and his long research in mainland Greece leave no doubt that he was very wealthy.[49] Travel was expensive: Apuleius used up most of his fortune of about one million sesterces on a stay in Athens and a 'grand tour' through the east of the empire.[50] Pausanias himself takes great wealth for granted:

> As for those places that were exceedingly wealthy in ancient times, Egyptian Thebes, Minyan Orchomenos and Delos, which was once the trading centre of all of Greece, they are now less prosperous than a private man of moderate means.[51] (Paus. 8.33.2)

At least Thebes and Orchomenos still existed as communities in Pausanias' time, and from this statement we have to assume that Pausanias' idea of merely 'moderate means' implies considerable wealth. The contrast between ancient and contemporary circumstances is probably exaggerated to give a dramatic description of the downfall of great cities, but it takes the perspective of a very wealthy man to illustrate such an argument with this particular comparison. It is likely that Pausanias belonged to the provincial élite of Asia Minor, probably one of the leading families of Magnesia. His comment on the poverty of smaller cities reminds us that in all but the most prosperous places a few eminent citizens were likely to have more disposable income than their whole community. Greek cities in this period relied on their private benefactors, and it was seen as the duty of a wealthy man to contribute generously. Plutarch, probably the most eminent man in the small city of Chaironeia a few decades before Pausanias' visit, was very aware of his responsibilities, and decided to resist the temptation of moving to one of the intellectual centres which would have welcomed a man of his calibre with open arms and a grant of citizenship.[52] Not all wealthy men, however, were equally conscientious. Pausanias' close contemporary Aristeides, for example, saw offers of grand honours by Smyrna and his native city Hadrianoi as cumbersome and expensive duties that he wanted to avoid.[53] Pausanias, in commenting on the fourth-century orator Isokrates, states that it is best not to be involved in public affairs.[54] This view may well have been shaped by similar experiences, although he does not discuss the matter of public service in his own time. He does, however, also show some appreciation for the positive influence of contemporary private benefactors on some sites in Greece.[55]

Wealth meant access to a good education, and Pausanias was clearly a well-educated man with many intellectual interests and an intimate knowledge of a wide range of literary works, in short, a *pepaideumenos*.[56] His Greek contemporaries shared an ideal of *paideia*, a word which is usually translated as 'education', although it implies more, namely a sense of Hellenic culture informed by learning and active involvement in intellectual activities. A higher education focused on rhetorical exercises, philosophy and literature, particularly the thorough study of a canon of archaic and classical Greek texts which served as a general frame of reference.[57] In a circle of *pepaideumenoi* one could allude to these texts without further explanation, and they would come to mind when an appropriate argument or literary comparison was needed.

This common ground of Greek culture, *paideia*, informs most of the Greek literature of the period from Nero to the end of the Severan dynasty, which is today classified as the Second Sophistic, a label taken from Philostratos' *Lives of the Sophists*.[58] Our impression of the cultural activities of the period is dominated by the 'sophists', highly paid professional intellectuals who used their *paideia* to impress as public orators and teachers of rhetoric.[59] These high-profile individuals were exceptional, but many of their contemporaries shared their interests and ideals. Texts of the period convey a sense of continuous peer competition focusing on, and conducted through, *paideia*. The hallmark of educational distinction was a proficiency in Attic Greek, an artificial language based on the literary idiom of classical texts and far removed from the colloquial language of the day. Educated men were greatly concerned with the fine details that characterised appropriate language, and the pitfalls that could lead to embarrassment.[60] Pausanias' language and style have long been criticised as inferior to the usual high standards of Second Sophistic authors.[61] Pausanias must have been aware of the ongoing debates about the correct form of Greek language and style.[62] In fact, his prose is too artificial and consistent to be the result of mere incompetence. Like his contemporaries, he deliberately chose a style based on the imitation of earlier authors, creatively combined to present something new. The result is idiosyncratic and quite different from other Second Sophistic texts, with an emphasis on a variety of expression and material, while the artificial hallmarks of Attic Greek are kept to a minimum.[63]

A *pepaideumenos* also had to be able to prove his credentials by showing his intimate knowledge of literature, if possible well beyond the educational canon. An encyclopaedic knowledge of facts from various fields of ancient learning was also useful to impress one's peers.[64] Pausanias was aware of this competitive environment for any kind of intellectual activity, and he meets the challenge on his own terms.

> I have done the most diligent and careful work to determine the date of Homer and Hesiod, but I do not like to write about this subject because I am aware of the quarrelsome nature of some people, at present especially those who specialise in epic poetry.[65] (Paus. 9.30.3)

Pausanias speaks as a *pepaideumenos* who is not just a mere consumer of learning: he claims to have done research into areas that were central to the literary canon. He decides against muscling into such a crowded field, but not without asserting his intellectual prowess. The *Periegesis* offers a wide range of information, some site-specific, some connected by free association and presented in a *logos*. Discussions of general topics often include examples from outside Greece, and sometimes they provide handy lists of noteworthy facts.[66] Not all of these remarks are concerned with scholarly analysis. As with sites and monuments, Pausanias is looking for remarkable details, things worth talking about. There was a whole genre of *variae historiae* (varied enquiries) which collected material from earlier texts, particularly books that were not easily available, and arranged it in some engaging way.[67] Some scholars have argued that the *Periegesis* is just a particularly elaborate example of this genre, with fictitious site descriptions serving as a framework.[68] Pausanias' topographical accuracy shows that this theory is preposterous, but the consistently important role of informative digressions in his work deserves attention. Just as *variae historiae* presumably found an interested audience, the additional comments in the *Periegesis* were likely to be attractive to 'sophisticated' readers who wanted to expand their educational horizons and for whom knowledge was a form of entertainment.[69]

Many Second Sophistic texts, especially Philostratos' *Lives of the Sophists*, describe an intellectual network which included most of the major cities around the eastern Mediterranean, and some eminent places in the west. Pausanias grew up close to three major centres of Greek learning, and he visited many others. He must at least have known a few star sophists of his time, and would presumably have witnessed their performances.[70] Pausanias is, however, not a name dropper, and he mentions only a few contemporaries. Apart from the Roman emperors, he refers to two benefactors who paid for public buildings, namely Herodes Atticus and a senator Antoninus (Sextus Iulius Antoninus Pythodorus). He also mentions Hadrian's favourite Antinoos, a Messenian notable, Claudius Saethidas, and two contemporary Olympic victors.[71] It is also difficult to say whether any of the intellectuals of the time knew Pausanias. There is little evidence that the *Periegesis* was read in antiquity,[72] but this does not say much because few Second Sophistic authors are mentioned in other ancient texts. One reference in Aelian's early third-century work *Varia Historia* was dismissed by an early editor, seemingly without good reason.[73] Increased scholarly attention to the texts of the Second Sophistic has led to some suggestions that other authors may also be drawing on Pausanias, for example Philostratos, Longus, Lucian, Pollux and Athenagoras.[74] None of these possible allusions to the *Periegesis* can be identified for certain, but at least it is now accepted as a distinct possibility that Pausanias' work was recognised by other intellectuals of his own time.

The world of Pausanias and of the Second Sophistic was shaped by the

Romans, albeit Romans with an increasing interest in Greek culture. Roman buildings adorned the cities, Roman taxes, laws and magistracies had a strong influence on an individual's public life, and Roman sanctuaries and festivals, particularly those connected to the imperial cult, were introduced alongside older Greek traditions. Life in the Roman empire of Pausanias' time meant security, prosperity and, for the provincial upper class, a growing influence within the empire. In this period an increasing proportion of the provincial élite obtained Roman citizenship, and it was no longer impossible for a Greek to reach senatorial status, or even the consulship.[75] Pausanias seems particularly impressed with Antoninus Pius for allowing Roman citizens to leave their fortune to sons who did not themselves have citizenship.[76] It seems likely that Pausanias had some personal interest in this particular change in the law, but this is all he ever says about Roman citizenship – not enough to allow any conclusions about his own citizen status.[77]

Pausanias' attitude to the Romans has long been a matter of discussion. Individual conclusions depend on the interpretation of a number of seemingly inconsistent remarks in the *Periegesis* which are easily emphasised, interpreted or dismissed to create a particular impression. Pausanias' approach clearly does not follow a single line: he reports historical events and gives his judgement according to the circumstances.[78] The Romans' role in Greek history, with particular reference to specific individuals, is seen in a rather negative light,[79] and it was regrettable that Greece was no longer free, especially because, for Pausanias, freedom was key to the great cultural achievements of Greece which still defined the culture and intellectual pursuits of educated Greeks in his own time.[80] The Romans are, however, not blamed for the downfall of Greece. The actual cause of decline was Greek disunity and treachery as well as the actions of the Macedonians.[81] Pausanias deplores the Roman practice of looting ancient art, particularly when sacred images were taken for art collections.[82] The imperial cult is usually mentioned only in passing, but sometimes it appears as an intrusion in older historical or sacred spaces, and, as we have already seen, Pausanias thought that the deification of human beings in his own time was mere flattery, a pale imitation of earlier myths.[83] New Roman cities such as Patrai and especially Nikopolis, both founded by Augustus, are criticised because the settlement process brought about great changes in the surrounding regions.[84] Pausanias actually speaks about 'those whose inhabitants moved because of the misfortune of Roman rule'.[85] Pausanias' strong statement is possible in the context of his indignation about Augustus' foundations and it need not refer to the situation in his own time, but it shows that Pausanias could find it appropriate to connect 'misfortune' and 'Roman rule'. In other respects, however, Pausanias had come to terms with the Romans of his own time: whatever the grim facts of the past, the ruling power had made amends for its wrongdoings and Pausanias has only praise for the emperors of his life-time.[86]

Pausanias' complex attitude should be understood in the context of the general situation in the Greek east of the Roman empire. The literature of the time shows a wide range of opinions about Rome. While some, most notably Plutarch, had excellent relationships with the ruling power and showed an interest in Roman culture and history, others avoided refer-ences to all things Roman or to the Latin language, and some flaunt a remarkable indifference to Rome and its history.[87] Most authors, however, show some ambiguity in their attitudes: provincial élites of the Roman empire had to reconcile the fact that the Romans had deprived their ancestors of their freedom with the need for co-operation with the imperial power on which their own privileged position depended. In Greece this situation was further complicated by a sense of cultural superiority, which was reinforced by the admiration of Greek culture shown by many Ro-mans.[88] Greek cities and individuals therefore had an extra incentive to stress their great past, but this would evoke comparisons between the political freedom of the classical *polis* and life in the Roman provinces. Even if cities were still contending for freedom (*eleutheria*), now a privilege bestowed by the emperor, Greeks knew that they were no longer free in the same sense as their forebears in the classical period.

Pausanias was often faced with this contrast between a great past (real or perceived) and the sometimes disappointing situation in his own time.[89] His picture of Roman Greece is, however, not all bleak. Many have commented on the fact that he seems almost exclusively interested in the past,[90] but in spite of its focus on archaic and classical monuments, the *Periegesis* presents an image of a contemporary Greece. Pausanias did not dream himself into a fantasy version of a Greece before Alexander: his Greece is quite explicitly that of his own time, and his interest in the past expresses itself by recording the traces that remained, be they memories or monuments, as he found them in his own time.[91] In fact, without the *Periegesis* we would know much less about Roman Greece, and even taking into account the relatively recent interest in the Roman layers of older Greek sites, the situation in the province of Achaia would probably look quite bleak, at least outside a few thriving centres. The *Periegesis* may not offer much information about contemporary life, but it provides insights into the cultural activities and identities of numerous small cities in the Roman period.

Mythical/historical tradition and religious activities were very impor-tant for Greek cities under Roman rule. Their élites may no longer have been involved in what we might call actual politics, but they were still directing their community's internal affairs and conducting inter-state relations with other cities. These activities could bring considerable re-sults, for example when a city managed to convince the emperor to grant them freedom from taxation, and cities competed to assert their importance. Smaller cities needed to make an effort to attract benefactors to ensure their survival. There were no longer wars between neighbouring states, but a small community might still find itself, or part of its territory, absorbed by a wealthier neighbour.[92] Many of these activities were conducted through (in the widest sense) cultural activities. An illustrious past, impressive ancient monuments and remarkable festivals were crucial for a city's self-presentation to the outside world.[93] The orators of the period stressed these aspects when they praised a city in their speeches, and a similar focus can be seen in monuments and inscriptions of the Greek east of the Roman empire.[94] Relations between cities were cemented by 'discovering' ancestral links, and cities welcomed research, or fiction posing as research, to back up their claims.[95] Hadrian tapped into this mode of 'inter-state' relations when he founded the Panhellenion, an organisation of Greek cities which had to prove their Greekness based on mythical links with mainland Greece.[96] Greek identity outside mainland Greece was ultimately always in some way related to the old motherland, either through ancient migration stories, for example in Ionia, or through founding heroes. At the same time, many of the places in mainland Greece were known to every educated Greek, because many are mentioned in the most widely read texts, be it the Catalogue of Ships in the *Iliad* or the classical historians.

The information gathered in the *Periegesis* is therefore not merely antiquarian. Details about the history, cults and local traditions of communities were valuable commodities, especially in mainland Greece. Pausanias' wealthy and educated peers, members of the élite of their cities, would have been well-versed in maintaining, celebrating, using and perhaps even manipulating the cultural heritage of their own cities. The wealthy élite had the education to interpret the local past and to link it to widely known Greek traditions such as the epics or the Attic tragedies. They were also responsible for maintaining and setting up new monuments, and they paid for local festivals. In return for their efforts they had most to gain if their community managed to attract the attention of people in high places who might be of some assistance. Many of Pausanias' informants in Greece were probably members of the local élite who were themselves involved in the same activities.[97] In fact, if we take into account the crucial importance of *polis* life and local culture for the Greeks, it should come as no surprise that in all but the smallest places Pausanias found someone willing to explain the most noteworthy features of their city's heritage. Greek culture viewed with the *polis* in mind is not uniform: on the contrary, it is characterised by a great variety of cultural expression in different cities, albeit within a common framework.

The *Periegesis* sets out to map Greece, and by so doing it (re-)constructs Greekness like a jigsaw, as a big picture that is made up of many small details which emphasise the variety and local individuality of Greek city-states. It is clear from the text that this work involved a lot of meticulous research on site and in libraries. Pausanias was very thorough, but we should not see him as an eccentric scholar detached from the real world. On the contrary, as we shall see in the next chapter, Pausanias' research required a man who engaged with the world, interacting with people on every new site, listening to informants and sharing opinions. At the same time, he engages in the intellectual discourse of his time, demanding respect from his fellow *pepaideumenoi*. The *Periegesis* responds to specific needs and interests of Pausanias' potential readership, the well-educated, Greek-speaking élite of the Roman empire. At the same time it recognises the value of the information that could still be discovered in Greece. In a way, Pausanias' efforts continue a cultural dialogue between mainland Greece and the many Greeks overseas that had been going on since the Dark Ages.[98]

The Importance of Travelling

> In Egyptian Thebes I crossed the Nile to the so-called Pipes (Syringes), and I saw a seated statue which gives out a sound. The many (*hoi polloi*) call it Memnon, and they say that he advanced into Egypt and even as far as Susa. The Thebans, however, say that it is not a statue of Memnon, but of a native named Phamenoph, and I have also heard that it is Sesostris. Kambyses broke the statue in two, and now it has been cast down from the head to the middle. What remains, however, is seated and every day at sunrise it makes a noise which is best compared to the sound of a kithara or lyre when a string has been broken.[1] (Paus. 1.42.3)

Pausanias was a seasoned traveller who had visited many places outside his native Ionia and the part of Greece covered in the *Periegesis*. He refers to journeys through most of Asia Minor and Syria as far east as the Euphrates. In the west he visited Sicily and parts of Italy, especially Rome, which he knew relatively well. In Egypt he went to the sanctuary of Ammon at Siwah, saw the pyramids and travelled up the Nile at least as far as Thebes.[2] We can assume that for the man who embarked on the project to describe Greece, travelling was nothing unusual, and in this he was not alone: travel was a standard part of élite life in the Roman empire.

The *Periegesis* is not a travelogue, but the text is in many ways influenced by the realities of travel at the time. Sometimes it is possible to see how Pausanias' actual experiences in Greece influenced his work, and he provides some insights into the process of collecting information on site. This line of enquiry is limited by his reluctance to speak about the actual process of travelling or to mention specific incidents on his journeys. Beyond Pausanias' own experience his informed assumptions about the collective habits and interests of the educated Greek traveller also had an influence on the shaping of the *Periegesis*. The whole book is arranged as an itinerary which subtly invites readers to imagine themselves journeying along those routes, and individual site descriptions respond to the interests of educated travellers of the period. Pausanias also had to bear in mind that many of his potential readers might know at least some of the sites he was describing. The role of travel as an integral part of Second Sophistic culture will be at the centre of this discussion: I investigate the habits and preferences of ancient travellers, and relate them to corresponding features of the *Periegesis*.

Travelling had been a part of the common Greek consciousness as long as anyone could remember. There had been Greeks overseas since the

3. The Importance of Travelling

Bronze Age, and the foundation of numerous Greek cities around the shores of the Mediterranean and the Black Sea in the eighth and seventh centuries was a part of the process that formed Greek culture as we know it. When Herodotos speaks of sixth-century Egypt, he mentions that many Greeks were already there at that time, some as mercenaries, some traders, and others who had come to see the country.[3] Travelling also plays a pivotal role in the earliest Greek literature: the *Iliad* deals with a large overseas campaign while the *Odyssey* follows its hero on his long journey home. Even the apparently sedentary Hesiod seems to regard a journey by ship as a normal, if undesirable, part of a farmer's life around 700 BC.[4] These early texts were very influential, and, as we shall see in the next chapter, Greek literature continued to engage with the experience of travel in a variety of ways. From the beginning the act of travelling and the encounter with foreign lands also had a great impact on Greek self-definition, for example in the foundation stories of cities that explained connections to the ancient motherland, or in texts about foreign lands that reflect and define Greek values by discussing strange cultures.[5]

In Pausanias' time the Romans guaranteed peace around the Mediterranean and travelling was easier and safer than it had been ever before. Aelius Aristeides' *Praise of Rome* offers an enthusiastic assessment of the situation:

> Now it is indeed possible for Greek or non-Greek, with or without his belongings, to travel easily wherever he wants to go, just as if passing from fatherland to fatherland. The Kilikian Gates hold no terror, and neither does the narrow, sandy route to Egypt which runs through Arab country, nor inaccessible mountains, great stretches of river or savage barbarian tribes; but for security it suffices to be a Roman, or one of those under your [i.e. Roman] rule. Homer speaks of an 'Earth common to all', and you have made it come true. You have measured the whole inhabited world, you have spanned rivers with all kinds of bridges, and cut through mountains to make way for traffic. You have filled deserts with posting stations and you have made all areas accustomed to a settled and orderly way of life.[6] (Aristeides 26.100-1)

This eulogy may be exaggerated to fit the purpose of the speech, but Aristeides' audience would not have found his description unrealistic. The imperial infrastructure did not just provide safe roads and shipping routes: it also meant that around the whole Mediterranean a traveller could get by with the same currency and just two languages. The Roman empire depended on good communications and was willing to invest in maintaining security and a good infrastructure. Rome and other large urban centres needed a steady stream of overseas imports, and the administration required smooth movement of personnel and information. Travelling was part of life for members of the Roman ruling élite, including many of the emperors and their families. As Aristeides' comments show, however, Roman officials and traders were not alone in enjoying the advantages of safe communications.[7]

Many of the travellers we hear about in the ancient sources were comparatively wealthy, but it was not just the well-off who travelled on a regular basis.[8] Some sanctuaries, particularly those of Asklepios, attracted constant streams of visitors from all backgrounds. Prime historical sites saw an increase in visitors, and high profile festivals such as the Olympic Games drew larger crowds than ever before. The historical sites of Greece and Asia Minor were particularly attractive, especially those that could boast an important role in the Greek past. Egypt offered safe and comfortable access to an exotic culture and impressive ancient monuments.[9] Famous sites had many visitors from all parts of the Roman empire as is best documented in visitors' graffiti from Philae in Upper Egypt and in the tombs of the Valley of the Kings, called Syringes ('Pipes') in antiquity. This epigraphical evidence also supports the impression that the second century AD offered the best opportunity to travel: a majority of the inscriptions are from this period.[10] This phenomenon is often described as 'ancient tourism', but this term is problematic, because it conjures up images of modern mass tourism. The Grand Tours of the eighteenth century offer a better comparison to the activities of educated ancient travellers who went to see significant sites.[11] Pausanias' trip to Egypt, mentioned in the passage that opens this chapter, was certainly not exceptional. He went to Thebes and saw the Valley of the Kings and the 'statue of Memnon', a colossal statue of Amenhotep III which broke apart around 27 BC and subsequently emitted a sound at sunrise which quickly turned it into a first-rate visitor attraction. It, too, has admirers' inscriptions on it, but apparently only high-class travellers were allowed to leave their mark there, usually an expression of their amazement at hearing the statue's sound.[12] By identifying the statue as Memnon, a hero who featured prominently in the epic tradition surrounding the Trojan War, Greek visitors had brought their own myths to explain the statue and its unique properties. Pausanias, probably deliberately responding to Herodotos' description of Egypt, turns to local, ostensibly older traditions to challenge this Greek interpretation.

In spite of the dangers of shipping in antiquity, long voyages were usually undertaken by ship, which was faster and more comfortable than travel on land.[13] Pausanias' itinerary in the *Periegesis* sometimes takes to the sea and follows the coastline in the manner of a *periplous* (literally 'circumnaviagation'), an archaic Greek mode of describing geographical features and settlements along a coast. As Hutton points out, Pausanias has a tendency to make unusual topographical mistakes when he describes sea routes, quite possibly because he copied some of these passages from existing geographical works.[14] Most of the *Periegesis* stays firmly on land, following roads from one site to the next. As a whole the itinerary used to organise the text is clearly artificial, but it seems that at some point Pausanias actually travelled along most of the routes he is describing. He mentions the state of a road only when it does not conform to usual standards, and these occasional comments suggest that Pausanias expected to find single-track roads fit for a carriage with two draught animals.[15] Greece did indeed have a well-established road system which made even rather remote and mountainous areas accessible for wheeled transport. Carriages were a standard means of transport for the wealthy, who would usually travel with a number of attendants and substantial baggage.[16]

Practicalities of ancient travel have had some bearing on the discussion about Pausanias' potential readership. Ancient readers probably could have found the *Periegesis* worth their while without actually travelling to Greece, but did Pausanias expect that some would use his work on site? It is never explicit whether he imagines his readers at home or somewhere on a site in Greece.[17] Intellectuals did take books and writing materials on their journeys, but there is no evidence that travellers used guidebooks.[18] At first sight Pausanias' plain topographical information, for example comments on roads or springs, seems designed for a travelling reader, but in fact it is rarely sufficient to serve as a practical guide.[19] Simple directions are clearly not Pausanias' priority, but the work certainly stood up to a confrontation with the realities of a site, as far as we can tell today. For example, Pausanias' description of Olympia contains details of hundreds of statues: this provides an interesting trawl through centuries of Greek history when read at home, but on a bewildering site with probably thousands of statues Pausanias' selection of noteworthy objects would surely have been of particular value.[20] There has been some discussion as to whether it would have been too cumbersome to handle ancient scrolls while walking around sightseeing.[21] This approach takes for granted the most common modern way of using guidebooks, namely carrying them around a site to help with organising a tour or to find explanations for interesting features as one comes across them. Ancient travellers did not need to use guidebooks in quite the same way, because exact directions and essential details about monuments were easily available in most places. The *Periegesis* does not replace the services of a tourist guide, it is more concerned with adding to the information that was easily available on site. For this purpose the book would not have to be carried around while sightseeing, but a traveller might find it useful to have it on hand to consult it in preparation for a site visit. Pausanias' travelling readers would be ready to face their informants with ideas about which sites to see and which questions to ask about local tradition.

Any ancient traveller would take communication with local people for granted. The slow pace of travel meant that visitors would usually stay for longer than most modern tourists and communication was easy because a visitor's Greek or Latin would be understood in almost the whole known world. In Pausanias' time there were tourist guides at sites that could expect a steady stream of visitors, possibly offering their services for money. Ancient authors seem to have a rather low opinion of such guides. For example, Plutarch's *De Pythiae Oraculis* is a philosophical dialogue presented as a tour around Delphi where the learned discussion is frequently interrupted by tourist guides offering standard information about monuments and traditions.[22] Pausanias was prepared to consult local guides, but he does at times express disapproval, especially when he suspects that they are manipulating local history.[23] The exact status of his guides is usually impossible to determine, and it is likely that because local history was valued so highly in this period even smaller communities had recognised experts who were eager to offer their assistance.[24]

Wealthy, well-educated travellers probably also depended on local *pepaideumenoi* for information. Members of the élite preferred to rely on the hospitality of their peers rather than to stay at inns, and letters of introduction could open doors in places where one did not have personal friends.[25] Pausanias mentions only one guest-friend (*xenos*) of his, a man in Larisa in Thessaly,[26] but after years of travelling he probably had an extensive network of acquaintances in Greece. In most smaller cities this would give him access to the wealthiest and best-educated local families, the same people who were actively involved in maintaining local monuments and traditions. Plutarch's philosophical tour of Delphi takes it for granted that educated locals would show around visiting friends, and as a priest in Delphi he probably did so himself on numerous occasions.[27] Pausanias' guides usually remain anonymous, but in Olympia he mentions an Aristarchos who was possibly the member of an ancient priestly family. In Athens he may have known the Lykomidai, an important family with connections to Eleusis, while in the city of Elis he talked to a man with the title *nomophylax Êleiôn*, presumably a local official.[28] Sometimes Pausanias hints at learned conversations he had on a site, usually when he felt compelled to comment on the local tradition or to question the information he had been given, but he was also prepared to engage in philosophical discussion.[29]

Travel was essential for the educated Greek élite of Pausanias' time, both for their activities as leading figures in their cities and to enhance their credentials as *pepaideumenoi*. Although Greek culture was still firmly tied to life in the *polis*, the role of the ancient city-state had changed fundamentally since the beginning of the Hellenistic period. Leading families carried on with their local, civic duties alongside political or cultural activities on a supraregional level. Sophists in particular had to keep moving to maintain their status among their competitive peers. They would do most of their teaching in a particular city, but they travelled to give rhetorical performances, and the most distinguished orators could expect invitations to address crowds at festivals or to perform in front of the emperor.[30] In most parts of the empire, well beyond the Greek world, the élite shared a similar lifestyle and ideals and a distinguished traveller's status would be recognised wherever he went. Notables of the eastern part of the empire often had widespread family ties and connections through acquaintances, and they used their links on behalf of their cities. Expressing local patriotism was still expedient under certain circumstances, but realities of élite life brought about more cosmopolitan attitudes. Greek culture and education, rather than a particular location, became the focus of identification for some. As Philostratos' Apollonios puts it: to the wise man Greece is everywhere.[31]

Travelling had always been recognised as a way of acquiring knowledge: Odysseus is introduced as a man 'who saw many cities and became acquainted with the customs of many peoples'.[32] The Greeks were aware that there were places with civilisations far more ancient than their own and that Egypt in particular had records and monuments dating back many centuries.[33] By the early classical period, 'travelling to see' (*theôria*) was firmly linked with acquiring wisdom (*sophia*). For example, Herodotos' king Kroisos introduces a philosophical question by referring to Solon's experience:

> Our Athenian guest, we have heard much of you, because of your wisdom and your wanderings, travelling far to seek knowledge and to see much of the world. Now, therefore, I would like to ask you if you have ever seen a man more blessed than everyone else.[34] (Hdt. 1.30)

Many of the men who were particularly famed for their wisdom or learning were thought to have travelled extensively, for example Solon and Pythagoras. Apollonios of Tyana, sage *extraordinaire* of the early Roman imperial period, is a late representative of this group: no longer satisfied with Egypt or Syria and Mesopotamia, hardly exotic destinations in his time, it was said that he travelled as far as India. Even a barbarian could acquire wisdom through travelling, as is shown in the long tradition of the Scythian sage Anacharsis, a character who allowed Greek writers to adopt an 'outsider's view' of their own culture.[35] A wandering existence could therefore be seen as appropriate for a wise man, and in this way even exile could be presented as a virtue.[36]

In the Roman imperial period the process of acquiring a higher education was itself inextricably linked with an individual's mobility.[37] For many young men a long life as a habitual traveller would start in their teens when their educational needs could no longer be met in their home town.[38] To reach the status of a true *pepaideumenos* they needed to study with a distinguished sophist, usually in one of the larger cultural centres. Philostratos stresses that the most prominent sophists had pupils from the whole Roman world.[39] Some successful Greek sophists came from unlikely places and were probably not even native speakers of Greek, for example Lucian of Samosata in Syria, Favorinus of Arelate in Gaul or Apuleius from Madauros in North Africa: for them, travelling to study with a

37

sophist literally meant to acquire Greekness.[40] Aspiring *pepaideumenoi* had the chance to hear the great sophists on their lecture tours, or they travelled to become acquainted with different rhetorical schools. As a consequence, this most elevated form of *paideia* meant membership of a network of people who would know each other well, so much so that insiders could produce and recognise parodies of other sophists' rhetorical styles.[41] Many would also embark on a Grand Tour to Greece, Asia Minor and Egypt to complement their literary studies with a knowledge of the most famous ancient sites. This allowed them an encounter with locations they already knew from the classical texts. Such educated tourists probably shared many interests with Pausanias, especially regarding new insights in the interpretation of the literary tradition. Classical art and architecture were also of interest to educated travellers, and celebrated works of the old masters attracted large numbers of visitors.[42] In fact, art connoisseurship was essential to maintain one's credentials as a true *pepaideumenos*, and in order to acquire a good working knowledge of the most famous masterpieces and artists' styles most would have needed to visit a number of key sites.[43]

The travelling habits of the Greek élite also had an impact on the way in which they assessed and presented information in their texts, particularly in historical or geographical works, where personal research and travelling experience were increasingly seen as indispensable. Polybios is particularly outspoken about the subject, and, like Thucydides, he felt that his own involvement in important historical events was a special incentive to write about contemporary history.[44] He stresses the importance of original research, and his ideas about developments in the field of historical and geographical studies are closely connected with the rapid expansion of the Roman empire and the conquest of the Hellenistic world in his lifetime.

> In our own time, however, the regions of Asia have been opened up for travel by land and sea by the empire of Alexander, and the other regions through the rule of Rome. Men with practical experience have been freed from the need to strive for excellence in war or politics and have therefore found many good opportunities to concentrate their efforts on the knowledge of the areas already mentioned, and we can therefore expect to have a better and more accurate understanding of what was formerly unknown. I am especially determined to give the curious full information about these matters, because it was for this reason that I faced the dangers and discomforts of my travels in Libya, Iberia and Gaul, as well as of the sea which washes the western shores of these regions; so that I might correct the ignorance of those who have gone before, and acquaint the Greeks with these parts of the inhabited world.[45] (Polyb. 3.59)

Considering that Polybios' political career ended when he was taken to Italy as a hostage this statement seems over-enthusiastic, but he clearly had a sense that in the face of Roman domination the Greeks needed to reconsider their role. He saw an opportunity in the meeting of a long intellectual tradition with a rapidly changing and more accessible world.[46] These thoughts seem to anticipate aspects of the discourse about the role of Greek intellectual pursuits in the Roman empire that we see in the Second Sophistic three centuries later.

Polybios' main concern in this passage is, however, the role of original research in scholarly works. After all, an author's claim to *autopsia* – personal experience, or, literally, 'seeing for oneself' – could enhance his credibility. As we shall see in the next chapter, this issue had long been a concern for any author dealing with foreign lands or travel experiences. Some 'travel writers' were less than truthful, and accounts of journeys were central to many works of fiction. As a larger part of the world became accessible, and travelling became safer and easier, fantastic stories would have to be set in the past or in the remote corners of the world. An author who, like Pausanias, wrote about an area which was not out of reach, describing sites which some of his readers were likely to know, would have to be particularly careful in his claims of personal knowledge. In fact, it is quite clear that his research was thorough and very detailed, and he carefully separates anything he has personally verified from information he knows only from hearsay.[47]

Pausanias' comments about his enquiries provide valuable insights into his research methods. He was prepared to make an effort to investigate a potentially interesting site, even if it was difficult to reach and visiting it required a significant detour.[48] Pausanias also demonstrates that his interests and patience extended to rather unlikely causes:

> Among the fish in the Aroanios there is one kind called speckled fish. These fish, it is said, make a sound like a thrush. I have seen such fish caught, but I have not heard them sing, although I stayed by the river until sunset, which is when they were said to sing most.[49] (Paus. 8.21.2)

His patience may not have been rewarded in this case, but this willingness to pay attention to detail and to explore anything that just *might* be of interest does result in uncommonly thorough descriptions. Moreover, his interests go far beyond the obvious, such as buildings or art works that were famous or aesthetically pleasing. Pausanias' attention to inscriptions provides the best evidence of his dedication. He was mainly interested in names mentioned in inscriptions, be they those of heroes, politicians, artists, athletes or sometimes cities, and therefore dedications and artists' signatures are more frequently cited in the *Periegesis* than historical documents such as treaties or decrees. Most importantly, however, Pausanias valued inscriptions as a source of information that could be used to complement or correct local oral tradition.[50] No wonder, then, that Pausanias went to some length to discover epigraphical evidence.

Not far from the market-place is a theatre, and nearby are pedestals of bronze statues, but the statues themselves are no longer there. On one pedestal is an elegiac inscription which states that the statue was that of Philopoemen.[51] (Paus. 8.49.1)

Here we see Pausanias walking around the centre of Tegea, looking at a number of empty statue bases until he discovers a description of historical significance, and he made similar discoveries in other places, too.[52] It is anyone's guess how many inscriptions he investigated for any one recorded in the *Periegesis*. Many inscriptions were worn with age or damaged, and Pausanias learned to cope with archaic scripts and dialects.[53]

Pausanias was also keen to collect local, oral tradition, and, as we have already seen, it was probably not difficult to find informants on most sites. He assessed local stories in the light of the literary tradition or alternative evidence, and he was not always satisfied with what he heard, engaging in discussion with his informants.[54] In some places Pausanias looked for alternative information, for example by talking to the oldest inhabitants who might remember details that were otherwise forgotten.[55] Comments on questions the locals could not answer to his satisfaction highlight main areas of enquiry. Local history prompted questions about genealogies, eponymous heroes or founders and *aitia,* stories that explained particular aspects of local culture.[56] When faced with a monument Pausanias asked about artists and dedicators, the meaning of images or sculptures and the history of the monument.[57] He was also specially interested in minute details of cult practice and the historical background of any unusual features of local religion.[58]

Pausanias' personal knowledge of Greek sites is no longer a matter of dispute, but his original research is still questioned in many areas, for example recently the issue of written sources for his many details on mythical traditions has been raised again.[59] Did Pausanias use specialised handbooks as sources for his accounts of myths, foundation stories or information about local cults? There is no doubt that such material was collected and published in antiquity, and since Pausanias complemented his research by consulting many literary sources it seems likely that he also consulted appropriate reference books. In fact, there are many parallels between particular details in the *Periegesis* and the information found in fragments of ancient mythographical works, but it is still possible that he could have heard the same information on site. Educated élites everywhere in the Greek world would have been very aware of the traditions circulating about their city, and their own versions of the local past could take literary sources into account: a certain uniformity of Greek myths would therefore not be surprising. The consistency of Pausanias' focus on particular themes and questions has also been presented as evidence for his use of specific reference books as a main source. Again, however, this feature of the *Periegesis* (which is, incidentally, easily exaggerated) could also be due to Pausanias' own process of research and writing. After all, his questions and interests would have prompted particular answers from his informants, and further adjustments to the material could have been made when the text was composed. The most problematic issue, however, is the exact nature of those books that are said to have served as source for large amounts of material included in the *Periegesis*. There is no good evidence for the existence of any work which would have provided the consistency as well as breath and depth of coverage of any topic that is central to Pausanias' work, especially since much of this information is specifically tied to the contemporary monumental landscape of sites in a particular part of mainland Greece. Ultimately, we cannot just pass the source question from one existing literary work to a series of hypothetical books: either the handbooks in question would have been compiled in an admirably consistent manner from disparate literary sources, or we have to postulate that there was another author whose project of travelling around Greece to collect this kind of information would have been quite similar to Pausanias' activities. Moreover, too much reliance on works that were several hundred years old would have been problematic in conjunction with Pausanias' description of Roman Greece, because local tradition is by no means static and adjusts to contemporary circumstances.[60] Any handbook that could have served as a major source could hardly have been created more than a few decades before the *Periegesis*: many changes had been made to the Greek memorial landscape during Pausanias' own lifetime, especially under the influence of the emperor Hadrian. Since we already know without doubt that Pausanias visited the sites he writes about and investigated them in great detail, he does seem the best candidate for the man whose research also provided much of the additional local material presented in the *Periegesis*. Any other interpretation seems to be an unnecessary complication.

Given Pausanias' thorough investigation, every site visit would have resulted in large amounts of material, including excerpts from inscriptions, lists of characters depicted on monuments, or genealogical sequences.[61] His thorough descriptions seem impossible without extensive notes taken on site visits. Pausanias may not have carried out this work on his own, just as Aristeides ordered his slaves to record his measurements of Egyptian monuments.[62] Nevertheless, the process would have required Pausanias' presence to interpret and select what he wanted recorded. Even if we assume that most of the collected material was included in the *Periegesis*, the investigation of a middle-sized city would have taken days. The detailed record of hundreds of art works and monuments at Olympia could hardly have been produced without a lengthy investigation, probably on numerous visits, and the note taking must have taken several weeks at least.

What was the incentive for such efforts? As we have seen, Greek identity and the ideals of *paideia* are closely connected to the long tradition of travel and enquiry. For a man who wanted to display his intellectual prowess this alone could have been a good reason to investigate mainland Greece. Ancient travellers, however, aimed not only to increase their knowledge or *paideia*: they were also looking for the experience of encountering landscapes or monuments that had a special cultural significance for them. This aspect of ancient travel has become the focus of attention because of an increased interest in ancient pilgrimage.[63] The term pilgrimage in the context of Graeco-Roman culture is contentious, but the concept can be useful to analyse reactions of ancient travellers if one avoids a narrow, essentially Christian definition.[64] It is also worth remembering that 'pilgrimage', if one chooses to adopt this terminology, does not need to have exclusively or even principally religious aims.[65] Although ancient religions did not, unlike Christianity or Islam, offer a widely recognisable ideology of pilgrimage, there were many who sought to visit places that were meaningful to them in some way.

When Elsner suggested that Pausanias' *Periegesis* could be seen as a pilgrim's account written for pilgrims he provoked strong criticism, but he has also opened new avenues of enquiry.[66] Pausanias comes closest to a conventional pilgrim's account when, with palpable awe, he reports the complex and intense rituals required for a consultation of the oracle of Trophonios at Lebadeia. The report ends with the statement that he himself consulted the oracle, followed by a note that everyone who did so had to dedicate an inscribed tablet. We are therefore led to assume that, like many pilgrims and tourists everywhere, he left his own trace in the sacred and monumental landscape, almost as a challenge for readers to go and see for themselves whether his account is true.[67] Uniquely, this passage clearly reflects a specific religious experience, but even here Pausanias relates the process of consulting the oracle in impersonal terms. In this respect the *Periegesis* is quite unlike 'conventional' pilgrimage texts which focus more explicitly on the impact that encounters with particular places have on a specific individual. As an opaque synthesis of many trips with varying characteristics carried out during several years or decades, the *Periegesis* makes it difficult to chart a 'pilgrim's progress'.[68]

Pausanias' impersonal account shifts the focus away from the author, so as to let readers forget that they are experiencing Greece through an intermediary. Nevertheless, Pausanias' approach to the landscape shares some characteristic features with pilgrims' attitudes and experiences.[69] A *pepaideumenos* travelling around Greece would encounter a landscape that was already very familiar from the literary tradition, and would therefore find his imagination confronted with reality. Hutton suggests that Pausanias' focus on sacred sites and monuments of the archaic and classical age shows how an imagined landscape embued with a strong significance by texts or tradition can influence a traveller's perception of an actual place: in some cases he may have been prone to finding what he already expected.[70] Moreover, Pausanias illustrates what made Greece a

3. The Importance of Travelling

very special destination for many of his contemporaries. In the *Periegesis* the sacred and the historical are intimately connected, and the determined quest for authentic traces of the past is often similar to a search for some spiritual truth. There is also a special sense of closeness to the ancients when Pausanias stresses that some feature of local culture survives down to his own time: the encounter with a continuous ancient tradition offers a unique connection to the past, and to the roots of Greek identity.[71]

4

Greek Travel Writing: Between Report and Invention

> ... In the old days poets, historians and philosophers wrote much that is miraculous or mythical. ... One of these is Ktesias, son of Ktesiochos of Knidos, who wrote about India and its characteristics without seeing it himself or hearing about it from anyone who was telling the truth. ... Many others with similar aims have written about their imaginary wanderings, journeys and adventures of theirs, and they talk about huge beasts, cruel men and strange ways of life. Their guide in these falsehoods is Homer's Odysseus, who tells Alkinoos and his court about captured winds, one-eyed men, cannibals and savages, and talks about animals with many heads, and the transformation of his comrades which was achieved with drugs.[1] (Lucian *VH* 1.2-4)

According to Lucian, ancient Greek travel writers could not be trusted. This attack on real or imagined travel writing is humorously exaggerated, and serves as an introduction to the *Verae Historiae* ('True Stories'), a rare ancient example of a fantasy story that never claims to be anything else but a figment of the author's imagination. As far as we can tell, such honesty about fictionality was rare in ancient literature, and distant regions in particular had become a convenient setting for the fantastic.[2] Serious scientific pursuits such as ethnography and geography, however, had to rely on reports of explorers who had reached distant lands, even if their accounts were less than trustworthy, and many unrealistic details about far away regions were handed on reverently from one scientific work to the next. At the same time, the scepticism about 'tall stories' displayed by Lucian also had a long tradition, and heated debates about the world and distant regions were well established probably as early as in the late archaic period.[3] Any author embarking on a work of travel literature in the widest sense could hardly avoid skirting along the blurred boundary between fact and fiction, and an account of ancient travel literature must necessarily follow in their footsteps. It should therefore come as no surprise that works with doubtful factual credentials, namely the Homeric epics and a number of Lucian's satirical writings, will have to play a crucial role in a discussion of Pausanias' literary context.

This chapter introduces main themes in Greek literature that are connected to travelling. Modern travel literature most commonly focuses on individuals' encounters with a place or region and personal experiences of specific journeys.[4] In addition one might also consider a wide range of texts that offer information about particular sites or regions, either general guidebooks or books catering to specific interests, such as specialist guides and sometimes literary works or compilations that constitute appropriate reading for a particular place. The ancients had neither a clearly defined genre of travel writing, nor a notion of books specifically written for travellers; on the contrary, the texts discussed here were variously associated with different genres such as historiography, geography, epic poetry and narrative literature, and many relevant texts survive only in fragments. This may explain why a comprehensive discussion of ancient travel literature has never been attempted. Is it worthwhile to use a modern category, namely 'travel writing', to analyse a set of ancient texts which were not perceived as belonging to one common group in antiquity? In such a situation one has to be careful to avoid assumptions about connections that ancient readers would perhaps not have made themselves. Nevertheless, the works I am discussing in the next two chapters all have something in common: they tackle the problem of representing geography, landscape and travellers' observations and experiences as a text. A comparison of different approaches illustrates the range of options available to an ancient writer who set out to create a piece of travel writing, and the implications of choosing a particular mode of describing a journey or region.

As we shall see, Pausanias' reaction to different traditions of ancient travel writing is complex: he avoids association with some kinds of travel report, while he depends on conventions established to describe foreign regions and customs in historical or geographical texts. There are parallels in other ancient texts to most aspects of Pausanias' project, but nothing suggests that he considers his work as part of a specific genre of travel literature; neither, in spite of the unique scope and complexity of the *Periegesis*, do his statements about plans and methods give the impression that he intended to establish a new genre. If Pausanias expresses affinities with any genre, it is historiography. In the next two chapters I juxtapose the *Periegesis* with other travel texts to analyse the choices Pausanias made in designing his description of Greece. The implications of different conventions of travel writing for an author's credibility will be central to this discussion.

I begin with texts that deal with travellers' experiences and personal observations. This category of literary works contains many examples that are difficult to separate from fiction and fantasy. In order to get a full view of the connections between ancient Greek literature and individual or collective travel experiences we have to cast the net wider, looking at a rather disparate group of texts that, like Pausanias' *Periegesis*, explicitly draw on the knowledge acquired through travelling without dwelling on the process of specific journeys. Many genres and branches of ancient learning benefited from a knowledge of the wider world. Geography and ethnography were naturally dependent on information about far-flung places, and ever since Herodotos historiographers were almost expected to depend on material gathered by travelling. Stories about the customs of barbarians in distant lands became a matter of discussion for philosophers, and accounts of plants and animals offered comparisons for flora and fauna at home as well as material for ethical debates.[5] There was a long and varied tradition which provided models for literary encounters with a historical landscape while also requiring an author to bear in mind readers' prejudices and expectations. I shall return to Pausanias' *Periegesis* at the end of this chapter to assess how it relates to general aspects of Greek travel writing. The following chapters will introduce further Greek texts which offer comparisons to Pausanias' handling of geography and landscapes, history, city topographies and works of art.

As Lucian suggests in the passage that introduces this chapter, the tradition of ancient Greek travellers' accounts starts with Odysseus.[6] As the only surviving eyewitness, the hero relates much of his own journey from Troy to Scheria[7] where the poem 'listens in' on his dramatic report to Alkinoos and the Phaiakians. Lucian may criticise these stories as unbelievable, but the *Odyssey* presents them as the true account of actual events.[8] Odysseus himself, however, makes clear that he cannot always be trusted: his own story shows how he cunningly concealed his true identity from Polyphemos.[9] Later, after his return to Ithaka, Odysseus' credentials as a man who 'tells lies as if they were the truth' are demonstrated even more clearly.[10] The first person he meets is Athena in disguise, and he introduces himself as a Cretan fugitive. The goddess responds by showing him up as a habitual liar:

> Anyone who would outdo you in all kinds of trickery would have to be cunning and crafty indeed, even if it were a god who met you. You are bold, full of various wiles and always out for deceit. Although you are now in your own land it does not look as if you are going to stop lying or inventing artful stories which you love from the bottom of your heart.[11] (Hom. *Od.* 13.291-5)

More such elaborate 'Cretan tales', all well adapted to purpose, audience and circumstances, are presented to Eumaios, Penelope and Laertes.[12] Penelope in particular shows some scepticism about travellers' stories: she tests Odysseus' false account, but his tale is constructed to stand up to her scrutiny, demonstrating how fiction can be made to resemble fact. Most worryingly, these 'Cretan tales' seem much more realistic than the 'actual' events which attracted Lucian's complaints about stories of monsters and miracles. Odysseus' 'Cretan' personas do not talk about marvellous adventures: their comfortable lives were disrupted by events such as family strife, aristocratic rivalry, war and ordinary shipwrecks, all quite plausible at least at the time when the epic was written down. The audience is almost invited to ask why these stories which the poet labels as lies should be less believable than the much more fantastic 'truth': Odysseus, the paradigmatic traveller and adventurer, is also the ultimate unreliable narrator. Greek travel literature would never lose its connection with its epic but dubious beginnings, and travellers' reports, even those that were perhaps truthful descriptions of faraway regions, often attracted doubts from learned commentators. This may explain why, in spite of the importance of travelling for the literary élite, few 'respectable' authors ever wrote detailed accounts of their journeys, except, perhaps, in the guise of different literary genres, particularly history.

Modern travel literature often focuses on emotional responses to a journey and gives much room to the transforming impact of the experience on an individual's character, knowledge or spiritual state. There are few ancient Greek accounts of actual journeys that focus on a traveller's experience and personal reaction in a similar way. As we have seen in the last chapter, Greeks saw travelling as a means of acquiring knowledge and wisdom, and there are stories about the journeys of famous wise men, although few could qualify as travel literature. Philostratos' *Life of Apollonios* includes a fantastic account of the sage's trip to India, which focuses on relating his reflections on what he saw on the journey and his philosophical conversations with people he met along the way, such as the Indian sophists.[13] Pilgrimages are journeys that emphasise a traveller's personal experience, but there are few extensive texts that could be interpreted as a record of the reflections and reactions of pagan Greek pilgrims.[14] The most extensive surviving example, Aelius Aristeides' *Sacred Tales*, is a kind of memoir offering a uniquely personal view of the author's activities with a special emphasis on his relationship with the god Asklepios during a long struggle with various real or imagined illnesses. This text includes accounts of many journeys, some routine trips of a sophist at the top of his profession, and others undertaken in search of healing, usually on the advice of Asklepios. Aristeides' comments document various aspects of travelling, from mundane practicalities and complaints about uncomfortable transport to ideas about the personal spiritual meaning of particular journeys.[15]

Travel experiences play a more significant role in Greek fiction, particularly in the novels, a genre originating in the Hellenistic period. A majority of the preserved examples follow their main characters on a series of journeys, with pirates, storms and shipwrecks as crucial plot devices. The narrative rarely leaves the confines of the familiar world of the Greeks and their neighbours around the Mediterranean, and the exotic is usually represented by 'familiar' barbarians such as Persians or Egyptians, strange people who nevertheless had clear characteristics well-known from classical literature. There is some variation in how the different authors use travel as a narrative device, but, on the whole, the stories pay comparatively little attention to geographical or ethnographical detail, and there is little comment on the process of travelling, unless it is directly relevant to the plot.[16] Greek novels seem almost exclusively interested in those aspects of travelling that 'real' travellers' accounts ignore: they focus on the adventure and the dangers of travelling, and dwell on the hardships that a traveller might endure, including the separation from one's home, family and true love. In the process the characters themselves change: they become more experienced and acquire new knowledge, not scientific expertise of any kind, but rather knowledge about themselves or other characters in the story. Apuleius' *Metamorphoses*, a Latin adaptation of a Greek novel also known from a version preserved among the works of Lucian, offers an extreme example of a traveller changed by his experience. The main character and narrator, Lucius, is turned into an ass, which allows the author to explore a unique angle on the process of travelling, by telling most of his story from the perspective of a beast of burden. The main transformation of the character, however, occurs only when he has regained his human form: his ordeal, followed by a divine epiphany, leads him to become a devout follower of the goddess Isis.[17]

Such an interior perspective remains exceptional: most Greek travel accounts almost exclusively focus on geographical or ethnographical information, describing what the traveller saw, rather than relating personal feelings or reactions to specific events. Many of these texts are reports of explorers or adventurers, and the boundary between reality and invention is decidedly blurred. It is difficult to tell whether the available sample is representative, because many relevant fragments are found in the context of geographical discussions, particularly in Strabo's *Geography*. Our knowledge of ancient explorers' reports is probably biased towards those dealing with the most distant and exotic regions because these required most discussion in geographical works. Strabo's summaries of scientific debates in the Hellenistic period demonstrate that ancient scholars could hardly agree on which texts should be discarded as fiction. The most extensive debate concerned the *Odyssey* and its geographical setting, and there were a number of different theories concerning the location of particular episodes of the story. Most geographers agreed that the epic was essentially a factual account with some poetic embellishment, and Eratosthenes' view that it had nothing to do with actual geography remained an extreme position.[18] There was less agreement about other authors who did not have the benefit of Homer's venerable authority. As Strabo's examples of such debates show, opinions differed so much that almost every account of far-off regions had at some point been labelled as fiction and as fact in different scholarly works.[19]

The tradition of written travellers' accounts probably began with seafarers' logs, preserving information about distances, landmarks and harbours to facilitate orientation for future voyages. This seems to be the origin of the *periplous*, an ancient genre of texts describing coastlines.[20] Most *periploi* are plain lists of places and the distances between them, sometimes with a few added details about settlements or landscapes. Some explorers used this form to record specific, unique journeys, producing early versions of logbooks or travelogues. The best preserved of these texts is Hanno's account of a voyage along the African coast, probably in the early fifth century BC. This report was believed to be a Hellenistic Greek translation of Hanno's original Punic votive inscription, dedicated in a sanctuary in Carthage after his return. Although it is possible that the peoples around the archaic Mediterranean developed similar literary forms of seafarers' reports, and that there was some connection between similar genres in different languages, it is still remarkable that a text derived from a Carthaginian epigraphical source should conform so well with the specific tradition of the Greek *periplous*. In any case, the text is usually seen as a relatively realistic account, and modern scholars have attempted to match up the places Hanno describes with landmarks on the coast of West Africa.[21]

> We took interpreters from them [the Lixites], and we sailed south along the desert shore for two days, and then one day towards the east. There, in the recess of a bay, we found a small island with a circumference of five *stadia*. We called it Kerne and founded a settlement. We calculated from our route that this place lies opposite Carthage, for the length of the journey from Carthage to the Pillars and from there to Kerne was the same.[22] (Hanno 1.8)

Hanno was sent out to found colonies and he notes several such foundations, as well as reporting specific adventures, particularly encounters with native peoples. At the same time he also offers basic geographical information, such as notes on the duration of different stages of his voyage and comments on the weather conditions, resources and potential dangers on the coast. The *periplous* could still be used to great effect in Pausanias' time: Arrian presents his *Periplous of the Black Sea* as a letter he wrote to Hadrian when he was governor of Cappadocia. He uses the ancient literary form to portray his journey as an encounter between Greek, Roman and Barbarian, with many meaningful links to the past.[23]

Before the Roman conquests in north-western Europe the main source of information about the European Atlantic coast was the a work called *Peri tou Okeanou* (On the Ocean) by Pytheas of Massalia, which recorded a voyage probably undertaken in the 320s BC. He circumnavigated Britain and reached some coast further north, perhaps Iceland or Scandinavia, as well as visiting part of the northern coast of the European mainland. The text provided information about the topography of coastlines, and it also offered some observations about native peoples, weather conditions and local plants and animals, often grappling with phenomena which were completely unknown to the Greeks and were therefore difficult to put into words. Both Polybios and Strabo criticised Pytheas' report as untrustworthy, but modern commentators tend to accept the work as a record of an actual voyage because much of Pytheas' information is unique for his time and can be made to match up with actual conditions around the North Sea.[24]

During much of the archaic and classical periods access to the most distant regions of Asia depended on good relations with the Persians, and reports about India in particular were transmitted by Greeks who were in the service of the Great King. Around 500 BC Skylax of Karyanda was commissioned by Dareios I to explore the Indus. He sailed down the river and then continued westward along the coast until he reached the Red Sea. The literary account of this journey described a world full of monstrous animals and strange races which were not quite human.[25] More miraculous stories about the east were provided by Ktesias, a Greek physician at the Persian court around 400 BC. His *Indike* was supposedly based on accounts of travellers, but Photios' summary of this lost work suggests that this text was a collection of marvellous phenomena, presenting an India more miraculous and strange than that of Skylax.[26] In fact, even where Ktesias could rely on first-hand information, in his *Persian History*, he produced a highly unreliable account.[27] Since the *Odyssey* was generally considered at least partly factual there was a venerable precedent for introducing such fantastic elements in descriptions of distant regions.

While some authors merely embellished their reports, others went further and focused on purely imaginary regions and peoples. The earliest 'traveller's report' of which we know any detail is the *Arimaspeia* of Aristeas of Prokonnesos, an epic poem probably written in the early sixth century BC.[28] This man had already attained mythical status in Herodotos' time, and, as far as we can tell, his journey to the lands beyond the Scythians included plenty of fantastic material, such as the one-eyed Arimaspians, gold-guarding griffins and the mythical people of the Hyperboreans. This fictional tradition of explorers' tales was an inspiration for later authors who wrote utopian fiction about fantastic journeys to islands at the edges of the earth, beyond the confines of the known continents, or even places outside the world, such as the underworld or the moon.[29]

By the late classical period anyone who planned to write about their experiences on a journey to remote places must have been very aware that they would have to work hard to establish their trustworthiness. Military campaigns into hitherto little known regions gave rise to a new kind of travel account which was more akin to historiography than to the old adventurers' tales. While historical works often commented on movements of people or gave descriptions of particular regions, they would not usually provide a detailed account of a particular journey. Military campaigns into unknown regions offered the opportunity to present what was essentially an explorer's tale as a historical account which could claim more credibility than the tales of a lone seafarer, not least because there would be many eyewitnesses who, like the readers, shared the author's education, wealth and high class.[30]

Xenophon's *Anabasis* records the adventures in 401-399 BC of the Greek mercenaries hired by the Persian prince Cyrus for his attempt to overthrow his brother, King Artaxerxes II. While the fragments of most explorers' tales focus on describing foreign regions and unusual discoveries, the *Anabasis* is presented as a historical narrative which chronicles the Greek mercenaries' campaign to northern Mesopotamia and their bid to return home through the unknown hostile territory of eastern Anatolia. Once the Black Sea coast and therefore familiar Greek territory is reached,[31] the text reverts from a travel account to a more historical mode, focusing on events involving the Greeks, rather than on their movements and observations. Throughout the work, Xenophon maintains a strictly impersonal authorial voice, never betraying the fact that he is, in fact, identical with one of the central characters of the story. Nevertheless, this text is the longest and most extensive personal account of an actual journey that survives from antiquity. The work was probably written decades after the events and it is not clear whether Xenophon had an original travelogue as a source for the minute details he is recording.[32] He includes specific information about distances, routes and topography as well as comments on weather conditions, flora and fauna. When Xenophon talks about the settlements and people they came across on the way, his perspective is clearly not that of an explorer encountering unknown cultures but rather that of an army commander most concerned with security and provisions. He also conveys a sense of the men's reactions to danger, hardships and successes, and the text includes moments of high emotion, most famously the scene when, after a long, difficult march through mountainous inland territory, the Greeks finally catch a first glimpse of the sea.[33]

When Alexander started his campaign against Persia he was determined to make history, and by taking a historian, Kallisthenes, he made sure that there would be an official record. History was, however, not his only concern: there were also experts tasked with recording distances and information relating to geography, ethnography or the natural sciences.[34] It is not clear how far Alexander expected to go when he set out, but he clearly assumed that he would pass areas which had not been explored properly. In this he may have been influenced by Aristotle whose work shows a particular concern with collecting, revising and extending knowledge in various scholarly fields. Alexander set out to make history in a political as well as in a scientific sense, and when he left the centres of the Persian empire to continue towards Baktria and India his conquest did indeed turn into the exploration of regions about which the Greeks knew hardly more than miraculous stories. Alexander's epic undertaking made such an impression that it inspired a number of participants to write their own version of the story.[35] None of these accounts is preserved, but, like

Xenophon before them, most of these probably focused on the historical events while leaving some room for details about the regions and peoples they encountered.

Alexander's scientific staff were credited with significant advances in obtaining reliable knowledge about the east, although their original records apparently did not survive for long, so that Strabo, around the beginning of the Common Era, knew them only through another source.[36] A number of officials who served under Alexander and his immediate successors also wrote about India. The best known of these accounts is Nearchos' *Indike*, which was the main source for Arrian's work of the same title. Nearchos' work dealt with Indian geography, peoples, customs and animals, followed by a *periplous*-style account of his voyage from the Indus to the mouth of the Tigris in the Persian Gulf. For Strabo, Nearchos and his fellow naval commander and geographical author Onesikritos were men who 'speak the truth, but with a stammer':[37] the results may not have been very reliable, but at least they were trying to represent India in a realistic manner. In the long run, however, Alexander's exploits apparently did not have a lasting impact on how travellers described distant regions of Asia: Strabo scathingly cites Megasthenes and Deimachos, ambassadors to the court of the Maurya kings in the late fourth and early third century BC, as examples of authors for whom personal experience was apparently no obstacle to a return to the old well-rehearsed reports of miracles and monstrous people.[38] In fact, Alexander himself soon became the hero of the Alexander Romance, a tradition that produced a collection of fantastic adventures among the strange peoples of an imaginary east, a return to epic fiction that was now set in an India that owed more to the colourful early reports of Skylax and Ktesias than to the sober accounts generated by his own campaign.[39]

Away from the murky waters of untrustworthy travellers' tales, there was a long tradition of texts about places or regions which did not talk about travelling at all. The earliest example is the Catalogue of Ships in the *Iliad*, which simply lists the names of many Greek tribes and cities in a roughly geographical order. Many place names are given epithets such as 'sandy', 'well-built fortress' or 'rich in sheep', but these sparse attributes, though usually quite appropriate, are clearly not intended to provide a meaningful description of a place or landscape. This list could be seen as the beginning of factual geography, because it provides a geographical framework which remained an authoritative source for Greek historical topography.[40]

We have already encountered the *periplous* as an early form of travellers' account, but the norm of the genre was probably a coastal description listing places without reference to a particular voyage.

> After the Megarians are the cities of the Athenians. And the first in Attica
> is Eleusis, where the sanctuary of Demeter is, and a fortification. By this is

the island of Salamis, with a city and a harbour. Next the Piraeus and the Legs [the Long Walls?] and Athens. And the Piraeus has three harbours. Anaphlystos, a fort with a harbour; Sounion, a promontory with a fort; a sanctuary of Poseidon; Thorikos, a fort with two harbours; Rhamnous, a fort. And there are many other harbours in Attica. Circumnavigation of the Athenian territory: 1140 *stadia*: from the Iapis territory to Sounion 490 *stadia*, from Sounion as far as the borders of the Boiotians 650 *stadia*.[41] (Pseudo-Skylax 57)

This description of Attica is taken from the anonymous *Periplous of the Great Sea* which dates from the late fourth century BC and was falsely attributed to Skylax of Karyanda. The work describes the whole Mediterranean, following the coasts in a long clockwise route from Spain via the coasts of Italy, Greece and Syria to North Africa. The author focuses on the most basic features, and even a place as famous as Athens hardly distracts him from his purpose. A similar literary genre, the *stadiasmos*, listed places and distances along overland routes.[42]

These texts represent the beginning of Greek geographical writing, and as a literary equivalent to maps they may well have contributed to the development of early cartography in sixth century Ionia.[43] In the same period Hekataios of Miletos wrote his *Periodos Ges* (*Journey Around the World*) which recorded geography in the manner of a *periplous* but also established geography as a science concerned with the shape of the earth and the position of the continents. Later geographers paid more attention to overviews, using geometrical comparisons to explain better how different places related to each other in space. Nevertheless, geographical works remained concerned with describing the world by listing regions and places, even if, as we can observe in Strabo's *Geography*, they might allow more space for additional material such as descriptions of the landscape, historical details or information about the life of the locals.[44] The ancient mode of describing the world by listing places with a few attributes did not, however, become obsolete: in the second century AD a certain Dionysios composed a work entitled *Periegesis of the Inhabited World* which described the whole world in about 1,200 epic verses.[45]

Texts dealing with specific regions or sites in greater detail are particularly dependent on knowledge gained by a visit. Pausanias' work was not the first to offer descriptions of sites and monuments: from the late classical period there were books that dealt with particular sites. These included at least three books on Athenian monuments by a Diodoros dating from the fourth century, and a number of works by Polemon of Ilion, for example on the Athenian Acropolis, monuments of Sparta, treasuries in Delphi and three books on his native city, written probably in the early second century BC. As far as we can tell, these works presented monuments together with accounts of local history and customs. The fragments suggest that their interests are similar to the topics Pausanias includes in his *logoi*, but since we are dealing with whole books on single sites the descriptions must have been more detailed or the additional information much more extensive. It has traditionally been assumed that there was a *periêgêsis* genre of such site descriptions, but recently Hutton has disputed this theory.[46] None of these works is preserved, and the only surviving work that focuses on one site is Lucian's *Dea Syria*, written at about the same time as Pausanias' *Periegesis*.[47] A different approach to Greek cities, with an interest in contemporary landscapes and a satirical perspective of the local people can be found in the fragments of Herakleides Kritikos (formerly known as Pseudo-Dikaiarchos), probably written in the third century BC.[48]

Last but not least, travel was seen as essential for the work of a historian, and standards set by historiographers affected authors' use of personal research in many genres and disciplines. After all, Herodotos, the 'Father of History', presents his work as *Historiai* – Enquiries, and he leaves no doubt that, for him, information gathering meant extensive travelling.[49] He included long ethnographical *logoi* and local stories from many places in his work, and his source criticism often takes the form of comparisons between different peoples' versions of events. From the beginning, therefore, original research was seen as essential for a historian, and historiography also set the standards for the scrutiny and critique of evidence gathered in this way. Thucydides set a lasting trend for a narrow focus on political history, but historiography continued to depend on sources from different places and a good knowledge of geography and local circumstances also remained essential for understanding and explaining specific events.[50] The debate about the value or necessity of autopsy for historiographers became increasingly relevant when historians began to draw on an ever-growing literary tradition. Few openly shared Diodoros' view that a lack of personal involvement guaranteed a healthy detachment, while authors who, like Polybios or Josephus, were participants or eyewitnesses of historical events they were describing were particularly keen to stress the value of personal experience.[51] Lucian's discourse *How to Write History* shows that the subject was still a crucial issue in the Parthian Wars of the 160s AD, when historians rushed out to write accounts of the current events.[52] The importance of stressing one's autopsy was acknowledged by other scholars as well: Strabo, for example, boasts about his travel experience:

> You could not find one other geographical writer who has travelled over much more of the distances just mentioned than I, but those who have seen more in the west have not covered as much in the east, and others for whom the opposite is true lag behind in the west. The same is true with regard to regions in the north and south.[53] (Strabo 2.5.11)

Despite this proud statement, most commentators agree that Strabo does, in fact, display surprisingly little knowledge even of many core areas of the

Mediterranean world. Statements about personal research on location had apparently become an indispensable means of establishing the credibility of a scholarly work, whether they were accurate or not.[54] Second Sophistic authors used real or bogus reports of their own experience in various contexts, from Aristeides' discussion of the Nile which reports his efforts to measure Egyptian monuments to Dio's elaborate travel stories that serve as context for philosophical discussions.[55] Lucian parodies this tradition when his hero Menippos visits the underworld and the heavens to solve philosophical problems by seeing the evidence for himself.[56]

Autopsy and travel experience are at the centre of Pausanias' *Periegesis*, providing a basic structure and a motivation for detailed research, but, just as in other texts, they are also a source of authority:

> I will not deny that the Tantalos who was the son of Thyestes or Broteas (both versions are given) and who was married to Klytaimnestra before Agamemnon is buried here; but he who, according to tradition, was the son of Zeus and Plouto is buried on Mount Sipylos – I know because I have seen it (*idôn oida*), and the grave is worth seeing.[57] (Paus. 2.22.3)

Pausanias settles an argument about conflicting mythical stories simply by asserting his personal knowledge: 'I know because I have seen it.'[58] Other Second Sophistic authors' cavalier attitude to statements of autopsy led some scholars to suspect that the *Periegesis* was just a compilation of second-hand information presented as original research, and it is likely that similar suspicions could have arisen in antiquity.[59] Pausanias must have been aware that autopsy as an overused literary *topos* had become almost meaningless, and he went to great lengths to indicate that his research was authentic and recent. Numerous references to the current state of Roman Greece, including the description of many hardly impressive sites or ruined monuments, give an impression of immediacy which would be difficult to achieve in a compilation from earlier texts. Reports about disappointments add to this picture of authenticity, for example when a long trip to Phigalia to see an unusual statue of Demeter results in the discovery that it had been destroyed some decades earlier.[60] Pausanias can therefore juxtapose his own description of contemporary circumstances with the outdated information that inspired this particular trip.

It is quite clear that in his efforts to authenticate and evaluate his sources Pausanias takes his lead from historiography. Many readers of the *Periegesis* feel immediately reminded of Herodotos, and there is no question that the similarities are deliberate. Arrian and Lucian produced texts in Herodotos' Ionian Greek, but Pausanias decided not to go so far.[61] He follows the historian in a more subtle way, by imitating his manner of establishing credibility through personal experience. Pausanias' text resembles Herodotos' *Histories* most closely when he reports his reaction to what he has seen, and when he demonstrates how he uses his informed judgement to evaluate and interpret his material. This particular mode of imitating Herodotos was by no means a conventional or safe choice. After all, Herodotos was respected for his graceful style, but many doubted his credibility, and his manner of presenting and juxtaposing stories had become a particular cause for suspicion.[62]

Journeys recorded in travel texts usually led to distant, strange places which needed to be understood by highlighting how different they were to Greek cultural norms. There were also stories about travellers who had come the other way, most famously the legendary Scythian sage Anacharsis, which allowed Greek writers to reverse their standards of ethnographical interpretation by presenting a barbarian's view of Greece. Either way, travel accounts allowed Greeks to reflect upon their own identity by exploring differences between foreign cultures and their own.[63] Pausanias' *Periegesis* introduces a new angle to this cultural discourse: it is the account of an outside observer, but one who essentially shares his cultural background with the local people.[64] He is therefore able to relate all but the most unusual aspects of local tradition to a common Greek history and heritage. Whatever might appear strange here is actually Greek by definition. The observer cannot distance himself from what he does not understand, but whatever he sees, however strange, is an aspect of his own culture because it is, after all, located in the old motherland of Greece. Unlike most travellers before him, Pausanias seeks, and finds, answers about the nature of Greek culture where it is most at home: in the most ancient heartlands of the Greek world.

5

A Sense of Space: Landscape and Geography

> The Isthmos of Corinth stretches on one side down to the sea at Kenchreai, and on the other to the sea at Lechaion, and this is what makes the land inside [i.e. in the Peloponnese] mainland. He who tried to turn the Peloponnese into an island gave up before he had dug through the Isthmos. And the place from where they began to dig can still be seen, but they never advanced into the rock. Thus the Peloponnese is still mainland, as it is by nature.[1] (Paus. 2.1.5)

This is Pausanias' description of one of the most remarkable geographical features in the area covered by the *Periegesis*. In antiquity the Isthmos of Corinth was seen as a significant boundary between two distinct parts of Greece,[2] and in Pausanias' *Periegesis* it marks the point where the text embarks on the seven books which deal with the Peloponnese. There is no introduction to this major section of the work, and an overview of the peninsula's regional divisions is offered only much later, at the beginning of Book VIII.[3] Pausanias apparently did not find it necessary to focus on the special geographical situation of Corinth (Fig. 6). He does say that the Isthmos is bounded by the sea in two places, but the covert reference to Nero's failed canal project is the only reminder of the fact that this narrow stretch of land separated two gulfs which were several days' dangerous sea voyage apart. Instead Pausanias refers to Kenchreai and Lechaion, the Corinthian ports which are introduced properly only a few paragraphs later. Even in this context it is not explained that one harbour faces towards the Corinthian Gulf and the Adriatic while the other offered access to the Saronic Gulf and Aegean, and we are never told explicitly which harbour lies on which side of the Isthmos.[4] Every educated Greek would know about the unique location of Corinth and the almost proverbial wealth that it had once brought to the city.[5] It is quite possible that in describing such a famous region Pausanias was keen to avoid anything that might seem commonplace to an informed reader.

We can see a slightly more methodical approach in Strabo's *Geography*, written about 180 years earlier. Strabo based most of his work on second-hand information, but he did know Corinth from personal experience, which means the two authors are, for once, on a level playing field.[6]

> The coast begins on one side at Lechaion, and on the other at Kenchreai, a village with a harbour about seventy *stadia* from the city. The latter is used by those from Asia, and Lechaion serves those from Italy. ... The shore

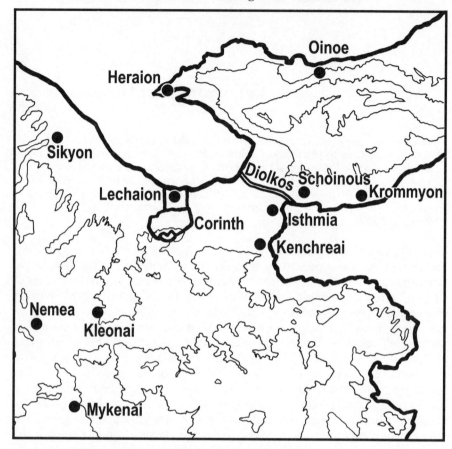

Fig. 6. The Isthmos of Corinth.

continues from there to Pagai in the Megarid and it is washed by the Corinthian Gulf. It is curved and forms the Diolkos, the slipway towards the other shore at Schoinous near Kenchreai. Halfway between Lechaion and Pagai there was once the oracle of Akraian Hera, and Olmiai, the promontory which forms the gulf where Oinoe and Pagai are situated: both are forts, the former belongs to Megara, and Olmiai is Corinthian. From Kenchreai you come to Schoinous at the narrow part of the Diolkos and then to Krommyonia. Before this coast lies the Saronic Gulf and the Eleusinian Gulf, which is almost the same, and it is adjacent to the Hermionic Gulf.[7] (Strabo 8.6.22)

Without a map and some idea of the geography it may still be difficult to visualise the topography of the Isthmos from this description, but Strabo provides much more detail than Pausanias and he manages to convey some sense of the location of different places along the coasts on each side.

5. A Sense of Space: Landscape and Geography

Just like Pausanias, Strabo wrote for an educated audience, but the author of a geographical work was almost obliged to pay attention to such a striking topography, however well-known. Pausanias' *Periegesis* is clearly not following the same rules, even if it uses geography as an organising principle.

Pausanias fails to mention that the Isthmos of Corinth is not just an interesting geographical feature, but also a unique landscape which offers spectacular views. Travellers following Pausanias' route would approach from the Megarid in the north-east, and before descending to the Isthmos they could take in the view, as Edward Dodwell did in autumn 1806:

> In forty minutes we reached an elevated part of the mountain, which commands a most extensive and animating view. The whole circumference of the spacious horizon seemed occupied with classical regions of high renown and of deep interest. Below us appeared the Isthmus, the Acrocorinthos, the Saronic and Crissaean gulfs. The more remote prospect unveiled the soft and undulating lines of the Attic coast and mountains, fading into the receding distance of the Sunium promontory, which was distinguished as a speck upon the blue aether of the terminating sky. The beautifully varied coast of Argolis, the abrupt and pointed promontory of Methana, with the islands of Kalauria, Aegina, and Salamis, and other insular rocks, embellish the surface of the Saronic gulf. Beyond the Corinthian sea are distinguished the hills of Achaia, surmounted by the loftier summits of Arcadia glittering with snow. (Dodwell (1819) II.183, 30 November 1806)

Dodwell travelled through late Ottoman Greece where little survived of what Pausanias had seen, and the evocative ancient place names he uses in this passage to restore Corinth's pivotal place in Greek historical topography were only just beginning to take hold again.[8] The physical landscape, however, was still the same, and where neither Strabo nor Pausanias found it necessary to comment on the scenery, Dodwell manages to convey a sense of an impressive view. At the same time, he acknowledges the geographical significance of the Isthmos, and as he scans the view from east to west he uses his vantage point to provide the reader with a comprehensive overview that connects areas he has already seen with places he is about to visit.[9]

These three descriptions of the same area illustrate that there are many different ways of turning a landscape into text. An author has to choose from a set of defining characteristics, be they topographical features, flora and fauna or aspects of human geography, such as settlements, monuments, agricultural landscapes and road networks. Other aspects of the landscape might not be immediately visible but they are nevertheless important, such as connections with myth or history, or a special religious significance. The author communicates his or her selective image of a landscape to allow the readers to create an image in their minds which may or may not be similar to what the writer has seen, or to what other

59

readers might imagine. It is not enough to list all the interesting places, but in order to produce more than a catalogue an author also needs to explain how different locations relate to each other. Topography is an obvious organising principle for a travel text, but it is not the only way in which a landscape can be evoked and recreated in words: to some travellers the meaning of particular places may appear more important than their physical location.

Pausanias' description of the Isthmos offers neither a geographical overview nor a visual impression, although this area offers a particularly good opportunity for both. One passage is not sufficient to draw conclusions about a literary work as extensive and complex as the *Periegesis*, but this example illustrates that Pausanias' text does not always conform to our expectations of what is appropriate or necessary for the description of a particular place. Modern readers are used to visualising landscapes with maps and images, and most travel books will include such illustrations. The communication from travel writer to reader is heavily influenced by such habits of visual representation. Today's travel writers are likely to think of topographical relations between places with a map in mind, and descriptions of the scenery will be influenced by the experience of taking and viewing photographs of landscapes. Since the *Periegesis* shares important features with a familiar genre of contemporary travel writing, modern readers are likely to approach the text with similar expectations. Editions and studies of Pausanias regularly challenge the norms of classics publications because it is difficult to present this text to a modern audience without offering at least maps, and, if at all possible, images as well. We need to recognise, however, that Pausanias' ancient readers did not share our familiarity with maps or our easy access to pictures of regions we have not visited ourselves. In fact, our way of visualising landscapes based on maps or images may often make it difficult to notice what Pausanias does *not* say, and one needs to pay attention to realise that the *Periegesis* rarely offers the complete representation of the landscape which we would expect from a modern travel text.[10]

Anyone who knows Greece will be struck by Pausanias' apparent indifference to even the most impressive scenery. The landscape is usually just mentioned in passing, for example when directions for a route are given, or when topographical features are connected to local stories or cults. Such references generally acknowledge the presence of a mountain, spring or forest, but any information that would suggest what a place actually looks like is exceptional. In Pausanias' text features of the landscape, natural or man-made, become 'visible' only when he considers them worth mentioning. Mere natural beauty was not sufficient to qualify for that category, because the focus of the *Periegesis* is firmly on places that are historically or culturally significant, with a particular interest in sacred sites.[11] The description therefore includes apparently inconspicuous items such as trees, rocks or wells which had interesting stories to tell, while impressive aspects of scenery might not be mentioned at all.

The valley of the Styx in northern Arkadia was worth a visit because of its important role in Greek myth as a river of the underworld by which the gods swore their most solemn oaths. Pausanias uses a whole chapter (8.18) to discuss traditions about the Styx, while his comments on the route take up only a few lines.

> As you leave Pheneos towards the west, the left road leads to Kleitor, and on the right is the road to Nonakris and the water of the Styx. In ancient times Nonakris was a town (*polisma*) of the Arkadians, named after the wife of Lykaon, but in our time it is in ruins, and most of these are hidden. Not far from the ruins is a high cliff: I know of no other that reaches such a height. A water trickles down the cliff, and the Greeks call it the water of the Styx.[12] (Paus. 8.17.6)

This visit could not be made without considerable effort, because the route from Pheneos to Nonakris leads through extremely mountainous territory. Pausanias does not mention that these few lines describe a tour of at least a day's travel each way over passes and through narrow valleys which bear little resemblance to a cultivated Mediterranean landscape. Nevertheless, in this passage Pausanias does at least acknowledge the landscape in its own right, perhaps because it was such an apt setting for the legendary river. In his commentary, Frazer, who visited the area in autumn 1895, tried to give readers a better sense of what Pausanias might have seen:

> The path winds up the glen, keeping at first high on the right bank. The bed of the stream here is prettily wooded with poplars and other trees ... the water of the Styx, as seen from above, appears to be of a clear light blue colour, with a tinge of green. This colour, however, is only apparent, and is due to the slaty rocks, of a pale greenish-blue colour, among which the river flows. In reality the water is quite clear and colourless. In about twenty minutes from leaving the village [Solos] we come in sight of a cliff over which the water of the Styx descends. It is an immense cliff, absolutely perpendicular, a little to the left or east of the high conical summit of Mount Chelmos. The whole of this northern face of this mountain is in fact nothing but a sheer and in places even overhanging precipice of grey rock – by far the most awful line of precipices I have ever seen. ... The cliff down which the water comes is merely the lower end of this huge wall of rock. Seen from a distance it appears to be streaked perpendicularly with black and red. The black streak marks the line of the waterfall ... In the crevices of the cliffs to the right and left of the fall great patches of snow remain all the year through. (Frazer (1898) IV.250)

Frazer could draw on a well-established tradition of landscape description in literature, and he is catering for the expectations of contemporary readers. In his time the description of scenery played an important part in fiction, where it could set the mood of the story or reflect the emotional state of a character.

Ancient Greek literature did not develop such a strong tradition of comprehensive, evocative landscape descriptions, although some writers did discuss the scenery. Travel accounts often dealt with exotic, distant regions, and they tend to focus on the unusual or marvellous without attempting to give a clear general impression of the surroundings. Familiar Mediterranean landscapes offered more scope for writers to pay attention to particular aspects and to tailor their description to suit the purpose of the text. The *Odyssey* introduces Ithaka from three different perspectives: the narrator sees the island from the point of view of the approaching ship, describing the harbour and its surroundings and the cave where the Phaiakians land to leave the sleeping Odysseus. When the hero wakes up he does not recognise his homeland, and he perceives a rather inhospitable natural landscape, with high mountains and forests, and a coast full of sheltered bays. Finally, when Athena reveals to him that he has finally reached his home she evokes the cultivated landscape by praising its suitability for agriculture and pasture.[13] Beginning with the Homeric epics, Greek poets drew material for similes from specific aspects of Mediterranean landscapes, which are often observed in loving detail. In Hellenistic bucolic poetry such references are used systematically to suggest a pastoral setting, and at times they evoke a specific landscape, such as Theokritos' Sicily.[14]

Dio Chrysostom frames part of his discussion on kingship with a story about his wanderings in the Peloponnese. Dio does not intend to inform his audience about Greece, but he needs a suitable context for a mythical story which forms part of his argument.

> On my way from Heraia to Pisa I walked along the Alpheios following the road for a while, and then I got into woodland and rough terrain with paths leading to flocks and herds, but I met no-one and could not ask the way. ... I saw a clump of oaks on a hill which looked like a sacred grove and I made my way there, hoping that from there I might discover some road or house. I found stones roughly set together, hanging hides of animals that had been sacrificed and some clubs and staffs, all apparently dedications of herdsmen.[15] (Dio Chrysostom 1.52-3)

This description of a Greek landscape could not be much more different from Pausanias' perspective. The setting is somewhere on the boundary between Arkadia and Elis, but apart from the place names which locate Dio's adventure in the western Peloponnese there is no indication of anything that would be specific to these particular places. The description of the cult place consists of pastoral stereotypes, and it seems to owe more to bucolic poetry than to reality.

In terms of genre and attention to local detail, Herakleides Kritikos' Hellenistic description of Attica and Boiotia[16] offers the closest comparison to the *Periegesis*. Herakleides' different perspective is, however, reflected in his approach to the landscape.

> From there to Tanagra it is 130 *stadia*. The road runs through olive groves and woodlands, wholly free of any fear of highwaymen. The site of the city is high and rugged. It looks white and chalky, but the fronts of the houses with their painted decorations make it look very beautiful.[17] (Herakleides F1.8 (Pfister))

Herakleides is interested in contemporary life, and his description reflects the general visual impression of the landscape. He gives his readers an idea of what Tanagra looks like as one approaches, without attaching deeper meaning to any of the features he is mentioning. There is no passage in the *Periegesis* which offers a similar image of a city and its surroundings. When Pausanias is on the move, he keeps his eyes firmly on the route he is following. The reader encounters locations that are 'worth seeing' at the point when they are reached on the road, without the benefit of a previous glimpse ahead from a distance. The contemporary human landscape barely registers at all: although there are a few references to agricultural produce and the general state of settlements in the *Periegesis*, there is no parallel to Herakleides' description of olive groves and houses in Tanagra.[18]

Pausanias may not have known Dio's or Herakleides' texts, but it is likely that he was aware of the different options a writer had when he wanted to describe a landscape. His decision to pay little attention to the scenery and to emphasise those features that were relevant to his particular interests is likely to be deliberate. In fact, Pausanias' selective approach bears some resemblance to the way in which historians integrate geographical information within their narrative, and this should not come as a surprise, because the study of historical texts and their techniques of narration and description were part of the standard rhetorical education.[19] Ancient historiographers focus on specific features in the landscape where they are relevant to the story, particularly in the context of warfare, for example to explain the route of a campaign or the layout of a battlefield. As the events unfold, details are mentioned when they become relevant, and the reader is rarely provided with a comprehensive overview, let alone an impression of the scenery.[20] Pausanias was clearly familiar with this aspect of historiography: his own historical narratives include topographical references, and he also made some effort to relate earlier historical accounts to the landscape when he visited the locations of important events.[21]

Topography was much more important to Pausanias' *Periegesis* than the visual impact of the scenery, especially because the whole work is organised along geographical lines. The reader had to be able to follow the description and to understand the links between different places. Modern readers will soon discover many shortcomings in Pausanias' topographies, but it is important to understand his efforts in the context of ancient attitudes to geography. It is hardly possible to overestimate the influence of maps on how descriptions of landscapes are perceived today. To us, the outlines of continents and countries have become familiar icons, and we are used to thinking of landscapes with that overview in mind.[22] The Greeks created their first maps of the world in the sixth century BC, and it seems that early cartography was particularly important in philosophical discussions about the shape of the world and the definition of the continents. More commonly, however, geography depended on verbal description rather than on maps.[23] During the Hellenistic and Roman period geographical knowledge was refined, particularly after many areas became more accessible and better known through conquest and exploration. The *Geography* of Pausanias' close contemporary Ptolemy summarises the results of this long process as a set of co-ordinates and cartographical instructions, and, while the areas close to the edges are vague, the resulting outline of the Mediterranean regions bears a close resemblance to the familiar contours of modern maps.[24] As we can see in Strabo's work, geographical overviews could also be provided by comparing regions and coastlines with geometrical shapes to which one could add measurements of crucial distances.

> The shape of the Peloponnese resembles the leaf of a plane tree. Its length and width are nearly equal, each about 1400 *stadia*, that is from west to east, namely from Cape Chelonatas through Olympia and the territory of Megalopolis to the Isthmos, and, from south to north, from Maliai though Arkadia to Aigion. The circumference, without counting the bays, is 4000 *stadia*. ... At the Diolkos where they draw ships overland from one sea to the other the Isthmos is 40 *stadia* wide.[25] (Strabo 8.2.10)

Strabo's description of the Peloponnese coincides relatively well with the visual impression we get from maps, but this system of describing regional geography can become rather cumbersome. The complex topography of Greece as a whole, for example, proves a major challenge for Strabo, who opts to divide it into a sequence of 'peninsulas' divided by imaginary lines from coast to coast (see Fig. 7).

> The first of these peninsulas is the Peloponnese, closed in by an isthmus which is forty *stadia* wide. The second includes the first, and its isthmus extends from Pagai in the Megarid to Nisaia, which is the naval station of the Megarians; the passage across this isthmus is 120 *stadia* from sea to sea. The third peninsula also comprises the last, and its isthmus reaches from the interior of the Krisaian Gulf to Thermopylai. The line we imagine between these is about 508 *stadia*, including within it the whole of Boiotia and cutting through Phokis and the territory of the Epiknemidians. The fourth peninsula has its isthmus between the Ambrakian Gulf, through Mount Oita and Trachinia to the Malian Gulf, about eight hundred *stadia*.

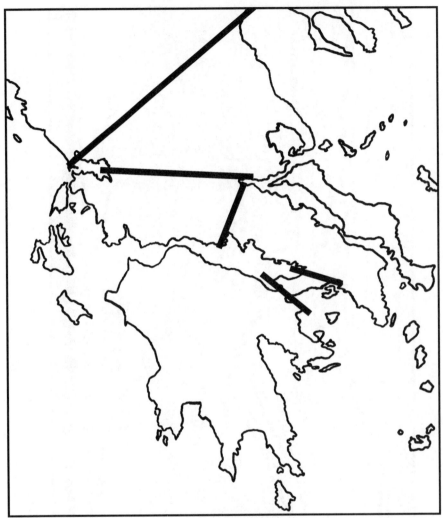

Fig. 7. Divisions of Greece: Strabo 8.1.3.

There is another isthmus of over a thousand *stadia*, from the Ambrakian Gulf through Thessaly and Macedonia to the bay of the Thermaian Gulf.[26] (Strabo 8.1.3)

It seems that such efforts to gain an overview of the shapes of coastlines and regions were mainly a matter for geographical theorists, while detailed discussions of particular regions were handled quite differently.[27]

Most ancient descriptions of landscapes never attempt to give a comprehensive sense of spatial relations between places. They follow a route or

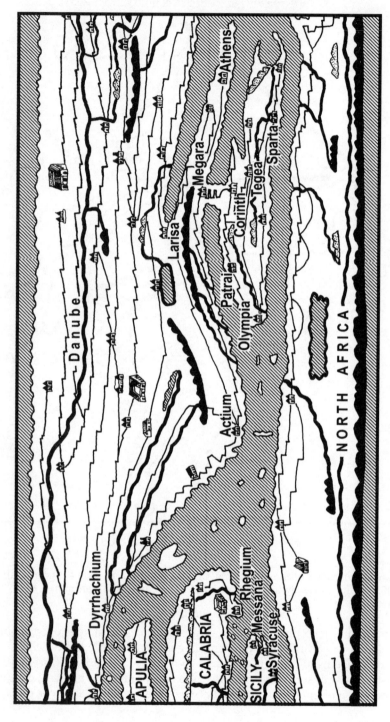

Fig. 8. The Peutinger Table, Section VII.2-VIII.1 – Southern Italy, Sicily, Greece. Based on Miller (1962).

coastline listing place names or landmarks, in linear fashion, but they hardly provide any sense of the layout of the landscape in two dimensions, as a modern map would do. Travellers plodding along the road at hardly more than walking speed were more concerned with the next inn or fork in the road than with the general lie of the land, and it seems that their linear view of the world, together with the sailor's focus on coastlines, continued to define how most people thought about topography. The *Peutinger Table*, a medieval copy of a late antique Roman road map, provides a visual representation of this literally pedestrian perspective (Fig. 8).[28] It was drawn some time after Ptolemy's map and includes a similar area, namely the Roman empire and Asia as far as India. The results are, however, very different: the regions around the Mediterranean appear as three parallel strips of land, with central Europe on top, Italy turned sideways to fill most of the centre, and Africa at the bottom. Like a modern diagram of a public transport system, the *Peutinger Table* is not concerned with reproducing actual topography; instead it focuses on the communication lines, indicating which roads lead to particular places, the number of stations between large cities and points where routes intersect. Geographical features are included to indicate where roads meet with coasts, mountain ranges or rivers, but they do not add up to a comprehensive overview of a 'global' geography. In literature the *periplous* stood at the beginning of this long tradition of describing landscapes in linear fashion.

The early Hellenistic *Periplous of the Great Sea* and its sparse description of Attica were introduced in the previous chapter. It describes coasts in some detail, including smaller harbours and landmarks, but the inland is ignored almost completely.

> Arkadia lies in the interior and comes down to the sea below Lepreon. There are cities inland, and the biggest ones are these: Tegea, Mantinea, Heraia, Orchomenos, Stymphalos. There are also other cities. The coastal voyage of the Lepreates' territory is 100 *stadia*.[29] (Pseudo-Skylax 44)

The author of the *Periplous* justifies a quick tour of the interior of the Peloponnese because Arkadia had some claim to Triphylia, a region on the west coast of the Peloponnese. The Arkadian cities are listed in no apparent geographical order. One might be surprised that a text that describes a coastal voyage mentions an inland region at all. For the Greeks, whose cities lined up around the coasts of the Mediterranean 'like frogs around the pond',[30] there were not many inland regions worth writing about, but mainland Greece was something of an abnormality in this respect, because some of its famous ancient cities were not located close to the coast.

Strabo's treatment of Greece shows a strong influence of the *periplous* approach. Although he aims to provide a universal geography his grasp of inland regions remains surprisingly vague.[31] Again, Arkadia provides a good test case:

> Arkadia lies in the middle of the Peloponnese, and it contains most of the mountainous areas. ... Because of the complete devastation of this region it is not necessary to say much about it. The cities have been destroyed by continuous wars, although they were once famous, and the farmers have abandoned the countryside at the time when most cities were united to found Megalopolis. And now Megalopolis itself has become what the comic poet describes as 'the Great City is a great desert'.[32] (Strabo 8.8.1)

The description of the whole region takes up all of two pages of Greek text in the Teubner edition, comparatively little by Strabo's standards, and quite insufficient if we consider Pausanias' substantial Book VIII (110 pages) which shows that about 180 years later there was plenty to write about in Arkadia. Strabo provides 'scientific' geographical overviews, but as soon as he 'zooms' in on particular regions to provide more detailed descriptions he reverts to a traditional linear approach. He stays close to the coast with occasional short tours into the interior. Strabo states that in focusing on the coastline he is following Ephoros, whose description traced the coasts of Greece from west to east, just like the *Periplous of the Great Sea*.[33]

Pausanias organises his description of Greece in a completely different way, focusing on the inland areas and dividing them by regions and cities instead of following the coasts. This approach is rarely found in ancient texts: Herakleides follows overland routes and the *Iliad*'s Catalogue of Ships lists the contingents of the Greek army in tribal or regional groups, presenting individual communities or cities within these areas in a roughly geographical order.[34] Pausanias is more methodical in organising his description along a clearly-defined route, usually following roads between cities with only a few passages that describe a coastline in *periplous* fashion.[35] As he moves along his route, he provides information about distances and directions, but the quality and quantity of these statements is rarely consistent.

> Apart from the roads already mentioned there are two others which lead to Orchomenos. On one is the so-called Stadium of Ladas ... and by it is a sanctuary of Artemis, and on the right of the road is a high mound of earth. They say that it is the tomb of Penelope. ... Next to the grave is a small plain, and in it lies a mountain on which there are still the ruins of ancient Mantinea. Today this place is called Ptolis. As you go a bit further north there is a spring named Alalkomeneia, and thirty *stadia* from Ptolis there are the ruins of a village called Maira. ... Finally, there is the road to Orchomenos which passes Mount Anchisia, and the tomb of Anchises lies at the foot of the mountain. ... Near the tomb of Anchises are the ruins of a sanctuary of Aphrodite, and the boundary between Mantinea and Orchomenos is at Anchisiai.[36] (Paus. 8.12.5-9)

There are many topographical details in this passage, but as soon as one tries to follow Pausanias' directions to understand the layout of the landscape, it becomes clear how much vital information is missing. At one point we are told that the road continues north, so we might (correctly) imagine that we are moving in a northerly direction. Rather than referring to the points of the compass Pausanias usually prefers to give directions by simply naming the next major stage on the road, which does not provide an objective geographical overview. Pausanias' notes on distances seem to be based on his own observations and tend to be reasonably reliable, but they are rarely continuous.[37] In the example above we find out that it is thirty *stadia* from Ptolis to Maira, but distances for the other stages are given in only vague terms, if they merit any comment at all, and it is impossible to find out from the text how far it is from Mantinea to the boundary, or to the city of Orchomenos.[38] The description may not provide comprehensive directions, but it does manage to give the reader a sense of the route, and it would at least be possible to draw imprecise linear diagrams of Pausanias' roads with all the landmarks they pass on the way. The reader is, however, not given enough detail to gain even a vague sense of the layout of the landscape. Anyone trying to draw even a very simple map of the topography would need a good deal of additional information; my example of a visual representation of Pausanias' text (Fig. 9) illustrates his description of the Argolid. In the passage above, we are not told how the two roads from Mantinea to Orchomenos relate to each other in the landscape. Which route is on the left and which on the right? Do the two roads take completely separate routes or is there a single road that forks at some point? Where does the first route reach the boundary? Where exactly is Mount Anchisia located, and how does the second route get there from Mantinea?[39]

It seems ironic that a work with such incomplete directions served as the main travel guide to Greece for early modern travellers, particularly from the seventeenth to the nineteenth century, and that topographical researchers continue to rely on the *Periegesis*.[40] Pausanias may have assumed that any reader who needed exact directions could consult local people who would be familiar with all the features named in the text, but modern travellers did not have this advantage and often had to rely on the text alone. It took the diligent efforts of many to understand how the *Periegesis* relates to the topography and extant ancient remains, and the results of these efforts make up much of the material included in the various Pausanias commentaries. As it turns out, in most cases it is possible to identify locations which seem to match the topographical information in the *Periegesis*, even if Pausanias' directions are incomplete.[41] It is important to remember that in spite of all the shortcomings which can be identified by comparison with modern travel guides or maps Pausanias still provides by far the most comprehensive information about sites and landscapes in any extant ancient text. His approach is dictated by an aim to produce a readable text rather than a scholarly handbook or list of geographical data and it is informed by an understanding of topography which differs considerably from our own.

Like most ancient Greek writers Pausanias generally shows little interest in spatial relationships between the places he is describing. When he encounters large topographical features such as mountains or coastlines he does not take the opportunity to explain the wider geographical context: we are not told what lies behind a mountain range or further along a coastline, unless the text is actually headed in that direction. He makes an occasional exception when he encounters a river and lists places along its course.[42] This approach to the landscape is reminiscent of the *Peutinger Table* which shows a similar tendency to neglect an accurate depiction of two-dimensional geography in favour of a representation of roads and sequences of settlements along routes. It has been suggested that Pausanias may have used a similar map to organise his text, but the *Peutinger Table* includes only the most important routes in Greece, and there is no evidence for the existence of ancient maps that could match the detailed coverage of the Greek landscape presented in the *Periegesis*. The *Peutinger Table* represents an ancient alternative to a conventional map, and it suggests that, rather than being eccentric, Pausanias' way of organising the landscape by routes may have been familiar to his readers.[43]

Since Pausanias was describing inland regions he needed to find a way of achieving a comprehensive coverage of the territory. A *periplous* could pursue one long linear itinerary along the coasts, but in the interior roads formed a complex network which had to be represented in the *Periegesis*. In every region Pausanias follows a main itinerary, but when he reaches a city he describes the major roads in all directions as far as the border before he continues to the next major settlement. These secondary routes may not be described in full, but they give the impression of a dense set of connections between the major cities, including routes that cross boundaries between regions. Pausanias may be doggedly linear in his approach when he follows a road, but on a regional level he combines his routes into a network which constitutes a much more sophisticated representation of a two-dimensional landscape than the traditional *periplous*. At the same time, he is surprisingly selective when it comes to turning aside from his main route to establish these spatial connections. He is capable of passing close by a site which he has described in another context without pointing out the connection between his present route and one he has discussed earlier. For example, much of the Argolid is described in a long tour which almost comes full circle at Tiryns and Asine, both in the vicinity of Nauplia. When Pausanias finally reaches Nauplia on another route he does not mention that he has already been in the same area twice before (Fig. 9).[44] Close proximity or the fact that one place might be easily visible from another site are less important to Pausanias than the connections he creates by including a site in a particular itinerary.

For Pausanias, connections between places are not a mere matter of topographical coverage: they also indicate the relative importance of different sites, particularly in historical and mythical terms. For example,

Fig. 9. Pausanias' Argolid. Based on Paus. 2.24.5-38.7.

Pausanias' network of routes is organised around places he considers cities, and his topography therefore evokes the traditional world of Greek *poleis* as independent states with their individual relations to neighbours.[45] At the same time, Pausanias' topographical organisation emphasises the importance of regional centres. Most of Boiotia is described in routes starting at the gates of Thebes, almost as if it were just the Theban countryside. After all, Thebes was the location of some of the most famous Greek myths and it dominated the region politically for much of the classical period. Pausanias acknowledges that after several devastating destructions in the Hellenistic period the contemporary city no longer lived up to its great history, but his description unearths traces of its former stature, and restores its position as the leader of Boiotia. These topographical hierarchies are adapted to every region, with Argos as a centre of the south-eastern Argolid and Sparta unsurprisingly dominating Lakonia, while Arkadia is organised in one long circular route without a regional centre. Pausanias' ideas about the relative importance of sites can override topographical realities. For example, Delphi is presented as the focal point of Phokis, and Pausanias emphasises its links with other Phokian cities by following a number of difficult mountain routes. His description acknowledges the mountainous territory but it does not reflect how the Parnassos range which dominates the region affected connections between its cities.[46]

Pausanias' description does not provide a clear representation of the physical world, but it does draw the readers' attention to other aspects of the Greek landscape: we are presented with a parallel reality which takes into account the past and contemporary significance of different places. While scenery and contemporary settlements were there for all to see and discover for themselves, the meaning of particular places needed to be unearthed and explained. For Pausanias the physical, visible landscape is just a framework for a much more complex topography of myth, history and sacred places.

6

A Sense of Time: Pausanias as Historian

The island of Sphakteria lies in front of the harbour just as Rheneia is off the anchorage at Delos. It seems that places that were once unknown have achieved fame through the fortunes of men: Kaphereus in Euboia is famous because of the storm that came over the Greeks with Agamemnon on their voyage from Troy, and Psyttaleia by Salamis we know from the destruction of the Persians there. In a similar way the Lakedaimonian defeat made Sphakteria universally known.[1] (Paus. 4.36.6)

Apart from the Spartan defeat in 425 BC there was nothing worth recording about Sphakteria: the island was uninhabited and without its association with a memorable episode in Thucydides' account of the Peloponnesian War it would probably have remained 'invisible' to readers of the *Periegesis*.[2] Pausanias almost seeks to justify his reference to Sphakteria, and he discusses other historical locations where the contrast between an unimpressive site and the momentous events that took place there was particularly striking. There is no doubt that the past has a strong influence on how Pausanias views the contemporary landscape: history can make a place worth seeing, even if strictly speaking there is nothing interesting to see. Geography serves as the main organising principle of the *Periegesis* because it determines the order in which the information is presented. History, however, plays an equally important role as the main criterion for Pausanias' selective approach to the landscape. The past (in the widest sense, including myth) often determines what is worth recording, and it defines the identities of cities and regions that give structure to the work as a whole. It is this combination of past, present and landscape that is so characteristic of Pausanias' Greece.

A close connection between history and geography was not new. Herodotos includes much information that we would consider geographical or ethnographical, and both Polybios and Strabo show that by the Hellenistic period geography was seen as closely related to history: much depended on whether scholarly enquiries (*historiai*) were presented spatially or chronologically, and which aspects of the material were emphasised, but both disciplines had an interest in similar cultural themes.[3] Compared to geographical works, however, the *Periegesis* gives more room to the past, and in several places narrative accounts almost overwhelm the topographical framework. Pausanias not only handles a variety of historical material from different sources, he also displays some versatility in presenting the past in different ways, and in adapting his accounts to particular contexts. He clearly did not set out to produce a purely historical work, let alone a political history in the strict Thucydidean sense, but his emphasis on local detail and on his personal enquiries deliberately echoes Herodotos' *Histories*. The close integration between history and landscape in the *Periegesis* will be explored further in Chapter 7, but first it is necessary to consider Pausanias' efforts as a historian, namely his ways of using, selecting and presenting accounts of the past to serve various purposes within his work.

Pausanias' histories reach down to his own lifetime,[4] although he gives more space to earlier times, particularly the Hellenistic period and the remote past. Any discussion of Pausanias' historical activities needs to take into account the fact that for the ancient Greeks the earliest mythical times merged into history without clear distinction.[5] When I speak of history, therefore, I refer to the whole past as Pausanias and his readers would have seen it, with no distinction between 'real' and mythical events. Mythical stories were attached to a wide range of cultural phenomena, for example the many traditions about legendary ancestors and founders which defined local identities and explained the nature of sanctuaries, cults or local customs.[6] In the *Periegesis* all these aspects of Greek culture are therefore also historical phenomena, and religion in particular becomes an integral part of this historical past, all the way back to the birth of the gods. It is also important to remember that the great past of Greece, or at least an idealised and selective version of it, was thoroughly familiar to every *pepaideumenos* who had grown up with classical Greek literature. Pausanias expects his audience to recognise oblique historical references just as they would understand obscure literary allusions in the texts of the period: a connection with a particular battle or the name of a hero would suffice to indicate the historical context. History provided common ground between Pausanias and his readers, because most educated Greeks had similar ideas about the significance of particular events and the merits of the major historical accounts.

History in the *Periegesis* comes in many shapes and sizes. There are several long narrative accounts which offer the best opportunity for Pausanias to show his credentials as a historian. Introductions to particular regions allow him to focus on specific periods, for example the Messenian Wars in Book IV and the history of relations between the Achaian league and Rome in Book VII. In Lakonia and Arkadia Pausanias provides detailed royal genealogies which form a framework for regional history.[7] Extensive narratives can also be attached to a particular site or monument, for example several long excursuses on Hellenistic history which are included in the description of Athens, the account of the Gallic invasion in Delphi and the biographies prompted by memorials of Aratos, Philopoimen and Epameinondas.[8] For his introductions to cities of some importance Pausanias developed a particular form of historical outline: before he launches into his description he provides an account of 'high-

74

lights', usually a summary of foundation myths followed by a series of concise references which connect the community with well-known events such as the Trojan War or the Persian Wars.[9] Additional historical material is integrated with the description of landscape and sites: almost every item described by Pausanias is in some way provided with a specific historical context. These links are often established in a matter-of-fact way, for example by a reference to a founder or aetiological story. Both lengthy historical set pieces and city introductions have seen a good deal of scholarly attention, because they offer some insight into Pausanias' methods and attitudes to particular periods. It is, however, important to see the many comments included in the descriptions of monuments and sites as integral to Pausanias' efforts as a historian.

Pausanias' handling of historical information changed while he was writing the *Periegesis*: he developed summaries of historical highlights as introductions to larger sites and regions, and these were increasingly focused on a particular set of events which he came to consider especially important.[10] An analysis of how this aspect of the *Periegesis* developed is complicated by the fact that Pausanias starts his work in Athens which dominated the canonical classical texts and was therefore central to Greek education and culture in the Roman period. A *pepaideumenos* would pride himself in a detailed knowledge of Athenian history and monuments, at least as far as they played a role in literature. Whole books had been written on the monuments of the Acropolis alone, and since the late classical period Athenian history had been the subject of a distinct sub-genre, namely Atthidography.[11] Pausanias' description would have to include the familiar while avoiding too many details that might seem commonplace. Just as the text launches into the description of Attica without an introduction there is also no attempt to provide a historical overview. All information about the past of Athens is integrated in the description by tying it to particular sights on the way. Early on in his first book Pausanias offers a rare statement about his intentions concerning historical digressions.

> But as to the age of Attalos [I] and Ptolemy [II], it is more ancient, so that tradition about them no longer remains, and those who were with these kings in order to record their achievements in writing were neglected even earlier. Therefore it occurred to me to describe their deeds and the manner in which their fathers came to rule over Egypt, the Mysians and the people living nearby.[12] (Paus. 1.6.1)

This much-quoted passage marks the beginning of one of several lengthy excursuses on Hellenistic history in the first half of Book I. We are introduced to a number of important rulers of the period apart from Attalos I and Ptolemy II: Ptolemy I and VI, Lysimachos, Pyrrhos of Epeiros and Seleukos I. Pausanias also deals with the sack of Athens by Sulla and the Lamian War, and there is an account of the invasion of the Gauls in the early third century, an event revisited at greater length as part of the description of Delphi in Book X.[13] It is not clear whether post-classical history, particularly that of Alexander's early successors, was in fact as neglected as Pausanias maintains, because he is not the only Greek writer of the Roman period to tackle Hellenistic history, even if the subject rarely features in the rhetorical texts of the Second Sophistic. Pausanias' explicit statement so early on in the *Periegesis* and the sheer amount of Hellenistic history included in his work suggest that he thought that a focus on this period, or perhaps more generally any historical information that was not part of the mainstream classical canon, was likely to impress or interest his potential readership.[14]

Most of the Hellenistic history presented in Book I is included in the description of the Athenian agora. This passage, with its many long digressions, makes it quite difficult to follow the complicated route around the site and its many distinguished monuments. The description of the agora is shaped by two distinct aims: Pausanias uses a topographical framework, and he wants to include extensive historical accounts which, in this case, are designed to combine to give a fairly comprehensive overview of a particular period. These ambitious goals cannot be reconciled without compromising the overall effect. In fact, these digressions are not particularly well integrated with the description of the site because Pausanias focuses on classical monuments and ignores important post-classical additions to the Athenian market-place, most notably the monumental Stoa of Attalos.[15] This selection did not offer convenient or conspicuous anchors for all the Hellenistic narratives that needed to be included, and in order to link particular historical events or figures to the topography Pausanias seeks out smaller monuments, including appropriate honorary statues which may not have been very conspicuous among the hundreds of sculptures that had probably accumulated in the centre of Athens by this time.[16] The Athenian agora underwent many significant changes in the post-classical period, but it is unlikely that a visitor in the second century AD would have perceived the site as the focal point of Hellenistic history which it becomes in Pausanias' text.

The discussion of local history was bound to become easier once Athens was left behind, because in other places the amount of material worth recording was more easily manageable. The histories Pausanias presents in most cities consist of a few key episodes such as a founding hero, stories connected to the activities of Herakles and his descendants and events connected with the Trojan War, while later periods are often summarised by references to a handful of instances where local history coincided with major events that affected all of Greece. He develops historical introductions which offer an overview of these main defining points in a city's past. A 'typical' mode of historical introduction emerges slowly, starting in the first book when Pausanias ventures outside the city of Athens and encounters places whose past or present identities were not indisputably Attic. Oropos, Salamis and Megara therefore receive historical introductions which focus on mythical founders and conquests to explain their traditional links with Athens and Attica.[17]

By the time he embarked on his second book Pausanias had apparently abandoned his original plan of connecting all historical information with particular features of a city's memorial landscape. Introductions to larger sites represented a space where history could be presented in chronological order without interfering with the general topographical scheme. The description of the Argolid and adjacent cities in Book II was bound to encourage further experiments with this formula, because it dealt with an area which did not have one common regional or tribal identity:[18] it was therefore particularly important to establish every city's ancestral connections. The sequence of heroes, family relations and mythical conquests that defined most cities' identities could be set out relatively concisely in a historical introduction, while it would be more difficult to give the reader a comprehensible overview if the same material was presented as a set of stories attached to monuments. Regional historical introductions probably developed from Pausanias' city histories: the earliest book with such a general introduction is Book III on Lakonia where Sparta was so dominant that the city's history is almost identical to that of the whole region. After Lakonia, every new region receives a historical introduction.[19] Pausanias' increasing flexibility in his handling of historical narratives in relation to site descriptions was particularly useful in those regions where he found less material on site. The historical introductions of Messenia and Achaia therefore became the dominant part of Books IV and VII respectively, which allowed Pausanias to try his hand in extensive historical narratives.[20]

In the earlier books Pausanias' historical introductions are mainly concerned with mythical events that define a city's or region's identity, and specific historical events are discussed as part of site descriptions. In the course of the *Periegesis* the scope of historical introductions is expanded beyond the essential account of mythical origins, and in the later books actual historical events become a regular feature in Pausanias' summaries.[21] Usually he selects only two or three examples, but the introduction to Arkadia provides a comprehensive list of the historical events he found most worth mentioning.

> The Arkadians as a whole have achieved memorable deeds: the most ancient is their participation in the Trojan War, and next comes their support for the Messenians in their struggle against Sparta. They also took part in the action against the Persians at Plataia. It was obligation rather than approval that made them fight with the Spartans against Athens and cross over to Asia with Agesilaos; they also followed the Lakedaimonians to Leuktra in Boiotia. ... They did not fight with the Greeks against Philip and the Macedonians at Chaironeia, nor later against Antipater in Thessaly, but neither did they oppose the Greeks. They say that the Spartans kept them

from taking part in the struggle against the threat of the Gauls at Thermopylai, because they feared that the Spartans might devastate their land while
their adult men would be absent. The Arkadians were more enthusiastic
members of the Achaian League than any other Greeks.[22] (Paus. 8.6.1-3)

Pausanias never discusses his selection of historical highlights, but it
seems that while he was working on the *Periegesis* his sense of what
defined a city's identity underwent a significant change. As the work
progresses he increasingly emphasises those events where Greeks stood
together to defend their freedom against threats either from the outside
(Persians, Macedonians, Gauls, Romans) or from large Greek powers with
imperialist intentions, particularly Sparta.[23] These struggles for a free and
united Greece are added to the mythical stories that usually served to
describe a community's place in the world. The freedom of the Greeks and
their individual cities becomes a defining characteristic of the periods that
made Greece great and turned it into a centre of cultural achievements
that were relevant to all educated Greeks even centuries after its heyday.

The key events that dominate Pausanias' historical introductions do not
represent a simple set of criteria to define Greekness: the Greek identity
of the cities described in the *Periegesis* is never in question, although most
of the places that are introduced in this way did not succeed in backing the
Greek cause at every turn. What all these events have in common,
however, is that they were crucial in defining and maintaining a strong
Greek identity far beyond mainland Greece, which made them relevant to
anyone who claimed a part in Greek culture. To a visitor with a sense of
this great heritage, the contrast between the momentousness of events
such as the Persian Wars or the Gallic invasion and the small size and
poverty of many of the communities that were known to have played a
significant part in them must have been striking. All over the ancient
world, cities which claimed some Greek ancestry could point to foundation
myths and stories of migrations or wandering Greek heroes, but the cities
in mainland Greece had played a much more significant role in shaping a
history that was relevant to Greeks everywhere. Any role in these pivotal
events in Greek history, even as a neutral bystander or as an ally of the
enemy, adds more depth to the history and identity of a particular *polis* or
region. Pausanias' selection of historical events highlights the importance
and almost heroic quality of those moments when Greek states fought
together, and emphasises the importance of mainland Greece for all
Greeks.

The historical introductions provided space for (more or less) systematic
overviews, but Pausanias continued to attach information about the past
to his descriptions of monuments and sites. The summaries of pivotal
moments in a city's history made it easier to place objects into the local
historical framework with just a short reference, but there was still ample
room to introduce more narrative detail while guiding the reader around

the most memorable sights. Historical *logoi* embedded in the descriptions give a special meaning to particular monuments, but they can also expand on a narrative that has been given only in outline. A specific place can enhance an account significantly, especially when a historical event is discussed on location and in context with related monuments. Pausanias' Greece was full of opportunities to explore the topography of historical events, particularly on battlefields where one could compare historical accounts with the landscape and with monuments connected to the event, and perhaps also discover a few local stories that could add to what was already widely known.[24] A good example is the account of the death of Epameinondas at the battle of Mantinea in 362 BC. This event is presented twice, once in its context on the battlefield south of Mantinea, and then again as part of the short biography of the general presented in his native city of Thebes, where his end is merely mentioned in one sentence.[25] The account presented as part of the description of Mantinea shows how even a well-known story can be enhanced within its local context. Pausanias adds a few details which were part of the local tradition, pointing out relevant locations on the battlefield with its significant place names and evocative topography, and there was also the general's grave where the emperor Hadrian himself had left particular marks of his esteem. The treatment of the battle and Epameinondas' death at Mantinea goes beyond mere narrative, commenting upon the relevance of the event in different contexts and periods.

As we have already seen with the accounts of Hellenistic history included in the description of Athens, direct local relevance was not always a necessary condition for a historical digression. Although Pausanias became more systematic in the treatment of history within his work as it progressed, he continued to include long accounts of events that were not strictly speaking part of local history, but that were in some way linked to a monument.[26] Just as in Athens Pausanias includes an overview of early Hellenistic history which goes beyond what is relevant to the site itself, so the *Periegesis* as a whole continues to provide more than just local perspectives, covering aspects of general Greek history from the earliest beginnings down to Pausanias' own time. It has been suggested that different sections of his work focus on particular historical periods and themes.[27] In Athens the focus on the Hellenistic period is clear, but there is little to suggest that the description of every other book or region was meant to be dominated by a set of specific ideas. In some places Pausanias' description does indeed emphasise a particular issue or historical event, but this often reflects immediate literary concerns or the state of the actual memorial landscape, for example his unusual interest in Roman monuments at Mantinea.[28] Similarities between disparate passages in the *Periegesis* cannot be ignored, but it is important not to over-interpret apparent connections. Pausanias reacts to common habits of constructing local histories and similar interests of local informants, and many of the recurring themes in the *Periegesis* are due to this source material rather than to an overarching and somewhat artificial literary scheme.

The location of historical *logoi* is a result of conscious decisions about the structure of the text and the relevance that should be attached to particular monuments or locations, and such considerations can lead to results that seem counter-intuitive to a modern reader. For example, Pausanias had to find an appropriate location for the biography of Philopoimen, a citizen of Megalopolis and general of the Achaian League who was assassinated in Messene. In his descriptions of Messene and Megalopolis Pausanias mentions Philopoimen, but each time he deliberately interrupts his account of local history, postponing his discussion of the great man with a cross-reference.[29] A lengthy biography is finally presented as part of the description of Tegea, a city that had no particular connections with Philopoimen, except that there was a pedestal with a noteworthy epigram in his honour.[30] We have come across this passage before: Pausanias discovered the epigram when investigating inscriptions on empty statue bases outside the theatre of the city. Since an empty statue base is hardly a monument worth writing about, it seems likely that the biography of Philopoimen was postponed to justify the inclusion of this epigraphical discovery.

Pausanias' efforts as historiographer have often been dismissed as inferior, and traditionally scholarship was mainly concerned with identifying his literary sources. The *Periegesis* contains a lot of historical information that is unique, particularly for the Hellenistic period, and there are many details that are not found elsewhere, which potentially makes it an important source. Pausanias' historical accounts, however, have also attracted justified criticism because there are numerous factual errors which he should have been able to avoid by consulting the literary sources available at the time.[31] Some of these problematic passages can be understood in the context of his aims, his use of local sources and his willingness to include details that differed from what could be found in well-known literary works.[32] Nevertheless, every piece of historical information in the *Periegesis* needs to be evaluated with particular care, a process of scholarly scrutiny that has been going on for a long time and which is well-documented in the different commentaries. Mere fact-checking, however, should not stand in the way of investigating Pausanias' methods as a historian. On the following pages I investigate how he tackles crucial aspects of historiography, namely source criticism, chronology, the interpretation and presentation of his material and his thoughts on the causes of historical events.

As we have seen in Chapter 3, Pausanias' research in Greece allowed him to hear many stories on site, local tradition that was tied to particular places or monuments and could still be adapted and changed every time it was presented to an audience. A large amount of such material is included in the *Periegesis*, and the process of integrating oral tradition with the written record presented special challenges for Pausanias as a historio-grapher.[33] He had to evaluate his material, and he needed to make sure that his readers would be able to understand and appreciate these local stories in the context of mainstream Greek history. Such accounts were of vari-able quality, and there were often different, even contradictory, versions of the same events.[34] Wherever possible Pausanias uses alternative evi-dence to reconstruct 'what really happened' and then he assesses whether a particular account is a truthful representation of these 'actual events'.[35] Pausanias' ultimate criterion in any assessment of historical information is his sense of what is plausible, probable or possible. If a story does not seem plausible he tries to reconstruct the 'historical truth' by rational interpretation, a widely accepted method with a long tradition in Greek scholarly writing.[36] Pausanias believes that the tradition is often manipu-lated by individual writers and the general public who desire to make their history more impressive by adding exaggerations and miracles, and he tries to reconstruct the 'original version' by removing what he identifies as later inappropriate additions.[37] Many details are included in the *Periegesis* although they are identified as implausible or wrong, and often there are alternative versions of a story; readers are invited to come to their own conclusions.[38] This approach is clearly modelled on Herodotos' *Histories*, but it is particularly appropriate for the *Periegesis* because many of the stories it records enhance the site descriptions and give meaning to specific monuments, regardless of their value as historical evidence.

During his research in Greece Pausanias learned to deal with a wide range of historical material, and he shows exceptional versatility in com-bining diverse types of sources. He appreciated the potential of buildings, art works and inscriptions as historical sources and sometimes he also considers local customs, rituals or dialects to support his arguments.[39] Pausanias found additional historical information in the literary sources, especially historical texts and epic poetry, and he stresses his particular trust in Homer as a work of historical reference.[40] We as readers can know only as much about Pausanias' historical research as he allows us to see, namely the material he *did* consider worth recording, together with occa-sional comments on the value of particular sources and on the efforts he made to present a full and truthful account. Such remarks are designed to fill the reader with confidence and perhaps admiration, and they are therefore likely to present Pausanias' ideas about the ideal way of ap-proaching history and a selection of what he thought his best arguments.[41]

I wanted to make the effort to find out which children where born to Polykaon by Messene, and I read the so-called *Eoiai* and the epic *Naupaktia*, as well as the genealogies by Kinaithon and Asios. However, they do not provide any information about this matter, and although I know that the *Great Eoiai* says that Polykaon, son of Boutes, married Euaichme, daughter of Hyllos, son of Herakles, it makes no mention of the husband of Messene or of Messene herself.[42] (Paus. 4.2.1)

In this passage Pausanias admits that he could not find out a specific detail of mythical genealogy. Instead, almost as an excuse for his failure to provide an answer, he shows just how much research could be involved in solving such problems. In this context Pausanias has every reason to present his hard work in the best light, but it is unlikely that all historical accounts in the *Periegesis* were researched with similar diligence. In fact, Pausanias' explicit statements about his effort (*polypragmosynê*) in discovering historical details do not seem to be consistent: for example, in one case he stresses his diligent research, only to present information which seems to be based on a simple reference in the *Iliad*, while the same claim seems more credible in the case of the material he collected for his Arkadian genealogy, which includes local tradition gathered on site.[43] It is often difficult to tell what kind of material Pausanias has in mind when he talks about his sources and there is rarely a clear distinction between library research and what he may have heard on site.[44] Like any educated man of his time Pausanias would know at least the Homeric epics by heart, and it is likely that he could rely on his memory for extracts from many other classical texts, particularly Herodotos. The classics provided a good framework for the myths and history of mainland Greece which could be complemented by additional reading. The passage quoted above seems to suggest that Pausanias read several books to solve this particular problem, but all the authors he mentions are cited in other contexts as well. Like other writers of his time, Pausanias probably read such works to mine them for information and then relied on notes or his memory when he needed a particular detail to back up an argument.[45]

Many authors, among them numerous historians, are mentioned in the *Periegesis*.[46] Pausanias' local stories are probably often based on oral tradition, but literary sources provided additional material, and his longest historical accounts seem largely compiled from books. Pausanias frequently provides references when an author is in disagreement with his own or a third opinion, but the basic sources for a historical account usually remain anonymous. Not all his sources are credited: Polybios, for example, appears only as a historical figure, and Plutarch's name is never mentioned at all.[47] Where it is possible to identify Pausanias' sources it seems that he preferred to use the standard works for the period in question, often accounts written soon after the events he describes.[48] The historical accounts in the *Periegesis*, with their focus on particular regions or cities, could rarely simply be copied from one particular work, and Pausanias needed to combine different accounts to produce the narrative he needed. Literary sources are subjected to scrutiny just as are the stories collected on site, and he is particularly aware that some written accounts may be biased.[49] A discussion of the main sources for his Messenian history offers a rare insight into Pausanias' approach to the literary evidence. It was impossible to reconcile the history of the First Messenian War by Myron of Priene and Rhianos of Bene's epic about the Second Messenian

War because both works had the same main hero, Aristomenes, although two generations were thought to have passed between the two wars.[50] Pausanias decides to follow Rhianos' chronology, mainly because he considers Myron as less trustworthy as an author, and his work seemed to contradict some of the information supplied by the poet Tyrtaios who was contemporary to some of the events. For once, Pausanias allows us an insight into his activities as a historiographer, and he shows himself capable of complex historical reasoning. It is not, however, clear how Pausanias finally combined these sources to create his history of the Messenian Wars: he seems to have followed his own chronology, but his narrative is probably an adaptation of both Myron's and Rhianos' accounts, with additions from other sources such as Tyrtaios. As Auberger has shown, the account is carefully shaped to reflect Pausanias' own views.[51]

The chronological framework for the *Periegesis* was particularly complex. Every city description includes numerous sights and stories which had to be provided with some form of date, and local tradition often came without links to a generally intelligible chronology. Pausanias works with a combination of different chronological systems which allows him to provide a rough date for the thousands of monuments and stories contained in his work. Such chronological information is often not given explicitly, but it can usually be deduced from a story or name attached to a particular feature of the landscape.[52] The guiding principle of chronology in the *Periegesis* is genealogy. This system is based on generations which could be roughly translated into years by equating one century with three generations. For the mythical past this was the only system available, and most local stories could be placed within a particular generation by establishing their relationship with pivotal 'events' and their participants from different areas of the Greek world. An example is the expedition of the Argonauts and the Trojan War.[53] Wandering heroes such as Herakles provided further convenient connections. Pausanias could expect his readers to know the basics of this framework, especially for the heyday of the Greek mythical past, roughly from Herakles to the first generation after the Trojan War.[54] Most regions and cities could fit some of their own stories into this system, and more connections could be established through genealogies of local heroes, often mythical royal families. The most extensive of these genealogies, particularly Pausanias' Spartan and Arkadian king lists, span many generations, offering a connection between the earliest heroes and periods which are historical in the modern sense.[55]

The introduction of Book III provides the most elaborate genealogical account in the *Periegesis*: Pausanias presents the two Spartan royal lines separately, essentially trawling through Lakonian history twice, but each time with a slightly different angle on particular events.[56] Pausanias explains that he keeps the two families apart because their generations did not coincide. This would not matter much if he just wanted to provide an introduction to regional history, but these genealogies are much more important because they provide a chronological framework for the whole *Periegesis*. The Spartan genealogies run from Herakles to the late third century BC, including all the periods which are particularly interesting to Pausanias. Sparta's prominent role in Greek history also meant that its kings often became involved in events in most of the areas covered in the *Periegesis*, particularly in the Peloponnese. The Spartan king lists therefore connect events well beyond Lakonia, and they were also closely linked to many classical texts. Pausanias uses this genealogy extensively, not just for mythical times, but also when he deals with the classical and Hellenistic periods. Where the main genealogies do not provide enough information Pausanias constructs complex genealogical links to provide a date, and pivotal events such as the Persian Wars or the battle of Leuktra serve as basic reference points. The attempt to date a work of the sculptor Onatas once set up in Phigalia is a particularly fine example of this method. Pausanias cites a signature of the artist on a monument set up by Deinomenes of Syracuse to commemorate an Olympic victory of his father Hieron. He knows (presumably from Herodotos) that Hieron's predecessor Gelon was a contemporary of the Persian king Xerxes and concludes that Onatas, the contemporary of Deinomenes, lived two generations (c. 60 years) after the Persian Wars, in our terms roughly around 420 BC. Unfortunately, this is incorrect: Hieron succeeded Gelon just a year after the end of the Persian Wars and died soon after his Olympic victory in 468 BC. Onatas probably made the monument, one of his latest works, just over ten years after the end of the Persian Wars, in the early 460s, and therefore about half a century earlier than Pausanias' date.[57] One has to appreciate Pausanias' imaginative combination of genealogical data with epigraphical and literary evidence, but his error illustrates that genealogy is a very inexact science and therefore not best suited to periods where precise dates were readily available.

There are very few absolute dates in the *Periegesis*. When Pausanias gives the exact year for an event he usually provides an Olympiad date combined with the name of the eponymous archon at Athens. There are only twenty such dates in the whole work[58] and the events that are singled out in this way are the beginnings or ends of wars, important battles, the foundation or destruction of cities and the destruction of important temples. The uniformity of these dates suggests that Pausanias took this information from a chronographical source, although it is possible that he adapted some to fit his own ideas.[59] Alternative dating systems, as used in different cities, do not usually feature in the *Periegesis*, although Pausanias must have found such dates mentioned in inscriptions: there is one example where Pausanias adds the name of a Delphic magistrate, a *prytanis*, to the usual formula.[60] Extensive chronological lists and histories with a precise annalistic structure such as Diodoros' *Bibliotheke* were available in the second century AD, and it seems that Pausanias had access to such works. His preference for a vague genealogical chronology is therefore deliberate, again rejecting developments in historiography initiated by Thucydides in favour of a more archaic, Herodotean approach.[61]

Once the material was selected, evaluated and firmly placed into context Pausanias could start to compose his text. It is particularly difficult to assess his efforts as a historical writer because the *Periegesis* deals with the past in many different ways and contexts. Pausanias adapts his material to fit his purpose within a particular section of the text, which allows him to demonstrate his versatility as a writer and the wide range of his historical knowledge. He covers various subjects, ranging from the mythical and miraculous to recent political history, and he includes romantic tales and legends as well as descriptions of battles and political developments or genealogical lists. Pausanias could choose from a wide range of historiographical styles and methods, and he could expect his erudite readers to recognise echoes of different writers or historical episodes. The presentation of a historical narrative could therefore depend on the effect he wanted to achieve in a particular context.

In a few cases Pausanias tells the same story twice, and he also had to deal with many types of events that recur in Greek history, such as battles or sieges, and the repetitive traditions about some mythical figures.[62] Pausanias adjusts the style and focus of his accounts, and rather similar events can be treated very differently. I compare his accounts of the sack of Kallion by the Gauls and of the destruction of Corinth by the Romans, which are of about the same length and deal with devastating conquests of cities by foreign aggressors.

> What Komboutis and Orestorios did to the Kallians is the most atrocious crime ever heard of, and no man has ever dared to do anything similar. All males were put to the sword, old men were butchered as well as children at their mothers' breasts; as they killed the fattest of these infants the Gauls drank their blood and ate their flesh. Women and adult virgins who had any spirit killed themselves before the city was captured. Those who survived were subjected to every kind of extreme outrage perpetrated by men equally devoid of pity and love. Every woman who happened to find a Gallic sword committed suicide; the rest were soon to die of lack of food and sleep as the unrestrained barbarians took turns in raping them, and they even assaulted the dying and the dead.[63] (Paus. 10.22.3-4)

This passage is written in the tradition of dramatic historiography which aimed to evoke strong emotions in the reader by including striking anecdotes and graphic descriptions of cruel scenes in the narrative. Polybios expresses particularly strong criticism of this mode of historical writing because he thought that such effects borrowed from tragedy were not appropriate for a serious historical work. In his opinion any historian of integrity should include only information based on fact, while dramatic historians would usually have to invent their lurid details.[64] Pausanias' comments on the behaviour of the Gauls should be seen in the context of his whole account of the Gallic invasion and the sack of Delphi: the atrocities at Kallion emphasise the image of reckless, impious barbarians who were defeated by an alliance of brave Greeks. After all, the defence against the Gallic invasion was one of Pausanias' core events in Greek history.[65]

The account of the sack of Corinth in 146 BC comes at the end of an extensive account of relations between the Achaian League and Rome, and it marks the completion of the Roman conquest of Greece.

> As soon as it was night, the Achaians who had escaped to Corinth during the battle fled from the city, and many of the Corinthians did likewise. Although the gates were open, Mummius initially hesitated to enter Corinth, because he suspected that an ambush had been prepared inside the walls. On the third day after the battle he stormed the city and set it on fire. Many of those left in the city were killed by the Romans, but the women and children Mummius sold into slavery. He also sold the liberated slaves who had fought with the Achaians and who had not immediately died in the battle. Mummius carried off the votive offerings and art works which attracted most admiration; those that were not as highly valued he gave to Philopoimen, the general of Attalos. Even in my time there are Corinthian spoils at Pergamon.[66] (Paus. 7.16.7-8)

In this case Pausanias concentrates on the bare outline of events, leaving the gruesome details to his readers' imagination. There was no need to establish that the sack of Corinth was a terrible disaster: it was an infamous example of the worst behaviour of Roman conquerors, and even Romans criticised Mummius' actions as excessively harsh.[67] Pausanias' account seems to be inspired by Thucydides who demonstrated that an understated, matter-of-fact report of horrific events can be more effective in evoking outrage or pity in the reader than any graphic depiction of cruel scenes.[68] Thucydides' terse report of the destruction of Melos at the end of the Melian dialogue required no explicit condemnation of Athenian cruelty. In the same way, Pausanias' concise account of the fall of Corinth at the end of a long account of deteriorating relations between Achaians and Romans does not imply that he is trying to excuse Mummius' actions. Nevertheless, a comparison between his comments on the fates of Kallion and Corinth illustrates a clear distinction between Gauls as stereotypical barbarians at their most ferocious, and Romans whose behaviour is violent, but not outside the norms of Greek warfare.

Pausanias shows his versatility as a historical writer, which makes it difficult to come to general conclusions about his historical *logoi*: where one passage seems to be distinguished by certain qualities there is often another account where the same features are conspicuously absent. At the same time, this variety of historiographical styles allowed Pausanias to suggest associations and interpretations to his readers without having to make his intentions explicit.[69] Echoes of Herodotos' style and approach are particularly common in the *Periegesis*,[70] and this can lend a certain archaic weight to events that might otherwise seem less conspicuous. Pausanias is not always content with subtle literary echoes, and he has a number of ways of suggesting particular interpretations of historical events. His second and more elaborate account of the Gallic attack on Delphi in 279 BC is designed to emphasise the parallels between this barbarian invasion and those of the Persians in the early fifth century BC.[71] Pausanias rarely chooses to impose his own interpretation quite so forcefully, but in this passage he employs a number of devices to guide the reader towards a particular point of view. The location of the digression is carefully chosen to underline Pausanias' interpretation: he passes by a number of relevant monuments, but the narrative is finally attached to the main temple, following a reference to the shields dedicated by the Athenians after the battle of Marathon. The report is distinctly Herodotean, deliberately reminiscent of the definitive account of the Persian invasion and the Greek defence effort in 480/479 BC, and the description of the Gauls and their behaviour is frequently achieved by comparison or contrast with Herodotos' Persians. Moreover, Pausanias includes explicit comments on the similarity between the two barbarian invasions, and on the comparative threat faced by Greece in each case, both in his own authorial voice and when he reports the views of the Greek forces at the time.[72]

Historians are usually committed to one coherent narrative, and they are therefore likely to aim at a certain unity of style and approach. Pausanias, however, is not constrained by such conventions, because he deals with many accounts in a variety of contexts. He is therefore free to experiment with the format of his historical passages, and he can link events or historical figures that might not otherwise be connected. Different periods and events are juxtaposed whenever monuments with different historical associations are described side by side.[73] Sometimes Pausanias deliberately explores connections or comparisons between historical events, usually in order to illustrate his opinions on particular events or general aspects of Greek history. The best example is a list of benefactors of Greece which allows Pausanias to explore his views on Greek freedom and unity. Similar ideas are expressed when he discusses those historical characters whose treachery did much damage to the Greek cause.[74] Historical comparisons or precedents can also suggest new interpretations of events. For example, Augustus' decision to punish the Tegeans for opposing him by taking their most revered sacred image is accompanied by a list of conquerors who took ancient cult statues. Pausanias usually abhors such heavy-handed treatment of Greek sanctuaries, but his discussion of historical precedents in this instance suggests that the emperor was merely following a long established custom.[75]

When he is writing history Pausanias is sometimes unusually open about his opinion, and he can express his views, especially moral judgements, very forcefully. He has praise for courage, piety and patriotism, but criticism is more common, and many individuals are censured for their crimes, particularly those considered as corrupt, impious or guilty of treason.[76] A failure to live up to Pausanias' moral standards can lead to harsh condemnation:

> Philip [II] might be considered as having accomplished greater exploits than any Macedonian king before or after him. But nobody in their right mind would call him a good general, because more than any other man he always trampled on sacred oaths, violated treaties and broke his word on every occasion.[77] (Paus. 8.7.5)

In fact, it is very difficult to see how anyone in their right mind could *not* call Philip II of Macedon a good general, but for Pausanias morally sound behaviour counts more than the shrewd diplomacy and excellent tactics of the Macedonian king. Divine retribution for Philip's crimes is presented as a decisive factor in the history of fourth century Macedonia:

> The wrath of heaven was not long delayed, it came earlier than any we know of. Philip was only forty-six years old when he fulfilled the oracle that Delphi gave him when he enquired about the Persians: 'the bull is crowned, its end is near, and the sacrificer is present'. Not long afterwards it became clear that the oracle did not refer to the Persians, but to Philip himself.[78] (Paus. 8.7.6)

This argument is then pursued further with a summary of the subsequent fate of the Argead family, namely Alexander's premature death and the murder of all close family members. Pausanias' closing comments return to Philip's original crimes:

> If Philip had taken into account the fate of the Spartan Glaukos, and remembered the verse 'the family of the man who keeps his oaths will prosper hereafter' during each of his actions, then, it seems to me, some god would not have so ruthlessly put an end to Alexander's life and, at the same time, to the heyday of Macedonia.[79] (Paus. 8.7.8)

Seen in this light, Philip's qualities as a politician and general are indeed insignificant, because the direct consequences of his perjury rapidly reversed all advantages he gained during his lifetime. Pausanias' whole interpretation of Philip II and his activities is dominated by his moral judgement and his view that serious crimes will be subject to divine retribution. This allows him to create a causal link between a number of crucial events that shaped the fate of the Hellenistic world.

The causes of historical events, though central to historiography, are often not systematically explored in the *Periegesis*. Pivotal developments are usually recorded as a fairly simple sequence of events, without further comments about their connections with other aspects of the narrative.

Where an explanation is offered, it can remain rather vague. Pausanias is rarely concerned with long-term political developments or complex historical factors, preferring to show how particular actions of individuals or states influence history. For example, Pausanias' history of the Achaian League in the Hellenistic period and during the Roman conquest of Greece is among his most elaborate historical narratives.[80] Nevertheless, most of the developments presented in this account are influenced by the personal interests and initiatives of a few flawed individuals. Ultimately the main cause of the Roman victory over the Achaian League appears to be the treachery and ineptitude of three Greek politicians combined with the ambition and bias of a few Roman notables. Pausanias' references to the political situation scarcely give an impression of the complex interactions between Rome, Macedonia, the Achaians and numerous other states that shaped Greek history in the first half of the second century AD. As we have already seen in Pausanias' comments on Philip II, he considered divine retribution as a plausible explanation for historical developments. He is not thinking of particular gods exacting personal revenge, but there is a clear notion that impious actions can have a negative influence on the fate of the perpetrator and his family or associates. Divine retribution features as a factor in many historical events, even down to relatively recent times, for example when Sulla's harsh treatment of Greece is connected to his fatal illness, or when he hints at a connection between the fate of Caligula and Nero and their orders to remove the statue of Eros from its temple at Thespiai.[81]

Pausanias' preferred mode of historical writing emphasises a continuity of the Greek past from a remote antiquity to his own time. Herodotos may be seen as the 'Father of History', but Thucydides' adaptation of the original formula had a lasting influence on the genre. He introduced a new form of authoritative account that combined an unambiguous narrative with in-depth political analysis and a precise chronology. Recent history could be treated in this way, but Thucydides consigns earlier periods to a short introduction because of a lack of precise information.[82] Few ancient historians lived up to Thucydides' exacting standards, but many at least professed to share his aims.[83] Pausanias, too, is influenced by this cautious approach to source criticism, and, as we have seen, some passages in the *Periegesis* echo Thucydides' style and historiographical technique.[84] Pausanias has a notion of an early heroic age about which little can be known, but this refers to a period which is much more remote than Thucydides' 'prehistory'.[85] It was easier to adapt Herodotos' less rigid mode of reporting the past to Pausanias' project because it includes contradictory traditions and does not require a clear distinction between vague mythical accounts and later events that were documented more precisely. As we have seen, Pausanias also prefers a chronological framework that can accommodate all eras, from the earliest heroic age to the Roman empire. He leaves room for the divine and the miraculous in his accounts, particularly when making divine retribution a crucial factor in historical events, and when he presents oracles that correctly predicted events even in the Hellenistic and Roman period. Sometimes he is even ready to admit that heroes or gods could be actively involved in history.[86] At the same time, information about all ages is scrutinised with the same critical attitude, suggesting that stories about remote antiquity are to be taken just as seriously as the sources for more recent events. Pausanias' historical method therefore helps to emphasise the notion that Greece had a continuous history with direct, tangible links between past and present – a land where the remote past was never far away.[87]

Pausanias' historical accounts show his great versatility as a writer and as a collector of diverse examples of tradition and historical evidence. His stories are sometimes inaccurate, but close attention to their context can often lead to a better understanding of how they have come about. It is important to remember that Pausanias' histories have a purpose beyond providing information to the reader. They give meaning to the landscape, both for Pausanias and his readers, and their value in this context does not always depend on historical accuracy. References to the past explain why it was worthwhile to visit all those remote places in mainland Greece, and they can imbue the most inconspicuous monuments with great significance. There is no long, uninterrupted narrative, but the many small details add up to a grand picture of the Greek past, more than just a linear progression, but a complex set of individuals, events and developments which are connected in many different ways, through stories, memories, rituals, places and monuments. Ultimately, Pausanias the historian can be fully appreciated only in connection with the Greek memorial landscape.

7

Describing a City

> From Chaironeia it is twenty *stadia* to Panopeus, a city (*polis*) of the
> Phokians, if one can call it a city, seeing that they have no government
> offices, no gymnasium, no theatre, no market-place, and no water descending
> to a fountain, but live right above a ravine in mere shelters, just like cabins
> in the mountains. Nevertheless, their territory has defined boundaries with
> their neighbours, and they send delegates to the Phokian assembly. ...
> Looking at the ancient city walls I estimated their length at about seven
> *stadia*. I was reminded of Homer's verses about Tityos, where calls the city
> 'Panopeus with beautiful dancing floors', and in the battle over the body of
> Patroklos he says that Schedios, the son of Iphitos and king of the Phokians,
> lived in Panopeus.[1] (Paus. 10.4.1-2)

Rarely is Pausanias as scathing about the current state of a site as he is
in this passage. He saw many ancient cities in a state of decline, and his
description of such places usually conveys a sense of nostalgia or historical
inevitability paired with respect rather than the disdain shown here.[2]
Panopeus is an extreme example that allows some insight into Pausanias'
approach to individual cities. In this chapter I focus on a few sites to
demonstrate how monuments, local stories and Greek literature add up to
characteristic images of particular places. Geography and history have so
far been discussed separately, but a closer look at Pausanias' site descriptions shows how he integrates landscape and history to create his distinctive vision of Greece.

Pausanias' comments on Panopeus have traditionally been seen as a
catalogue of minimum requirements for a city, a list of basic amenities
which he expected to find in any settlement that deserved to be classified
as a *polis*.[3] This close attention to the typical components of ancient urban
infrastructure is, however, unusual for Pausanias. He occasionally mentions such public buildings, but they rarely receive more than a passing
comment, while private houses are almost completely absent from the
Periegesis. Why did he choose to comment on these aspects of a city here,
where they were absent or particularly unimpressive? There was a sim-
pler way of dealing with places where there was nothing worth describing:

> Fifteen *stadia* from Amphikleia is Tithronion which lies in a plain. There is
> nothing memorable there. From Tithronion it is twenty *stadia* to Drymaia.[4]
> (Paus. 10.33.12)

91

Although there was perhaps not much more to *see* in Panopeus than in Tithronion, there was still a lot more that could be said about it. When Pausanias notes that Panopeus still has boundaries and sends delegates to the Phokian league he acknowledges that it has the status of a *polis*, a city-state with what qualified as 'foreign relations' in the Roman period. The question of what constitutes a *polis* in the *Periegesis* is important because the text is organised by city territories. Pausanias may therefore have decided the status of some of his sites to suit the structure of his books, but these choices could not be completely arbitrary. Scholarly discussion about Pausanias' definition of a *polis* revolves mainly around borderline cases. Large cities are easy to categorise, but it is more difficult to understand where he draws the line between a *polis*, a small city or town (*polisma*) and a village (*kômê*). In the case of Panopeus, membership of the Phokian assembly was sufficient to make a few huts perched above a ravine a *polis*, but another member of the Phokian League, Ledon, did not qualify because there the core settlement was completely abandoned.[5] A deserted town could, however, also be given *polis* status: as excavations have shown, by the second century AD there was only limited settlement activity at the site of Stymphalos, but Pausanias speaks of the 'city of my own time', suggesting that Stymphalos is a functioning *polis*. His description, however, seems to reflect the reality, because it is largely concerned with a rural landscape.[6]

This inconsistency between different passages in the *Periegesis* is quite typical: Pausanias' decision about a settlement's *polis* status was clearly not made with a well-defined checklist of buildings in mind. His judgement of a site depends on its physical appearance in conjunction with its status in the Greek literary tradition; often history, rather than monuments, seems to be the decisive factor. In Panopeus, for example, Homeric 'history' was particularly important. Many cities on the Greek mainland were mentioned in the Catalogue of Ships, but Panopeus is singled out because, apart from that standard reference, it also appears as the residence of Schedios, a king and notable warrior, and the poet even describes it as famous (*kleitos*). Even more remarkably, it was mentioned in the *Odyssey*, too, where we hear that Leto was on her way to Delphi, passing the 'beautiful dancing places' of Panopeus.[7] Other cities had stories, monuments and customs which were connected to such important episodes of their history, but Panopeus had little to show for its Homeric distinction. Pausanias had to resort to his own research to find appropriate links to the epic tradition. He points to the large, ancient city walls and strategic position of the settlement to explain why such a place might have been an attractive location for the residence of a Homeric king: Panopeus has clearly seen better days.[8] In the end, Pausanias could at least find a contemporary Athenian tradition which suggested that the *Odyssey*'s reference to the 'beautiful dancing places' of Panopeus was still applicable, because every other year Athenian women went to Mount Parnassos for a special festival, and on the way they stopped at Panopeus to perform dances.[9] Pausanias' efforts to discover these traces of a Homeric past suggest that the most disappointing feature of the town was not the poor settlement, but the lack of tangible connections with its apparently impressive history. In Stymphalos a similar approach led to a deceptively favourable representation of a site in decline because there were still some sights and stories worth recording. Pausanias presents some local traditions, and there was one temple which provided a satisfactory link to the famous story of Herakles' hunt of the Stymphalian birds. The poor state of the contemporary community, if there were any inhabitants left at all, is never mentioned.

In Panopeus and Stymphalos past and present were hardly compatible, so that Pausanias had to decide how to evaluate their relative importance. Pausanias' reaction in each case shows that what he writes about a city is strongly influenced by his sense of the connections between the past and the contemporary landscape.[10] In what follows I use the city of Tegea to illustrate how Pausanias organises the description of a city, and how he integrates the physical landscape with the past.[11] Tegea was a middle-sized city in Arkadia which had received some notice in the major Greek texts, for example an entry in the *Iliad*'s Catalogue of Ships and a small but notable role in the historical accounts of Herodotos, Thucydides and Xenophon.[12] The most widely known feature of the city was its temple of Athena Alea, a sanctuary of supraregional importance.[13] Pausanias reports that an ancient temple on the site had burned down in 395 BC, and that it was replaced by a new building, designed by the eminent artist Skopas.[14] This temple of the mid-fourth century was excavated in the 1880s, and further work between 1985 and 1992 investigated the remains of the archaic temple and uncovered traces of continued cult activity on the site going back to the early Iron Age at least.[15] The urban settlement itself is less well-known, in spite of extensive excavations on the ancient agora which remain unpublished. In recent years the area of the city has also been investigated by intensive archaeological field survey, which has clarified some aspects of the general layout of the town (Fig. 10).[16] Major features of the urban landscape can therefore be located, but it is impossible to determine the exact location of most of the monuments described in the *Periegesis*.

In small towns Pausanias selects only a few notable sights, without much attention to their location, but larger sites with many monuments had to be organised in some way. In Athens some features of the landscape are grouped together thematically, but the usual pattern in the rest of the *Periegesis* is a topographical description. By the time Pausanias reached Elis he expected his readers to take this for granted, because when he arranges the monuments of Olympia by type rather than location he stresses several times that he is abandoning his usual practice of following routes around the site.[17] The topographical descriptions of sites probably

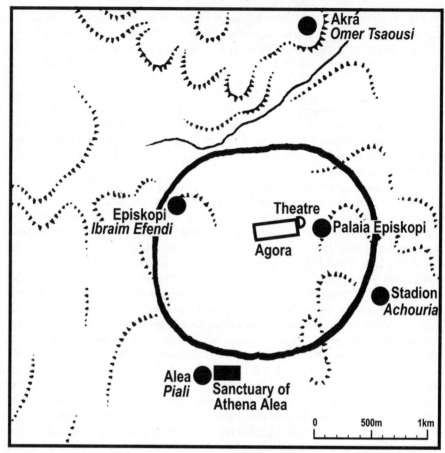

Fig. 10. Tegea: known remains of the city; conjectural location of the city-wall. Based on Jost & Marcadé (1998) 271, modified according to new findings of the Norwegian Arkadia Survey (Ødegård pers. comm.).

made sense when the monuments were still standing and locals could be asked for further information, but Pausanias' directions on their own are not sufficient to give a realistic idea of a site's topography.[18] Today the problem of understanding site descriptions arises when the *Periegesis* is analysed in conjunction with archaeological evidence. Pausanias has been very useful for identifying individual buildings and monuments in prominent sites such as Olympia and Delphi or the Athenian agora. In these places monuments are concentrated in a relatively small space, and archaeology, inscriptions and ancient literature offer enough additional information to analyse Pausanias' description. An abundance of independent evidence is indeed necessary to trace Pausanias' route, but even in these best-documented sites the identification of individual monuments can be a matter of scholarly dispute.[19] Most ancient cities pose a much more complex problem: very few settlement sites have been investigated in sufficient detail to allow a study of urban topography beyond the most prominent public spaces. Moreover, Pausanias' imprecise directions, combined with his habit of ignoring residential quarters, often do not offer enough guidance to warrant a systematic search for the remains of monuments he is describing. Apart from Athens, which is altogether exceptional, there are only a few cities where the urban topography described in the *Periegesis* can be reconstructed with some confidence, and Corinth is the best example.[20] Hutton's meticulous analysis demonstrates that Pausanias' description there follows a plan which echoes his way of organising the countryside, and it is likely that he treated other cities in a similar way. The tour usually starts in the agora and then follows radial routes as far as the city walls, describing everything that is worth noting along the way.[21] This system was not rigid, but could be adapted to local circumstances.

In Tegea the starting point is the temple of Athena Alea rather than the market-place, which emphasises its status as a prominent ancient sanctuary and the city's most famous attraction. Pausanias does not indicate its location south-west of the city, just outside the walls.[22] The description continues with a few sights 'not far from the temple', namely the stadium, a spring 'north of the temple' and a temple of Hermes three *stadia* from the spring. This is followed by a discussion of the temple of Athena Poliatis ('of the City') which one would expect to find inside the city walls.[23] The remark that the spring was north of the sanctuary of Athena Alea suggests that Pausanias is on his way towards the agora. The subsequent description of the town begins with the monuments around the market-place and then moves on to the theatre, which is 'not far from the agora'. Here the description halts for four chapters to accommodate the biography of Philopoimen.[24] After this, further notable monuments are listed, apparently in other parts of the town, but the text offers no more than a very vague idea of their locations. The following extract contains all the topographical information provided in this final part of the description of the city.

> The Tegeans have four images of Agyieus, one set up by each tribe. ... There is also at Tegea a temple of Demeter and Kore, whom they call Fruitbringers, and close by is one of Paphian Aphrodite. ... Not far from it are two sanctuaries of Dionysos, an altar of Kore, and a temple of Apollo with a gilded image. ... Next to Apollo stands a stone statue of Cheirisophos.
>
> The Tegeans also have what they call the Common Hearth of the Arkadians. In this place there is an image of Herakles. ... The high place with most of the altars of the Tegeans is called the place of Zeus Klarios. ... I also saw the following things in Tegea: the house of Aleos, the tomb of Echemos, and, engraved on a stele, the fight between Echemos and Hyllos.
>
> As you go from Tegea towards Lakonia, there is on the left of the road an altar of Pan, and another of Zeus Lykaios.[25] (Paus. 8.53.6-11)

Some sights are presented without any information about their location, but at first Pausanias seems to follow a route, describing monuments in relation to each other. The elevated place (*chôrion hypsêlon*) with the altars has not been identified, since there are no notable hills within the territory of the ancient city, but Pausanias' usual mode of city descriptions suggests that he is still inside the town. The point where he moves on to the countryside is reached suddenly, but it is clearly marked by indicating the road to Lakonia. This description provides only a very vague notion of the layout of Tegea, and we get no sense of what the city looked like.[26]

Pausanias' mental site maps become far more structured and distinct once their historical component is taken into account. The noteworthy objects described at a site may not be well located in space, but usually they are linked to a particular point in time. An object does not itself need to date to the correct period to represent a specific aspect of the past: it is usually enough if it evokes a relevant memory, as may a work of art that is much later than the period in question but that depicts an important character or aspect of the story. These chronological links are rarely explicit and they may not always be immediately apparent to a modern reader. Almost every monument comes with a story or at least a reference to a prominent figure or event, which would allow an ancient *pepaideumenos* to connect it with a particular generation or period. In addition, Pausanias' genealogies and historical accounts provide a chronological framework which accommodates most of the events or characters he mentions in his site descriptions. This combination of *theôrêmata* and *logoi*, description and comments, is characteristic for the *Periegesis*, and in order to understand the structure of Pausanias' Greek landscape it is important to consider them together, as the author intended. Monuments or stories are not just fixed in the local topography: they are also assigned their place in time. In the larger cities this produces a mental map with historical layers which surface in different locations in the town or the surrounding countryside wherever a place is in some way connected with a particular period or story.

I return to Tegea to illustrate how Pausanias' text reflects the historical topography. The description starts with a typical historical introduction which summarises a few highlights of the city's past without attempting a continuous narrative.

> The Tegeans say that under Tegeates, son of Lykaon, only the region was named after him, and the inhabitants lived in villages (*dêmoi*) ... In the reign of Apheidas a ninth deme, called Apheidantes, was added. Aleos was the founder of the modern city. Apart from the events in which they participated together with the Arkadians, which include the Trojan War, the Persian Wars and the battle at Dipaia against the Spartans, and, apart from what has already been mentioned, the Tegeans have the following famous deeds of their own: in spite of his wounds Ankaios, the son of Lykourgos, stood up to the Kalydonian Boar. ... When the Herakleidai returned to the Pelopon-

nese, the Tegean Echemos, son of Aeropos, beat Hyllos in single combat. The Tegeans were the first of the Arkadians to resist an attack of the Spartans, and they took most of them prisoner.[27] (Paus. 8.45.1-3)

There are some significant omissions in this summary, but the events that are included represent an uncontroversial selection. A foundation myth was obligatory and, as so often in cities of mainland Greece, the Tegean story is not very distinctive. All other episodes mentioned were familiar to educated Greeks because they were well represented in the Greek literary tradition. The Tegean king Aleos played an important part in the story of Telephos, a hero who was part of the cycle of stories connected with the Trojan War. Aleos' daughter Auge was raped by Herakles, and after her son Telephos was born she and her child were driven out of Tegea to be killed. They survived and came to Asia Minor, where Telephos opposed the Greeks on their way to Troy. This story was the subject of plays by Sophokles and Euripides which are now lost, and Telephos' fame further increased with the rise of Pergamon, which claimed him as its founding hero.[28] The Kalydonian boar hunt is often referred to in ancient literature, and besides its main characters Meleager and Atalante it could feature a variable cast of participants. The Tegean version predictably emphasised the role of a local hero.[29] The reference to the Trojan War refers to Tegea's entry among the Arkadian forces in the Catalogue of Ships. The stories of Echemos' fight with Hyllos, the victory over the Spartans, Tegea's involvement in the Persian Wars and the battle of Dipaia are all mentioned in Herodotos' *Histories*.[30]

The wider context for most of these events is provided by the list of Arkadian kings presented at the beginning of Book VIII:[31] Lykaon, Apheidas, Aleos, Lykourgos and Echemos are all part of the mythical Arkadian royal family. References to the Kalydonian boar hunt and to the death of Hyllos, son of Herakles, establish connections to well-known myths. The Spartan defeat is a specifically Tegean event which readers might find less easy to place within the wider Greek tradition. Pausanias provides appropriate connections: the event is mentioned in his Spartan chronology, and later on, in the course of the description of Tegea, a rough date is provided by naming the defeated Spartan king.[32] The reference to 'common Arkadian achievements' serves as a reminder of the list of historical exploits presented in the regional introduction at the beginning of Book VIII, perhaps also with a nod to readers who knew about these events from the *Iliad* and Herodotos and expected them to be included.[33] Pausanias' focus in this passage is on those episodes of Tegean history that were also particularly well represented in the monuments and stories he was about to record.

Equipped with this framework of major events in local myth-history, the reader is ready to set off to explore the sights. The temple of Athena Alea was Tegea's major sanctuary, which attracted many visitors from outside and was therefore a particularly important location to present the community at its best. This was already the case in the fifth century, when Herodotos mentions two significant exhibits in the temple, namely the fetters of the Spartan captives and the manger of Mardonios, taken as booty from the Persian camp after the battle of Plataia.[34] When the temple was built in the fourth century, its pediments were designed to show a local version of the Kalydonian boar hunt and the fight between Telephos and Achilles.[35] As in many Greek sanctuaries, a collection of noteworthy dedications was exhibited in the temple. Pausanias mentions a sacred couch of Athena which is given no historical significance, but the other exhibits mentioned are all duly linked with highlights of Tegean history: the fetters of the Spartan prisoners were still there, and there was also the shield of Marpessa, a woman who had fought the Spartans. Pausanias also saw the remains of the hide of the Kalydonian boar and an image of Telephos' mother Auge.[36] He seems to be in no doubt that the ancient objects could have survived the fire that destroyed the earlier temple. The archaic image of Athena and the tusks of the Kalydonian boar had been taken by Augustus and could now be seen at Rome. By adding a description of these venerable objects in their new location Pausanias does his best to restore them to his version of the Tegean memorial landscape.[37]

Beyond this focal point of Tegean self-presentation reminders of the past are dotted about the urban and rural landscape, and different aspects of one story can be attached to several locations. For example, Herodotos reports that the Spartans received an ambiguous Delphic oracle which seemed to promise them the land of Tegea. They attacked, bringing chains for the prisoners they were expecting to make, but were defeated and bound with the fetters they had brought.[38] Pausanias never tells the whole story at length, but the full significance of the Tegean tradition becomes clear only when Herodotos is taken into account, particularly when we are presented with the very chains of the Spartans which the historian had seen about six hundred years earlier. We also get a sense that there were more than just one battle between the two neighbours, which coincides with Herodotos' vague reference to continued Spartan defeats.[39] With the classical account in mind Pausanias moves around Tegea, reminding readers of the story wherever he finds an appropriate memorial and adding new local details. He connects a particular festival to a Spartan winter attack and a rather confusing stratagem that brought the Tegeans success. A statue of Ares Gynaikothoinas ('he who entertains women') on the agora evokes a story of Tegean women who donned armour and helped to bring about the capture of the Spartans with their king Charillos; we have already come across the shield of the women's leader in the temple of Athena Alea.[40] Apart from votives in the temple there was also the Halotia (Capture) festival celebrated in the stadium to commemorate the Tegean success. As Pausanias is leaving Tegea on the road to Thyrea he mentions the empty tomb of Orestes: this is a reference to the conclusion of Herodotos' account where the Spartans finally gain the upper hand over Tegea by bringing the bones of Orestes to Sparta.[41]

The story of Auge and Telephos also left several traces in the Tegean landscape. In this case objects in the temple provide only additional references, and the places where parts of the story had actually taken place are more significant. A statue of Herakles with a wound sustained in a battle against the sons of Hippokoon is a reminder of the reason why the hero came to Tegea: he was on his way to attack Sparta and asked Aleos for support.[42] Pausanias points out a spring where Herakles subsequently raped the king's daughter. The story continues at a temple of Eileithyia in the agora: Aleos had found out that his daughter Auge was pregnant and ordered her to be exposed at sea. The sanctuary marked the place where she gave birth as she was being dragged away, and it was therefore called 'Auge on her knees'. Mother and child were then put into a wooden chest which was thrown into the sea, which, incidentally, is a long way from Tegea. There was another version of the story in which Auge secretly gave birth to Telephos and the child was exposed alone, surviving because he was suckled by a deer (*elaphos*) which conveniently supplied an etymology for his name.[43] The Tegean landscape also had room for this alternative version: on the road to Argos there was a sacred precinct (*temenos*) of Telephos which marked the place where the infant had been found. Pausanias notes the contradiction between the stories, but he does not declare either of them invalid and he notes that both versions were current among the Tegeans. The existence of monuments supporting each version made it difficult to come to a definite conclusion.[44]

Other historical 'layers' of the Tegean landscape can be identified, especially a range of monuments connected to the three founding heroes.[45] Pausanias' choice of monuments and his historical introduction represent the same selection process, probably a combination of his own preferences and choices made by the locals over the centuries. A few items without links to these main themes were also included, namely the memorial of Philopoimen, monuments honouring Tegean lawgivers and an Olympic victor, and a temple of Artemis Hegemone dedicated by a man who ousted Aristomelidas, an otherwise unknown tyrant of Orchomenos.[46] These examples show that Pausanias' scheme was not so rigid that it would have prevented him from including anything that seemed of sufficient interest. There are sites where the monumental landscape represents a wider range of events than at Tegea. Nevertheless, most cities of sufficient size offered Pausanias an opportunity to present groups of monuments with connections to those aspects of the past that were particularly significant for the local community.

Every city in the *Periegesis* has its own unique selection of historical highlights. The crucial question is whether it is Pausanias who is doing the selecting, or whether many of his choices were made for him by the local people who remembered, adapted and indeed forgot aspects of their

99

local history, a process which went on for centuries and which had shaped their memorial landscape. In local oral tradition, history is not static: it is selected, interpreted and manipulated, and therefore develops with the community's sense of identity. Herodotos, six centuries earlier than Pausanias and in so many ways his model, took it for granted that there would be different local versions of historical events, and he accommodated them in his work.

In Roman Greece the past was more important than ever because the Greeks, collectively as well as in communities and as individuals, often needed to emphasise their impressive history to maintain their status of cultural superiority.[47] As the perception of the past changed, new monuments were set up and old ones were re-interpreted or abandoned. In Athens a number of classical temples and altars were even moved to the agora to create a new memorial landscape with 'genuine' historical roots.[48]

Pausanias' *Periegesis* reflects the results of such selective processes. For example, at Tegea he mentions the Persian Wars in the historical introduction, but he does not present a single monument that commemorates this crucial event. This omission is surprising because most cities prided themselves on their Persian War record and Herodotos emphasises the valiant role of the Tegeans, particularly in the battle of Plataia.[49] This gap in Pausanias' Tegean history probably reflects an actual peculiarity of the local memorial landscape, the result of a selection process that took place over time. It seems that the Tegeans preferred to present themselves as implacable enemies of their dominant southern neighbour, Sparta, and this version of the past could hardly be reconciled with the image of the Tegeans as a loyal Spartan ally which emerges from Herodotos and other major classical texts.[50] The complete absence of any connections to the Persian Wars is particularly uncharacteristic for Pausanias, who shows so much interest in both Herodotos and the struggle for Greek freedom. He does not discuss the issue, but it seems unlikely that he did not notice the fact that of the two dedications Herodotos saw in the temple of Athena Alea the shackles of the Spartan prisoners had survived, while the monumental bronze manger captured in the Persian camp after the battle of Plataia had disappeared. For anyone familiar with Herodotos the gap would be conspicuous without needing further comment. As we have seen at Panopeus, such a discrepancy between the literary tradition and the memorial landscape could be deeply disconcerting for Pausanias. Tegea, however, was still a sizeable city with plenty of material to collect and report, which probably made it easier to pass over this obvious gap in the local tradition without discussing it further.

Pausanias had to work with the monuments and stories he found on site, but this would still have left him with a good deal of freedom to select and emphasise what he found worth recording. Ultimately, the literary image of the memorial landscape is essentially his creation, even if it echoes local preferences.[51] Pausanias' selectivity is a standard subject of scholarly comment, with an emphasis on his tendency to ignore the history and monuments of the Hellenistic and Roman periods.[52] At Tegea the only monument that is explicitly Hellenistic is the statue of Philopoimen. The story of the man who killed the tyrant of Orchomenos, if historical at all, is also likely to be Hellenistic, and with it presumably the temple of Artemis Hegemone.[53] Both episodes are isolated within the monumental landscape of Tegea. Only one event in three hundred years of Roman rule was worth recording, namely Augustus' decision to take away the image of Athena Alea because the Tegeans had not taken his side against Mark Antony, and no single monument or building is identified as Roman. Nevertheless, Pausanias is not attempting to present a fantasy image of Greece centuries before his own time. The ruins reported in the country-side around Tegea are a stark reminder that we are indeed seeing the landscape of the Roman imperial period.[54] In fact, it is likely that a number of the monuments described in Tegea were indeed of a late date, but this was not in itself of sufficient interest, and in the text they serve as references to earlier periods while their own date is never discussed. Pausanias did not set himself a rule to ignore later monuments. As in Tegea, most of his city descriptions focus on objects that cluster around important aspects of local history. In some cities, for example Corinth or Tegea's northern neighbour Mantinea, this includes episodes of Roman or Hellenistic history. In the light of the general preference for earlier periods among Pausanias' contemporaries, however, it is not surprising that the major themes in most cities' memorial landscape revolved around myths or archaic and classical history.

The quality and interest of the material are also important aspects of the selection process. Pausanias was particularly attracted by items that were in some way connected to the common Greek tradition, and his readers were likely to find a story or monument more impressive if they could relate it to the classical texts that they all knew. Well-known narratives gained a sense of location and intensified reality when physical remains and traces were considered, and there was a chance that new aspects of a story could be discovered where it had actually taken place.[55] The *Periegesis* therefore often focuses on features in the local memorial landscape that could be linked to famous events or that involved well-known mythical or historical characters. Monuments are also particularly attractive if they can be attributed to a well-known artist. Again, Pausanias' local informants were likely to agree with such preferences, because their tradition played a crucial part in their interaction with outsiders, and widely recognised stories were likely to have a greater impact.[56] At Tegea, we can observe that the adaptation and selection of local tradition to correspond to well-known texts had been going on for some time. For example, the themes selected for the pediments of the fourth-century temple, Telephos and the Kalydonian boar hunt, both involve prominent Tegeans, but they are also part of mainstream Greek

101

tradition, and the boar hunt was probably adapted to include more local heroes.[57] The contradictory stories and monuments connected with the fate of Auge and the infant Telephos also seem to indicate a willingness to accommodate the literary tradition. The local variants of the story documented by Pausanias were probably influenced by the versions of Sophokles and Euripides. In fact, it is likely that Telephos, the king of the Mysians in Asia Minor, originally had no connections with Arkadian Tegea at all, although by the end of the sixth century BC the link had been established.[58] The historical landscape of Tegea therefore reflects a communication between local, mostly oral, tradition and the literary tradition that all Greeks had in common. Pausanias selects what seems most noteworthy to him, not least in the light of what was known from the classical texts, but the local tradition he found was already adapted to suit such interests.

Pausanias' city descriptions are further enhanced by his many comments on sacred sites and ritual practice. This aspect of the landscape is distinctive, but it is also closely integrated with local history because most sanctuaries are connected to myths or even historical events. At the same time, rituals and cult activities helped to define the monumental landscape. This is particularly striking in Olympia, where Pausanias decides to organise his description of the many altars in the sanctuary in the order in which the Eleans used to sacrifice on them.[59] A description of the sacred precinct at Olympia was a complex task because the space between the larger buildings was crowded with altars and statues which were not arranged in any clear topographical order. Pausanias tries to control the chaos by describing altars, statues of Zeus and statues of Olympic victors separately. His decision to list the altars in the traditional order of sacrifice does not just restore a link between monuments and topography: it also reminds us that tradition and ritual give meaning to a site that would otherwise merely appear as a chaotic collection of ancient objects. The influence of local rituals on the format of Pausanias' city descriptions is less apparent, but information about the religious significance of particular places, and comments on local cult practice, add extra depth to the description. This is particularly clear when Pausanias encounters rather inconspicuous places, simple caves or trees for example, which gain great importance because of their role in local religion. From the earliest days of the Greek city, rituals had also been used to strengthen spatial connections between different parts of a community's territory as well as between sanctuaries in different cities. Such connections could be marked by processions or, in the case of sanctuaries that were further away, sacred embassies and pilgrimage.[60] Myths, particularly foundation stories, and similarities between divinities, cult images or ritual practice further added to the network of sacred links between cities and sanctuaries. For example, a number of cities celebrated mysteries of Demeter similar to those of Eleusis, and there was usually a myth which explained their relationship with the Athenian sanctuary.[61] Pausanias reports many such sacred relationships, establishing topographical connections which transcend mere geography. Such links can also reach far beyond mainland Greece, and through their many monuments that defined such connections Olympia and Delphi in particular offered him an opportunity to survey much of the Greek world.[62]

There is one ancient text which shares many of the typical traits of Pausanias' city descriptions, namely Lucian's *Dea Syria* which deals with the sanctuary of Atagartis at Hierapolis in Syria. This text is written in a language that imitates Herodotos' Ionic Greek, but, like Pausanias, it focuses on monuments, history and rituals. Lucian's narrator presents himself as a devout Hellenised Syrian who has researched the history of the monuments and rituals at Hierapolis in order to present them to a Greek audience.[63] The description is almost overwhelmed by the amount of information about mythical history and details about the cult, but it follows a route from the entrance of the precinct to the temple which receives most of his attention, and then it discusses the monuments outside the temple while proceeding to the sacred lake. The narrator expresses a personal religious investment in the site which we sometimes also glimpse in the *Periegesis*, as, for example, at the oracle of Trophonios.[64] Compared with the *Dea Syria*, however, Pausanias' site descriptions seem sober and restrained. Parts of the account provide realistic details about Hierapolis but some passages seem ludicrously exaggerated.[65] Lucian's work almost seems like a parody of the *Periegesis* because it echoes many of Pausanias' mannerisms and usually exaggerates them just a little so as to make them seem absurd. Lucian was a close contemporary of Pausanias, and it is possible that he knew at least part of the *Periegesis*, although there is no conclusive proof of a direct connection between the two authors.[66] The similarities between the two texts can be explained by their common model, Herodotos. Lucian's choice of Ionic Greek supports the idea that the work is a deliberate pastiche of the ethnographical digressions in Herodotos' *Histories*. The *Dea Syria* shares more similarities with the *Periegesis* even than does Herodotos because both Lucian and Pausanias apply their model to detailed site descriptions, and they are equally influenced by the interests and scholarly traditions of their own time.

Pausanias' preoccupation with monuments, history and local tradition was not unusual for an educated Greek in the second century AD. Every Greek was intimately familiar with the monuments and stories of his own city, not least because the identity of every *polis* was so closely connected with its memorial landscape. A *pepaideumenos* would also have a thorough knowledge of Athens and perhaps a few other prominent sites.[67] What is unique about the *Periegesis* is Pausanias' careful investigation of the objects and traditions of so many communities which could be achieved only by meticulous and personal exploration. Pausanias' Greece is more than a sum of all these local details, but his approach recognises that the variety of individual polis identities characterised Greekness just as much as the many cultural traits that all Greeks had in common.

8

Considering Works of Art

As you enter the temple they call the Parthenon, the sculptures in the pediment represent the birth of Athena, and those on the other side show the quarrel over the land between Athena and Poseidon. The cult statue itself is made of ivory and gold. The image of a sphinx is set upon the middle of her helmet ... and on either side of the helmet are griffins. ... the statue of Athena is upright, with a *chitôn* (tunic) that reaches to her feet, and on her breast she has the head of Medusa worked in ivory. She holds a statue of Nike which is about four cubits [2 metres] high, and she has a spear in her hand; by her feet lies a shield, and near the spear is a serpent. This serpent would be Erichthonios. The birth of Pandora is shown on the base of the statue.[1] (Paus. 1.24.5, 7)

This is Pausanias' description of one of the most significant temples in the Greek world, in his time as well as today. The details he provides are valuable: this passage was instrumental in understanding the remains of the pedimental sculptures of the Parthenon and it supported the identification of replicas of Pheidias' famous chryselephantine statue.[2] A closer consideration of this passage, however, also shows just how much Pausanias does not tell us. The description of the image focuses on the material, basic posture and attributes of the statue, without giving readers a sense of style or expression. While the statue is lost, the temple itself and its elaborate sculptural decorations are very well-known. The statue groups of the pediments and particularly the frieze with its depiction of a Panathenaic procession caused a sensation when they were exhibited in London in the early nineteenth century. The Italian sculptor Canova was consulted on the artistic value of the marbles, and he could hardly have expressed his admiration in more enthusiastic terms:

I admire in [the marbles] the truth of nature combined with the choice of beautiful forms: everything about them breathes animation, with a singular truth of expression, and with a degree of skill which is the more exquisite as it is without the least affectation of the pomp of art, which is concealed with admirable address. The naked figures are real flesh, in its native beauty.[3] (A. Canova, 10 November 1815)

In spite of their damaged state, detached from their original setting and without their original colouring, Pheidias' designs made a great impression and they are still considered seminal works of western art. Pausanias had a chance to see the Parthenon complete and in a good state of repair,

105

but his only reference to the sculptures is a quick note on the theme of the pedimental sculptures. Did he even see the frieze, placed high up on the wall behind the outer colonnade? What did he make of the style and composition of the sculptures?

Pausanias' descriptions are often surprising and at times disappointing, and, although his work had a significant impact on the development of modern art history, his approach has little in common with today's methods of art analysis.[4] In this chapter I investigate Pausanias' descriptions of art in their contemporary cultural context. Art, that is to say sculpture, painting and architecture, played an important role in the lives of Greek communities and their educated élites. The presentation of art works in the *Periegesis* depends on the display and perceived significance of the original on site, and the text also needed to be shaped to accommodate the interests and previous knowledge that could be expected from potential readers. In antiquity, discussing art meant much more than just commenting on an artefact's appearance and interpreting the artist's methods and intentions: works of art could serve as the basis of learned discussions that went far beyond straightforward description, and some had a deeper meaning, particularly when they were displayed in a sacred context. Pausanias could draw on a long literary tradition of *ekphrasis*, the description of art, which reached a particularly high degree of sophistication in the second century AD. The many references to works of art have an important role to play as a characteristic ingredient of the *Periegesis* as a literary creation.

Many Greek cities of the Roman period would have had a lot of art on public display: architecture, particularly temples, as well as a variety of sculpture including honorary statues, sacred images, relief *stêlai* and architectural sculpture. Paintings were displayed in temples or other public buildings, alongside a mix of miscellaneous objects, from works of art and elaborate cult equipment to historical war booty and fossilised bones.[5] This image of a typical city's collection of artefacts could be pieced together from ancient literature without the *Periegesis*, but Pausanias offers by far the most detailed overview, providing information about the setting of public art in numerous sites of Roman Greece, and about its meaning for the local community. Individual examples are often mentioned only in passing, but the sheer amount of material adds up to a comprehensive picture. Caylus, an eighteenth-century French artist who read Pausanias to learn more about Greek art,[6] counted 'about 2827' statues mentioned in the *Periegesis*, but this was not a reliable number because Pausanias often just passes through a public space with a note that there are 'some statues'. As already noted, in Olympia alone Pausanias records about two hundred statues of Olympic victors, and that was, as he tells us quite clearly, just a selection of the most noteworthy specimens. According to Caylus, the *Periegesis* also records 50 reliefs, 24 chariots, 40 statues of animals, 131 paintings and 713 temples.[7] When

Pausanias describes buildings he is most likely to comment on the sculptural decoration, and if he discusses the architecture at all he might merely identify the architectural order or point out unique features. Only a very small fraction of ancient art survives, but there are enough examples of buildings and statues to give us an impression, while for paintings we rely almost entirely on descriptions in ancient texts. Pausanias mentions a significant number of paintings, and in a few cases he discusses an art work in detail.[8]

Art description in the *Periegesis* follows the same principle of variety that we have already observed in Pausanias' treatment of history. In many cases he simply mentions the existence of an artefact, and if he provides additional information he often just gives the artist's name or identifies a subject or theme. Remarks about the size or the material of statues are relatively common and sometimes he notes individual attributes, especially if the work has a sacred function or meaning. There are, however, also a few 'set piece' examples of *ekphrasis* where the detailed description of a particular work of art takes up several pages of text. The most extensive examples deal with Polygnotos' paintings in the Lesche (Clubhouse) of the Knidians at Delphi and with the scenes on the Chest of Kypselos, an exhibit in the Heraion of Olympia which probably dated to the seventh century and featured a large number of images with mythical themes.[9] Pausanias' descriptions in these cases are so elaborate that reconstructions of the images have been attempted.[10] On both art works the depicted mythical figures were identified by inscriptions.[11] Pausanias gives a long list of all the people shown, with short remarks about their iconography and positioning and a discussion of the meaning of individual scenes.

All these descriptions were written for a readership which was thoroughly familiar with public art in Greek cities, but Pausanias could probably offer information that was not widely known, such as references to lesser-known works of famous masters, and details about unknown artists: after all, he mentions 179 sculptors and 16 painters, and many have more than one work to their credit.[12] In spite of persistent Roman looting, Greece still offered fascinating examples of archaic or classical art, sometimes tucked away in the dark corner of some temple and hardly known to educated circles beyond the local community. Art connoisseurship ranked highly as an élite pursuit, because it was part of the higher education that marked the true *pepaideumenos*. For members of the wealthy élite, however, an understanding of art was more than just an academic subject, because they were also actively involved in the commissioning of public art or buildings.[13] When Second Sophistic authors displayed their expertise in art history they could confidently expect that their readers would understand the subject. Pausanias uses complex comparisons of style, material and technique to interpret works of art and to determine relative dates.[14] He expects his readers to accept that it is possible to identify the works of particular artists, and his descriptions seem to assume a familiarity with individual artists' styles as well as a more general idea of the development of Greek art.[15]

This assumption of a knowledge about art that all educated Greeks shared is implicit in the *Periegesis*, but Lucian's *Eikones* (*Images* or *Pictures*) illustrates just how much could be expected. Lucian evokes the image of an ideal woman by assembling aspects of well-known statues and paintings: this creative exercise in art connoisseurship could achieve its full effect only if readers could draw on their own knowledge of these works to recreate the image in their minds.[16] An expertise in art history and a familiarity with different artists' styles can be acquired only by comparing and analysing many examples. In the absence of cheap, easily transportable reproductions such as photographs, aspiring art experts had to rely on originals or high quality copies. The locations of famous masterpieces were therefore on the itinerary for an aspiring *pepaideumenos* who was travelling to increase his knowledge. Surviving examples of ancient sculpture suggest that copies of classical statues were common, at least in Italy, and there were also replicas of celebrated paintings.[17] It is likely that in the large cultural centres it would have been possible to find good copies of many well-known works of art, although there is no evidence of systematic collections for educational purposes.

> There is also a sanctuary of Apollo which is very old, as are the sculptures on the pediments. The wooden image (*xoanon*) of the god is also ancient; it is nude and of a very large size. None of the locals could name the artist, but anyone who has already seen the Herakles of Sikyon would assume that the Apollo of Aigeira is a work by the same artist, namely Laphaes of Phleious.[18] (Paus. 7.26.6)

Pausanias was confident of his own expertise in assessing art. His extensive travel and detailed research in many Greek sites are likely to have resulted in a knowledge of Greek art well beyond the most famous masterpieces. In the passage above a comparison between two similar statues is used to identify the artist of an uncredited work.[19] Pausanias could draw on many comparative examples and he realised that stylistic analysis is useful to categorise works of art. Such a judgement relies on the assumption that artists have individual styles which can be identified by an experienced viewer. He describes styles in terms that were probably generally recognised, for example the name of the architectural orders, and regional styles of sculpture such as Attic or Aeginetan.[20] The criteria that allow the identification of a particular style are never fully explained, and the closest he comes to discussing the characteristics of a specific style is when he states rather vaguely that Daidalos' works are 'rather unshapely to look at but nevertheless the divine is manifest in them'.[21]

It is likely that Pausanias knew literature about art and artists, although he does not discuss his own theoretical thoughts on art criticism.[22] Pollitt presents a collection of specialised Greek terms that were used to describe the qualities of art. Pausanias uses a fair range of words to describe what he has seen, but his technical vocabulary is less varied than that of authors more interested in matters of style and expression, be it in art or literature, especially Lucian.[23] In fact, Pausanias is rarely interested in matters that were central to ancient art criticism, for example the effect of an art work on the viewer, or the analysis of an artist's methods of *mimesis*, the imitation of the natural world. Lucian comments on problems of focus in some art descriptions:

> There are some who leave out or just touch upon the great and memorable events, and, through lack of education or taste and because of their ignorance of what to mention and what to leave out, they expound extensively and laboriously on the smallest details. This is just like someone who overlooks the overall beauty of the Zeus of Olympia and fails to praise and describe it for those who do not know it, while admiring the good workmanship and finish of the footstool and the fine proportions of the base, describing them with the greatest attention to detail.[24] (Lucian *Hist. Conscr.* 27)

This example of a 'failed' description of a great work of art is uncannily close to a summary of Pausanias' description of Pheidias' Zeus at Olympia. Pausanias gives a quick overview of the posture and attributes of the god, in much the same manner as in his description of the same artist's Athena Parthenos at the beginning of this chapter, but he adds a meticulous discussion of the reliefs on the throne and footstool. There is no conclusive evidence that Lucian knew Pausanias' work, but he shows that some ancient *pepaideumenoi* with a special interest in sophisticated art criticism may have found Pausanias' approach wanting, just as art historians do today.

When Pausanias describes the appearance of an art work he often starts with the material of which it was made, especially if it was in some way different from the norm. He comments on building materials, for example the colourful marble so fashionable in his own time, but he also distinguishes different types of the more conventional white marble, and he mentions local limestone, fired brick and mud brick.[25] Details about material and technique were particularly relevant for the description of statues. Bronze statues were the standard, and many were made of white marble, which is sometimes identified as coming from a particular source, such as Pentelic or Parian, while coloured marble was comparatively rare in sculpture.[26] Pausanias was particularly interested in wooden statues because to him this simple material usually indicated that they were particularly ancient.[27] Some statues were made of a combination of materials, such as gold and ivory mounted on a wooden substructure (chryselephantine statues), or wooden torsos with hands and faces made of stone (acroliths). Special attention is paid to extraordinary materials, for example a statue of gold and hippopotamus teeth or one of amber.[28] In this latter case the ambiguous meaning of the Greek word for amber, *êlektron*, leads to a comment on amber and on the alloy of gold and silver that was known under the same name. Pausanias also examines the properties of other materials: for example there is a list of the types of wood that could be used for statues and a discussion of the merit of brick walls for defence purposes.[29] The description of the Zeus of Olympia ends with an excursus on the upkeep of ivory statues followed by an enquiry into the nature of ivory.[30] He was interested in the technical process involved in the making of sculpture, and sometimes he discusses how a statue was made, especially if the technique was ancient or unusual.[31] A special technique could raise a statue into the category 'worth seeing' and therefore earn it an entry in the *Periegesis*: once he even recommends a statue to 'anyone who prefers workmanship to mere antiquity', and another is noteworthy because it is made of iron, which is especially difficult to work.[32]

Many references to works of art in the *Periegesis* are, as has been said, very short; if an object is described at all, the text often includes only a few essential aspects. As soon as Pausanias embarked on a more extensive description, however, he was following an ancient literary tradition which would have been familiar to his audience. *Ekphrasis* was an ingredient of Greek literature from its very beginning in the Homeric epics. The most impressive example is the extensive description of Achilles' shield in the *Iliad*, but there are many passages in the *Iliad* as well as in the *Odyssey* which give some details about a variety of artefacts.[33] Hellenistic poetry added to the tradition by emphasising the experience of an observer discovering and decoding a work of art.[34] In Pausanias' time *ekphrasis* became part of the well-stocked literary toolkit of orators and writers. Rhetorical exercises (*progymnasmata*) for aspiring sophists included such descriptive accounts which could be useful in many contexts, because they did not only deal with works of art but also with places, circumstances, events, persons, animals and various objects.[35] There are, however, a number of works of the Second Sophistic period in which the description of art takes pride of place. *Ekphrasis* was probably a routine part of the activities of a performing orator: it would be useful in the standard topic of praising a city, but references to art could serve to illustrate an argument in many contexts and were easy to include because speeches would usually be delivered in public places filled with works of art. Lucian's *De Domo* presents a rhetorical contest between orators who discuss the influence of a magnificent building on their performance. Their arguments include references to their surroundings and one participant provides short descriptions of the paintings displayed in the hall.[36] *Ekphrasis*, however, primarily has the power to create an image of an object that is not present, and it was therefore not dependent on a particular location or context. In historiography the description of buildings in particular can be useful to set the scene.[37] Narrative texts such as the Greek novels included descriptions of art works as literary devices, for example to enhance the interpretation of events or to foreshadow what was going to happen next.[38] In rhetorical texts works of art could be introduced to underline a specific point or to illustrate a line of argument, while also giving the author a chance to show his credentials as a connoisseur.[39] Finally, there are texts that concentrate on *ekphrasis*, most prominently the *Eikones* of the older and the younger Philostratos.[40] These texts ostensibly follow a tour around an art collection, with descriptions of a series of paintings.

Rhetorical handbooks suggested that the main purpose of *ekphrasis* was to allow the audience to visualise the object that was being described.[41] It may therefore come as a surprise that only a few of the surviving examples in Second Sophistic texts attempt, let alone achieve, this goal in the literal sense of allowing their reader to imagine what the object in question actually looks like. The *Eikones* of the Philostrati demonstrate the main focus of ancient art description: instead of exploring the visual aspects of a painting, they are mainly concerned with deciphering its content and with exploring its meaning and effect on the reader.[42] The author may discuss the expressions of figures or the setting of a scene, but the image is often described as if the viewer were observing a real event, looking at real people or objects: we are told what happens in the scene, or what a person looks like and what feelings their face and gestures are expressing. Ancient *ekphrasis* is rarely concerned with how the painter has created the image and what visual means were employed to generate a particular impression, and frequently the reader is not even given a clear idea of the composition of the picture. These texts are, however, quite clear about the fact that they are dealing with images rather than real life, because they explore how the viewer interacts with art. The *Eikones* comment on the contrast between the artificial nature of a painting and the realistic impression it can achieve, they respond to a viewer's questions about the content and meaning of an image, and they expand on the themes that arise from this discussion. In this way, literary *ekphrasis* attempts to enhance the viewer's (and the reader's) encounter with an image, and it progresses well beyond a purely visual experience.[43]

Of all the authors of the period, Lucian is most sensitive to visual details and therefore comes closest to our own mode of art analysis. He uses all the devices of conventional ancient *ekphrasis*, but when he describes a painting he can also pay attention to the painter's technique and the composition of the image.[44] Lucian's most comprehensive description deals with Zeuxis' painting of a family of centaurs. The context is a discussion of the relative merit of unusual ideas and technical skills, which gives Lucian a reason to focus on the way in which the painter creates a particular visual impression, while the theme of the work remains secondary.[45] The description focuses on aspects of the image that are particularly complex, such as the complicated position of the female centaur as she lies on the ground feeding her children. Lucian explains how Zeuxis carefully combines appropriate aspects of the bodies of human and horse to depict the wildness of the male in contrast with the more refined appearance of the female, while also making the centaurs seem like coherent characters. The text also notes how the interaction between the different figures is depicted, and offers comments on the finer points of the design, such as the precise lines, a good use of colour, shadows, perspective, proportion and symmetry.

Pausanias' extensive descriptions do not exhaust the possibilities of ancient *ekphrasis*, let alone those of Lucian's exceptional example. Apart from aspects of material and technique he shows some interest in iconography, which usually serves to support the interpretation of a work of art: Pausanias' main concern is to decipher the content of an image, and he rarely pays attention to the impact of an art work on the viewer.[46] The most complex *ekphrasis* in the *Periegesis* is the description of Polygnotos' paintings in the Lesche of the Knidians at Delphi.[47] Pausanias faithfully lists all the characters that were included in every part of the painting, giving barely more than their names, which were supplied by inscriptions. His main aim is to understand what the image can tell him about individual characters and the story as a whole.[48] There are few references to the painter's visual interpretation of the scenes, but Pausanias comments on iconographical details, noting, for example, the clothing, hairstyle and attributes of some figures, and occasionally he also mentions the colour of particular features. The viewer is guided through the image, moving from scene to scene, and Pausanias' directions provide some information about the composition of the painting, as when he points out that some scenes are depicted *above* others. This suggests that the painting loosely arranged its figures and scenes in several tiers, as can be seen on some classical vases. Pausanias does not actually attempt to convey what the picture looked like – Stansbury-O'Donnell's reconstruction reproduces the order and approximate location of the scenes as they are described in the text, but for its design has to rely on appropriate vase paintings – and it is completely impossible to imagine colours and shading.[49] This disregard for the visual aspects and artistic qualities of art works is most striking in Pausanias' most extensive *ekphraseis*, but it characterises his general approach to art. In fact, Pausanias' complete silence on design, expression or style is even more remarkable in the case of his description of the Chest of Kypselos.[50] Here he was dealing with a style that must have seemed unusual and thrillingly ancient, but although Pausanias clearly wrestles with an unfamiliar iconography, and though he describes the archaic design of the inscriptions, he mentions only one aspect that betrays the high age of the images, namely a centaur with human forelegs.[51] The closest Pausanias ever comes to an analytic description of the archaic style are his comments on an athlete's statue in Phigalia which he describes as 'ancient, not least in its posture: the feet are not far apart, and the arms hang down by the side as far as the hips'.[52]

Pausanias' most extensive examples of *ekphrasis* are not inviting the reader to admire the works of art for their visual qualities. In fact, he begins his description of the throne of Apollo at Amyklai by saying that he will not describe all the reliefs in detail because that might bore his readers.[53] What follows is a list of mythological themes which are depicted, and this reflects Pausanias' attitude: when he focuses on an artefact he often presents it as a valuable collection of mythological themes which illustrate the viewpoint of a particular time and place. He approaches monuments which include many details almost as if he were deciphering a complex text, and he was willing to take some time to understand and record the information that could be derived from art works. Pausanias' description of the Chest of Kypselos hints at his efforts to decode unfamiliar iconography and inscriptions, probably in discussion with his local guides.[54] In this case his hard work was rewarded not just with an insight into an ancient interpretation of mythology: he was able also to record verse inscriptions which he assumed to be the work of the Corinthian poet Eumelos.[55] The investigation of this exhibit by such a learned visitor may well have developed into a complex discussion of art, archaic poetry and a whole range of mythical traditions. In the text at least, Pausanias uses the images and inscriptions to gain an insight into the interpretation of many crucial Greek myths in archaic Corinth. Polygnotos' work in the Lesche of the Knidians was less ancient, but the themes of the paintings made them attractive to Pausanias. The painting of the Underworld included characters from different famous stories which would evoke many associations to a learned viewer or, indirectly, to the readers of the *Periegesis*. The *Iliou Persis* (*Sack of Troy*) was not the subject of the canonical Homeric poems, and there were numerous stories about the fate of the many well-known characters involved in the war on both sides. Polygnotos' painting of the scene offered a particular interpretation which was worth discussing. Pausanias considers some of the inscriptions, and he compares the interpretation suggested by the paintings with relevant texts, just as he might compare different versions of written and oral narratives.[56]

This habit of 'reading' some works of art almost like texts should not come as a surprise, for many authors of Pausanias' time acknowledge close parallels between art and literature. Writers who explored theories of literary style used art as a comparison to illustrate their ideas.[57] One major focus of discussion was the question of whether it was easier to express complex ideas through words or through images. Dio Chrysostom explores this issue in his *Olympic Discourse*. He introduces Pheidias into his speech and lets the artist himself discuss how he managed to create a depiction of Zeus that was generally thought to capture the essence of the god's character and majesty. The artist argues that poets have a greater freedom of expression, and therefore find it easier to represent character, let alone actions and movement. In fact, the statue is such a success, Pheidias/Dio argues, because it tries to depict the image already created by Homer.[58] Philostratos, however, had a higher opinion of the power of art, rating the powers of poets and painters as equal:

> Anyone who does not appreciate painting does injustice to the truth and to all the wisdom of poets, for both contribute equally to our knowledge of the deeds and the look of heroes. He also fails to praise the harmony of proportions (*symmetria*) through which art approaches reason.[59] (Philostratos *Eikones* 1.1)

The idea is that painters, just like poets, are able to express their insights about characters and stories in unique ways and that through their creativity they can, paradoxically, produce a new interpretation of an ancient tradition that is at the same time closer to the truth. The description of art can cross the boundary between literature and visual arts and allows a writer to combine insights gained through both media. Pausanias would probably have approved of Philostratos' emphasis on the value of paintings and poetry as sources for mythical stories. As we have seen, Pausanias investigates monuments to discover local traditions and unique interpretations of mythical stories: the visual arts often allow him to explore new aspects of the Greek past. As sources works of art can be scrutinised in similar ways to texts, often using alternative evidence to assess the value of the information.[60] Inscriptions and local informants could supply names of depicted characters, which often allows Pausanias to expand the cast of a story beyond a few widely known individuals. He also saw iconography as a crucial means for an artist to represent ideas and interpretations, and he often focused on such details, for example the attributes of gods and heroes.[61]

In order to accommodate works of art and associated traditions within his memorial landscapes Pausanias had to pay some attention to chronology. The actual date of an art work and the period it is used to illustrate are often not identical, for many monuments commemorated events long before their own creation. Pausanias does not, therefore, always provide a date for the work itself, preferring to explore significant historical associations rather than the history of the actual monument. Nevertheless, he is interested in the chronology and development of Greek art, and he handles art history in a way similar to his treatment of mythical and political history: dates are rarely discussed directly, but they are often implicit in the information provided in the description. Again Pausanias depends on a system of generations, in this case teacher-pupil relationships between artists that can form a kind of genealogy. Additionally, points of contact between artists and historical characters or references to historical events provide links to a wider chronological framework.[62] The development of

114

artistic techniques is also tied in with this rough chronology, because Pausanias often names innovators or inventors, and technique could therefore be used to verify or refute local traditions about the date of a monument.[63] The hallmarks of the earliest examples of Greek sculpture were particularly fascinating. Those included aniconic objects that served as images of divinities, or *xoana* – wooden statues which were often thought to be particularly ancient.[64] Once the great age of such an artefact was established, the statue could be appreciated as an awe-inspiring tangible link to a remote past. Pausanias believed that there were authentic works by artists such as Daidalos and even the god Hephaistos. He clearly accepted that artefacts created by such mythical characters survived in Greece down to his own day, and he judged them on merit: in one case a claim is rejected because the technique seemed anachronistic for Hephaistos, but other works of the god are considered authentic, and Pausanias lists a number of artefacts he accepts as works of Daidalos.[65]

It has long been noticed that Pausanias' selection of art works for his book was strongly influenced by their age. Larger cities could have thousands of statues cluttering their public spaces, and most sites probably had so many monuments that Pausanias had to select a small sample of the most noteworthy pieces.[66] A majority of the works of art mentioned in the *Periegesis* date from the archaic and classical periods, and few are securely dated to a period after the middle of the second century BC.[67] In fact, some very conspicuous buildings of the Roman and Hellenistic periods are omitted altogether, such as the Stoa of Attalos in Athens or the Nymphaion of Herodes Atticus in Olympia.[68] This preference for the archaic and classical periods is in line with the tastes of Pausanias' contemporaries. One should, however, consider this apparent neglect of later periods with some caution.

As we saw in the last chapter, most cities' local histories emphasised particular periods, and although many focused on their earlier history, there were places where Hellenistic or even Roman events were crucial. In the same way, Pausanias has no qualms about filling some of his cities with works of art or buildings which are clearly postclassical or even fairly recent, while elsewhere later monuments are omitted or perhaps described without any hints to their actual date.[69] There is no general attempt to deny the existence of all later artefacts, but in some places they clearly did not fit the image that Pausanias wanted to present, an image that was often determined by local history. Some art works provided valuable evidence for local traditions, or they could serve as convenient anchors for various *logoi*. Age or artistic value was probably secondary if there was a good story to tell. All we can say is that Pausanias often did not find it worthwhile to discuss the date of Hellenistic or Roman monuments. Where the history of the monument itself seemed neither interesting in its own right nor relevant for explaining its historical significance he tends to omit details that might indicate its date. Historical relevance is not the only reason to include a monument. Some were worth mentioning because of a connection with a known artist, while others merited discussion because they were rare examples of a special technique or special material. In any case, the visual and physical properties of a monument could be taken into account, but mere visual impact was not enough to secure an entry in the *Periegesis*. Pausanias' selection and interpretation of art works suggest how he saw the role of art in Greek culture, and perhaps also what art meant to him personally. He presents art in many contexts, but, apart from their importance as historical monuments, he most commonly singles out objects for their religious significance and, more generally, for their role as symbols of Greek culture.

Greek religion was inextricably linked with art, especially because divinities were usually represented by anthropomorphic images. In his *Olympic Discourse* Dio explores the origins of the human conception of the divine and he names four main sources: human instinct, poetry, laws and art. The discussion that follows focuses on poetry and art, and here it is the artist who has the advantage over the poet, because his work is more easily accessible even to those who are not able to appreciate poetry.[70] The ancients were aware of the fact that through statues that served as cult images the interpretation of an artist could influence many people's concept of the divine.[71] For Pausanias, cult images provide evidence for the countless variants of the gods all Greeks had in common, and a few divinities that were unique to particular communities. The choice of representation and attributes could provide some idea about the aspects of a god or goddess that were particularly important, and they could illustrate local interpretations that had little to do with mainstream Greek ideas.[72] In the *Periegesis* sacred art represents a crucial aspect of the variety of cultural expression that characterises Pausanias' Greece.

It would be difficult to conceive of this imaginary landscape without the many works of art that populate Pausanias' cities and sites. Public art gave shape and meaning to the memorial landscapes explored in the previous chapter, both in the *Periegesis* and in the 'real world'. Art was a sign of prestige which conferred an air of culture, history and general significance on a community, and it was no doubt a hallmark of Greekness which would be easy to recognise well beyond the Greek world. It may not be possible to gain much information about the exact appearance of the many buildings, statues and paintings described in the *Periegesis*, but we do get a sense of the significance and function of art in Greek cities of the Roman world. Yet that impression is likely to be exaggerated. Pausanias probably did indeed see almost every object he includes in his work, but it is important to remember just how emphatically his work focuses on public art while many other aspects of ancient city life remain almost invisible. The *Periegesis* therefore creates an impression of a Greece where even the poorest communities could often display sublime examples of classical art by the most illustrious old masters, and where art is central to community life. This seductive but scarcely realistic image had a strong impact on later ideas about Greece and Greek art which will be considered in the following chapters.

Pausanias and his Readers

We cannot refrain from expressing the hope that we may yet see a worthy
English translation of the *Periegesis*. No edition annotated by the light of
modern archaeological discovery exists, we believe, in any language. When
we recall the splendid illustrations that the excavations of the last quarter
century – nay, even the last decade – have prepared for such a work, we
cannot fail to perceive what a fine field of research and erudition awaits the
scholar who should undertake an edition of Pausanias on the lines of Canon
Rawlinson's *Herodotus*. To be worthily executed such a work would demand
the labour of more years than most men are willing to devote to a single
object; but once accomplished, it would ensure its author an honourable and
lasting name in literature.' (G.F. Bowen in Murray (1884) 94)

This demand to make Pausanias finally accessible to those without a full
classical education was made in the introduction to one of the earliest
modern travel guides to Greece.[1] The author was thinking of the value of
the *Periegesis* for interested travellers, but he expected that its impact
would not be confined just to this specialised sphere. Little did he know
that in the same year J.G. Frazer had just started to work on his translation and commentary that were to answer his wishes in a more than
adequate manner, although the completion of his work was to take fourteen years. Bowen's statement illustrates the general interest, partly
fuelled by new archaeological discoveries in Greece, that would lead to
about twenty years of intensive research and scholarly discussion of the
Periegesis. The story of Pausanias appreciation, however, began much
earlier. After his work came to Europe in the early fifteenth century it was
translated into several languages, including English. In fact, the earliest
translation into Latin appeared in 1500, several years before the first
printed edition of the original text (Musurus, 1516). Another Latin translation was published around 1547, followed by an Italian one in 1593. The
eighteenth century saw further translations into French (1731-3), German
(1765-6, 1798-9), two into English (1780 and 1793), and a new Italian
version (1792-3), with further editions and translations in the nineteenth
century.[2] Pausanias clearly had many readers long before it became
relatively easy to test the qualities of his description by visiting Greece.
Many who wanted to find out more about ancient Greek culture, particularly mythology, art and religion, read the *Periegesis* with interest.

A full study of Pausanias' readers and their reactions to the *Periegesis*
since its re-discovery in the early Renaissance is beyond the scope of this

book. This chapter therefore offers a discussion of a few highlights in the reception of Pausanias during the last six hundred years to illustrate how his work influenced particular areas of modern thought. Much work is yet to be done in this field, and it is striking how little attention some commentators on relevant authors pay to Pausanias as a crucial source.[3] It is true that at first sight his work often appears to be not much more than a faithful quarry of information about ancient Greece, but once ideas and interpretations are investigated further it becomes clear that his influence was at times much more profound. The most evident effect of the *Periegesis* is without doubt its influence on perceptions of Greece, which will be discussed in the next chapter. Pausanias has, however, also been an important source of inspiration for crucial advances in scholarly thought. Most remarkably, the *Periegesis* had a formative influence on two works that are among the most influential books of the eighteenth and nineteenth centuries, namely J.J. Winckelmann's *Geschichte der Kunst des Alterthums* (*History of the Art of Antiquity*) of 1764 and J.G. Frazer's *Golden Bough* (1890).

The story of Pausanias' *Periegesis* in western Europe starts with a single manuscript copy that reached Italy from Constantinople soon after AD 1400. Its owner was Niccolò Niccoli of Florence, an avid collector of ancient manuscripts, and the first we hear of his copy of Pausanias is in a letter of 1418 which shows that he had agreed to lend it to an acquaintance in Venice. This is where Guarino Veronese of Padua may have encountered the *Periegesis*. In any case, he became Pausanias' first known reader in western Europe and he was highly satisfied with what he saw, as is recorded in a letter he wrote to Niccoli to express his pleasure in reading Pausanias' Corinthian book.[4] Niccoli's original Byzantine manuscript disappears from our record at some point in the sixteenth century, but by that time several copies had been made, and these are the basis for all printed editions of the text, beginning with Musurus (1516).[5]

Since the *Periegesis* is presented in geographical order it is not easy to extract information on particular subjects which might be scattered throughout its ten books, but this apparently did not deter scholars from using Pausanias as a source for various aspects of ancient culture. One early professor of Greek, Demetrios Chalkondyles, was reputed to have memorised the whole work. In fifteenth-century scholarship, the *Periegesis* usually supplied evidence to support scholarly arguments about matters that could be quite unrelated to its themes or aims. For example, Domizio Calderini, who attempted the first translation into Latin, also included references to Pausanias in his works on Ovid, Martial and Statius, and Marcus Musurus, the editor of the first printed version, quoted the *Periegesis* in his lectures on the *Anthology*.[6] This mining of Pausanias for the many valuable details in his work continues to this day, but as new aspects of Greek culture came to the attention of scholars it turned out that there were many subjects where Pausanias could contribute arguments and suggest interpretations. One field of classical studies where this became particularly apparent was art history.

The beginnings of modern art history can be traced back to the Renaissance, with a collection of artists' lives, Vasari's *Vite* of 1550, as one of the earliest landmark works which dealt with the lives of medieval and Renaissance artists down to his own day. Interest in Greek and Roman art also developed around the same time, fuelled by contemporary artists who learned from ancient models combined with the ongoing research into ancient literature and culture. In this period an increasing number of Roman works of art were discovered in Italy, and by the eighteenth century collections of ancient artefacts also contained examples of Egyptian and Etruscan art, as well as some pieces which were identified as Greek.[7] Since the fall of Constantinople in AD 1453, which also led to the Ottoman conquest of most of Greece, few western travellers had visited the country, but in the seventeenth century the first reports of visits became available. Some travellers discussed the ancient remains in some detail, and the first images of Greek sites reached western Europe, most notably the drawings of the Parthenon before its partial destruction in 1687.[8] Nevertheless, very few original examples of Greek art were known at the time, and most theories about the subject had to be based on ancient literary evidence.

In the introduction to his *History of the Art of Antiquity* Winckelmann gives a scathing verdict of writers who had tackled the subject before him:

> Some writings with the title *History of Art* have appeared, but art has played only a small part in them; for their authors were not sufficiently acquainted with art and therefore could not offer anything they had not gleaned from books or hearsay. Almost no writer guides us to the essence and the interior of art, and those who deal with antiquities either only touch upon subjects where they can show their learning, or, if they talk about art, it is in part only with general compliments.[9] (Winkelmann (1764))

Given the circumstances, it is hardly surprising that few writers before the mid-eighteenth century had much direct experience of original ancient art works. Winckelmann himself admits that in his own time it was still difficult, if not impossible, to write a substantial work on ancient art without living in Rome for several years, although interest in art was growing and access to collections was becoming easier.[10] Earlier writers relied almost exclusively on the ancient texts, and Pausanias was among their crucial sources. Iunius' *De Pictura Veterum (The Visual Arts of the Ancients)* of 1637[11] is a good example because it was one of the most influential works on ancient art before Winckelmann's *History of the Art of Antiquity*, and its argument mainly relies on numerous citations and quotations from ancient texts. The main part of the work discusses the origins and development of art, particularly of painting and sculpture, and the factors that lead to perfection in art. There is also a *Catalogue*, which is essentially a lexicon of artists, engineers and architects as well as patrons of the arts, presented in alphabetical order. In the theoretical parts of his work Iunius relied mainly on ancient authors who dealt with art in a systematic way, for example Pliny's chronological overview of the development of Greek art,[12] and a number of ancient authors who discuss art and style, such as Vitruvius, Quintilian, Cicero, Frontinus, Athenaios and Philostratos.[13] Pausanias is used extensively, especially in the *Catalogue*, mainly as a source of information about particular art works and artists.

In the eighteenth century more original ancient works of art became known, and the study of Greek and Roman art could start in earnest. At the same time, the influence of ancient art on contemporary art became a matter of discussion, and therefore the study of original works was relevant beyond a merely antiquarian interest.[14] In France, Caylus, who had a special interest in the theory of art and style, published seven volumes on ancient art. These collections of engravings depicted hundreds of ancient art works to make them available for comparison and analysis. Caylus' commentary shows that, since Iunius' work, attitudes to ancient art had shifted considerably. The artefacts were now the centre of attention, and wherever possible texts supplied only additional information. In fact, Caylus suggests that ancient artefacts could clarify details that were not sufficiently explained in the literary sources, and add to the incomplete understanding of antiquity that could be achieved through the texts.[15] He was one of the earliest art critics to move away from tracing developments through individual artists' biographies and to concentrate on the changes in what we would call style.[16] He talks of his aim to understand the characteristic 'taste' (*goût*) of ancient peoples which changes over time, and in his view these changes in national 'taste' can be traced by the careful analysis and comparison of surviving works of art.[17] The examples in his collections are therefore presented in separate sections for Egyptian, Etruscan, Greek, Roman and Gallic remains. Caylus' highest admiration is reserved for the elegance of Greek art, although he concedes that there were comparatively few original examples.[18] This problem was exacerbated by the fact that the numerous Greek vases which had been found in Etruria were yet to be classified as imports from Greece.[19]

Now that art critics had started to base their judgements about technique, expression and style on their own observations, they were no longer exclusively dependent on descriptions of lost masterpieces or ancient art theory. At the same time, it became more important to understand the meaning of ancient art works in their original context. Caylus leaves no doubt about his main source: for him 'nothing is more capable of corroborating our ideas about the magnificence of the Greeks and about their manner in which they cultivated the arts than Pausanias' report.'[20] Where other ancient authors, especially Pliny, document only the admiration for classical Greek art, often outside its original context, Pausanias described the environment in which such extraordinary progress had actually taken place.[21] It seems that Caylus knew the *Periegesis* when he began his work, but he read it carefully only after volume I was finished. As a result the introduction to the Greek part of volume II contains enthusiastic remarks about Pausanias' usefulness and a long discussion of the nature of ancient Greece.[22] As we saw in the last chapter, Caylus carefully recorded and counted the many works of art mentioned in the *Periegesis*, and tried to gain a sense of the methods and personality of its author. Pausanias is represented as reliable, and the fact that he appears too credulous at times supports the assumption that he is reporting truthfully what he saw and heard.[23] Caylus complains that Pausanias did not pay enough attention to 'the sublime of Greek art', but he appreciates his stylistic judgement.[24] It seems that Caylus was an early subscriber to the 'dependable dullard' image of Pausanias.

The *Periegesis* also supplies Caylus with ideas and material for a discussion of the history of Greek art, particularly in its earliest phase. In volume I Caylus refutes ancient claims that the Greeks invented art, pointing towards connections with Egypt. He supports this argument with references to temples of Egyptian gods in Greece, mostly of a late date as we know now. From the beginning, the *Periegesis* supplies most of this evidence, but at this early stage Caylus suggests that Pausanias was reluctant to contemplate the beginnings of Greek sculpture.[25] This view has changed considerably in volume II, where we are still presented with the argument about Egyptian temples in Greece, but there is now also a discussion about the affinity between the styles of Greece and Egypt.[26] Pausanias' comments on the earliest Greek statues are the prime evidence for this line of argument since few other ancient authors discuss the beginnings of Greek art in any detail. Caylus switches from a purely historical approach to one which focuses on the development of style, an early example of art-historical analysis, and he does so under the influence of the *Periegesis*. Pausanias himself never adopts the systematic methodology of an art historian, but he used style, material and technique to identify artists and to establish rough chronological links, and this approach resonated with those who were now beginning to categorise ancient works of art by similar means.

Around the time that Caylus' first volumes were published, Winckelmann was also turning his attention to ancient art.[27] In 1755 he moved to Rome to study the many works of art on display there, and focused on ancient sculpture. In Caylus' work we have already seen the beginnings of an analytical examination of ancient art, but Winckelmann must be credited with underpinning this new approach with the theoretical framework that stands at the beginning of modern art history. His efforts belonged to a wider scholarly trend of his time which saw representatives of various disciplines describe, catalogue and systematise large amounts of material in order to gain a better understanding of the world.[28] Winckel-

mann introduced an analytical method of describing art which pays special attention to technique and expression and he was the first to divide
Greek art into distinct periods defined by particular aspects of style. He
also linked this evolution of artistic style to Greek history, and he explained the nature and development of Greek art with reference to its
cultural and historical background.[29] Winckelmann was aware that his
theory was problematic: after all, he was speculating about the nature of
Greek art although almost all the original evidence was lost. In fact he was
the first to recognise that most 'Greek' sculptures preserved in Italy were
actually Roman copies of lost originals, which made it even more difficult
to decide whether his few examples were representative of a particular
phase of Greek art.[30] Winckelmann's definition of periods of Greek art
therefore relied mainly on texts that rarely mentioned the often minute
details that his analysis of surviving art had identified as crucial.

Although the art works themselves were firmly at the centre of
Winckelmann's attention, he had to rely on texts to understand the
cultural and historical context of Greek art. He had enjoyed a thorough
classical education and had read widely among both Greek and Roman
literature.[31] His study is therefore based on a wide range of sources,
especially Pliny, who supplies the framework for the historical development of Greek sculpture, just as in earlier works on ancient art. We do not
know when Winckelmann first encountered the *Periegesis*, but in February 1756 he reported that he had drawn up a plan for a 'treatise on the
taste of Greek artists' and that this had prompted him 'to re-read the
whole Pausanias'.[32] There is no doubt that he knew the *Periegesis* very well
indeed; as his many references show, it was rarely far from his mind while
he was writing his *History of the Art of Antiquity*.[33] In one case Winckelmann suggests an emendation of the text, arguing on the basis of
Pausanias' idiosyncratic style, and he describes him as 'Cappadocian',
which suggests that he had engaged with the problem of Pausanias'
background.[34] Within the work the *Periegesis* provides evidence for crucial
arguments and it is used to establish the context and meaning of art works
in antiquity: where were statues set up, and what was their function?
Which types of art were sacred?[35] Pausanias also supplied evidence about
the material of art works, the iconography of statues, and, more generally,
the subjects of ancient sculptures. Winckelmann was, in fact, one of the
first to suggest that most ancient sculpture did not deal with Roman
history, but depicted Greek mythological subjects.[36] Finally, like Caylus he
found Pausanias useful for his (limited) thoughts on the earliest stages of
Greek art.[37]

It is likely that, rather than merely serving as a mine of information,
the *Periegesis* played a role in shaping Winckelmann's new approach. As
we saw in the last chapter, Pausanias was capable of stylistic comparison,
and he had some sense of chronological criteria which could be applied to
sculpture in particular. Winckelmann respected Pausanias' judgement on

style and his sense of chronology, and he was ready to base crucial conclusions on the *Periegesis*.

> That the style of the art of the last period was very different from the ancient style is implied by, among others, Pausanias, when he says that a Priestess of the Leukippides ... had the antique head of one of the two statues removed, because she believed that she could make it more beautiful, and had a new head made for it which, as he says, was 'fashioned according to today's art'.[38] (Winckelmann (1764))

A similar conclusion arises from an argument about the date of the sculptor Kallimachos. Pausanias ranks him below the greatest artists, which suggests to Winckelmann that the sculptor must have lived in the period when Greek art reached its high point, because otherwise it would not be necessary to say this at all. He seems to assume that Pausanias not only thought in historical epochs but was also capable of assigning artists and their creations to the appropriate periods, even those that did not reach the full potential of their age.[39] This assessment of Pausanias' chronological method is probably too generous, but it shows how closely Winckelmann associated the ancient author's approach with his own.

Further parallels between the two authors arise from an analysis of Winckelmann's conception of Greek history and culture. In his view all Greek art was public, just as one would expect from reading the *Periegesis*, and he notes that all Greek cities were involved in commissioning art for temples and public spaces.[40] He also rejects all ancient evidence which suggests that artists were seen as lowly craftsmen and he insists that they were honoured and admired, a view which reflects the attitude of the Second Sophistic with its reverence for classical art, backed up by numerous references to Pausanias. For Winckelmann the most important ingredient for an environment conducive to great achievements in art is political freedom, and therefore the high point of Greek art is reached in the fifth and fourth centuries, the period we still call 'classical'.[41] The decline starts with Macedonian control in the early Hellenistic period and continues after the Roman conquest, with occasional signs of recovery when Greece was allowed some freedom by its rulers.[42] Winckelmann's emphasis on freedom as a crucial precondition for a people to reach its full potential should be seen in the context of intellectual developments in his own time: many thinkers of the Age of Enlightenment were contemplating the issue of political freedom, and we are just a few decades away from the French revolution. Nevertheless, Winckelmann's ideas were also based on his ancient sources. The notion of the decline of Greek art during the Hellenistic period is quite typical for ancient texts of the Roman imperial period, most significantly Pliny,[43] and this coincides with a general preference for the archaic and classical period in most Second Sophistic texts.[44] Pausanias more or less agreed with this idea, and he had particularly strong views about the importance of Greek freedom. Unlike Winckelmann, he does not directly connect the political status of Greece with the achievements of its artists, but his work offers an opportunity to contemplate the loss of Greek freedom together with information about a decline in art and the cultured ways of the classical Greeks.

Winckelmann's approach provided the basis for the study of ancient art, a crucial part of classical archaeology. Moreover, he had a great impact on attitudes to antiquity in general, especially in Germany. His interpretation of art as part of Greek culture contributed to a more holistic approach to the history and culture of antiquity (*Altertumswissenschaften*) which developed particularly in Germany alongside purely literary studies (classical philology).[45] Soon after Winckelmann's death (1768), however, attitudes to ancient Greece were to change significantly. The last decades of Ottoman rule in Greece saw the looting of a number of important antiquities, especially sculptures from the Parthenon, Bassai and the temple of Aphaia in Aigina. The analysis of originals as well as Roman copies progressed rapidly, so that many of Winckelmann's conclusions soon seemed hopelessly outdated. At the same time a more sober image of Greece replaced the romantic and idealistic notions of the Age of Enlightenment.[46] An increasing number of travellers visited Greece in the early years of the nineteenth century, and after the foundation of the modern Greek state the country and its archaeological sites became increasingly accessible. Research into ancient Greek art and culture no longer relied exclusively on texts. Attitudes to the *Periegesis* were bound to be particularly affected, since it could now be measured against real artefacts and landscapes.

Early travellers used Pausanias as a travel guide which, though out-of-date by over sixteen hundred years, still proved useful for their purposes. Excavations provided new evidence which illustrated Pausanias' approach to particular sites. By the latter part of the century the general esteem for the *Periegesis* had grown significantly, as demonstrated by the call for a new translation that opens this chapter. Soon there was a new English translation and a German multi-volume edition, followed by Frazer's monumental translation and commentary.[47] At the same time there was also a backlash to this enthusiastic reception: Wilamowitz and a number of his pupils emphasised Pausanias' 'ineptitude' as a writer and suggested that much of his work was a compilation of earlier literary sources. These arguments were refuted almost instantly, but the debate remained influential for several decades. Arguments about Pausanias' reliability were further fuelled by problems with the identification of recently excavated monuments on sites described in the *Periegesis*.[48] The 'Pausanias boom' of the late nineteenth century therefore included a good deal of heated debate.[49]

Frazer is a crucial figure in this period of Pausanias studies. His valuable if somewhat eccentric commentary is still important, and it will remain a crucial source for the state of Greece and of classical scholarship around 1900 even if some aspects of his work have now been superseded by more recent editions and commentaries. Like Winckelmann, Frazer tapped into intellectual trends of his own time and discovered a new way of reading Pausanias, as well as opening up a new field of scholarly enquiry which had an impact well beyond classics. Frazer's association with Pausanias can be traced back to 1884 when he signed a contract to publish a translation of the *Periegesis*. By this time the steadily increasing tourism to Greece meant that such a work was likely to find many readers, as the quotation at the beginning of this chapter shows. By 1886, however, Frazer had changed his mind: he now wanted to add a commentary which, to the disquiet of his publisher, was steadily growing in size. There was no doubt that there was a need for a full commentary which would take into account the recent developments in Greek archaeology.[50] By 1888 the Pausanias project had ground to a halt: Frazer had been sidetracked – he was now preparing 'a work on comparative mythology', the extraordinarily influential *Golden Bough*, published in its earliest version in 1890.[51] Ackermann shows that Frazer had long been interested in anthropology, a subject constantly fuelled by new observations from many parts of the planet which were becoming more easily accessible, but were as yet little affected by western culture. In 1884, around the time when he started to work on Pausanias, Frazer formed a close friendship with Robertson Smith, a biblical scholar and anthropologist, and this seems to have triggered his own extensive enquiries in this field.[52]

This new interest was to keep Frazer occupied for the rest of his life, but this did not mean that Pausanias was set aside. On the contrary, the *Golden Bough* would not have been possible without Frazer's work on the *Periegesis*, because at its centre is the desire to find a new interpretation of ancient myths and rituals, and Pausanias was a major source of material for these anthropological studies. The idea of adding a commentary to the translation was, in fact, probably a reaction to his new anthropological interests, and many of the notes that were included in Frazer's *Pausanias* when it finally appeared in 1898 are distinctly '*Golden Bough*-ish'. Frazer's argument focuses on similarities between Greek traditions and the countless details about non-western cultures that researchers were collecting all around the world. His studies drew on a wide range of ancient sources, but there is no doubt that the *Periegesis* was crucial for this line of enquiry, because unlike many other ancient texts, it presents myths and religion in their local context. In fact, Pausanias' interest in comparisons between different versions of Greek myths and his attempts to explain some of the more unusual rituals he found in Greece coincide with major themes of most Victorian explorers' enquiries. Frazer's new approach led to an image of Greek culture that differed significantly from earlier ideas: where Pausanias' eighteenth-century readers had found cities full of art works, inhabited by a people that had reached the pinnacle of human cultural achievement, Frazer looked at the many myths and rituals recorded in the *Periegesis* and discovered that they had much in common with the customs of the 'savages' of his own day. For a modern reader many of his comparisons seem to be drawn from various backgrounds without any examination of their validity. In Frazer's day this was justified by the assumption that all cultures went through similar stages of evolution, and that, therefore, similarities between 'primitive cultures' anywhere and at any time were more than just mere coincidence.[53] Frazer's method was discredited by the next generation of anthropologists, but it was very influential as one of the foundations of comparative ethnology, and it also had a profound impact on the English literature of the period.[54]

Frazer was not the only scholar to discover the affinities between the study of Greek culture and late Victorian anthropology. In 1890, the year the *Golden Bough* came out, Harrison and Verrall published a selection of translated passages from Pausanias' Book I with an extensive archaeological and historical commentary. Harrison boldly states that she is 'regarding the myth-making Greek as a practical savage rather than a poet or philosopher'.[55] Her anthropological eye discards many of the romantic notions of antiquity which were still one of the foundations of classics, a discipline mainly preoccupied with the most distinguished examples of ancient literature. This 'anthropological' approach particularly affected the study of cultural history: pure *Realienkunde*, the collection and analysis of relevant literary sources, was now complemented with comparative material, and the ancient evidence could be investigated with methods that had been developed for other disciplines. Harrison herself was to follow up her work on Pausanias with a number of studies on Greek religion which pursued new avenues of anthropological, psychological and proto-feminist interpretation of Greek cults and their origins.[56] Her somewhat eccentric approach was never fully accepted by the academic establishment, and ultimately it was a much more sober work, Farnell's *Cults of Greek States*, that became the standard work on Greek religion for the early twentieth century. This work discusses the Greek gods one by one, collecting evidence for cult buildings and epithets: a less revolutionary approach, but this, too, claimed its roots in archaeology, anthropology and the ancient texts, above all again Pausanias.[57]

As Beard and Henderson have demonstrated, the 'Pausanias boom' around 1900 coincided with a complex debate over the nature and future of classical studies, in the wake of the many archaeological discoveries in Greece.[58] The question was whether classics was essentially the study of ancient literature or whether its focus should be ancient culture, which would mean that archaeology would have to become an integral part of the discipline. The *Periegesis* was right at the centre of this debate: it had never been one of the chief texts of classical studies because of its perceived lack of literary quality, but now it increasingly received scholarly attention in connection with excavations and topographical research in Greece. Back in the ivory towers of western Europe, far from the physical evidence, Pausanias allowed scholars to deal with the material remains of ancient Greece without having to contemplate new approaches that could challenge the role of the literary tradition as main source for ancient culture: the idea that ancient texts can be an obstacle to the interpretation of the material evidence was to become a matter of debate in Greek archaeology only several decades later.[59] In Britain the earliest archaeology lectures did, in fact, focus on choice passages in Pausanias, which could then lead to discussions of new material evidence.[60] At the same time, however, all but the most determined armchair scholars had begun to see a visit to Greece as essential to their studies. Frazer spent a good part of the eight years between the publication of the *Golden Bough* and the completion of his six-volume commentary collecting archaeological evidence, and he eventually realised that he needed to go to Greece to make sure that his information was up to date and correct.[61] His two visits became much more than mere fact-finding missions. Frazer discovered the landscape of Greece which so rarely gets a mention in the *Periegesis*, and his commentary turned into a hybrid between notes on the text and a report of his own travels in the footsteps of Pausanias, often filling perceived gaps in the ancient description. In the footsteps of his ancient guide, Frazer followed ancient roads, looked for ancient sites and investigated monuments, and in the process he also developed an image of Pausanias which was in many ways similar to his own travelling, researching self.[62] Frazer's *Pausanias* broke with the tradition of classical scholarship because it did not include the original text, let alone a new critical edition based on the manuscripts,[63] but it firmly established the idea that Pausanias needed to be read with the Greek landscape in mind.

The boundaries between classics and archaeology have never been fully broken down, and attitudes to Pausanias during much of the twentieth century reflect this continuing divide. By 1900 Pausanias was firmly established as the crucial text for the study of Greek religion as well as for archaeological work in mainland Greece. Beyond these specialised fields the *Periegesis* remained peripheral to classicists' interests: a text of inferior quality which would at times be useful as a source for out-of-the way information about Greece and its culture. The renewed interest in Pausanias since the 1980s is closely connected to a radical reassessment of Greek literature under the Roman empire: it seems that yet again the *Periegesis* has become a useful resource for a new line of enquiry. As we have seen, during the six hundred years since Pausanias was re-introduced to western Europe, his work, though always at the edges of the canon of 'respectable' ancient texts, has proved a versatile resource in the changing trends of scholarly interests. Most of the scholars discussed in this chapter had access to a wide range of ancient texts, but often it is clear that Pausanias played a central role in their enquiries and served as more than just as a quarry of information. The *Periegesis* has had a profound influence on how the ancient Greeks are perceived in the modern western world, and it has been instrumental also in shaping the disciplines of classics and classical archaeology. Through his many readers Pausanias has become part of the fabric of the discipline: many aspects of his approach inform the basic assumptions and methods that underlie the study of ancient Greece.

Discovering Greece with Pausanias

I return to Pausanias. The details I have presented on the basis of his work must strike the imagination and give a good impression of the genius of the Greeks. One might be surprised to find so many things of beauty united in a land which is rather mediocre in size, and this is even more surprising when one considers that these works of art were generally masterpieces, created with taste, genius and in the most grandiose manner. Finally, Greece was the temple of the arts, and ... everywhere she presented a perfectly arranged art gallery, even more superb because all the works of art which imitated beautiful nature were placed in a way that doubled their merit. No part of the world has ever offered a sight to equal it. ... We can therefore only preserve with much sorrow and much diligence the little of the monuments that remain of these rare and superior people. (Caylus (1752-86) II.109-10)

From the seventeenth century onwards most educated travellers who visited Greece would have arrived with clear expectations of what might still be found in that ancient landscape. Ideas about the achievements of Greek culture were based on the classical texts, combined with the idealistic image created by many authors of the Second Sophistic. Pausanias, however, connected the art, literature and mythology of the ancients with specific places, and offered a glimpse of Greek cities and countryside well beyond Athens. Before western Europeans even set foot on the Greek mainland they would therefore have expected a landscape full of poignant associations. Few would have shared Caylus' utopian view, which has little to do with Greece in any period of antiquity, but his enthusiastic musings stand for the more romantic notions that Pausanias inspired in his readers, ideas that inevitably defined their approach to Greece, its landscape, people and ancient remains.[1]

The *Periegesis* has had a major influence on the complex discourse between Greeks and outsiders, and between ancient tradition and historical reality that was, and to an extent still is, central to the identity of modern Greece. This influence is most manifest in the memorial landscape of Greece today, which, through rediscovery as well as invention during the last four hundred years, has acquired numerous place names, sites and specific monuments which are directly related to the *Periegesis*. Both Greeks and outsiders, particularly the writers of early travel reports and later on archaeologists and historical topographers, have contributed to this process, which started in the Ottoman period and gained momentum after the foundation of the Greek state in 1821. This complex story deserves a more extensive treatment than it can receive in this context, but I shall introduce a few poignant voices and developments to illustrate how the *Periegesis* itself has become instrumental in investing places and landscapes with ancient (but actually new) meanings and memories.

The rediscovery of ancient Greece in western Europe at the beginning of the Renaissance began in southern Italy, which was then still partly inhabited by native speakers of Greek, but it was also aided by connections with the remnants of the Byzantine empire. In the late fourteenth and early fifteenth centuries, still before the fall of Constantinople in 1453, the first antiquarians travelled to the east to find unknown ancient Greek manuscripts for collectors, among them probably the single Byzantine Pausanias manuscript that reached the west.[2] Most scholars who were interested in antiquity were, however, satisfied with studying the ancient texts, both reappraising works that had always been known, and investigating material that had been newly discovered. Travellers usually had other interests, and early references to Greece tend to be short notes on a few harbours where ships stopped on their way elsewhere, usually the Holy Land.[3]

The first traveller who fully recognised the potential of the Greek landscape and its ancient remains as an object of antiquarian studies was Cyriac of Ancona.[4] Cyriac, a merchant and largely an autodidact in classical studies, travelled widely and was involved in the complex politics of the time just before the fall of Constantinople: he knew the last Byzantine emperor, had connections at the Ottoman court and was a close associate of the cardinal who became Pope Eugene IV.[5] Cyriac came to recognise his extensive travelling activities as an opportunity to collect information about ancient sites and artefacts, and he has been called the 'medieval Pausanias' as well as the 'father of classical archaeology'.[6] He approached the Greek landscape with an antiquarian eye, trying to identify ancient places and recording ancient artefacts, particularly inscriptions, he discovered along the way.

> We wanted to see whether anything remains in our day of the destroyed city of Mycenae ... first we saw on the Argive plain traces of ancient monuments, and especially some slabs of shining marble with the most beautiful images which had been taken in the past by Christians to adorn churches of our religion from a very ancient temple of Juno; they are thought to be from among the works of Polykleitos. On the most outstanding of these slabs, on a stone that was partially broken, we found the following ancient inscription in Latin ...
>
> We searched for ancient remains of Mycenae among the old, uninhabited Argive villages which provide some traces of the temple of Juno ruined so long ago. Finally, not far from it and no more than about seven miles from the city of Argos, towards the north and less than forty *stadia* from Nauplion, we saw the remains of the fortress of Mycenae on a steep hill with a rocky top. Some parts of its ancient walls survive, together with traces of towers and gates. They are also conspicuous because of the beautiful workmanship

of the architects and were well worthy of our attention. (24 March 1448).
(Cyriac in Bodnar (2003) 336-8)

As it happens, the site Cyriac visited was in fact not the ancient Mycenae we know today.[7] Nevertheless, there is no doubt about his pioneering approach to the remains of antiquity, complete with a sense of how artefacts are dispersed and reused in later centuries. He talks about his own travel experience, and he particularly likes to boast about his eminent acquaintances, but when he turns to the landscape he deals almost exclusively with monuments, sites and inscriptions. Cyriac travelled with his own manuscript copies of Thucydides, Pliny's *Natural History*, and the geographical works of Strabo, Pomponius Mela and Ptolemy.[8] One book that is conspicuously absent from his collection and his comments on Greece is Pausanias' *Periegesis*.[9] The news of its recent discovery apparently never reached Cyriac, and we are left to speculate what he could have achieved travelling in Greece with Pausanias, as his like-minded successors did in centuries to come. Nevertheless, he raises all the issues that have dominated 'cultured' travel in all areas of Graeco-Roman antiquity ever since the beginning of the Renaissance. Cyriac, like so many travellers in regions not covered by the *Periegesis*, demonstrates that without Pausanias, an antiquarian mind faced with a Greek landscape would still be asking questions about the identity of ancient sites and connections between artefacts and the ancient tradition. The *Periegesis*, however, covers such topics in more detail than any other ancient text, not least for the part of the Argolid that Cyriac was trying to explore in the passage quoted above. Cyriac's predicament shows why few educated travellers after him would venture into the Greek landscape without consulting Pausanias.

These promising beginnings of antiquarian travel in Greece were cut short just a few years after Cyriac visited the Argolid: Constantinople fell in 1453, and almost all Greece became part of the Ottoman empire. Few learned travellers visited Greece for some time afterwards, and the first texts that demonstrate that the *Periegesis* was put to the test in the Greek landscape date to the seventeenth century, when foreign contacts with Greece were again increasing, notably through the foundation of the English Levant Company in the late sixteenth century. In the seventeenth century Catholic orders established monasteries in Athens where the Capuchins in particular became well-known for their hospitality to foreign visitors. They even produced the first plan of Athens, and in 1674 a Jesuit, Jacques Babin, published the first topographical account of Athens to be based on personal knowledge of the site.[10] Although travel to Greece now became easier, a surprising number of seventeenth-century texts dealing with Greek topography were still entirely based on literary sources, compiled by authors who had probably never visited themselves.[11]

In the late seventeenth century Olfert Dapper produced learned compilations of this kind on Africa, America and various parts of Asia, as well as descriptions of the Greek islands and the Peloponnese (Morea).[12] He has much more comparatively recent information about the islands than about the Greek mainland, and the interior was apparently almost completely unfamiliar to westerners.[13] It was the usual practice of geographers at the time to supply details about unknown areas by relating hearsay or reporting any information that could be found in ancient texts. The Old World could offer comparatively rich sources because here it was possible to draw on Greek and Roman literature, and information about the little known interior of central and southern Greece could be found in Strabo and particularly Pausanias.[14] In Greece the abundance of sources presented a difficult challenge: in the preface Dapper explains that he had planned to describe the Peloponnese in detail, but there was so much ancient literature and its landscape was so full of history and ancient sites that he could not include it all.[15] Many classical texts, particularly the historical works, refer to the Peloponnese, but the overabundance of attested sites is a problem unique to Pausanias' Greece. Dapper cites him extensively; the first division of the Peloponnese that comes to his mind is that of the *Periegesis*, although he was aware of other geographical approaches, and Strabo supplies much of the general framework.[16] Dapper also included maps that illustrate his approach particularly well. He offers two versions, one based on Blaeu, which attempts to provide contemporary place names but has to resort to a mix of ancient and modern (probably partly invented) names to fill the interior. The other map, credited to Meursius, seems to focus on the ancient topography; it features the most important cities as well as smaller settlements and even small rural sites referred to by Pausanias (Fig. 11). Both maps are geographically inaccurate, but although they draw on more than one source they essentially represent an early attempt to represent Pausanias' Greek topography through cartography.

Personal travel experience, however, soon became an essential precondition for a description of Greece: the 1670s saw a controversy over Georges Guillet's widely read work on ancient and modern Athens, *Athènes ancienne et nouvelle*.[17] The text is presented as a personal travel account, complete with exact information about travel companions and dates for particular stages of the journey. Guillet even records that he was overwhelmed by his first view of Athens, 'struck by a sentiment of veneration for the wonders of antiquity'.[18] Unfortunately for Guillet, Jacob Spon acquired a copy of the first edition when he was on his way to Greece and discovered that it did not stand up to scrutiny when compared with the actual site of Athens, ancient or modern. Guillet answered Spon's initially mild criticism with an attack, claiming that Spon himself had not been to Greece. This resulted in an elaborate refutation in which Spon addressed specific problems to prove that *Athènes ancienne et nouvelle* was nothing more than a skilful compilation based on other travellers' reports and the

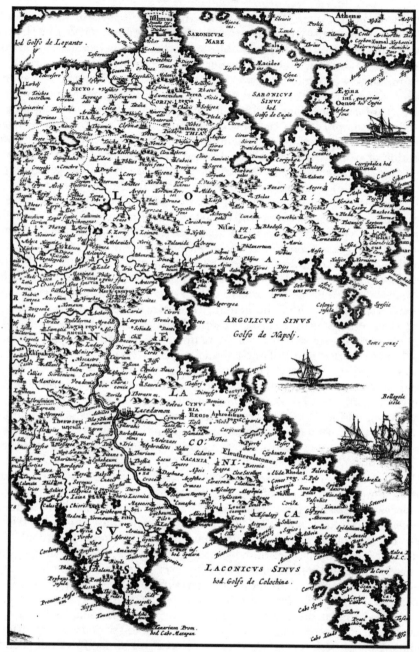

Fig. 11. Dapper (1688), map *Peloponnesus sive Morea apud Iac. Meursium* (follows p. 40). Image supplied by the Bodleian Library, University of Oxford (Mason T.130).

traditional collections of relevant texts.[19] In spite of his methods, however, Guillet had shown the right instinct: autopsy was again becoming crucial to establish a travel writer's credibility, just as it had been in antiquity.

Spon produced the first detailed account of a journey through Greece; this was followed by an English version by his travel companion George Wheler.[20] They visited Athens and investigated its monuments but they were also the first to use Pausanias as a guide for journeys through the Greek countryside, from the Corinthian Gulf via Delphi through Boiotia to Attica, and then again on a trip from Athens to Corinth. Inscriptions usually serve to identify ancient remains, but Pausanias supplies the basic topographical information about ancient sites and sometimes even helps to locate individual monuments.[21] Spon and Wheler apparently recalled crucial passages of the *Periegesis* from memory: they did not have a copy of Pausanias with them, as we find out when we read that a particular question had to be postponed until they could consult a copy that belonged to the British consul at Athens.[22] Spon's original French travel account combines comments on their own travel experiences and research activities with details found in the literary sources. Most sites are introduced with an overview of local history – just as in the *Periegesis* – and Pausanias supplies most of the material for these passages.

Spon and Wheler are at the beginning of a long tradition of travellers who used Pausanias as a travel guide to Greece and its ancient remains. British travellers in particular began to produce travel accounts that focused on the historical topography.[23] Wherever they follow Pausanias' route their description of the landscape almost inadvertently becomes a commentary on the ancient text, comparing the *Periegesis* with the landscape they saw themselves, commenting on the remains of monuments it mentions and 'updating' its information. The most notable travel accounts of this kind were written by Richard Chandler, who visited Greece in the 1760s, and three travellers who toured individually in the first years of the nineteenth century, namely Edward Dodwell, William Gell and William Leake.[24] At this point, recent travel accounts still could not replace the *Periegesis*, and classically trained western visitors had little hope that the local people would supply valuable information about their illustrious past.

> A traveller must not expect to derive any information whatever from the generality of Greeks upon the antiquities of their country, but must extricate himself as well as he can, from the dark mazes of conjecture and uncertainty, by the topographical light of Pausanias, and by the few scattered materials of some other authors. (Dodwell (1819) II.403-4)

The traveller's own observation is therefore always juxtaposed with the ancient text, often without much interest in contemporary circumstances. Gell points out that by the early nineteenth century an author almost needed an excuse for publishing yet another travel book about Greece.[25] These major travel accounts of the early nineteenth century did, however, make an important contribution to the understanding of Greek historical topography, because they attempted to approach the landscape and the relevant ancient texts with scholarly rigour. As Wagstaff has shown, Leake's research is particularly noteworthy in this respect, since he combined a thorough scrutiny of Pausanias' text with exact measurements and a particularly detailed and methodical approach to the topography and the ancient remains.[26] His discussions of Greek topography[27] mark the transition to the systematic archaeological investigation of Greece which began in earnest in the second half of the nineteenth century. Leake was fully aware of how much there was still to do:

'The more I see of the Peloponnesus, and the more I read its description by Pausanias, so much the more do I regret the shortness of the time that I have it in my power to bestow upon its geography; ...Of perseverance, it must with gratitude be admitted, that we have an excellent example in our guide Pausanias, even without omitting the consideration, that, instead of exploring unknown and deserted sites, he was travelling in an ordinary manner, over the roads of a civilised country, from one celebrated place to another, in each of which he found an exegete to assist him in all his researches. So complete, however, were these researches, and so ardent his curiosity, that it requires the most detailed inspection of the country to be assured that one has not overlooked some still existing proof of his accuracy .... I have every day occasion to remark instances in which it is impossible correctly to understand him, or to translate his words, without actually following him through the country, and examining the spots described, and it is not always that a single visit to a place is sufficient. (Leake (1830) II.288-90)

For Leake, Pausanias and the Greek landscape are so closely connected that neither can be fully understood without the other. He saw similarities between his own research and Pausanias' investigations: at some points in his book he conveys a sense of familiarity, as between colleagues who essentially do the same work, and his experience informs his interpretation of the *Periegesis*.[28] This close connection between modern travellers and Pausanias' description deserves further investigation. From the beginning, the *Periegesis* influenced perceptions of Greece, but its impact was so great exactly because it answered to so many of the modern antiquarian's concerns and preoccupations.

The landscape itself represents the most tangible connection between Pausanias and his travelling readers in a later age. One has to assess texts outside the regions he covers to understand how the *Periegesis* enhanced the experience of travelling through central and southern Greece. Cyriac of Ancona used Strabo to provide geographical information and some background while other ancient texts could add a special meaning to particular sites. He shows that even before Pausanias was rediscovered mainland Greece was particularly rich in such historical associations and its landscape had great potential as the subject of antiquarian exploration because it contained so many places that played a major role in the classical historical texts and the most prominent mythical cycles. It takes more than a passing reference in an ancient text, however, to make a place really meaningful to later visitors: very little was known about most sites, not least because the preserved ancient literature puts an overwhelming emphasis on Athens. In spite of the shortcomings of his directions and landscape descriptions Pausanias offers more geographical information than Strabo or any other ancient writer, and he often provides enough topographical details to challenge an inquisitive traveller to look for a particular location. Strabo's *Geography* never became completely obsolete as a source of additional information about Greece because it offered a more comprehensive geographical overview than the *Periegesis*, and in some places Strabo provides an alternative perspective, such as his description of Corinth or the extensive discussion of Homeric geography in some regions.[29] Pausanias, however, does not just provide the most detailed topographical information, he also gives a special significance to countless places in Greece. In the areas covered by the *Periegesis*, travellers no longer had to seek out a few places with historical associations; rather, they could expect that, as they moved along one of Pausanias' routes, every few miles would afford them an opportunity to search for ancient remains or at least some notable topographical feature.

With Pausanias as a guide even a first-time visitor could feel that he was not entering a completely unfamiliar landscape. Foreign travellers therefore approached regions and sites with clearly defined expectations, and many were determined to make the contemporary landscape match Pausanias' ancient topography.

> Pausanias ... mentions so many temples and curiosities at Phlious, that we were particularly anxious to discover its situation, and I know not by what fatality we missed it, as we must have been within a very short distance of it; but I suspect that our guides and agogiates were as anxious to arrive at Argos as we were to discover ruins of ancient cities. (Dodwell (1819) 212)

The combined efforts of travellers and topographers looking for Pausanias' sites slowly produced a map of central and southern Greece that is full of exactly located ancient sites. Research that focuses on topographical features mentioned in ancient texts continues to this day.[30] Few other landscapes can boast such a high concentration of known ancient place names. The early travellers were aware that this abundance of identified sites was unusual, and as soon as they knew themselves outside 'Pausanias country' they readjusted their expectations:

> We observed some ancient traces and large blocks of stone; and a little farther on, several foundations on a hill, probably the Acropolis of the small city which was in the plain. It is useless to conjecture its ancient name: there

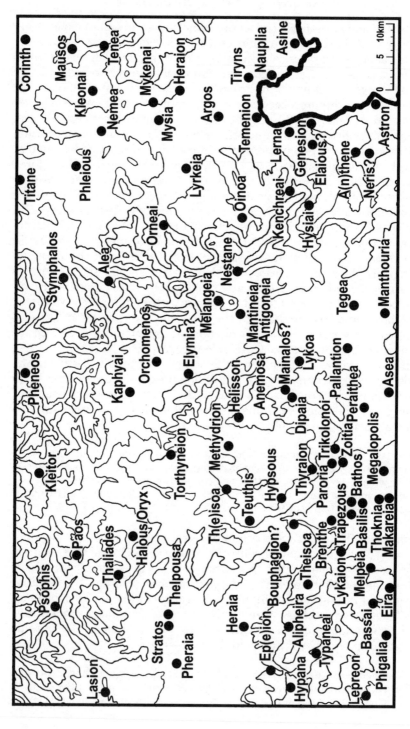

Fig. 12. Securely located ancient place names in Pausanias' Greece: central/north-eastern Peloponnese, part of Paus. II and VIII. Based on the Barrington Atlas: Camp & Reger (2000).

is a great vacuum in the history of this country, though bordering on the classical shores of Phocis, and within view of Parnassos itself. (Dodwell (1819) 144)[31]

A comparison between maps of similar areas in the Peloponnese (Fig. 12) and Asia Minor (see Fig. 5, p. 22) demonstrates the difference: my maps are based on the Barrington Atlas which aims to document all ancient sites that are reasonably securely located: although my sample area of Greece includes the mountainous inland area of Arkadia there are still many more well-identified ancient sites than in the coastal area around the great cities of Smyrna, Pergamon and Pausanias' own home, Magnesia on Sipylos. However, the high density of known ancient place names in the Greek landscape has its own pitfalls: there is a temptation to attach a name to every newly discovered spot with ancient remains, even if it means stretching the meaning of the ancient texts to find an appropriate reference. Only recently have field surveys been able to uncover such a large number of sites that it is no longer possible to look to the *Periegesis* to identify them all. At the same time Pausanias' emphasis on historical monuments, works of art and sacred sites no longer defines the sole focus of archaeological research in Greece, and more attention is given to a wider range of ancient remains.[32]

Visitors to Ottoman Greece had combined their observations with Pausanias to establish a basic framework of identified ancient sites, but the *Periegesis* was a stark reminder of the many sites that still needed to be explored, and at the same time it also raised expectations of magnificent finds. Caylus' Pausanias-induced utopian view of Greece which opened this chapter also translated into great expectations for Greek archaeology:

> In Greece, if the Turks were to permit excavations, one could still find under the scattered ruins of many famous cities some remains of those masterpieces which once represented their beauty and ornament. (Caylus (1752-68) I.iv)

Over a century later the first excavations showed that his prediction had not been far from the mark: sensational finds such as Schliemann's royal tombs at Mycenae or the buildings and sculptures of Olympia seemed to be particular confirmations of Pausanias' descriptions. Archaeologists continued to approach sites with the *Periegesis* in mind and were largely successful in discovering what they expected to find.[33] Pausanias' selective approach, however, also suggests what we should *not* be interested in, and his preferences and silences sanctioned an emphasis on the classical and archaic remains while the 'less interesting' Roman remains were often neglected or simply removed. There is no question that many excavations did indeed uncover sites and monuments that were a remarkable match for Pausanias' descriptions, but it is also worth remembering that the presentation of every site, particularly once it is restored and opened to visitors, is a matter of interpretation and selection. In Greece these decisions were often guided by Pausanias' description and therefore also influenced by his preferences.[34]

The *Periegesis* also had a profound impact on how travellers wrote about the Greek landscape. A learned travel account would include references to relevant ancient sources as a matter of course, and all the major descriptions of Greece combine paraphrases of notes made en route with carefully selected information from ancient texts and earlier modern travel books. Just like Pausanias, many later travel writers chose to provide a historical overview before they embarked on the description of a site, and the *Periegesis* often supplies the main details for these introductions. Moreover, Pausanias creates an imaginary Greece which combines the visible landscape with monuments and memories that were lost, and his travelling readers in modern times would have found this approach very familiar. Their descriptions of the Greek landscape often contain much more than a traveller could actually still see on the surface: most writers combine their own observations with Pausanias' description, and it is not always made clear when we move from the present landscape into the past. The following passage is Dodwell's description of the way from Mantinea to Orchomenos, a route we have already encountered in Chapter 5.

> On quitting Mantineia on the 9th [March 1806] for the ruins of Orchomenos, we traversed the middle of the ancient city, and were thirteen minutes in going from the western wall. We here crossed the ditch formed by the Ophis, and, proceeding in a northern direction through the middle of the plain, in an hour and four minutes from the walls of Mantineia, came to the foundations of a building composed of large stones. Pausanias [8.12] mentions two roads from Mantineia to Orchomenos, on one of which were the stadium of Ladas, a temple of Diana, and a lofty tumulus of earth, which some believed to be the tomb of Penelope. In this vicinity a mountain was covered with the ruins of the ancient Mantinea, near which rose the fountain Alalkomenia. Thirty *stadia* from the town were the ruins of the village Maira. On the other road the topographer mentions the monument or tomb of Anchises, and a temple of Venus at the mountain called Anchisia, which separated the Orchomenian and Mantinean territories. (Dodwell (1819) 424)

This is clearly presented as the record of an actual journey made in March 1806, but in fact, most of what Dodwell describes was not actually visible and is directly taken from Pausanias' text. Ancient place names are used matter-of-factly throughout, and, apart from the wall of Mantinea and the foundation of an ancient building, this description 'borrows' Pausanias' ancient landscape instead of describing that of the early nineteenth century. Not all travellers' accounts of this period achieved such a seamless transition between ancient and modern Greece, but most did at times lapse into descriptions that give distances in *stadia* or note art works that they clearly did not find on an abandoned site. Leake explains his reasoning behind presenting so much that was ancient and no longer visible:

> Although the description of the ancient cities of Peloponnesus, which I have extracted in an abridged form from Pausanias, relate in some instances to places, of which not a vestige now remains to illustrate the Greek topographer, I have nevertheless introduced them all, because, by the addition of a few pages, the present work is thus rendered more complete, and because the reader is thus enabled to compare every part of Peloponnesus as Pausanias found it, with the view which it presented to the follower of his steps, after an interval of sixteen centuries. I am, moreover, much inclined to believe, that the descriptions which the ancient traveller has given of the cities of Greece – of their distribution, mode of decoration, monuments, and productions of art, would, if better known, be useful to the cultivators of the fine arts in general; that they might have a tendency to assist the public discrimination on these subjects. (Leake (1830) viii-ix)

For Leake, Greece is not complete without Pausanias' ancient landscape, and he clearly estimates the didactic value of ancient cities as much higher than that of the landscape he saw in the last years of Ottoman rule. For visitors with antiquarian interests, Pausanias' description was an integral part of the landscape, and in their imagination his sites and monuments were as present as what they actually saw.

During centuries of travel writing about Greece, Pausanias has had a formative influence on general 'habits' that are shared by most texts that attempt to present a systematic account of Greek sites or landscapes. As Sutton has shown in her study of modern descriptions of Nemea, Pausanias can subtly dictate the agenda for a site, and his main themes and preferences echo even in recent travel guides which do not share the antiquarian outlook of earlier travellers.[35] More generally, the *Periegesis* had a strong influence on how Greece was presented in guidebooks. All early guides to Greece draw heavily on Pausanias. One of the earliest, the Baedeker guide of 1883, was edited from extensive notes compiled by H.G. Lolling on research trips in Greece between 1876-81.[36] Lolling's text and the Baedeker guide follow the tradition of integrating Pausanias' description with the contemporary landscape. Once an increasing number of excavations were under way, the combination of archaeological finds and Pausanias' detailed description also presented a niche for a new kind of guidebook, the 'cultural guide' which, like Pausanias, ignores practicalities of travel in order to focus on history and monuments. The earliest guide of this kind, *Mythology and Monuments of Ancient Athens* (1890) by Harrison and Verrall, was in fact intended as an archaeological commentary on Pausanias, but soon attracted many buyers who took it to Greece to enhance their visit to the ancient monuments.[37] The *Periegesis* continues to have a strong influence on modern guidebooks to Greece, as a source both for explanations of ancient sites and for mythical stories or details

141

about ancient cults that can be used to enliven the ancient remains. Much of this information is no longer directly based on Pausanias, but has been passed on from one travel guide to the next: the ancient description has become part of a 'canonical' literary tradition that is attached to particular sites and monuments.

The landscape was the most concrete connection between the *Periegesis* and its later readers, but modern travellers also empathised with Pausanias' approach to the heritage of Greece. The idealising views of Greek culture that dominated in the eighteenth and nineteenth centuries were inspired by ancient literature, and particularly by the texts produced in Pausanias' own cultural environment, the Second Sophistic. Compared to his modern readers, Pausanias is an insider explaining Greek culture to a distant audience. At the same time, however, he takes the stance of an outsider, the visitor from Asia Minor who is fascinated to discover a landscape full of associations and memories of a great past. Modern travellers, steeped in the classical tradition just like the *pepaideumenoi* of the Roman imperial period, therefore found it easy to sympathise with many of his interests and attitudes.

> In these volumes the ancient state of Greece is described, in order to illustrate the present and to add new interest to modern localities and customs, by identifying them with the events or the manners of a more early period. The reader must never forget, that a classic interest is breathed over the superficies of the Grecian territory; that its mountains, its valleys, its streams, are intimately associated with the intimidating presence of the authors, by whom they have been immortalized. Almost every rock, every promontory, every river, is haunted by the shadows of the mighty dead. Every portion of the soil appears to teem with historical recollections; or it borrows some potent but invisible charm from the inspirations of poetry, the efforts of genius, or the energies of liberty and patriotism. (Dodwell (1819) iv)

For Dodwell it is Greek history and the association with ancient literature that make Greece a worthwhile subject of description. The aims he sets out in this passage would be a reasonable description of Pausanias' approach, and the two authors would probably have agreed on the ancient texts they considered particularly relevant. The aim to discover and document the many connections between the memorial landscape and the past is at the centre of Pausanias' project. He uses site descriptions and historical or mythical accounts to emphasise the continuity of culture and tradition in mainland Greece, and there are numerous passages where he specifically states that an old custom or an ancient artefact was still in existence. Pausanias has a number of ways of emphasising such continuities but it is remarkable that these statements are so often expressed in the first person, 'down to my own time', which suggests some emotional response to the encounter with antiquity in the Greek landscape.[38]

142

Modern travellers knew that Pausanias had had the advantage of seeing most sites still intact, but their interests seemed so similar to his approach that it often just took a few identifiable remains of an ancient site together with the appropriate passage in the *Periegesis* to take them back to the glory days of ancient Greece. We have already seen how easily landscape descriptions could switch between antiquity and present: in their imagination Pausanias' travelling readers were not just restoring ancient monuments, but, more importantly, establishing connections between the contemporary topography and the ancient memorial landscape. For people who saw the classical tradition as the centre of their cultural identity this was a highly emotional business, and this was true in antiquity as well as in the eighteenth and nineteenth centuries.[39] Travel writers who followed in Pausanias' footsteps are often vocal about their enthusiasm.

> I cannot describe the sensations which I experienced, on approaching the classic shores of Greece. My mind was agitated by the delights of the present, and the recollections of the past. The land which had been familiar to my ideas from early impression, seemed as if by enchantment, thrown before my eyes. I beheld the native soil of the great men whom I had so often admired; of the poets, historians, and orators, whose works I had perused with delight, and to whom Europe has been indebted for so much of her high sentiment, and her intellectual cultivation. I gazed upon the region which had produced so many artists of unrivalled excellence, whose works are still admired as the models of perfection, and the standards of taste. All these ideas crowding into the mind, made a deep impression; and fixed me for some time, in a contemplative, but pleasurable reverie. (Dodwell (1819) 78)

In the Greek landscape a man with a classical education and some imagination needs just a moment's reverie to escape into an ancient world which is not dissimilar to the playfully constructed past of the Second Sophistic and Caylus' ideal view of the cities of ancient Greece.

There was, however, a flipside to these delightful connections between past and present that were so evident in the Greek landscape: travellers not only thought of the great past; they were also constantly and painfully reminded of the many glorious things that had been lost since antiquity.[40] Again, writers in the Roman imperial period had already begun to stress the many aspects of classical Greek culture that no longer existed in their own time, and both ancient and modern responses to Greece share a good deal of melancholy and nostalgia.

> Returning from Asia I sailed from Aigina towards Megara, and I began to look at the regions around: behind me was Aigina, before me Megara, the Piraeus to the right, and on my left was Corinth – towns which were once most flourishing, but are now lying prostrate and in ruins before one's eyes.[41] (Ser. Sulpicius Rufus to Cicero, March 45 BC. Cic. *Ad Fam.* 4.5.4)

Many modern visitors came to Greece already expecting to find a landscape where much was lost, and the ancient authors provided a template for their response. The decline, which was traditionally associated with Roman rule, could be easily compared with the development of the region under the Ottomans, only now the decline seemed even more pronounced, since the Greeks themselves appeared to have forgotten their great heritage.[42] Pausanias plays a double role in this discourse between ancient and modern: on the one hand, his work offered a detailed view of a glorious lost world which could serve as a contrast to the sad present state of the landscape, and on the other hand he himself was confronted with signs of decline, so that his observations often seemed to parallel the experiences of later travellers.

References to ruins, lost cities and missing artefacts are an integral part of Pausanias' project. After all, only a notion that traditions and physical remains are likely to disappear can inspire such a colossal effort of recording monuments and traditions. There needs to be a sense of distance and loss that separates the past from the present, and references to monuments that have disappeared or stories that have (almost) been forgotten add to a sense of complex layers in the memorial landscape.[43] Pausanias demonstrates a nuanced attitude to the lost heritage of Greece, and it is important not to overemphasise his sense of separation from a lost past. The *Periegesis* has often been called a nostalgic text which focuses on the decline of Greek culture under Roman rule, and, as so often in Pausanias, there is no lack of passages to support this impression.[44] This is, however, not the whole picture: Pausanias does not present an image of a deserted Greece; on the contrary, the emphasis is on monuments that are intact, traditions that are remembered and rituals that are still carried out faithfully. In fact, the *Periegesis* often offers a valuable alternative to ancient authors who suggest that Greece was almost completely deserted and in ruins.[45] It was probably easy to dismiss the whole region from a distance, or with the knowledge of a few poignant places. A ruin one encounters in the landscape is, however, always ambiguous: it is a testimony to the loss of a site, but at the same time it serves as a powerful memorial which keeps the ancient meaning of a place from being completely forgotten. Pausanias reacts to this ambiguity by adopting different modes of dealing with abandoned sites. Many ruins are just mentioned matter-of-factly to fill gaps in the memorial landscape. Where he decides to comment on the fact that a site is ruined Pausanias does sometimes reflect on the loss of a monument or site, but in other cases he emphasises the fact that some remains still survived in his own time, and he clearly appreciates the value of unimpressive remains in comparison to those sad places where he could not even discover ruins.[46]

Nostalgia is sometimes implicit in the *Periegesis*, particularly when great events in the past are juxtaposed with modest contemporary remains. There are a few instances where Pausanias comments on the fact that the heyday of Greece was well in the past, particularly in historical accounts that deal with the loss of Greek freedom.[47] In spite of his great patience with very modest sites and monuments he registers disappointment about the state of some Greek cities, most notably in his dismissive description of Panopeus.[48] The description of Megalopolis leads him to ponder the rise and decline of great cities:

> Megalopolis was founded by the Arkadians with great enthusiasm and it inspired the highest hopes of the Greeks, but it has lost all its splendour and ancient prosperity, and in our day it is mostly in ruins. I am not surprised because I know that heaven always wants to bring about something new, and also that all things, strong or weak, growing or perishing, are being changed by fortune, and she drives them with inevitable force according to her whim.[49] (Paus. 8.33.1)

This passage comes after Pausanias has already passed through a part of the countryside around Megalopolis with many settlements that had been abandoned when the new city was founded. The grand name would also have emphasised the less than impressive state of the town. For early modern travellers the contrast between the great classical past as they imagined it and the state of the landscape they found was much greater, and they were often vocal about their feelings of nostalgia and disappointment. The almost invisible remains of Delphi induced Spon to ponder the fall of the sanctuary that was once so famous:

> What I found most strange is that the most famous place on earth has seen such a reversal of fortune, so that we had to look for Delphi at the site of Delphi itself and to ask where the temple had been although we stood on its foundations. (Spon (1678) II.58)

Spon and Wheler were in fact the first to investigate the site of ancient Delphi and they were quite successful in identifying some of its main features. Spon's comments on these few unimpressive ruins echo Pausanias' thoughts on Megalopolis: both could draw on the same long tradition of thoughts about the rise and fall of great cities.[50] Spon leaves the site with another poignant comment:

> We had to leave the site and to content ourselves with what the books can convey about the riches and ornaments of that place, because there is no longer anything but misery there and all its splendour has passed like a dream. (Spon (1678) II.66)

In fact, the texts that describe the splendour of ancient Delphi are also the cause of Spon's nostalgia. The rich tradition that is tied in with the landscape makes a trip to Greece worthwhile, and it turns every visit to ancient remains into a quintessentially romantic encounter between a vanished past and resurrected memories.[51] Pausanias' *Periegesis* usually supplied the information that allowed travellers to evoke this bitter-sweet contrast between past and present.

For most travellers in early modern Greece the local people were a sore disappointment.[52] Westerners were looking for memories of the old myths or remnants of ancient customs. Cyriac of Ancona was luckier (or more sympathetic) than most when he discovered that in Lakonia people still used ancient building techniques, followed dietary habits he recognised from the ancient texts and had preserved ancient expressions. Their young men even engaged in sporting competitions.[53] Nevertheless, soon after reporting these signs of cultural continuity he expresses his grief about the decline of Greek cities, and laments the sad state of the people who had lost all traces of their original 'noble human virtue and renowned integrity of spirit'.[54] Later travellers who were faced with Greece as an Ottoman province found it even more difficult to discover evident parallels. Only occasionally did the locals manage to impress by displaying behaviour or knowledge that seemed sufficiently reminiscent of their ancient forebears to satisfy classically minded visitors with idealistic expectations.[55] Pausanias' Greece was inhabited by Greeks who were aware of their past and keen to continue ancient traditions. Nevertheless, his work, together with other Second Sophistic texts, suggested ways in which travel writers might approach the dilemma of Ottoman Greece. Many took their lead from Pausanias and focused on the topography and ancient monuments without paying much attention to contemporary circumstances and local people.[56] Pausanias often chooses to ignore the history and monuments of the last few centuries before his own time, and early modern travellers frequently decided to do the same. Medieval and Ottoman history is therefore rarely discussed at all, and there are few Turkish buildings that managed to attract special attention from the western visitors.

> We lose sight of the Venetians and Turks, of Dandolo and Mohammed II, and behold only the ruins of Sparta and Athens, only of the country of Leonidas and Pericles. For Greece has no modern history of such a character as to obscure the vividness of her classical features. A modern history she does indeed possess, various and eventful, but it has been (as has been truly observed) of a destructive, not of a constructive character. It has left little behind which can hide the immortal remains of the greatness of Hellenic genius. In all parts of the country the traveller is, as it were, left alone with antiquity: Hellas tells her own ancient history with unmistakable distinctness. (G.F. Bowen in Murray (1884) 8)

By the time Murray's travel guide was written this neglect of post-classical or post-Roman history and remains had become the standard approach to Greece, and the conspicuous gap between the end of antiquity (or sometimes the fall of Constantinople) and the foundation of modern Greece is still largely the norm in Greek public discourse and self-presentation as well as in most outsiders' imagination.[57]

146

Ancient texts stressed the decline of Greece under Roman rule, and their approach essentially defined western reactions to Ottoman Greece. If conquest by the Romans, who appreciated the superiority of Greek culture, had such a devastating impact on Greece, it was likely that the Ottomans, who were perceived as ignorant of the classical tradition, would cause an even more severe degradation. Travellers often came expecting the worst and they duly produced drastic reports of an ignorant, poverty-stricken people. Ancient writers, including Pausanias, left no doubt that the freedom of Greece was essential to her greatness. In the eighteenth century the idea of political freedom gained momentum, and with it the assumption that in Greece, more than in any other place, freedom was a crucial precondition for cultural achievement. At the same time, many also felt a nostalgic attachment and gratitude to Greece as the font of western civilisation. All these sentiments fuelled the western philhellenism which played an important role in the creation of the Greek state.[58]

The Greeks themselves, however, also relied on the ancient texts to define their identity, partly in reaction to western philhellenism.[59] Since 1821 Pausanias has served as a crucial link between modern Greece and its ancient heritage. This is particularly evident in the development of place names, where ancient toponyms have now largely replaced the old names of Slavonic, Turkish, Albanian or Italian origin that had come to dominate the landscape. Lolling documents just such a change in the 1870s:

> There is no doubt that the ancient city of Amphissa was situated in the same spot as modern Salona; in official language the new city is always referred to by the ancient name. (Lolling (1989) 245; manuscript written in 1876/7)

It is not clear whether he is aware that the ancient name was in fact completely forgotten when Spon and Wheler visited Salona two hundred years earlier. At that point some thought that Salona was ancient Delphi, and Spon and Wheler may have been the first westerners who identified the site correctly after discovering an inscription that mentioned Amphissa.[60] Place names were a particularly emotional issue, and some western visitors were reluctant to contemplate the possibility that the Greeks themselves no longer used or even knew the ancient toponyms.

> Many places in Greece, that are still known to the inhabitants only by their ancient appellations, are barbarously misnamed by foreign sailors. In these instances the Author has deemed it most expedient to retain those names which are at present in use in the country, which was the object of this tour. (Dodwell (1819) v)

Once Greece had become independent, the ancient Greek heritage became an important means of consolidating national identity.[61] The restoration of ancient place names is a particularly visible sign of a re-appropriation of

147

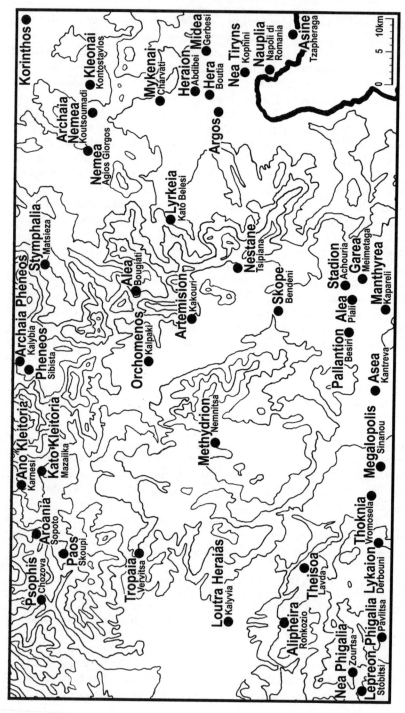

Fig. 13. 'Restored' ancient place names in Greece today (old names in smaller font): central/north-eastern Peloponnese. Based on Pikoulas (2001).

the past, and it seems to have been a slow process guided mostly by local initiative. The old names are sometimes still in use, but maps, documents and official road signs exclusively use the restored 'ancient' names. This process has been going on in many parts of Greece, but it has been most comprehensive in the regions covered by Pausanias: after all, in those areas it was easiest to find an appropriate ancient name for most modern settlements, even if the identification would not always stand up to expert scrutiny. In the area of ancient Tegea several villages have replaced the ancient city, and there was a lack of ancient toponyms. Two villages nevertheless opted for names based on the *Periegesis*, Piali, the site of the temple of Athena Alea, adopted the epithet of the goddess and became Alea, while Achouria opted for a feature that Pausanias just mentions in passing and is now known as Stadio(n). Two settlements in the vicinity, Garea and Manthyrea, have adopted names of Tegean villages (demes) mentioned in Pausanias.[62] In other places different communities stake rival claims to a prestigious ancient name, for example at Nemea or Pheneos. The result of all these changes in southern Greece is a map that suggests a remarkable degree of continuity (Fig. 13). Only a closer inspection reveals that we are, in fact, dealing with the construction of a whole new historical topography which is not always very accurate. Pausanias' text is no longer merely a description of Greece at a particular point in the past: it has actually shaped today's memorial landscape.

Finally, there are also signs that the *Periegesis* has become a crucial resource for local tradition. Foreign visitors with an interest in ancient history can encounter local people who are happy to summarise Pausanias' information about the area, and his stories are sometimes also adapted, re-interpreted and connected to particular topographical features. In some places, new interpretations of the *Periegesis* have even left tangible 'traces'. For example, on the way from Levidi to Klitoria (ancient Kleitor) there are signposts to a 'historical Pausanias vine tree'. The curious visitor finds an impressive ancient vine growing on a group of plane trees but there is no obvious connection with Pausanias, who passes through the area in a matter of a few sentences.[63] This site has all the hallmarks of a place that would make an interesting entry in the *Periegesis*: a unique natural feature has been connected with the authoritative literary source for ancient tradition although the place in question is not actually mentioned there, and the local community has snatched a share in the glorious past.[64] In fact, Pausanias records a very similar example: in Kaphyai, one of the Arkadian cities which was not mentioned in the *Iliad*, there was an impressive plane tree which was said to have been planted by Menelaos.[65] Local tradition in Greece seems to have come full circle: Pausanias himself has become a crucial source of local pride and self-identification, just as the Homeric epics were in his own day.

Epilogue: 'Solid Instruction and Refined Amusement'?

> In short, the philosopher and the historian, the critic and the naturalist, the poet and the painter, the statuary and the architect, the geographer and the antiquary, may find in this work an ample fund of solid instruction and refined amusement: for Pausanias had the art of aptly uniting conciseness with accuracy, and the marvellous of venerable traditions and mystic fables with all the simplicity of unadorned description. (Taylor (1794) vii)

How should modern readers respond to Pausanias' work? Today Taylor's idea of a wide readership among non-specialists seems surprising, and 'amusement' is rarely a word uttered in connection with the *Periegesis*. The work as a whole is not an easy read, and even the most enthusiastic Pausaniacs will have to admit that there is no easy shortcut to appreciating its appeal as a literary text. While it may seem relatively easy to mine the *Periegesis* for information, any closer look at the presentation and context of every detail opens up new questions and new insights. Every site description requires its own investigation to tease out the full implications of Pausanias' selection and interpretation, as far as they can be recovered at all. Much still needs to be done to appreciate the context of Pausanias and that of the many sites one encounters in his work. As the culture of the Greek east of the Roman empire becomes better known, especially through archaeological and epigraphic studies to complement the texts of the Second Sophistic, many aspects of the *Periegesis* will need re-evaluation. Readers also have to be alert to the particularly strong impact of Pausanias reception during the last five hundred years on how we see the text today, especially in connection with the Greek landscape. Long-established layers of interpretation may need to be stripped away to rediscover the author's original intentions.

What, then, makes the *Periegesis* worthwhile for further study at the beginning of the twenty-first century? It remains a core text for anyone interested in ancient Greece, especially mainland Greece, as a geographical and historical entity beyond the few places in the spotlight of general attention. Anyone seeking a realistic impression of Pausanias' work has to venture out of Athens and the big, famous centres such as Sparta, Corinth, Argos or even Thebes in its decline to visit the small cities of the Argolid, of Arkadia, Achaia, Boiotia or Phokis. Small-town Greece presented a challenge to the wealthy, educated visitors who were at home in the large,

151

well-developed centres around the Eastern Mediterranean. In the competition between these grand cities, imposing buildings, splendid monuments and the best infrastructure the Roman world could devise were taken for granted. Pausanias, however, patiently describes numerous towns that were less than impressive, and he pays attention to many details that seem small and inconspicuous. He takes time to tease out the significance of his discoveries, and finds a landscape so full of meaning and history that few places outside mainland Greece could compete. One of his most valuable discoveries is the great variety of myths, monuments and cults which could be found in different Greek cities. Pausanias documents how even small communities maintained, adapted and displayed their local traditions in this period to claim their place in the competitive world of Greek cities under Roman rule: what we get to see was of the greatest contemporary significance.

The variety and range of cultural expression in the cities of mainland Greece is crucial to Pausanias' project to investigate 'all things Greek'. It was well documented, particularly in the *Iliad* and Herodotos' *Histories*, that the conflict between individual communities' concerns and common Hellenic interests was a crucial aspect of Greek identity. The *Periegesis* is a complex account of local cultural expression within the wider context of the almost cosmopolitan interpretation of Hellenism favoured by the educated élite of the Second Sophistic. Rarely are the boundaries between the outsider's ethnographical gaze and the insider's observations in investigating his own identity as blurred as in the *Periegesis*. We can find the visitor mystified by traditions that seem strange and outlandish, but what he is observing is Greek by definition, because it is situated in the old motherland. At the same time, Pausanias as a *pepaideumenos* often felt that he understood Greek traditions better than his informants because he had an intimate knowledge of the literary tradition and an overview of many cities and regions. The result of this enquiry, then, is an insight into the many expressions of Greek identity with more depth and detail than can be found in any other ancient text. Pausanias charts a complex network of memories, myths and symbols centred on the old cities of mainland Greece that held the whole Greek world together and defined the place of individuals and communities in it. The *Periegesis* also allows us to observe a variety of responses to the Roman influence on Greece – Pausanias' own differentiated reactions as well as those of many communities he visited. The tensions between local and global perspectives emerging between cities, the Greek world and the Roman empire is central to the culture of the Second Sophistic, but it was never documented in a more complex fashion than in the *Periegesis*: Pausanias still has much to contribute to the study of the culture and literature of his period.

Pausanias has traditionally been seen as an outsider to the exclusive circle of Second Sophistic writers. Close study shows that he shares the concerns and intellectual interests of many of his contemporaries, and he could claim a special expertise in several areas, such as in art, mythology and archaic poetry. His work may seem eccentric, because he made conscious decisions not to follow the mainstream in all aspects of his writing, for example in respect of his literary style. We need also to remember that the *Periegesis* has affinities with a number of literary genres and scholarly disciplines that we can assess only in fragments. Pausanias addresses a whole range of cultural concerns of his time and he traces the central themes of Greek identity and history in every community he visits, however remote or small. The *Periegesis* offers many unique insights into the reception and use of literary and oral tradition in the Roman imperial period, demonstrating how commonly known texts and stories could become more than just a record of the past, but also a means by which ideas and meanings could be easily communicated among all those who had acquired Greek *paideia*. Without Pausanias we would know little about the complex layers of meaning and historical significance that were attached to numerous features of the landscape, be it urban or rural. Pausanias' landscapes with their allusions and learned associations can be read almost like Second Sophistic texts, and they can indeed be useful to illustrate the physical and imaginary environment which the *pepaideumenoi* in this period took for granted.

A close study of the *Periegesis* reveals complex layers of interpretation: Pausanias is not merely reporting, but he is shaping his own version of Greece. In this he is influenced by the cultural concerns of his time, but there is also a strong influence of personal preferences and interests. The authorial voice in the *Periegesis* is subtle, but nevertheless ubiquitous and distinct: it is not sound to mine the work for information without taking into account Pausanias' general aims and perspective, and his specific agenda in any specific passage or place. It is also crucial to remember that the information offered in the *Periegesis* is not universally applicable to all periods of Greek history: apart from his discussion of events and monuments that can be firmly dated, Pausanias offers very little reliable information about Greece before his own time, and often the past he describes is strongly influenced by contemporary ideas and interpretations. Claims about the long tradition of cultural practices such as cults should be treated with particular caution. Anyone using a passage of the *Periegesis* to support arguments about matters outside its immediate geographical or chronological context has to make a case for its general applicability.

A close reading of Pausanias can become a challenge for a modern classical scholar: the *Periegesis* invites us constantly to rethink our own attitudes to ancient Greece, its monuments and landscape. Watching Pausanias at work as he does his research in painstaking detail suggests a closer look at modern approaches to the same sites, monuments, texts or traditions. As Pausanias creates his very own version of the myth-histories of Greece, selecting what he finds most worth recording, we are led to consider what underlies modern interpretations of Greek histories and landscapes. Since the re-discovery of Greece and its ancient sites, the *Periegesis* has always been the one text that could not be fully understood without an investigation of the landscape, and it has presented archaeologists with the dilemma of how to investigate sites that are the subject of such a detailed ancient description. Pausanias continues to remind us of the fact that the divide in classical studies between literature and material culture has never been fully bridged. His varied interests challenge boundaries between disciplines and clearly demarcated fields of interest: studying Pausanias in depth requires us to take routes that we have never had to travel before. Since its re-discovery about six hundred years ago, this particular quality of the *Periegesis* has led to a number of crucial new perspectives on ancient Greek culture. Pausanias still has the potential to inspire new approaches in the future.

Notes

1. Approaching Pausanias' *Periegesis*

1. Paus. 1.1.1: Τῆς ἠπείρου τῆς Ἑλληνικῆς κατὰ νήσους τὰς Κυκλάδας καὶ πέλαγος τὸ Αἰγαῖον ἄκρα Σούνιον πρόκειται γῆς τῆς Ἀττικῆς· καὶ λιμήν τε παραπλεύσαντι τὴν ἄκραν ἐστὶ καὶ ναὸς Ἀθηνᾶς Σουνιάδος ἐπὶ κορυφῇ τῆς ἄκρας.

2. Elsner (2001a), Hutton (2005a) esp. 4-5, 22-3.

3. Poseidon: *IG* I² 310, 1.24; Aristoph. *Birds* 868, *Knights* 559; cf. Dinsmoor (1974) 233; See Pritchett (1999) 39-45.

4. Cf. Snodgrass (2001) 130, 135-7, Veyne (1988) 3.

5. E.g. Hutton (2005a) 24-5, 242-7, Alcock (1996) 244.

6. See pp. 141-2.

7. Diller (1956); Diller (1957), Marcotte (1992), Irigoin (2001); see p. 119.

8. Bowie (2001) 27-8.

9. See Diller (1957) 178: a manuscript giving '*Historiai*' as title; Trendelenburg (1911) 6-7, 18-19, (1914) 8-9 suggests *Hellênika* ('Greek matters') as original title, cf. Paus. 1.26.4.

10. See Diller (1957).

11. Steph. Byz. s.v. Haimonia (p. 50, 1.5 Meineke), s.v. Araithyrea (p.108, 1.16 Meineke), s.v. Sphakteria (p. 594, l. 23 Meineke) give the full title; there are eighty references in all. Cf. Habicht (1985) 5.

12. Paus. e.g. 1.39.3, 2.13.3, 2.15.1, 2.34.2, 2.34.10, 3.11.1, 5.21.1, 6.1.1-2, 6.17.1, 10.9.1.

13. Hutton (2005a) 247-55, Arenz (2006) 133-6, Bischoff (1938).

14. Hutton (2005a) 241-72, Habicht (1985) 3, Bischoff (1938) 727-8.

15. Paus. 1.26.4: Δεῖ δέ με ἀφικέσθαι τοῦ λόγου πρόσω, πάντα ὁμοίως ἐπεξιόντα τὰ Ἑλληνικά.

16. Hellas is the mainland south of Thermopylai: Paus. 1.3.5, 1.4.2, 3.4.8, 5.14.2; Epeiros part of Greece: 9.6.1; Epeiros outside Greece, Korkyra in Greece: 1.11.5-6; Ionia part of Greece: 7.10.1. 8.46.3; Ionia outside Greece: 7.5.13, 8.45.5. See Regenbogen (1956) 1011, Elsner (2001a) 5, Hutton (2005a) 57-61, esp. 57 n. 6.

17. Gurlitt (1890) 2-4, 68, Robert (1909) 261, Trendelenburg (1911) 8, Meyer (1954) 19, Habicht (1985) 5-6, Bearzot (1988) 90-112, Hutton (2005a) 55-68.

18. Hom. *Il.* 2.484-760; Homeric geography: Prontera (1993); e.g. Strabo 1.1.1-2, 1.1.10-11, Engels (1999) 115-20, Dueck (2000) 31-40; cf. Eratosthenes' critique: Strabo 1.2.17; Geus (2002) 264-7.

19. E.g. Paus. 8.25.12-13, cf. Hom. *Il.* 2.606; cf. Paus. 6.22.5-6.

20. Meyer (1954) 20, Habicht (1985) 5 (Achaia); Bearzot (1988) 108-12 (Amphiktyony), cf. Bultrighini (1990b).

21. Steph. Byz. s.v. Tamyna (p. 600 Meineke) with Meineke's commentary, followed by Gurlitt (1890) 68, Regenbogen (1956) 1011. Diller (1955) 274-5, Chamoux (1996) 48; Robert (1909) 261-4 suggests that up to four books are lost.

22. Habicht (1985) 7-8, Akujärvi (2005) 60-4 lists 155 cross-references; cf. Settis (1968) 61-3, Moggi (1993) 402-3.

23. Paus. 1.24.5, referring to 9.26.2-4.

24. Paus. 8.37.1, referring to 10.13.8; 5.15.4, referring to 8.37.9; some cross-references are less precise: e.g. Paus. 4.31.7: 'I will deal with the appearance [of the image of Artemis Laphria] elsewhere', referring to Patrai, 7.18.8, cf. 6.12.1 (referring to 10.34.8).

25. Bowie (2001) 21-3 (the shortest possible chronology, Book I finished by AD 165); Habicht (1985) 8-12 suggests that Book I was written in the 150s. Note Musti (1982) xii-xiii who suggests that Book I may have been published under Hadrian. See pp. 23-4.

26. Paus. 10.38.13. Habicht (1985) 6-7; end might be intact (cf. Hdt 9.122): Nörenberg (1973), Alcock (1996) 267, Sidebottom (2002) 499, Ellinger (2005) 207-21.

27. Heberdey (1894) 96, Gurlitt (1890) 67-8, Daux (1936) 180-1, Heer (1979) 46, 280-4.

28. Paus. 10.9.1-2: Ὁπόσα δὲ τῶν ἀναθημάτων εἶναί μοι λόγου μάλιστα ἄξια ἐφαίνετο, ποιησόμεθα αὐτῶν μνήμην. ἀθλητὰς μὲν οὖν καὶ ὅσοι ἀγωνισταὶ μουσικῆς τῶν ἀνθρώπων τοῖς πλείοσιν ἐγίνοντο μετὰ οὐδενὸς λογισμοῦ, οὐ πάνυ τι ἡγοῦμαι σπουδῆς ἀξίους· ἀθλητὰς δὲ ὁπόσοι τι καὶ ὑπελείποντο ἐς δόξαν, ἐν λόγῳ σφᾶς ἐδήλωσα τῷ ἐς Ἠλείους.

29. Paus. 6.1-18 (Olympia); 8.38.5, 8.49.1 (statue bases); on Pausanias' Phokis see Pritchett (1969-89) IV.147.

30. Paus. 9.23.7 (on Larymna, daughter of Kynos).

31. Hutton (2005a) esp. 25-8.

32. Hirschfeld (1882) 122, Gurlitt (1890) 21, Habicht (1985) 19-20, Hutton (2005a) 83-96.

33. Paus. 9.18.1-23.4, 9.23.5-24.5, 9.25.1-4; Hutton (2005a) 88-9, Musti (1988).

34. Paus. 3.11.1: Ὁ δὲ ἐν τῇ συγγραφῇ μοι τῇ Ἀτθίδι ἐπανόρθωμα ἐγένετο, μὴ τὰ πάντα με ἐφεξῆς, τὰ δὲ μάλιστα ἄξια μνήμης ἐπιλεξάμενον ἀπ' αὐτῶν εἰρηκέναι, δηλώσω δὴ πρὸ τοῦ λόγου τοῦ ἐς Σπαρτιάτας· ἐμοὶ γὰρ ἐξ ἀρχῆς ἠθέλησεν ὁ λόγος ἀπὸ πολλῶν καὶ οὐκ ἀξίων ἀφηγήσεως, ὧν ἕκαστοι παρὰ σφίσι λέγουσιν, ἀποκρῖναι τὰ ἀξιολογώτατα. ὡς οὖν εὖ βεβουλευμένος οὐκ ἔστιν ὅπου παραβήσομαι. Cf. 1.39.3.

35. Paus. 2.13.3, 2.15.1, 2.29.1, 2.34.11, 3.11.5, 5.21.1, 6.17.1, 6.23.1, 8.10.1, 8.54.7 (e.g. τὰ ἀξιολογώτατα, τὰ μάλιστα ἄξια λόγου, τὰ θέας ἄξια, τὰ μάλιστα ἄξια μνήμης).

36. Frazer (1898) I.xxxiii-xxxvi, Regenbogen (1956) 1090, Habicht (1985) 23-4.

37. Habicht (1985) 134-6, Arafat (1996) 37-8; Hutton (2005b) 299-317. E.g. the Nymphaion of Herodes Atticus at Olympia: Settis (1968), Gardiner (1925) 192, Herrmann (1972) 192, Bol (1984) 99-100, Jacquemin (2001) 291-2.

38. E.g. Paus. 1.6.1, 1.27.3, 10.17.13.

39. Paus. 1.39.3: Τοσαῦτα κατὰ γνώμην τὴν ἐμὴν Ἀθηναίοις γνωριμώτατα ἦν ἔν τε λόγοις καὶ θεωρήμασιν, ἀπέκρινε δὲ ἀπὸ τῶν πολλῶν ἐξ ἀρχῆς ὁ λόγος μοι τὰ ἐς συγγραφὴν ἀνήκοντα.

40. Paus. 8.10.10: Λεωκύδους δὲ τοῦ Μεγαλοπολιτῶν ὁμοῦ Λυδιάδῃ στρατηγήσαντος πρόγονον ἔνατον Ἀρκεσίλαον οἰκοῦντα ἐν Λυκοσούρᾳ λέγουσιν οἱ Ἀρκάδες ὡς ἴδοι τὴν ἱερὰν τῆς καλουμένης Δεσποίνης ἔλαφον πεπονηκυῖαν ὑπὸ γήρως· τῇ δὲ ἐλάφῳ ταύτῃ ψάλιόν τε εἶναι περὶ τὸν τράχηλον καὶ γράμματα ἐπὶ τῷ ψαλίῳ, "νεβρὸς ἐὼν ἑάλων, ὅτ' ἐς Ἴλιον ἦλθ' Ἀγαπήνωρ". Οὗτος μὲν δὴ ἐπιδείκνυσιν ὁ λόγος ἔλαφον εἶναι πολλῷ καὶ ἐλέφαντος μακροβιώτερον θηρίον.

41. E.g. Meyer (1954) esp. 8, Levi (1971), Harrison & Verrall (1890); cf. Pouilloux (1992) XIX-XX, Lacroix (1994) 76.

42. With the possible exception of Xenophon's *Anabasis*. Cf. Hutton (2005a) 5-7.
43. Elsner (1992), (1994), (1995) 125-55, (1997a), (1997b), (2001a), (2001b), Hartog (2001), Hutton (2005a), Hutton (2005b).
44. E.g. Spon (1678), Wheler (1682).
45. E.g. Dodwell (1819), Gell (1817), Leake (1830).
46. E.g. Olympia: Trendelenburg (1914), Delphi: Daux (1936), Mycenae: Schliemann (1878) 59-61, cf. Belger (1899).
47. Coins: Imhoof-Blumer & Gardner (1885), (1886), (1887). Inscriptions: Habicht (1984), Habicht (1985) 28-94, e.g. *IG* V.1.559 with Hutton (2005a) 19-20, Tod & Wace (1906), Wide (1893).
48. E.g. Athenian agora: Robert (1909) 330 (reconstruction of the site on the basis of the text alone), Vanderpool (1949) esp. 130 (Pausanias' 'route' reconstructed on the basis of excavations), cf. Wycherley (1959), (1963). See also Habicht (1985) 78-80, Hutton (2005a) 140-1.
49. Frazer (1898), Hitzig & Blümner (1896-1910).
50. Habicht (1985) 98-101, Meyer (1954) 8; e.g. Urban (1979) 38-45, cf. Pretzler (2005b).
51. Wilamowitz (1877) 344-7, Hirschfeld (1882), Kalkmann (1886), Deicke (1935) 33-53, Jacoby (1944) 40-1 n. 12, Fehling (1988). On Wilamowitz see Habicht (1985) 165-7.
52. Alcock (1996) 241, 260-5, Hutton (2005a) 22-3.
53. Frazer's commentary on Pausanias IV takes up fifteen pages for the twenty-nine chapters of Messenian history, while the remaining seven topographical chapters get forty-three pages of commentary. Frazer (1898) III.405-64.
54. E.g. Meyer (1939), Pritchett (1969-89) esp. I.122-34, III.1-142, IV.1-102, V.69-91, VI.91-111, Pikoulas (1999).
55. Regenbogen (1956), see also Reardon (1971) 221-4.
56. Alcock, Cherry & Elsner (2001) vii-viii, Henderson (2001a) 207.
57. Musti et al. (1982-), Casevitz et al. (1992-).
58. Bingen (1996).
59. Hutton (2005a); see also Elsner (2001a), Akujärvi (2005).
60. E.g. Alcock (1993), Engels (1990), several articles in Pirenne-Delforge (1998b), Swain (1996) esp. 330-56; cf. O. van Nijf & R. Alston's forthcoming volumes on the post-classical city.
61. Alcock (2001) 146-53, (1993) 172-5.
62. Veyne (1988) 100-1, Alcock (1996) 242, 265-7.

2. Pausanias: the Man and his Time

1. Paus. 8.2.4-5: Οἱ γὰρ δὴ τότε ἄνθρωποι ξένοι καὶ ὁμοτράπεζοι θεοῖς ἦσαν ὑπὸ δικαιοσύνης καὶ εὐσεβείας, καί σφισιν ἐναργῶς ἀπήντα παρὰ τῶν θεῶν τιμή τε οὖσιν ἀγαθοῖς καὶ ἀδικήσασιν ὡσαύτως ἡ ὀργή, ἐπεί τοι καὶ θεοὶ τότε ἐγίνοντο ἐξ ἀνθρώπων, οἳ γέρα καὶ ἐς τόδε ἔτι ἔχουσιν ... ἐπ᾽ ἐμοῦ δὲ – κακία γὰρ δὴ ἐπὶ πλεῖστον ηὔξετο καὶ γῆν τε ἐπενέμετο πᾶσαν καὶ πόλεις πάσας – οὔτε θεὸς ἐγίνετο οὐδεὶς ἔτι ἐξ ἀνθρώπου, πλὴν ὅσον λόγῳ καὶ κολακείᾳ πρὸς τὸ ὑπερέχον, καὶ ἀδίκοις τὸ μήνιμα τὸ ἐκ τῶν θεῶν ὀψέ τε καὶ ἀπελθοῦσιν ἐνθένδε ἀπόκειται.
2. Akujärvi (2005), Hutton (2005a) 11.
3. E.g. Paus. 2.26.1, 6.22.8, 8.15.8, 8.35.1; note 10.29.3, 10.31.1 where Pausanias 'moves' through Polygnotos' painting. Cf. Akujärvi (2005) 145-65.
4. Paus. 4.31.6: Μεσσηνίοις δὲ ἐν τῇ ἀγορᾷ Διός ἐστιν ἄγαλμα Σωτῆρος καὶ Ἀρσινόη κρήνη· τὸ μὲν δὴ ὄνομα ἀπὸ τῆς Λευκίππου θυγατρὸς εἴληφεν, ὑπορρεῖ δὲ ἐς αὐτὴν ὕδωρ

ἐκ πηγῆς καλουμένης Κλεψύδρας. θεῶν δὲ ἱερὰ Ποσειδῶνος, τὸ δὲ Ἀφροδίτης ἐστί· καὶ οὗ μάλιστα ἄξιον ποιήσασθαι μνήμην, ἄγαλμα Μητρὸς θεῶν λίθου Παρίου, Δαμοφῶντος δὲ ἔργον, ὃς καὶ τὸν Δία ἐν Ὀλυμπίᾳ διεστηκότος ἤδη τοῦ ἐλέφαντος συνήρμοσεν ἐς τὸ ἀκριβέστατον.

5. Bol (1978) 1; cf. Dio Chrysostom 31.

6. Cf. Paus. 5.11.10, commenting on methods of preserving ivory, without mentioning Damophon.

7. Paus. 2.5.5.: Ἐκ Κορίνθου δὲ οὐκ ἐς μεσόγαιαν ἀλλὰ τὴν ἐπὶ Σικυῶνα ἰοῦσι ναὸς ἐμπεπρησμένος ἐστὶν οὐ πόρρω τῆς πόλεως, ἐν ἀριστερᾷ δὲ τῆς ὁδοῦ. γεγόνασι μὲν δὴ καὶ ἄλλοι πόλεμοι περὶ τὴν Κορινθίαν καὶ πῦρ ἐπέλαβεν ὡς τὸ εἰκὸς καὶ οἰκίας καὶ ἱερὰ τὰ ἔξω τείχους· ἀλλὰ τοῦτόν γε τὸν ναὸν Ἀπόλλωνος εἶναι λέγουσι καὶ ὅτι Πύρρος κατακαύσειεν ὁ Ἀχιλλέως αὐτόν.

8. E.g. Paus. 2.3.7; although he is not consistent: see 2.2.6 where he accepts the authenticity of ancient statues in Corinth.

9. Paus. 2.1.2, 2.2.6; cf. 2.1.1; see also Hutton (2005b).

10. E.g. Paus. 2.12.3, 2.23.8, 2.26.2, 3.25.2. 5.5.3, 5.5.4, 8.47.4, 9.18.6, 9.38.7-8, 10.8.9.

11. Alcock (1996) 260-1 with Crapanzano (1986).

12. For a detailed study see Akujärvi (2005) 25-178.

13. E.g. Paus. 1.4.6, 1.9.3, 1.24.6, 1.26.4, 1.26.11, 1.33.7, 1.33.8, 1.36.1, 2.4.5, 2.28.3, 4.29.13, 5.3.1, 5.5.1, 8.6.1 (comments on digressions), 1.9.4, 1.20.4, 1.23.10, 1.26.6, 1.29.2, 1.34.2, 2.38.3, 3.17.7, 3.18.9, 4.24.3, 5.4.5, 5.4.7, 8.37.6 (pointing out that a topic will not be discussed), 1.6.1, 1.8.1, 2.37.6, 3.18.6, 8.17.4, 10.17.3, 10.19.5 (giving reasons for particular decisions); cf. Akujärvi (2005) 34-64.

14. E.g. Paus. 1.26.4 (intentions), 1.39.3, 3.11.1, 6.1.1, 10.9.2 (selectivity), 5.14.4, 5.14.10, 5.21.1, 6.17.1, 8.6.3, 10.19.5 (notes on the structure of the text).

15. E.g. Paus. 2.21.10, 4.2.1, 4.6.1-6, 8.37.12.

16. Paus. 8.53.4-5: Λέγουσι δὲ καὶ ὅσοι Τεγεάτου τῶν παίδων ἐλείποντο, μετοικῆσαι σφᾶς ἑκουσίως ἐς Κρήτην, Κύδωνα καὶ Ἀρχήδιον καὶ Γόρτυνα· καὶ ἀπὸ τούτων φασὶν ὀνομασθῆναι τὰς πόλεις Κυδωνίαν καὶ Γόρτυνά τε καὶ Κατρέα. Κρῆτες δὲ οὐχ ὁμολογοῦντες τῷ Τεγεατῶν λόγῳ Κύδωνα μὲν Ἀκακαλλίδος θυγατρὸς Μίνω καὶ Ἑρμοῦ, Κατρέα δέ φασιν εἶναι Μίνω, τὸν δὲ Γόρτυνα Ῥαδαμάνθυος. ἐς δὲ αὐτὸν Ῥαδάμανθυν Ὁμήρου μέν ἐστιν ἐν Πρωτέως πρὸς Μενέλαον λόγοις ὡς ἐς τὸ πεδίον ἥξοι Μενέλαος τὸ Ἠλύσιον, πρότερον δὲ ἔτι Ῥαδάμανθυν ἐνταῦθα ἥκειν· Κιναίθων δὲ ἐν τοῖς ἔπεσιν ἐποίησεν ὡς Ῥαδάμανθυς μὲν Ἡφαίστου, Ἥφαιστος δὲ εἴη Τάλω, Τάλων δὲ εἶναι Κρητὸς παῖδα. οἱ μὲν δὴ Ἑλλήνων λόγοι διάφοροι τὰ πλέονα καὶ οὐχ ἥκιστα ἐπὶ τοῖς γένεσίν εἰσι.

17. See also Paus. 1.38.7, 1.41.4-6, 4.4.3, 6.12.8 where, in a Herodotean manner, Pausanias explicitly leaves the decision between contradictory accounts to the reader.

18. Cf. Paus. 2.12.3-13.2, 4.2.3, 4.33.1, 9.16.7.

19. E.g. Paus. 1.23.7, 2.22.3, 4.16.7, 4.31.5, 4.35.8-12, 5.5.5-6, 5.7.5-6, 5.20.8, 7.18.13, 8.41.6, 9.39.14; cf. Akujärvi (2005) 90-103.

20. Unresolved questions: e.g. Paus. 1.19.2, 1.28.3, 1.42.4, 2.7.6, 2.7.9, 2.24.7, 2.26.1, 2.29.2, 2.30.8, 2.31.4, 4.33.6, 5.5.4, 5.5.9, 5.6.2, 5.15.7, 5.15.12, 5.16.1, 5.22.5, 6.9.1, 6.21.10, 7.5.5, 7.22.5, 7.26.6, 8.8.4, 8.42.5, 8.42.12-13, 9.2.4, 9.5.3, 9.26.7, 9.27.1, 9.35.1, 9.39.1, 10.2.1, 10.34.6; questions which occurred to Pausanias later: e.g. 5.24.10, 8.41.10, 10.2.1.

21. E.g. Paus. 1.5.4, 2.33.3, 4.9.6, 4.30.4-5, 8.24.3, 8.33.1-4 (fate); 1.13.9, 1.20.7, 1.36.3, 2.9.4-5, 3.4.5-6, 3.10.4-5, 3.12.7, 3.23.5, 4.17.2-6, 4.24.6, 4.26.4, 7.15.6,

Notes to pages 20-23

7.24.6-7, 7.25.1-2, 8.7.6-8, 9.2.3, 9.25.9-10, 9.27.2-3, 9.33.6, 10.11.2, 10.33.2 (divine vengeance). See pp. 88-9.

22. Paus. 8.42.11 explicitly points out that he did not sacrifice; cf. 2.30.4, 9.39.5-14. Insider at cults: 1.14.3, 1.37.5, 1.38.7, 2.3.4, 2.17.4, 2.37.6, 4.33.5, 5.15.11, 8.37.9, 9.25.5-6. On Pausanias' religious beliefs: Frazer (1898) I.l-lv, Heer (1979), 127-307, Habicht (1985) 151-9, Pirenne-Delforge (1998a).

23. Cf. Price (1999) 126-42.

24. See Jones (1986) 33-45, Lightfoot (2003) 184-208.

25. Aristeides, *Sacred Tales*; Behr (1968).

26. E.g. Paus. 2.17.4, 2.31.2, 3.19.5, 3.25.5, 6.8.2, 9.8.1, 9.10.1.

27. Paus. 3.15.11: Ἐπίκλησις μὲν δὴ τῆς Ἀφροδίτης ἐστὶν ἡ Μορφώ, κάθηται δὲ καλύπτραν τε ἔχουσα καὶ πέδας περὶ τοῖς ποσί· περιθεῖναι δέ οἱ Τυνδάρεων τὰς πέδας φασὶν ἀφομοιοῦντα τοῖς δεσμοῖς τὸ ἐς τοὺς συνοικοῦντας τῶν γυναικῶν βέβαιον. τὸν γὰρ δὴ ἕτερον λόγον, ὡς τὴν θεὸν πέδαις ἐτιμωρεῖτο ὁ Τυνδάρεως, γενέσθαι ταῖς θυγατράσιν ἐξ Ἀφροδίτης ἡγούμενος τὰ ὀνείδη, τοῦτον οὐδὲ ἀρχὴν προσίεμαι· ἦν γὰρ δὴ παντάπασιν εὔηθες κέδρου ποιησάμενον ζῴδιον καὶ ὄνομα Ἀφροδίτην θέμενον ἐλπίζειν ἀμύνεσθαι τὴν θεόν.

28. Cf. Paus. 2.24.3, 5.15.5, 7.23.7-8, 8.36.5, 10.37.3.

29. E.g. Paus. 2.17.4, 6.8.2, 9.8.1 (dismissing stories), 3.25.5, 9.2.3, 9.30.2-6 (rationalising myths), 8.8.3 (deeper meaning). Frazer (1898) I.iv-ix, Veyne (1988) 95-102.

30. Paus. 5.13.7: Πέλοπος δὲ καὶ Ταντάλου τῆς παρ' ἡμῖν ἐνοικήσεως σημεῖα ἔτι καὶ ἐς τόδε λείπεται, Ταντάλου μὲν λίμνη τε ἀπ' αὐτοῦ καλουμένη καὶ οὐκ ἀφανὴς τάφος, Πέλοπος δὲ ἐν Σιπύλῳ μὲν θρόνος ἐν κορυφῇ τοῦ ὄρους ἐστὶν ὑπὲρ τῆς Πλαστήνης μητρὸς τὸ ἱερόν, διαβάντι δὲ Ἕρμον ποταμὸν Ἀφροδίτης ἄγαλμα ἐν Τήμνῳ πεποιημένον ἐκ μυρσίνης τεθηλυίας· ἀναθεῖναι δὲ Πέλοπα αὐτὸ παρειλήφαμεν μνήμῃ, προϊλασκόμενόν τε τὴν θεὸν καὶ γενέσθαι οἱ τὸν γάμον τῆς Ἱπποδαμείας αἰτούμενον.

31. Gurlitt (1890) 56-7, 130, Regenbogen (1956) 1012-13, Meyer (1954) 15, Habicht (1985) 13-15, Bowie (2001) 24-5, Hutton (2005a) 9.

32. Paus. 1.20.5 (Magnesia in the Mithridatic Wars), 1.21.3, cf. 8.2.7 (rock of Niobe), 1.24.8 (locusts), 2.22.3 (tomb of Tantalos), 7.24.12-13 (an earthquake), 8.17.3 (eagles on Mount Sipylos).

33. Diller (1955), Gurlitt (1890) 56-7, Frazer (1898) I.xix, Robert (1909) 271-4, Regenbogen (1956) 1012, Heer (1979) 13-16, Habicht (1985) 13-17, Arafat (1996) 8.

34. Aristeides 23, *On Concord*; Bowersock (1969) 17-19, Habicht (1969) 15-18, 162-4. Pergamon: Paus. 2.11.7, 2.26.9, 3.26.10, 5.13.3 (Asklepieion) 1.4.5-6, 1.8.1. 1.11.2, 10.15.2-3 (history), cf. 5.13.8, 6.24.8, 7.16.8, 8.4.9, 8.42.7, 9.35.6, 10.18.6, 10.25.10. Smyrna: 7.5.1-3 (history), 2.26.9, 7.5.9 (Asklepieion), cf. 1.33.7, 4.21.5, 4.30.6, 9.11.7, 9.29.4, 9.35.6. Ephesos: 4.31.8, 7.5.4 (Artemision), 1.9.7, 6.3.15-16, 7.2.7-9, 7.3.4-5 (history), cf. 5.24.8, 7.5.10.

35. Paus. 7.2.3-5.13, especially 7.5.4, 7.5.10, 7.6.1.

36. Cf. Gurlitt (1890) 1-2, 58-62, Frazer (1898) I.xv-xviii, Robert (1909) 270, Comfort (1931), Meyer (1954) 18, Regenbogen (1956) 1012-14, Habicht (1985) 9-12, Bowie (2001) 21-4.

37. Pausanias' references to his own time: Habicht (1985) 176-9, Musti (2001); note Pothecary (1997); cf. Akujärvi (2005) 65-89.

38. Paus. 5.1.2: Κορίνθιοι μὲν γὰρ οἱ νῦν νεώτατοι Πελοποννησίων εἰσί, καί σφισιν, ἀφ' οὗ τὴν γῆν παρὰ βασιλέως ἔχουσιν, εἴκοσιν ἔτη καὶ διακόσια τριῶν δέοντα ἦν ἐς ἐμέ.

39. Paus. 7.20.6: Κεκόσμηται δὲ καὶ ἐς ἄλλα τὸ Ὠιδεῖον ἀξιολογώτατα τῶν ἐν

159

Ἕλλησι, πλήν γε δὴ τοῦ Ἀθήνησι· τοῦτο γὰρ μεγέθει τε καὶ ἐς τὴν πᾶσαν ὑπερῆρκε κατασκευήν, ἀνὴρ δὲ Ἀθηναῖος ἐποίησεν Ἡρώδης ἐς μνήμην ἀποθανούσης γυναικός. ἐμοὶ δὲ ἐν τῇ Ἀτθίδι συγγραφῇ τὸ ἐς τοῦτο παρείθη τὸ Ὠιδεῖον, ὅτι πρότερον ἔτι ἐξείργαστό μοι τὰ ἐς Ἀθηναίους ἢ ὑπῆρκτο Ἡρώδης τοῦ οἰκοδομήματος.

40. Travlos (1971) 378, Ameling (1983) esp. 84-94, Galli (2002) 32-44; cf. Philostratos *VS* 551.

41. Frazer (1898) xvi, Habicht (1985) 10-11, Bowie (2001) 21, Hutton (2005a) 18; early chronology: Musti (1982) xii-xiii.

42. Paus. 1.19.6 mentions Herodes' stadium in Athens, built after AD 139/40, see Galli (2002) 12-28; concrete plans for the *Periegesis* were probably conceived considerably later. Cf. Frazer (1898) I.xvii. Musti (1982) I.xii-xix, argues that the prominence of Hadrian in the *Periegesis* suggests an earlier date, but this argument is not conclusive.

43. Paus. 1.26.4, cf. 8.37.1, alluding to the length of the project.

44. Reynolds & Wilson (1974) 23; cf. Frazer (1898) xvii-xviii, on public readings see Bowie (2001) 29.

45. Paus. 2.27.6, with Habicht (1985) 10, Habicht (1969) 63-6, Halfmann (1979) 171-2, n.89, Roux (1958) 27. Other references to the 160s: 2.26.9, 7.5.9: Asklepieion in Smyrna, under construction in AD 151, finished by AD 166, Aristeides 50.102, 47.17, cf. Aristeides 17 and 21; Bowersock (1969) 36-40; Paus. 6.8.4: probably a reference to Peregrinus' suicide in Olympia in AD 165, see Settis (1968) 43-8.

46. Paus. 8.43.3-5 (Antoninus Pius), 8.43.6 (Marcus Aurelius). other references to the 170s: 5.1.2 (AD 174, see above), 10.34.5 mentions the invasion of the Costoboci, probably in AD 171.

47. Habicht (1985) 9-10, Bowie (2001) 22.

48. Paus. 8.46.4-5.

49. Habicht (1985) 17.

50. Apuleius *Met*. 11.27-8, *Apol*. 23.

51. Paus. 8.33.2: Τὰ δὲ ὑπερηρκότα πλούτῳ τὸ ἀρχαῖον, Θῆβαί τε αἱ Αἰγύπτιοι καὶ ὁ Μινύης Ὀρχομενὸς καὶ ἡ Δῆλος τὸ κοινὸν Ἑλλήνων ἐμπόριον, αἱ μὲν ἀνδρὸς ἰδιώτου μέσου δυνάμει χρημάτων καταδέουσιν ἐς εὐδαιμονίαν.

52. Plutarch *Demosthenes* 1-2, cf. Dio Chrysostom 44.6. Patterson (1991) 152-6, Alcock (1993) 154-7, Quaß (1993) esp. 184-95.

53. Aristeides 50.63-108. Bowersock (1969) 42.

54. Paus. 1.18.8, praising Isokrates for 'his wisdom in keeping away from politics and in not getting involved in public affairs' (σωφρονέστατον δὲ ὅτι πολιτείας ἀπεχόμενος διέμεινε καὶ τὰ κοινὰ οὐ πολυπραγμονῶν). Cf. 1.8.3 (a similar idea, and criticising democracy). Palm (1959) 69, Habicht (1985) 109-11, Bultrighini (1990a) 21-47; cf. Carter (1986) 155-94.

55. Paus. 1.19.6, 2.7.1, 6.21.2, 7.20.6, 10.32.1 (Herodes), 2.3.5 (Eurykles) 2.27.6 (Antoninus Pythodorus), 4.32.2 (Claudius Saethidas); cf. 8.9-10 (Podares: a mixed response); Bowie (1996) 223-9.

56. On the connection between status and *paideia* see Whitmarsh (2001b) 96-108.

57. Heer (1979) 92-108, Anderson (1993) 47-53, 135, Schmitz (1997) 39-66, Conolly (2001). Canon of texts: Dio Chrysostom 18.6-17.

58. Philostratos *VS* 507, Anderson (1986) 11-21.

59. Bowersock (1969), Bowie (1982), Anderson (1993) esp. 13-39, Brunt (1994), Flinterman (1995) 28-51, Robert (1909) 274, Pasquali (1913) 165 suggested that Pausanias was active as a sophist, but there is no evidence for this: Habicht (1985) 137-40, Arafat (1996) 32-3; cf. Diller (1955).

60. On Atticism see Anderson (1993) 86-94, Swain (1996), 17-64, Schmitz (1997) 67-90; cf. Lucian *Rhet. Praec.* 16-17.

61. Strid (1976) esp. 11-14, 47-66, 99-103, Pasquali (1913), also: Arafat (1996) 27-31, Heer (1979) 39-40, Robert (1909) 201-16, Gurlitt (1890) 15-21.

62. See Paus. 2.27.3, 2.37.3, 3.15.2, 4.27.11, 5.15.7, 5.19.10, 9.22.3.

63. Hutton (2005a) esp. 175-240. See also Strid (1976), Habicht (1985) 137, Auberger (1994), Arafat (1996) 30.

64. Athenaios' *Deipnosophistai* presents an exaggerated version of a competitive dinner conversation between sophists. Pausanias' knowledge of literature: Frazer (1898) lxxii-lxxv, Musti (1982) xxiv-xxxv, Bowie (1996) 211; also note Gaertner (2006).

65. Paus. 9.30.3: Περὶ δὲ Ἡσιόδου τε ἡλικίας καὶ Ὁμήρου πολυπραγμονήσαντι ἐς τὸ ἀκριβέστατον οὔ μοι γράφειν ἡδὺ ἦν, ἐπισταμένῳ τὸ φιλαίτιον ἄλλων τε καὶ οὐχ ἥκιστα ὅσοι κατ' ἐμὲ ἐπὶ ποιήσει τῶν ἐπῶν καθεστήκεσαν.

66. E.g. Paus. 1.35.5-8 (special relics of heroes), 2.1.5 (canal projects), 2.5.2-3 (connections between rivers), 4.27.9-10 (cities in exile), 4.34.1-3 (dangerous animals in rivers), 4.35.8-12 (properties of water), 4.36.6 (places known for single events), 5.7.4-5 (rivers that flow through lakes), 5.14.3 (plants growing by rivers), 7.24.7-13 (earthquakes), 7.25.1-3 (divine vengeance), 8.7.2-3 (springs under water), 8.10.4 (water rising in temples), 8.17.2 (wood used for statues), 8.17.3-4 (white animals), 8.28.2-3 (cold rivers), 8.38.9-10 (rivers called Acheloos), 8.46.1-4 (rulers who looted images), 8.48.2-3 (plants used as prizes), 9.21.1-6 (fantastic animals), 9.28.1-4 (poisonous snakes), 9.40.3-4 (works of Daidalos), 9.41.1-5 (works of Hephaistos, 10.12.1-11 (sibyls), 10.32.2-7 (remarkable caves), 10.35.2-3 (temples burned by the Persians). See also Arafat (1999).

67. E.g. Aelian, *Varia Historia*, Athenaios, *Deipnosophistai*, Plutarch *Quaestiones Graecae* and *Romanae*. Bowie & Krasser (1997) 850-3; Sandy (1997) 87-8.

68. Robert (1909) 6, 8, 110, Kalkmann (1886) 271-82, Pasquali (1913) 161, 193-6, see also Musti (1984).

69. Konstan (2001a) 58-60, Arafat (2000) 191.

70. Habicht (1985) 12-13, 18, 128-30. Pausanias' close contemporaries include the sophists Herodes Atticus, Polemon Aristeides, Lucian and Apuleius.

71. Hadrian is mentioned often, most notably in Paus. 1.5.5, Antoninus Pius: 8.43.3-6, Marcus Aurelius: 8.43.6, Herodes Atticus: 1.19.6, 2.1.7, 6.21.2, 7.20.6, 10.32.1, Antoninus Pythodorus: 2.27.6, Antinoos: 8.9.7-8, Claudius Saethidas: 4.32.2, Olympic victors: 2.11.8 (Granianus), 10.34.5 (Mnesiboulos). In 2.37.3 Pausanias mentions Arriphon, an otherwise unknown contemporary. Habicht (1985) 18, Bowie (1996) 221-9.

72. Schubart (1853), Diller (1956) 84-5, followed by Habicht (1985) 22, 24, 26.

73. Aelian, *VH* 12.61, referring to Paus. 8.36.6; questioned in Faber (1667). Cf. Bowie (2001) 29-30.

74. Philostratus *VA* 6.10-11 ~ Paus. 10.5.9-13 in Dickie (1997) 15-20; Longus *Daphnis and Chloe* 2.25.4-26. 1 ~ Paus. 10.23.1-7 in Bowie (2001) 30-2; Lucian *Dea Syria* 13, 23, 60 ~ Paus. 1.18.7, 1.22.1, 2.32.1 in Lightfoot (2003) 218 (see also 218 n. 612); Athenagoras *Leg.* 17 ~ Paus. 1.26.4 in Snodgrass (2003), Pollux 7.37 ~ Paus. 5.14.5 in Hanell (1938) 1560. Cf. Gurlitt (1890) 73 and Frazer (1898) I.xv.

75. Jones (1971) 43-6, Touloumakos (1971) 46-51, Forte (1972) 301-18, Halfmann (1979); cf. Ameling (1983) 48-83, Cartledge & Spawforth (1989) 97-112.

76. Paus. 8.43.5.

77. See Swain (1996) 332, 350.

78. Hitzig & Blümner (1896-1910) III.1, 206, Robert (1909) 32-3, Segre (2004)

98-112, Palm (1959) 63-74, Habicht (1985) 117-40, Tzifopoulos (1993), Arafat (1996) esp. 202-14, Swain (1996) 330-56. Cf. Jones (1996b) 462: 'the question (...) is overdue for retirement'.

79. Paus. 1.20.4-7, 9.7.5, 9.30.1, 9.33.6 (Sulla), 2.1.5, 5.25.9, 5.26.3, 7.17.3, 9.27.3-4, 10.7.1, 10.19.2 (Nero); see Arafat (1996) 92-105. See also Paus. 7.16.9-17.1 (Mummius' settlement), cf. 7.9.1-7, 7.11.1-2, 7.16.10, 7.17.3-4.

80. Habicht (1985) 104-8.

81. Greek traitors: Kallikrates, Menalkidas, Diaios and Kritolaos. Paus. 7.10.1-5, 7.11.7-12.3, 7.12.8-9, 7.14.6, 7.16.6.; Macedonians: 3.7.11; cf. 1.25.3, 8.52.3.

82. E.g. Paus. 9.27.3-4, 9.33.6. In 8.46.1-4 he surprisingly excuses looting.

83. Paus. 8.2.5; statues of emperors in inappropriate places e.g. 2.8.1, 2.17.3, but note Steinhart (2002a).

84. Nikopolis: Paus. 5.23.3, 7.18.8-9, 10.8.3, 10.38.4; Patrai: 7.18.6-9, 10.38.9.

85. Paus. 8.27.1: πλὴν ὅσων κατὰ συμφορὰν (ἐπὶ) ἀρχῆς τῆς Ῥωμαίων μεταβεβήκασιν οἰκήτορες. Palm (1959) 72-4, followed by Rocha-Pereira (1990), Casevitz and Jost & Marcadé (1998), inserts 'epi' to read 'misfortune *in the time* of Roman rule'. Habicht (1985) 120, Arafat (1996) 202, Moggi (2002), Steinhart (2002b) agree. Against the emendation: Bowie (1996) 217, Swain (1996) 353-6.

86. Trajan: Paus. 5.12.6, Antoninus Pius: 8.43.3-6, Marcus Aurelius: 8.43.6, Hadrian: 1.3.2, 1.5.5, 1.36.3; cf. 1.18.6, 1.18.9, 1.42.5, 1.44.6, 2.3.5, 6.16.4, 8.8.12, 8.10.2, 10.35.6. Cf. Jacquemin (1996).

87. See Anderson (1993) 122-4, Bowie (1974) 200-1.

88. Woolf (1994), Swain (1996) 9-13, 65-89, Saïd (2001) 286-95, Whitmarsh (2001b) 1-17; see also Zanker (1995) 206-42.

89. Alcock (1993) 24-32, see Paus. 8.33; cf. pp. 144-5.

90. Frazer (1898) xxxiii-iv, Regenbogen (1956) 1090, Bowie (1974) 188, Habicht (1985) 130-7; more differentiated views: Arafat (1996) 36-42, Hutton (2005b).

91. Akujärvi (2005) 88; see also Ma (2003).

92. Alcock (1993) 145-54, 207-12.

93. Alcock (1993) 145-54, 207-12; Stadter (1980) 152-5, Swain (1996) 66-79.

94. Frézouls (1991); city panegyrics: Dio Chrysostom 33.1 (describing the stereotypical praise of a city), Menander Rhetor I.2. p. 353.4-359.10. Bowie (1996) 229.

95. E.g. Robert (1977) 120-9, *SEG* 2.549: the Argives praise Antiochos of Aigeai in Cilicia for establishing an ancient relationship between Argos and his native city; cf. Elsner (1994), Lacroix (1994). On 'mythical relations' between cities see Curty (1995), Jones (1999).

96. Swain (1996) 75-6, Spawforth & Walker (1985) and (1986), Jones (1996a), Romeo (2002). The Panhellenion was founded in the 130s AD. Pausanias and the Panhellenion: Musti (1984) 12-13, Arafat (1996) 12-13.

97. Pretzler (2005a), Cameron (2004) 218-22, note that there were mythographical works that were organised by city or region: Cameron (2004) 227-8.

98. Cf. Lafond (2001); on Greek identity see Saïd (2001), Konstan (2001b), Alcock (2002) 36-98, esp. 96-8.

3. The Importance of Travelling

1. Paus. 1.42.3: Ἐν Θήβαις ταῖς Αἰγυπτίαις, διαβᾶσι τὸν Νεῖλον πρὸς τὰς Σύριγγας καλουμένας, εἶδον ἔτι καθήμενον ἄγαλμα ἠχοῦν — Μέμνονα ὀνομάζουσιν οἱ πολλοί, τοῦτον γάρ φασιν ἐξ Αἰθιοπίας ὁρμηθῆναι ἐς Αἴγυπτον καὶ τὴν ἄχρι Σούσων· ἀλλὰ γὰρ οὐ Μέμνονα οἱ Θηβαῖοι λέγουσι, Φαμένωφα δὲ εἶναι τῶν ἐγχωρίων οὗ τοῦτο ἄγαλμα ἦν, ἤκουσα δὲ ἤδη καὶ Σέσωστριν φαμένων εἶναι. ὃ Καμβύσης διέκοψε· καὶ νῦν ὁπόσον ἐκ κεφαλῆς ἐς μέσον σῶμά ἐστιν ἀπερριμμένον, τὸ δὲ λοιπὸν κάθηταί τε καὶ ἀνὰ πᾶσαν ἡμέραν ἀνίσχοντος ἡλίου βοᾷ, καὶ τὸν ἦχον μάλιστα εἰκάσει τις κιθάρας ἢ λύρας ῥαγείσης χορδῆς.

2. Paus. 4.35.9 (Thermopylai), 1.13.2, 6.5.2, 9.30.9 (Thessaly), 9.30.7 (Macedonia), 1.13.1, 1.17.5, 7.21.2, 8.23.5 (Dodona), 4.31.5 (Rhodes, Byzantion), 5.7.4, 4.35.9-11, 8.16.5, 8.33.3 (Syria), 1.42.3, 9.16.1, 9.36.5 (Egypt incl. Siwa), 5.12.6, 8.17.4, 8.46.4-5, 9.21.1, 10.5.11 (Rome), 4.35.12, 5.12.3, 8.7.3 (Campania), 2.27.4, 4.35.10 (Latium). Frazer (1898) xx-xxi, Regenbogen (1956) 1013, Meyer (1954) 15-16.

3. Hdt. 3.139.

4. Hesiod *Works & Days* 618-40.

5. Hartog (1988) 212-59, Hall (1989) 3-13.

6. Aristeides 26.100-1: Νῦν γοῦν ἔξεστι καὶ Ἕλληνι καὶ βαρβάρῳ καὶ τὰ αὐτοῦ κομίζοντι καὶ χωρὶς τῶν αὐτοῦ βαδίζειν ὅποι βούλεται ῥαδίως, ἀτεχνῶς ὡς ἐκ πατρίδος εἰς πατρίδα ἰόντι· καὶ οὔτε Πύλαι Κιλίκιοι φόβον παρέχουσιν οὔτε στεναὶ καὶ ψαμμώδεις δι᾽ Ἀράβων ἐπ᾽ Αἴγυπτον πάροδοι, οὐκ ὄρη ... δύσβατα, οὐ ποταμῶν ἄπειρα μεγέθη, οὐ γένη βαρβάρων ἄμικτα, ἀλλ᾽ εἰς ἀσφάλειαν ἐξαρκεῖ Ῥωμαῖον εἶναι, μᾶλλον δὲ ἕνα τῶν ὑφ᾽ ὑμῖν. καὶ τὸ Ὁμήρῳ λεχθὲν Γαῖα δ᾽ ἔτι ξυνὴ πάντων" ὑμεῖς ἔργῳ ἐποιήσατε, καταμετρήσαντες μὲν πᾶσαν τὴν οἰκουμένην, ζεύξαντες δὲ παντοδαπαῖς γεφύραις ποταμοὺς, καὶ ὄρη κόψαντες ἱππήλατον γῆν εἶναι, σταθμοῖς τε τὰ ἔρημα ἀναπλήσαντες, καὶ διαίτῃ καὶ τάξει πάντα ἡμερώσαντες.

7. Casson (1994) 121-7, 149-52, 163-75, Horden & Purcell (2000) 124-43, Friedländer (1919-21) I.316-88, Braund (1993) 204-10, Anderson (1984) 77, Hägg (1983) 114, Bowie (1982) 31-8, Bowersock (1969) 43-50; Roman officials: André & Baslez (1993) 103-18, Mitchell (1976) 111-12; emperors: Halfmann (1986) esp. 143-56, Millar (1992) 28-40. See also Holum (1990) 72-7.

8. André & Baslez (1993) 207-46.

9. Adams (2007), Casson (1994) 253-61, Friedländer (1919-21) I.389-488.

10. Adams (2007) 176-7, Casson (1994) 128-7, 271-85, Hunt (1984) 403-8; graffiti: Baillet (1926), dates: XX-XXVII, Bernand (1969), dates: 15-21.

11. See Cohen (1992).

12. Bernand & Bernand (1960); Adams (2007)171-6, Casson (1994) 272-8, Friedländer (1919-21) I. 439-41.

13. E.g. Pliny *Ep.* 10.17a.

14. Hutton (2005a) 122-5. E.g. Paus. 2.34.7-10, 3.25.4, 9.22.2-4; cf. 1.1.1. Other sea routes: 2.29.6, 3.23.2, 4.35.1, 7.22.10, 7.26.10, 9.32.1; see pp. 61-72 with Fig. 9.

15. See Paus. 1.44.6 (two lanes), 2.11.3 (only one draught animal), 8.54.5 (good carriage road, a *leophoros*), comments on the width of roads: 2.15.2, 2.38.4, 8.6.4-5. Routes not accessible for vehicles: 2.15.2, 10.32.2, 10.32.7; cf. 10.34.7.

16. Roads: Pikoulas (2007), Pikoulas (1999) 250-5, Alcock (1993) 121-4, Pritchett (1969-89) III.143-96, Pritchett (1999) 17-36, esp. 20-2; carriages: Casson (1994) 67-8, 179-82, see also Kourinou (2007). Retinue: Casson (1994) 176-8. Pausanias never mentions travel companions, except for an implicit reference in 9.39.13, but note the occasional use of 'we' when talking about his activities. Hutton (2005a) 27, Akujärvi (2005) 101.

17. Readers on tour: Paus. 6.17.1, 1.26.3, see also 6.7.1. Readers at home: 1.19.6; cf. Petersen (1909) esp. 487-8.

18. E.g. Pliny *Ep.* 3.5.14-16, cf. Aristeides *Sacred Tales* 4.4.

19. Snodgrass (1987) 77-86, Hutton (2005a) 24-5, 83-174, Bommelaer (2001); see pp. 68-9 and 135-7.

20. Bol (1978) 1-6.

21. Books on site impractical: Casson (1994) 263-4, cf. Habicht (1985) 21-2; books on site possible: Arafat (1996) 33. See also Hutton (2005a) 243-4. Elsner (2001a) 16 (with n. 54) notes that travellers may have taken books in codex form, cf. Martial 1.2.1-6 with Roberts & Skeat (1983) 24-53.

22. Plut. *Mor*. 394D-409D; cf. Pseudo-Lucian *Amores* 8, Longus *Daphnis and Chloe*, proem. See Casson (1994) 264-7, Frazer (1898) I.lxxvi-vii, both with a collection of references. For a more positive interpretation see Jones (2001).

23. Paus. 1.34.4 (Athens), 1.41.2, 1.42.4 (Megara), 2.9.7 (Sicyon), 1.13.8, 2.23.5-6 (Argos), 2.31.4 (Troizen), 5.18.6 (Olympia). The Greek term is usually *periegetes*, but Pausanias uniquely uses the word *exegetes*. See Pretzler (2004) 204-7, Jones (2001) 33-4.

24. E.g. Pausanias' 'people who remember the ancient traditions' (οἱ τὰ ἀρχαῖα μνημονεύοντες): 7.18.2 (Patrae), 9.18.2 (Thebes). Disapproval: 2.23.5-6, cf. 1.34.4, 2.30.5.

25. Casson (1994) 87-90, 197-209, Marasco (1978) 30-7, André & Baslez (1993) 449-65. E.g. Apuleius *Met*. 1.21-2, cf. Lucian *Ass* 1-2.

26. Paus. 9.30.11.

27. Jones (1971) 26, on the setting of philosophical dialogues see Tarrant (1999) esp. 188.

28. Aristarchos: Paus. 5.20.4-5, with Habicht (1985) 146; Lykomidai: 9.30.12, cf. 1.22.7, 4.1.5, 4.1.7, 9.27.2, with Heer (1979) 71-2; Elean official: 6.23.6, cf. 6.26.2 'the most respectable Eleans' (Ἠλείων τε οἱ δοκιμώτατοι ἄνδρες).

29. E.g. Paus. 1.35.7-8, 2.23.5-6, 7.23.7-8, perhaps also 2.30.5, 4.32.3, 5.6.2, 10.14.5-6.

30. Anderson (1993) 28-30; cf. Jones (1971) 42, Garnsey & Saller (1987) 98-103.

31. Philostratos *VA* 1.34; Favorinus *De Ex*. 10.4; Jones (1971) 40-7, Millar (1981) 69, Alcock (1993) 154-7, Whitmarsh (2001a) 301.

32. Hom. *Od*. 1.3.

33. Hartog (2001) 9-11; cf. Hdt. 2; esp. 2.4, 2.49-50, 2.58, 2.64, 2.99-144, see also Diod. 1.96. Texts claiming to draw on the ancient wisdom of Egypt: e.g. Plato *Timaios*, Dio Chrysostom 11 (*Trojan Oration*); see also Lucian *Philops*. 33.

34. Hdt. 1.30: Ξεῖνε Ἀθηναῖε, παρ᾽ ἡμέας γὰρ περὶ σέο λόγος ἀπῖκται πολλὸς καὶ σοφίης εἵνεκεν τῆς σῆς καὶ πλάνης, ὡς φιλοσοφέων γῆν πολλὴν θεωρίης εἵνεκεν ἐπελήλυθας· νῦν ὄν ἐπειρέσθαι σε ἵμερος ἐπῆλθέ μοι εἴ τινα ἤδη πάντων εἶδες ὀλβιώτατον.

35. Hartog (2001) 5, 90-1, 108-16, 199-209; Solon: Hdt. 1.29-33, Plut. *Solon* 25-8; Pythagoras: Porphyry *Life of Pythagoras* 7-8, 18-19, Dikaiarchos F.33 (Wehrli); Anacharsis: Hdt. 4.76-7; see also Philostratos *Life of Apollonios*. Other travelling wise men: Diod. 1.96.

36. Whitmarsh (2001a).

37. Pretzler (2007) esp. 127-8.

38. E.g. Apuleius (Madaurus to Carthage): Apuleius *Florida* 20.9-10, Sandy (1997) 18, Harrison (2000) 1-5.

39. Philostratos *VS* 518, cf. 516, 530, 591; Bowersock (1969) 17-18, Anderson (1993) 22-4.

40. See Lucian *Bis Accusatus* 27, *Somnium* 15; Jones (1986) 6-14, Goldhill (2002) 60-93.

41. Philostratos *VS* 586. Bowersock (1969) 17-27, 43-58, 76-100; Bowersock (2002).

42. E.g. the Aphrodite of Knidos: Lucian *Amores* 11, Dio Chrysostom 12, esp. 12.25; Casson (1994) 229-37.

43. See pp. 107-8.

44. Thuc. 1.1, Polyb. 3.4.

45. Polyb. 3.59: Ἐν δὲ τοῖς καθ᾿ ἡμᾶς τῶν μὲν κατὰ τὴν Ἀσίαν διὰ τὴν Ἀλεξάνδρου δυναστείαν τῶν δὲ λοιπῶν τόπων διὰ τὴν Ῥωμαίων ὑπεροχὴν σχεδὸν ἁπάντων πλωτῶν καὶ πορευτῶν γεγονότων, ἀπολελυμένων δὲ καὶ τῶν πρακτικῶν ἀνδρῶν τῆς περὶ τὰς πολεμικὰς καὶ πολιτικὰς πράξεις φιλοτιμίας, ἐκ δὲ τούτων πολλὰς καὶ μεγάλας ἀφορμὰς εἰληφότων εἰς τὸ πολυπραγμονεῖν καὶ φιλομαθεῖν περὶ τῶν προειρημένων, δέον εἴη καὶ βέλτιον γινώσκειν καὶ ἀληθινώτερον ὑπὲρ τῶν πρότερον ἀγνοουμένων. ὅπερ ἡμεῖς αὐτοί τε πειρασόμεθα ποιεῖν, λαβόντες ἁρμόζοντα τόπον ἐν τῇ πραγματείᾳ τῷ μέρει τούτῳ, τούς τε φιλοπευστοῦντας ὁλοσχερέστερον βουλησόμεθα συνεπιστῆσαι περὶ τῶν προειρημένων, ἐπειδὴ καὶ τὸ πλεῖον τούτου χάριν ὑπεδεξάμεθα τοὺς κινδύνους καὶ τὰς κακοπαθείας τοὺς συμβάντας ἡμῖν ἐν πλάνῃ τῇ κατὰ Λιβύην καὶ κατ᾿ Ἰβηρίαν, ἔτι δὲ Γαλατίαν καὶ τὴν ἔξωθεν ταύταις ταῖς χώραις συγκυροῦσαν θάλατταν, ἵνα διορθωσάμενοι τὴν τῶν προγεγονότων ἄγνοιαν ἐν τούτοις γνώριμα ποιήσωμεν τοῖς Ἕλλησι καὶ ταῦτα τὰ μέρη τῆς οἰκουμένης.

46. Bowie (1974) 175-8, Nicolet (1988) 79, Clarke (1999) 89-97, 114-20, Henderson (2001b).

47. E.g. Paus. 2.35.8, 5.5.6, 8.41.6.

48. Paus. 8.17.1 (ruined temple on Mt. Cyllene, 2360 m high), 8.38.3 (Mt. Lykaios, 1420 m high); 8.39.1, 8.41.4, 10.5.1, 10.32.2, 10.35.8. (difficult roads); 8.40.4-6, 8.42.11-13 (disappointments on a visit to remote Phigalia).

49. Paus. 8.21.2: Εἰσὶ δὲ ἰχθῦς ἐν τῷ Ἀροανίῳ καὶ ἄλλοι καὶ οἱ ποικιλίαι καλούμενοι· τούτους λέγουσι τοὺς ποικιλίας φθέγγεσθαι κίχλῃ τῇ ὄρνιθι ἐοικός. ἐγὼ δὲ ἀγρευθέντας μὲν εἶδον, φθεγγομένων δὲ ἤκουσα οὐδὲν καταμείνας πρὸς τῷ ποταμῷ καὶ ἐς ἡλίου δυσμάς, ὅτε δὴ φθέγγεσθαι μάλιστα ἐλέγοντο οἱ ἰχθῦς.

50. Zizza (2006) esp. 399-436, Tzifoloulos (1991), Whittaker (1991), Frazer (1898) I.lxxv-vi, Habicht (1985) 64-5 and *passim*, Habicht (1984), Bearzot (1995), Bommelaer (1999), Chamoux (2001). See Paus. 8.13.2-3; comparing local tradition with epigraphical evidence: 5.2.5, cf. 1.2.4, 2.9.8, 2.37.3, 5.27.7. Pausanias quotes fifty-four inscriptions and cites over two hundred. See Zizza (2006).

51. Paus. 8.49.1: Οὐ πόρρω δὲ τῆς ἀγορᾶς θέατρόν τέ ἐστι καὶ πρὸς αὐτῷ βάθρα εἰκόνων χαλκῶν, αὐταὶ δὲ οὐκ εἰσὶν ἔτι αἱ εἰκόνες· ἐλεγεῖον δὲ ἐφ᾿ ἑνὶ τῶν βάθρων ἐστὶ Φιλοποίμενος τὸν ἀνδριάντα εἶναι. The epigram is quoted in full at 8.52.6. Zizza (2006) n. 44, 333-8.

52. Paus. 8.30.5, 8.38.5, 8.49.1.

53. Zizza (2006) 101-14, Tzifoloulos (1991) 1-23. Badly preserved inscriptions: Paus. 6.15.8, 8.40.1; dialects: 2.37.3 (Doric dialect used as evidence for chronology), 2.27.3 (Doric), 8.11.8-9 (Boeotian), see Whittaker (1991) 171; ancient script: 5.17.6, 2.1.4, 5.22.3, 6.19.5, 6.19.6.

54. Jones (2001) 33, Pretzler (2005a) 241-3; e.g. Paus. 1.35.7-8, 2.23.5-6, 7.23.7-8, perhaps also 2.2.2, 4.32.3, 10.14.5-6 (discussions), 7.26.13, 8.25.7-11, 8.41.5 (knowledgeable locals).

55. Paus. 6.24.9, 8.42.12-13 (old men in Elis and Phigalia); cf. 1.18.5 (Athenian women).

56. *Aitia*: e.g. Paus. 2.24.7, 4.34.6, 9.5.3; heroes and genealogies: e.g. 2.29.2 2.30.8, 3.21.8, 4.33.6, 5.5.4, 6.21.10, 7.5.5, 7.22.5, 9.8.4, 9.39.1. Cf. Lacroix (1994).

57. Artists: e.g. Paus. 5.22.5, 5.23.5, 5.23.7, 6.10.5, 7.26.6, 8.42.5, 8.53.8; iconography: 1.33.8, 6.9.1; inscriptions and statues: 5.21.3-16, 6.4.8, 8.40.1; history of monuments: 2.7.6, 5.11.3, 8.42.12-13, 9.29.9.

58. Cult practice: e.g. Paus. 1.44.5, 5.24.10, 9.3.3, 9.27.1; local deities and epithets: e.g. 1.19.2, 1.42.4, 2.31.4, 5.15.7, 8.44.6.

59. Gaertner (2006), Cameron (2004) 233-7.

60. See Paus. 8.41, a rare example where he engages with outdated information.

61. Inscriptions: e.g. Paus. 5.23.1-3, 6.12.8, 8.27.2-8, 8.52.6, 9.15.6, cf. Whittaker (1991) 179-80, Habicht (1985) 65; descriptions of art works: e.g. 3.18.9-19.2 (Throne of Apollo at Amyklai) 5.11.1-11 (Zeus of Olympia), 5.17.5-19.10 (Chest of Kypselos), 10.25.1-31.12 (Lesche of the Knidians).

62. Aristeides 36.1.

63. Elsner & Rutherford (2005) esp. 1-30, Dillon (1997), cf. Hunt (1984).

64. Morinis (1992) 1-28; debate about definition: Elsner & Rutherford (2005) 1-9, cf. Scullion (2005) 121-30, Williamson (2005) 220-3, Hutton (2005b) 293-7.

65. Horden & Purcell (2000) 445-7.

66. Elsner (1992); opposition: Arafat (1996) 10, Swain (1996) 334. Further developments: Rutherford (2001), Hutton (2005b). See also Galli (2005) 260-5.

67. Paus. 9.39.5-14; compare Lucian *Dea Syria* 60, *Verae Historiae* 2.28.

68. Elsner (1992) 20-5, Oliver (1972), Veyne (1988) 95-102, Ellinger (2005) 182-6. See also Hutton (2005a) 273-324, Hutton (2005b) 295: the discussion traditionally focuses on Paus. 8.8.3, which is not conclusive when juxtaposed with relevant passages in other parts of the work.

69. Rutherford (2001), Hutton (2005b) 295-9.

70. Hutton (2005b) esp. 298-9; this phenomenon has been studied especially in connection with late antique/early medieval pilgrimage e.g. Galli (2005), Campbell (1991), Leyerle (1996), Sivan (1988a), (1988b), Campbell (1988) 20-33, Elsner (1995) 134-5, 144-5, Westra (1995), Wilkinson (1981) 1-48.

71. Akujärvi (2005) 65-77.

4. Greek Travel Writing: Between Report and Invention

1. Lucian *Verae Historiae* 1.2-4: Τῶν παλαιῶν ποιητῶν τε καὶ συγγραφέων καὶ φιλοσόφων πολλὰ τεράστια καὶ μυθώδη συγγεγραφότων, ... Κτησίας ὁ Κτησιόχου ὁ Κνίδιος, ὃς συνέγραψεν περὶ τῆς Ἰνδῶν χώρας καὶ τῶν παρ' αὐτοῖς ἃ μήτε αὐτὸς εἶδεν μήτε ἄλλου ἀληθεύοντος ἤκουσεν. ... πολλοὶ δὲ καὶ ἄλλοι τὰ αὐτὰ τούτοις προελόμενοι συνέγραψαν ὡς δή τινας ἑαυτῶν πλάνας τε καὶ ἀποδημίας, θηρίων τε μεγέθη ἱστοροῦντες καὶ ἀνθρώπων ὠμότητας καὶ βίων καινότητας· ἀρχηγὸς δὲ αὐτοῖς καὶ διδάσκαλος τῆς τοιαύτης βωμολοχίας ὁ τοῦ Ὁμήρου Ὀδυσσεύς, τοῖς περὶ τὸν Ἀλκίνουν διηγούμενος ἀνέμων τε δουλείαν καὶ μονοφθάλμους καὶ ὠμοφάγους καὶ ἀγρίους τινὰς ἀνθρώπους, ἔτι δὲ πολυκέφαλα ζῷα καὶ τὰς ὑπὸ φαρμάκων τῶν ἑταίρων μεταβολάς.

2. Romm (1992) esp. 172-214, Hartog (1988) 12-33, see also Romm (1989), Ní Mheallaigh (2008).

3. Hdt. 2.20-3, 4.36, Romm (1992) 32-41.

4. Campbell (2002).

5. Pausanias was well aware of these scholarly traditions, and he includes a lot of geographical and ethnographical material in his work. See Arafat (1999).

6. See Hartog (2001), Dougherty (2001), Jacob (1991) 24-30.

7. Hom. *Od.* 9-12.

8. Hom. *Od.* 11.362-72; cf. 23.306-41.

9. Hom. *Od.* 9.252-71.

10. Hom. *Od.* 19.203: ἴσκε ψεύδεα πολλὰ λέγων ἐτύμοισιν ὁμοῖα.

11. Hom. *Od.* 13.291-5: κερδαλέος κ' εἴη καὶ ἐπίκλοπος, ὅς σε παρέλθοι ἐν πάντεσσι δόλοισι, καὶ εἰ θεὸς ἀντιάσειε. σχέτλιε, ποικιλομῆτα, δόλων ἄατ', οὐκ ἄρ' ἔμελλες, οὐδ' ἐν σῇ περ ἐὼν γαίῃ, λήξειν ἀπατάων μύθων τε κλοπίων, οἵ τοι πεδόθεν φίλοι εἰσίν. Odysseus' tale: Hom. *Od.* 13.256-86.

12. Hom. *Od.* 14.199-359 (Eumaios), 19.172-307 (Penelope), 24.261-79, 24.304-14 (Laertes). Odysseus presents himself as a Cretan to Eumaios and Penelope, and for Laertes he invents a town Alybas as his home.

13. Philostratos *VA* 1.18-3.58, cf. 4.1-27 (a trip to the upper Nile), see Anderson (1986) 199-226.

14. See pp. 42-3. Christian pilgrimage texts are connected to ancient pagan literature – see Hunt (1984) – but they will not be discussed here because extant examples are significantly later than Pausanias' *Periegesis*.

15. See Behr (1968) 116-28; the *Sacred Tales* cover the period AD 143-71.

16. Morgan (2007), Rohde (1960) 178-310.

17. Millar (1981); see also Schlam (1992) esp. 113-22, Winkler (1985) 276-91.

18. Strabo 1.2.2-19; Romm (1992) 184-93, Prontera (1993) note Jacob (1991) 16-24 (Homeric geography is still an issue today!).

19. Romm (1992) 196-202.

20. Giesinger (1937), Janni (1984) 120-30, Hutton (2005a) 264-7.

21. Jacob (1991) 73-84, Oikonomides & Miller (1995), Carpenter (1966) 81-103, Seel (1961) 5-8, 49-55, Cary & Warmington (1963) 63-8, Aly (1927) 317-30, Blomquist (1979). Inscription: Hanno 1, Aristeides 48.12-13.

22. Hanno 1.8: Λαβόντες δὲ παρ᾽ αὐτῶν ἑρμηνέας, παρεπλέομεν τὴν ἐρήμην πρὸς μεσημβρίαν δύο ἡμέρας· ἐκεῖθεν δὲ πάλιν πρὸς ἥλιον ἀνίσχοντα ἡμέρας δρόμον. Ἔνθα εὕρομεν ἐν μυχῷ τινος κόλπου νῆσον μικράν, κύκλον ἔχουσαν σταδίων πέντε· ἣν κατῳκίσαμεν, Κέρνην ὀνομάσαντες. Ἐτεκμαιρόμεθα δ᾽ αὐτὴν ἐκ τοῦ περίπλου κατ᾽ εὐθὺ κεῖσθαι Καρχηδόνος· ἐῴκει γὰρ ὁ πλοῦς ἔκ τε Καρχηδόνος ἐπὶ Στήλας κἀκεῖθεν ἐπὶ Κέρνην.

23. Stadter (1980) 32-41, Silberman (1993), Bosworth (1993) 242-53, Braund (1994) 178-87, Liddle (2003); see also Hutton (2005a) 266-71, Pretzler (2007) 135-6.

24. Strabo 2.3.5, 2.4.1, Polyb. 34.5; Cunliffe (2002), Roseman (1994), Carpenter (1966) 143-98, Stichtenoth (1959), Mette (1952).

25. Hdt. 4.44, Tzetzes *Chiliades* 144; Romm (1992) 84-5.

26. Romm (1989) 125-31.

27. Romm (1992) 86-8, Bigwood (1989); Summary in Photios *Bibliotheke* 72.

28. Hdt. 4.13-16 dates Aristeas at least 240 years before his own time, cf. Suda s.v. *Aristeas* (A3900): an Olympiad date in the early sixth century BC. Romm (1992) 71-4, Bolton (1962), with Herington (1964). Pausanias comments on Aristeas in 1.24.6.

29. Romm (1992) 202-14. Lucian *Icaromenippos, Menippos, Verae Historiae,* Antonius Diogenes *Wonders Beyond Thule,* Plutarch *On the Face in the Moon* 26-30 (940F-945D); probably also lost works of Antiphanes of Berge, Euhemeros, Iamboulos, Theopompos.

30. E.g. Xenophon's *Anabasis* – possible alternative accounts? Diod. 14.19-31; possible sources besides Xenophon: Sophainetos of Stymphalos, Ktesias (via Ephoros). See Stylianou (2004), Cawkwell (2004) 60-2, Gwynn (1929), Westlake (1987); cf. Xen. *Hell.* 3.1.2: Themistogenes of Syracuse.

31. Xen. *Anab.* 4.8.22.

32. Roy (2007), Cawkwell (2004) 51-9, Stylianou (2004) 77-87.

33. Xen. *Anab.* 4.7.21-6. Note Rood (2004).

34. Strabo 1.2.1, 2.1.6.

35. Arrian *Anab.* proem; Pearson (1960).

36. Strabo 2.1.9.

37. Strabo 2.1.9; Pearson (1960) 83-149; Seel (1961).

38. Romm (1992) 94-109. Strabo 2.1.9.

39. Hägg (1983) 125-40.

40. Hom. *Il.* 2. 484-760; commentary: Allen (1921). See also Hom. *Il.* 2.815-77 (Trojan catalogue). 'Homeric Geography': Jacob (1991) 30-2, Prontera (1993). The issue is still a matter of discussion: see Milani (1988). See also Strabo 1.1.2.

41. Pseudo-Skylax 57: Μετὰ δὲ Μεγαρεῖς εἰσὶν Ἀθηναίων πόλεις. Καὶ πρῶτον τῆς Ἀττικῆς Ἐλευσὶς, οὗ ἱερὸν Δήμητρός ἐστι, καὶ τεῖχος. Κατὰ τοῦ τό ἐστι Σαλαμὶς νῆσος καὶ πόλις καὶ λιμήν. Ἔπειτα ὁ Πειραιεὺς καὶ τὰ σκέλη καὶ Ἀθῆναι. Ὁ δὲ Πειραιεὺς λιμένας ἔχει γʹ. Ἀνάφλυστος τεῖχος καὶ λιμήν· Σούνιον ἀκρωτήριον καὶ τεῖχος· ἱερὸν Ποσειδῶνος· Θορικὸς τεῖχος καὶ λιμένες δύο· Ῥαμνοῦς τεῖχος. Εἰσὶ δὲ καὶ ἄλλοι λιμένες ἐν τῇ Ἀττικῇ πολλοί. Περίπλους τῆς Ἀθηναίων χώρας στάδια αρμʹ· ἀπὸ Ἰαπίδος χώρας ἐπὶ Σούνιον στάδια υθʹ· ἀπὸ Σουνίου μέχρι τῶν ὅρων τῶν Βοιωτίων στάδια χνʹ. See Peretti (1979), Counillon (2004).

42. See also the *Periplous of the Erythraian Sea* with Jacob (1991) 133-46, Casson (1989), Huntingford (1980), and the *Periplous of the Black Sea*, with Diller (1952) 102-46.

43. Janni (1984) 23-8, 41-9, Janni (1998), Jacob (1991) 34-9.

44. Hekataios: Lanzillotta (1988), Tozzi (1963); Eratosthenes: Geus (2002) 361-88; Strabo: Jacob (1991) 151-66, Janni (1984) esp. 102-58. Pausanias in 'Geographer mode': Paus. 7.2.1-5.13 with Moggi (1996).

45. Bischoff (1938) 726-7.

46. Bischoff (1938), Hutton (2005a) 247-63. Also note the fragmentary Hawara *Periegesis*: Wilcken (1910).

47. See p. 103.

48. See pp. 62-3.

49. Gould (1989) 9-41, Hartog (1988) 260-94, Redfield (1985), Hdt. 1.183.2-3, 2.29.1, 2.99.1, 2.123.1, 2.147.1, 2.148.5-6, 4.16.1-2; cf. Thuc. 1.22.2-3. On Herodotos as geographer see Harrison (2007).

50. Sordi (1988), Lancillotta (1988), Jacob (1991) 91-4.

51. Diod. 1.1.2. Nenci (1953), Dewald (1987) esp. 155-9, Marincola (1997) 63-95, Clarke (1999) 85-7, 240-2. Cf. Polyb. 12.25-8 with Walbank (1962), Meister (1975) 44-8; cf. Josephus *Against Apion* 1.10.53-4, *Bellum Iudaicum* 1.1.3, 1.8.22.

52. Lucian *Hist. Conscr.* 47, cf. 29; Porod (2007).

53. Strabo 2.5.11: Οὐδὲ τῶν ἄλλων δὲ οὐδὲ εἷς ἂν εὑρεθείη τῶν γεωγραφησάντων πολύ τι ἡμῶν μᾶλλον ἐπεληλυθὼς τῶν λεχθέντων διαστημάτων, ἀλλ᾽ οἱ πλεονάσαντες περὶ τὰ δυσμικὰ μέρη τῶν πρὸς ταῖς ἀνατολαῖς οὐ τοσοῦτον ἥψαντο, οἱ δὲ περὶ τἀναντία τῶν ἑσπερίων ὑστέρησαν· ὁμοίως δ᾽ ἔχει καὶ περὶ τῶν πρὸς νότον καὶ τὰς ἄρκτους.

54. Strabo 2.5.11, cf. 1.2.2; Engels (1999) 28-32, Dueck (2000) 15-30.

55. Aristeides 36.1, cf. Behr (1968) 16-20; Dio Chrysostom 1.50-6, 7.1-7, 36.

56. Lucian *Verae Historiae* 1.4, *Ikaromenippos*, esp. 10, *Menippos*. esp. 6; Georgiadou & Larmour (1998) 22-44, Saïd (1994).

57. Paus. 2.22.3: Τὸν μὲν δὴ Θυέστου παῖδα ἢ Βροτέου – λέγεται γὰρ ἀμφότερα –, ὃς Κλυταιμνήστρᾳ πρότερον ἢ Ἀγαμέμνων συνῴκησε, τοῦτον μὲν τὸν Τάνταλον οὐ διοίσομαι ταφῆναι ταύτῃ· τοῦ δὲ λεγομένου Διός τε εἶναι καὶ Πλουτοῦς ἰδὼν οἶδα ἐν Σιπύλῳ τάφον θέας ἄξιον. Note that Pausanias is talking about Mount Sipylos, probably his own home.

58. Cf. Arafat (1996) 17-18, Pritchett (1999) 11-16.

59. Kalkmann (1886), Wilamowitz (1877) 341-7, cf. Habicht (1985) 163-8. Jacoby (1955) 60-5, Meyer (1978) 243-6; cf. Alcock (1996) 260-1 on autopsy as authentication device.

60. Paus. 8.42.1-13; Ellinger (2005) 173-86.

61. Esp. Arrian *Indike*, Lucian *Dea Syria*. Hutton (2005a) 195-203, Lightfoot (2003) 91-7.
62. Plutarch *De Maliginitate Herodoti*; Evans (1968), Momigliano (1975) 129-32.
63. Hartog (2001) 79-106, Jacob (1991) 64-72, Nippel (1996).
64. Note Elsner (2004a) 282-4, with Alcock (1996) 242.

5. A Sense of Space: Landscape and Geography

1. Paus. 2.1.5: Καθήκει δὲ ὁ τῶν Κορινθίων ἰσθμὸς τῇ μὲν ἐς τὴν ἐπὶ Κεγχρέαις, τῇ δὲ ἐς τὴν ἐπὶ Λεχαίῳ θάλασσαν· τοῦτο γὰρ ἤπειρον ποιεῖ τὴν ἐντὸς χώραν. ὃς δὲ ἐπεχείρησε Πελοπόννησον ἐργάσασθαι νῆσον, προαπέλιπε διορύσσων ἰσθμόν· καὶ ὅθεν μὲν διορύσσειν ἤρξαντο δῆλόν ἐστιν, ἐς δὲ τὸ πετρῶδες οὐ προεχώρησαν ἀρχήν· μένει δὲ ὡς πεφύκει καὶ νῦν ἤπειρος ὤν.
2. Strabo 9.1.6
3. Paus. 8.1.1-3, cf 5.1.1-2, a discussion of the ethnic divisions of the Peloponnese. 8.54.7 notes the end of the description of the Peloponnese.
4. Paus. 2.2.3.
5. Strabo 8.6.20, Thuc. 1.13.5, Hom. *Il.* 2.570.
6. Pretzler (2005c) 153-4, Engels (1999) 28-32; see also König (2001) esp. 156-60.
7. Strabo 8.6.22: Ἀρχὴ δὲ τῆς παραλίας ἑκατέρας, τῆς μὲν τὸ Λέχαιον, τῆς δὲ Κεγχρεαὶ κώμη καὶ λιμήν, ἀπέχων τῆς πόλεως ὅσον ἑβδομήκοντα σταδίους· τούτῳ μὲν οὖν χρῶνται πρὸς τοὺς ἐκ τῆς Ἀσίας, πρὸς δὲ τοὺς ἐκ τῆς Ἰταλίας τῷ Λεχαίῳ. ... ἐντεῦθεν δὲ παρεκτείνουσα ἡ ἠὼν μέχρι Παγῶν τῆς Μεγαρίδος κλύζεται μὲν ὑπὸ τοῦ Κορινθιακοῦ κόλπου· κοίλη δ᾽ ἐστὶ καὶ ποιεῖ τὸν δίολκον πρὸς τὴν ἑτέραν ἠόνα τὴν κατὰ Σχοινοῦντα πλησίον ὄντα τῶν Κεγχρεῶν. ἐν δὲ τῷ μεταξὺ τοῦ Λεχαίου καὶ Παγῶν τὸ τῆς Ἀκραίας μαντεῖον Ἥρας ὑπῆρχε τὸ παλαιόν, καὶ αἱ Ὀλμιαί, τὸ ποιοῦν ἀκρωτήριον τὸν κόλπον ἐν ᾧ ἥ τε Οἰνόη καὶ Παγαί, τὸ μὲν τῶν Μεγαρέων φρούριον, ἡ δὲ Οἰνόη τῶν Κορινθίων. ἀπὸ δὲ τῶν Κεγχρεῶν ὁ Σχοινοῦς, καθ᾽ ὃν τὸ στενὸν τοῦ διόλκου· ἔπειθ᾽ ἡ Κρομμυωνία. πρόκειται δὲ τῆς ἠόνος ταύτης ὅ τε Σαρωνικὸς κόλπος καὶ ὁ Ἐλευσινιακός, τρόπον τινὰ ὁ αὐτὸς ὤν, συνεχὴς τῷ Ἑρμιονικῷ.
8. See pp. 147-9.
9. Cf. Strabo 8.6.21, using the view from the Akrokorinthos in a similar way, and Herakleides 1.9 (Pfister): a view from Pelion.
10. E.g. Frazer (1889) I.xxiv, Chamoux (1974) 86 with the comments by Hutton (2005a) 24-5.
11. Lafond (1994), on natural features see Jacquemin (1991b); cf. Jost (2007) 108-10.
12. Paus. 8.17.6: Ἐκ Φενεοῦ δὲ ἰόντι ἐπὶ ἑσπέρας καὶ ἡλίου δυσμῶν ἡ μὲν ἀριστερὰ τῶν ὁδῶν ἐς πόλιν ἄγει Κλείτορα, ἐν δεξιᾷ δὲ ἐπὶ Νώνακριν καὶ τὸ ὕδωρ τῆς Στυγός. τὸ μὲν δὴ ἀρχαῖον ἡ Νώνακρις πόλισμα ἦν Ἀρκάδων καὶ ἀπὸ τῆς Λυκάονος γυναικὸς τὸ ὄνομα εἰλήφει· τὰ δὲ ἐφ᾽ ἡμῶν ἐρείπια ἦν, οὐδὲ τούτων τὰ πολλὰ ἔτι δῆλα. τῶν δὲ ἐρειπίων οὐ πόρρω κρημνός ἐστιν ὑψηλός, οὐχ ἕτερον δ᾽ ἐς τοσοῦτον ἀνήκοντα ὕψους οἶδα· καὶ ὕδωρ κατὰ τοῦ κρημνοῦ στάζει, καλοῦσι δὲ Ἕλληνες αὐτὸ ὕδωρ Στυγός.
13. Hom. *Od.* 13.96-112, 13.194-6, 13.236-49; cf. 9.106-55.
14. E.g. Theokritos 1, 5, 9, 11. Elliger (1975).
15. Dio Chrysostom 1.52-3: Καὶ δὴ βαδίζων ὡς ἀφ᾽ Ἡραίας εἰς Πῖσαν παρὰ τὸν Ἀλφειὸν μέχρι μέν τινος ἐπετύγχανον τῆς ὁδοῦ, μεταξὺ δὲ εἰς ὕλην τινὰ καὶ δυσχωρίαν ἐμπεσὼν καὶ πλείους ἀτραποὺς ἐπὶ βουκόλι᾽ ἄττα καὶ ποίμνας φερούσας, οὐδενὶ συναντῶν οὐδὲ δυνάμενος ἐρέσθαι. ... ἰδὼν οὖν ἐπὶ ὑψηλῷ τινι δρυῶν συστροφὴν οἷον ἄλσος, ᾠχόμην ὡς ἀποψόμενος ἐντεῦθεν ὁδόν τινα ἢ οἰκίαν. καταλαμβάνω οὖν λίθους

169

τέ τινας εἰκῇ ξυγκειμένους καὶ δέρματα ἱερείων κρεμάμενα καὶ ῥόπαλα καὶ βακτηρίας, νομέων τινῶν ἀναθήματα, ὡς ἐφαίνετο.

16. See Pfister (1952), Arenz (2006).

17. Herakleides 1.8 (Pfister): Ἐντεῦθεν εἰς Τάναγραν στάδια ρλ´· ὁδὸς δι᾽ ἐλαιοφύτου καὶ συνδένδρου χώρας, παντὸς καθαρεύουσα τοῦ ἀπὸ τῶν κλώπων φόβου. Ἡ δὲ πόλις τραχεῖα μὲν καὶ μετέωρος, λευκὴ δὲ τῇ ἐπιφανείᾳ καὶ ἀργιλλώδης· τοῖς δὲ τῶν οἰκιῶν προθύροις καὶ ἐγκαύμασιν ἀναθεματικοῖς κάλλιστα κατεσκευασμένη. See also Arenz (2006) 147-8.

18. E.g. Paus. 5.5.2, 8.35.8, 9.28.1, 10.32.19, 10.36.1-2, cf. 7.21.11, 8.26.1.

19. *Ekphrasis*, description, was part of the usual rhetorical exercises (*progymnasmata*), and this included the description of places and landscapes. Graf (1995) 143-9, Reardon (1971) 155-65.

20. Sordi (1988), Lanzillotta (1988) esp. 20-4.

21. E.g. Paus. 1.22.3-5, 1.36.1-2, 5.20.4-5, 8.11.5-10.

22. Bender (1999).

23. Jacob (1991) 35-63, Janni (1984) 15-19. On maps in general see Dilke (1985); note Gallazzi & Kramer (1998), Kramer (2001): a map of Spain(?) on papyrus.

24. Jacob (1991) 105-31, see also Bagrow (1954).

25. Strabo 8.2.1: Ἔστι τοίνυν ἡ Πελοπόννησος ἐοικυῖα φύλλῳ πλατάνου τὸ σχῆμα, ἴση σχεδόν τι κατὰ μῆκος καὶ κατὰ πλάτος, ὅσον χιλίων καὶ τετρακοσίων σταδίων· τὸ μὲν ἀπὸ τῆς ἑσπέρας ἐπὶ τὴν ἕω, τοῦτο δ᾽ ἐστὶ τὸ ἀπὸ τοῦ Χελωνάτα δι᾽ Ὀλυμπίας καὶ τῆς Μεγαλοπολίτιδος ἐπὶ Ἰσθμόν· τὸ δ᾽ ἀπὸ τοῦ νότου πρὸς τὴν ἄρκτον, ὅ ἐστι τὸ ἀπὸ Μαλεῶν δι᾽ Ἀρκαδίας εἰς Αἴγιον· ἡ δὲ περίμετρος μὴ κατακολπίζοντι τετρακισχιλίων σταδίων. ... ὁ δ᾽ Ἰσθμὸς κατὰ τὸν διολκόν, δι᾽ οὗ τὰ πορθμεῖα ὑπερνεωλκοῦσιν ἀπὸ τῆς ἑτέρας εἰς τὴν ἑτέραν θάλατταν, εἴρηται ὅτι τετταράκοντα σταδίων ἐστίν.

26. Strabo 8.1.3: Ἔστι δὲ πρώτη μὲν τῶν χερρονήσων ἡ Πελοπόννησος, ἰσθμῷ κλειομένη τετταράκοντα σταδίων. δευτέρα δὲ ἡ καὶ ταύτην περιέχουσα, ἧς ἰσθμός ἐστιν ὁ ἐκ Παγῶν τῶν Μεγαρικῶν εἰς Νίσαιαν, τὸ Μεγαρέων ἐπίνειον, ὑπερβολῇ σταδίων ἑκατὸν εἴκοσιν ἀπὸ θαλάττης ἐπὶ θάλατταν. τρίτη δ᾽ ἡ καὶ ταύτην περιέχουσα, ἧς ἰσθμὸς ἀπὸ τοῦ μυχοῦ τοῦ Κρισαίου κόλπου μέχρι Θερμοπυλῶν· ἡ δ᾽ ἐπινοουμένη εὐθεῖα γραμμὴ ὅσον πεντακοσίων ὀκτὼ σταδίων τὴν μὲν Βοιωτίαν ἅπασαν ἐντὸς ἀπολαμβάνουσα, τὴν δὲ Φωκίδα τέμνουσα λοξὴν καὶ τοὺς Ἐπικνημιδίους. τετάρτη δὲ ἡ ἀπὸ τοῦ Ἀμβρακικοῦ κόλπου διὰ τῆς Οἴτης καὶ τῆς Τραχινίας εἰς τὸν Μαλιακὸν κόλπον καθήκοντα ἔχουσα τὸν ἰσθμὸν καὶ τὰς Θερμοπύλας, ὅσον ὀκτακοσίων ὄντα σταδίων· πλείόνων δ᾽ ἢ χιλίων ἄλλος ἐστὶν ἀπὸ τοῦ αὐτοῦ κόλπου τοῦ Ἀμβρακικοῦ διὰ Θετταλῶν καὶ Μακεδόνων εἰς τὸν Θερμαῖον διήκων μυχόν.

27. Jacob (1991) 147-57.

28. Miller (1916), Pritchett (1969-89) III.197-288, Brodersen (2003) 186-7. Talbert (2004) shows that the *Peutinger Table* was shaped by a number of complex concerns (e.g. aspects of design, ideology, format of a papyrus scroll). My argument here is, however, purely concerned with its unique mode of turning physical topography into an abstract diagram.

29. Pseudo-Skylax 44: Καθήκει δὲ ἡ Ἀρκαδία ἐπὶ θάλατταν κατὰ Λέπρεον ἐκ μεσογείας. Εἰσὶ δὲ αὐτῶν πόλεις ἐν μεσογείᾳ αἱ μεγάλαι αἵδε. Τέγεα, Μαντίνεια, Ἡραία, Ὀρχομενός, Στύμφαλος. Εἰσὶ δὲ καὶ ἄλλαι πόλεις. Παράπλους δὲ τῆς Λεπρεατῶν χώρας στάδια ρ´.

30. Plato *Phaidon* 109a-b.

31. Strabo 8.1.3, 9.2.21; Dueck (2000) 40-3, see also Clarke (1999) 198-202, Pretzler (2005c).

32. Strabo 8.8.1: Ἀρκαδία δ᾽ ἐστὶν ἐν μέσῳ μὲν τῆς Πελοποννήσου, πλείστην δὲ χώραν ὀρεινὴν ἀποτέμνεται. ... διὰ δὲ τὴν τῆς χώρας παντελῆ κάκωσιν οὐκ ἂν προσήκοι

μακρολογεῖν περὶ αὐτῶν· αἵ τε γὰρ πόλεις ὑπὸ τῶν συνεχῶν πολέμων ἠφανίσθησαν, ἔνδοξοι γενόμεναι πρότερον, τήν τε χώραν οἱ γεωργήσαντες ἐκλελοίπασιν ἐξ ἐκείνων ἔτι τῶν χρόνων, ἐξ ὧν εἰς τὴν προσαγορευθεῖσαν Μεγάλην πόλιν αἱ πλεῖσται συνῳκίσθησαν. νυνὶ δὲ καὶ αὐτὴ ἡ Μεγάλη πόλις τὸ τοῦ κωμικοῦ πέπονθε καὶ "ἐρημία μεγάλη 'στὶν ἡ Μεγάλη πόλις".

33. See Strabo 8.1.3, 9.1.22. See Di Napoli (2005).

34. Hom. Il. 2.484-760; cf. Fig. 4, p. 7.

35. Paus. 1.1.1, 2.34.7-10, 3.25.4, 9.32.2-4, 10.34.2, 3.23.1-2, 3.24.3, 3.25.9, 7.22.10, 9.32.1; cf. Hutton (2005a) 122-5.

36. Paus. 8.12.5-9: Ἐπὶ δὲ ὁδοῖς ταῖς κατειλεγμέναις δύο ἐς Ὀρχομενόν εἰσιν ἄλλαι, καὶ τῇ μέν ἐστι καλούμενον Λάδα στάδιον, ... καὶ παρ' αὐτὸ ἱερὸν Ἀρτέμιδος καὶ ἐν δεξιᾷ τῆς ὁδοῦ γῆς χῶμα ὑψηλόν· Πηνελόπης δὲ εἶναι τάφον φασίν, ... τοῦ τάφου δὲ ἔχεται τούτου πεδίον οὐ μέγα, καὶ ὄρος ἐστὶν ἐν τῷ πεδίῳ τὰ ἐρείπια ἔτι Μαντινείας ἔχον τῆς ἀρχαίας· καλεῖται δὲ τὸ χωρίον τοῦτο ἐφ' ἡμῶν Πτόλις. κατὰ δὲ τὸ πρὸς ἄρκτον αὐτῆς προελθόντι ὁδὸν οὐ μακρὰν Ἀλαλκομενείας ἐστὶ πηγή, τῆς Πτόλεως δὲ μετὰ σταδίους τριάκοντα κώμης τε ἐρείπια καλουμένης Μαιρᾶς. ... λείπεται δὲ ἔτι τῶν ὁδῶν ἡ ἐς Ὀρχομενόν, καθ' ἥντινα Ἀγχισία τε ὄρος καὶ Ἀγχίσου μνῆμά ἐστιν ὑπὸ τοῦ ὄρους τοῖς ποσίν. ... πρὸς δὲ τοῦ Ἀγχίσου τῷ τάφῳ ἐρείπιά ἐστιν Ἀφροδίτης ἱεροῦ, καὶ Μαντινέων ὅροι πρὸς Ὀρχομενίους καὶ ἐν ταῖς Ἀγχισίαις εἰσίν.

37. Pritchett (1999) 1-22.

38. Cf. Hutton (2005a) 117.

39. Cf. the schematic map of Pausanias' Argolid, p. 71.

40. See pp. 35-9.

41. Frazer (1898) IV.221-2, Jost & Marcadé (1998) 184-6.

42. Paus. 8.30.1, 8.54.1-3, cf. 8.20.1, 8.22.3.

43. Jacob (1980) 41, Snodgrass (1987) 81-6, Hutton (2005a) 120.

44. Hutton (2005a) 118-22 on Paus. 2.25.8, 2.36.4, 2.38.2; cf. Snodgrass (1987) 84 on Paus. 9.26.4, 9.32.5.

45. Jost (2007) 112-14.

46. Hutton (2005a) 86-8; Paus. 10.32.1, 10.32.12-33.1, 10.33.3.

6. A Sense of Time: Pausanias as Historian

1. Paus. 4.36.6: Τοῦ λιμένος δὲ ἡ Σφακτηρία νῆσος προβέβληται, καθάπερ τοῦ ὅρμου τοῦ Δηλίων ἡ Ῥήνεια· ἐοίκασι δὲ αἱ ἀνθρώπειαι τύχαι καὶ χωρία τέως ἄγνωστα ἐς δόξαν προήχθαι. Καφηρέως τε γάρ ἐστιν ὄνομα τοῦ ἐν Εὐβοίᾳ τοῖς σὺν Ἀγαμέμνονι Ἕλλησιν ἐπιγενομένου χειμῶνος ἐνταῦθα, ὡς ἐκομίζοντο ἐξ Ἰλίου· Ψυττάλειάν τε τὴν ἐπὶ Σαλαμῖνι ἴσμεν ἀπολομένων ἐν αὐτῇ τῶν Μήδων. ὡσαύτως δὲ καὶ τὴν Σφακτηρίαν τὸ ἀτύχημα τὸ Λακεδαιμονίων γνώριμον τοῖς πᾶσιν ἐποίησεν.

2. Thuc. 4.8, 4.14, 4.26, 4.31-9.

3. Clarke (1999) passim, esp. 4-128.

4. E.g. Paus. 8.43.3-6, 10.34.5. See Lafond (1996), Arafat (1996).

5. Veyne (1988) 5-15, Chamoux (1996) 55-64.

6. Lacroix (1994).

7. Paus. 3.1.9-10.5 (Sparta), 8.1.4-5.13 (Arkadia).

8. Paus. 1.4.1-6, 1.6.1-8.1, 1.9.1-3, 1.9.5-10.5, 1.11.1-13.9, 1.16.1-3, 1.20.3-4, 1.25.2-26.3 (Athens), 10.19.5-23.14 (Delphi), 2.8.1-9.6 (Aratos), 8.49.2-51.8 (Philopoimen), 9.13.1-15.6 (Epameinondas).

9. Habicht (1985) 95-116, Regenbogen (1956) 1063-76, Segre (2004) 20-4, Ebeling (1913).

10. Hutton (2005a) 295-303.

11. E.g. Polemo of Ilion on the dedications on the Acropolis and on the Sacred Way, Diodoros on monuments and on demes of Attica, Heliodoros on the Acropolis. See Bischoff (1937). Atthidography: Jacoby (1949), Harding (1994) 9-52; see also Day (1980) esp. xv-xvii.

12. Paus. 1.6.1: Τὰ δὲ ἐς Ἄτταλον καὶ Πτολεμαῖον ἡλικίᾳ τε ἦν ἀρχαιότερα, ὡς μὴ μένειν ἔτι τὴν φήμην αὐτῶν, καὶ οἱ συγγενόμενοι τοῖς βασιλεῦσιν ἐπὶ συγγραφῇ τῶν ἔργων καὶ πρότερον ἔτι ἠμελήθησαν· τούτων ἕνεκά μοι καὶ τὰ τῶνδε ἐπῆλθε δηλῶσαι ἔργα τε ὁποῖα ἔπραξαν καὶ ὡς ἐς τοὺς πατέρας αὐτῶν περιεχώρησεν Αἰγύπτου καὶ ἡ Μυσῶν καὶ τῶν προσοίκων ἀρχή.

13. Paus. 1.4.1-6 (Gauls, cf. 10.19.5-23.14), 1.6.1-8.1 (Ptolemy I and II, Attalos I), 1.9.1-3 (Ptolemy IV), 1.9.5-10.5 (Lysimachos), 1.11.1-13.9 (Pyrrhos of Epiros), 1.16.1-3 (Seleukos I); cf. Hutton (2005a) 276.

14. Hutton (2005a) 275-95, Ameling (1996), Bearzot (1992), Regenbogen (1956) 1068-70, Segre (1927); On Hellenistic history in the Roman period also see Arafat (1996) 170-1, Hornblower (1981) 72.

15. Cf. Hutton (2005a) 275-95.

16. Paus. 1.3.5 (portrait painting in the Bouleuterion: Athenian commander against the Gauls, 1.6.1 (eponymous heroes, include Ptolemy and Attalos), 1.8.6, 1.9.5, 1.11.1, 1.16.1 (statues of Egyptian kings, of Lysimachos, Pyrrhos and Seleukos respectively).

17. Hutton (2005a) 296-8; Paus. 1.34.1 (Oropos), 1.35.2-3 (Salamis; includes a report of how the people of Salamis were expelled in the early Hellenistic period), 1.39.4-6 (Megara).

18. Hutton (2005a) 298-300, Hall (1997) 67-107.

19. Paus. 3.1.1-10.5, 4.1.1-29.13, 5.1.3-5.1, 7.1.1-17.4, 8.1.4-6.3, 9.1.1 (but note the substantial introduction to Thebes 9.5.1-7.6), 10.38.1-3 (Ozolian Lokrians).

20. Musti (1996) 16-17.

21. Earliest example in the *Periegesis*: 5.4.7-5.1; Hutton (2005a) 301-3.

22. Paus. 8.6.1-3: Κοινῇ δὲ Ἀρκάσιν ὑπῆρχεν ἐς μνήμην τὰ μὲν ἀρχαιότατα ὁ πρὸς Ἰλίῳ πόλεμος, δεύτερα δὲ ὁπόσα ἀμύνοντες Μεσσηνίοις Λακεδαιμονίων ἐναντία ἐμαχέσαντο· μέτεστι δὲ καὶ πρὸς Μήδους σφίσιν ἔργου τοῦ ἐν Πλαταιαῖς. Λακεδαιμονίοις δὲ ἀνάγκῃ πλέον καὶ οὐ μετ' εὐνοίας ἐπί τε Ἀθηναίους συνεστρατεύσαντο καὶ ἐς τὴν Ἀσίαν μετὰ Ἀγησιλάου διέβησαν, καὶ δὴ καὶ ἐς Λεῦκτρα αὐτοῖς τὰ Βοιωτικὰ ἠκολούθησαν. ... Φιλίππῳ δὲ καὶ Μακεδόσιν ἐν Χαιρωνείᾳ καὶ ὕστερον ἐν Θεσσαλίᾳ πρὸς Ἀντίπατρον οὐκ ἐμαχέσαντο μετὰ Ἑλλήνων, οὐ μὴν οὐδὲ τοῖς Ἕλλησιν ἐναντία ἐτάξαντο. πρὸς Γαλάτας δὲ τοῦ ἐν Θερμοπύλαις κινδύνου φασὶ Λακεδαιμονίων ἕνεκα οὐ μετασχεῖν, ἵνα μή σφισιν οἱ Λακεδαιμόνιοι κακουργοῖεν τὴν γῆν ἀπόντων τῶν ἐν ἡλικίᾳ· συνεδρίου δὲ τῶν Ἀχαιῶν μετέσχον οἱ Ἀρκάδες προθυμότατα Ἑλλήνων.

23. Hutton (2005a) 63-4, 302-3, Habicht (1985) 105-8, Alcock (1996) 251-60, Swain (1996) 333-8, Bearzot (1992) 17-20; general views at the time: Touloumakos (1971) 60-4, Segre (2004) 20-4.

24. E.g. Paus. 1.32.1-5 (Marathon), 1.36.1-2 (Salamis), 8.10.5-8, 8.11.5-10 (Mantinea), 9.2.5-6 (Plataia), 9.40.7-10 (Chaironeia). On battlefields and memorials see Alcock (2002) 75-81.

25. Paus. 8.11.5-12, 9.15.5.

26. E.g. Paus. 7.2.5-5.13 (Ionians), 8.7.5-8 (Philip II and his successors), 8.49.2-51.8 (Philopoimen).

27. Musti (1996) 17-18.

28. Paus. 8.7.1-12.9, esp. 8.8.12, 8.9.7-9, 8.10.1-2, 8.11.8.

29. Paus. 4.29.12 (Messenian history), 8.27.16 (Megalopolis).

30. Paus. 8.49.2-52.6. Pausanias' interest in epigrams: Chamoux (2001), on this epigram also Bearzot (1995) 707-9.

31. Habicht (1985) 95-97, 110, for examples of criticism see 98-100; e.g. Holleaux (1898) 193-206, (1938) I.187-93.

32. See Pretzler (2005b).

33. Pretzler (2005a) 241-3.

34. Paus. 1.38.7, 4.2.3, 4.33.1, 8.53.5, 9.16.7; see also 1.14.7, 2.1.6, 2.12.3, 2.20.5, 2.31.9, 2.32.2, 3.13.2, 4.4.3, 5.6.2, 10.6.5; Cf. Lucian *Philops.* 2-4.

35. E.g. Paus. 3.16.7-8, 8.11.5-6, see also 4.4.3.

36. Paus. 2.21.5, see also 3.25.5-6 (Hekataios' rationalised Kerberos, *FGrHist* 1 fr. 27), 9.2.3-4, 2.11.5.

37. E.g. Paus. 2.37.4, cf. Paus. 1.41.5, 2.1.6, 1.20.5, 2.26.7, 4.4.1-6, 5.1.9.

38. E.g. Paus. 2.17.4, 3.19.5, 5.5.9, 9.8.1, 9.10.1; cf. Lucian *Hist. Conscr.* 60.

39. E.g. Paus. 2.37.2-3 (dialect provides a rough date for an inscription and a ritual, the argument is taken from another author); see also 6.12.8-9, 6.4.6-7, 6.9.4-5 (combination of sources), 2.36.1, 5.21.3-16, 5.23.1-3, 8.42.9-10, 10.7.6, 10.33.9, 10 36.9 (inscriptions), 2.7.8, 7.19.9-10 (rituals), 2.30.6 (coins), 1.39.4, 5.8.6, 9.10.4 (artefacts).

40. Paus. 2.21.10, cf 1.38.7. Homer compared to other sources: 1.28.7, 3.24.10-11, 9.41.2-5; other authors compared: 2.1.1, 2.6.5, 9.18.6, 10.32.9.

41. Alcock (1996) 262-5.

42. Paus. 4.2.1: Πυθέσθαι δὲ σπουδῇ πάνυ ἐθελήσας, οἵ τινες παῖδες Πολυκάονι ἐγένοντο ἐκ Μεσσήνης, ἐπελεξάμην τάς τε Ἠοίας καλουμένας καὶ τὰ ἔπη τὰ Ναυπάκτια, πρὸς δὲ αὐτοῖς ὁπόσα Κιναίθων καὶ Ἄσιος ἐγενεαλόγησαν. οὐ μὴν ἔς γε ταῦτα ἦν σφισιν οὐδὲν πεποιημένον, ἀλλὰ Ὕλλου μὲν τοῦ Ἡρακλέους θυγατρὶ Εὐαίχμῃ συνοικῆσαι Πολυκάονα υἱὸν Βούτου λεγούσας τὰς μεγάλας οἶδα Ἠοίας, τὰ δὲ ἐς τὸν Μεσσήνης ἄνδρα καὶ τὰ ἐς αὐτὴν Μεσσήνην παρεῖταί σφισι.

43. Paus. 1.28.7; 8.6.1, cf. Roy (1968).

44. Paus. 2.4.5, 5.1.3, 7.17.5, 9.6.1; Chamoux (1996) 57-9.

45. Habicht (1985) 97-8, Cameron (2004) 236-7; cf. Stadter (1989) xliv-li.

46. Regenbogen (1956) 1070; see also Amboglio (1991), Eide (1992) 124-23. Studies of Pausanias' sources: Meadows (1995), Pearson (1962) esp. 408-14, Bearzot (1992), Segre (1927) 214-22, Fischbach (1893), Kalkmann (1886).

47. Habicht (1985) 97-8, Regenbogen (1956) 1070-1, Segre (2004) 113-24, 157-215, for Polybios see 205-11.

48. Meadows (1995), 113, Bearzot (1992) 283-4.

49. Paus. 1.9.8, 1.13.9, 6.7.7.

50. Paus. 4.6.1-6; Meyer (1978) 242-46, Marinescu-Himu (1975), Pearson (1962), Kroymann (1943), Ebeling (1892); cf. Tyrtaios frg. 5, Diod. 15.66.3-4.

51. Rhianos is quoted in Paus. 4.17.11, Tyrtaios is quoted in 4.13.6 and 4.15.2 and cited frequently. Auberger (2005) 138-9; cf. Auberger (1992) and (2000)

52. See Moggi (2001).

53. Examples where this system is used: Paus. 2.14.4 (note the alternative Arkadian genealogy: Pelasgos son of Arkas), 3.24.11, 8.5.1 (correcting 1.41.2), 8.15.6-7, 10.17.4.

54. Cameron (2004) 219, 237-8, 247-9.

55. Paus. 3.1.8-10.5 (Sparta), 8.1.4-5.13 (Arkadia). See Meadows (1995), Hiller (1927) 1-8.

56. Paus. 3.1.8-6.9 (Agiadai), 3.7.1-10.5 (Eurypontidai); see Meadows (1995).

57. Paus. 8.42.8-10, cf. Hdt. 7.145, 7.153-163. Zizza (2006) nn. 42-3, 328-32. Onatas worked during the Persian Wars. Hieron's monument was among his later works. See Lippold (1939). Other examples: Paus. 6.4.6-7, 6.9.4-5 with a similar mistake, see Frazer (1898) I.lxxv-vi; Paus. 10.36.9.

58. Paus. 2.24.7, 4.5.10, 4.13.7, 4.15.1, 4.23.4, 2.23.9, 4.24.5, 4.27.9, 6.5.3, 6.9.5, 6.12.2, 7.16.10, 7.25.4, 8.27.8, 8.39.3, 8.45.4, 10.2.3, 10.3.1, 10.5.13, 10.23.14.

59. E.g. Paus. 8.27.8 (foundation of Megalopolis, date: 371/70 BC), cf. Hornblower (1990), Hejnic (1961) 111-18. See also 7.16.10: fall of Corinth, incorrect date 140/39 BC), cf. Moggi & Osanna (2003) 421.

60. Paus. 10.2.3.

61. Thuc. 2.1.1; cf. Rood (1998) 109-30; cf. Cameron (2004) 238-43 on genealogical lists in mythographical works.

62. E.g. Paus. 1.4.1-6, 10.19.5-23.14 (Gallic attack on Delphi); 8.11.5-12, 9.15.5. (death of Epameinondas). Similar events treated differently: Paus. 8.10.5-8 (battle of Mantinea *c.* 250?), 8.11.5-7 (battle of Mantinea 362, focusing on Epameinondas' death). Cf. Xen. *Hell.* 7.5.18-27.

63. Paus. 10.22.3-4: Καὶ τὰ ἐς Καλλιέας Κόμβουτις οἱ ἐργασάμενοι καὶ Ὀρεστόριος ἦσαν, ἀνοσιώτατά τε ὧν ἀκοῇ ἐπιστάμεθα καὶ οὐδὲν τοῖς ἀνθρώπων τολμήμασιν ὅμοια. γένος μέν γε πᾶν ἐξέκοψαν τὸ ἄρσεν, καὶ ὁμοίως γέροντές τε καὶ τὰ νήπια ἐπὶ τῶν μητέρων τοῖς μαστοῖς ἐφονεύετο· τούτων δὲ καὶ τὰ ὑπὸ τοῦ γάλακτος πιότερα ἀποκτείνοντες ἔπινόν τε οἱ Γαλάται τοῦ αἵματος καὶ ἥπτοντο τῶν σαρκῶν. γυναῖκες δὲ καὶ ὅσαι ἐν ὥρᾳ τῶν παρθένων, ὅσαι μὲν φρονήματός τι αὐτῶν εἶχον, ἑαυτὰς ἔφθησαν ὡς ἡλίσκετο ἡ πόλις διειργασμέναι· τὰς δὲ ἔτι περιούσας ἐς ἰδέαν ὕβρεως πᾶσαν μετὰ ἀνάγκης ἦγον ἰσχυρᾶς, ἅτε ἴσον μὲν ἐλέου, ἴσον δὲ τὰς φύσεις καὶ ἔρωτος ἀπέχοντες. καὶ ὅσαι μὲν τῶν γυναικῶν ταῖς μαχαίραις τῶν Γαλατῶν ἐπετύγχανον, αὐτοχειρίᾳ τὰς ψυχὰς ἠφίεσαν· ταῖς δὲ οὐ μετὰ πολὺ ὑπάρξειν τὸ χρεὼν ἔμελλεν ἥ τε ἀσιτία καὶ ἡ ἀυπνία, ἀστέγων βαρβάρων ἐκ διαδοχῆς ἀλλήλοις ὑβριζόντων· οἱ δὲ καὶ ἀφιείσαις τὰς ψυχάς, οἱ δὲ καὶ ἤδη νεκραῖς συνεγίνοντο ὅμως.

64. Polyb. 2.56.5-12. See Walbank (1962).

65. Ameling (1996) 149.

66. Paus. 7.16.7-8: Ἀχαιῶν δὲ οἱ ἐς Κόρινθον ἀποσωθέντες μετὰ τὴν μάχην ἀπεδίδρασκον ὑπὸ νύκτα εὐθύς· ἀπεδίδρασκον δὲ καὶ αὐτῶν Κορινθίων οἱ πολλοί. Μόμμιος δὲ τὸ μὲν παραυτίκα, ἀναπεπταμένων ὅμως τῶν πυλῶν, ἐπεῖχεν ἐς τὴν Κόρινθον παρελθεῖν, ὑποκαθῆσθαί τινα ἐντὸς τοῦ τείχους ὑποπτεύων ἐνέδραν· τρίτῃ δὲ ἡμέρᾳ μετὰ τὴν μάχην ᾕρει τε κατὰ κράτος καὶ ἔκαιε Κόρινθον. τῶν δὲ ἐγκαταληφθέντων τὸ μὲν πολὺ οἱ Ῥωμαῖοι φονεύουσι, γυναῖκας δὲ καὶ παῖδας ἀπέδοτο Μόμμιος· ἀπέδοτο δὲ καὶ οἰκέτας, ὅσοι τῶν ἐς ἐλευθερίαν ἀφεθέντων καὶ μαχεσαμένων μετὰ Ἀχαιῶν μὴ εὐθὺς ὑπὸ τοῦ πολέμου τὸ ἔργον ἐτεθνήκεσαν. ἀναθημάτων δὲ καὶ τοῦ ἄλλου κόσμου τὰ μὲν μάλιστα ἀνήκοντα ἐς θαῦμα ἀνήγετο, τὰ δὲ ἐκείνοις οὐχ ὁμοίου λόγου Φιλοποίμενι ὁ Μόμμιος τῷ παρ' Ἀττάλου στρατηγῷ δίδωσι· καὶ ἦν Περγαμηνοῖς καὶ ἐς ἐμὲ ἔτι λάφυρα Κορίνθια. Cf. Paus. 2.1.2, 2.2.2, 5.10.5.

67. E.g. Cic. *Off.* 3.46. See Arafat (1996) 90-7.

68. E.g. Thuc. 5.116.3-4. Cf. Hutton (2005a) 219-21, Strid (1976), Fischbach (1893). Eide (1992) argues against a strong Thucydidean influence.

69. See Moggi (1993), Segre (1927) 207-14; cf. Auberger (2001) on Messenian history.

70. Hutton (2005a) 191-213, Bowie (2001) 26-7, Moggi (1996) 83-7, Ameling (1996) 147-9, Meadows (1995) 94-6, Musti (1984) 7-18, Heer (1979) 97-9, Segre (1927) 207-9, Segre (2004) 40-5, Gurlitt (1890) 15-20.

71. Paus. 10.19.5-23.14; cf. 1.4. See Ameling (1996) 148-52. See also Alcock (1996) 251-8.

72. Paus. 10.19.5, 10.19.11, 10.20.1-5 (Pausanias' comments), 10.19.12 (thoughts of the Greeks).

73. See Bowie (1996) 213-15.

74. Paus. 8.52.1-5 (benefactors), 7.10.1-5 (traitors). Cf. 7.25.1-4 (crimes against suppliants).

75. Paus. 8.46.1-4; cf. 7.18.8-9. 7.21.1, 9.27.3-4.

76. E.g. Paus. 1.6.7, 1.16.3, 1.17.1, 1.20.7, 1.36.3, 2.9.4-5, 3.4.5-6, 3.10.4-5, 4.17.3-5, 7.10.1-5, 9.2-3, 9.32.9-10.

77. Paus. 8.7.5: Φίλιππον δὲ βασιλέων μὲν τῶν πρὸ αὐτοῦ καὶ ὅσοι Μακεδόσι γεγόνασιν ὕστερον, τούτων μὲν πείθοιτο ἄν τις μέγιστα αὐτὸν ἔργα ἐπιδείξασθαι· στρατηγὸν δὲ ἀγαθὸν οὐκ ἄν τις φρονῶν ὀρθὰ καλέσειεν αὐτόν, ὅς γε καὶ ὅρκους θεῶν κατεπάτησεν ἀεὶ καὶ σπονδὰς ἐπὶ παντὶ ἐψεύσατο πίστιν τε ἠτίμασε μάλιστα ἀνθρώπων.

78. Paus. 8.7.6: Καί οἱ τὸ ἐκ τοῦ θεοῦ μήνιμα ἀπήντησεν οὐκ ὀψέ, πρῶτα δὲ ὧν ἴσμεν. Φίλιππος μὲν οὐ πρόσω βιώσας ἕξ τε καὶ τεσσαράκοντα ἐτῶν τὸ μάντευμα ἐξετέλεσε τὸ ἐκ Δελφῶν, ὃ δὴ χρωμένῳ οἱ περὶ τοῦ Πέρσου γενέσθαι λέγουσιν, "ἔστεπται μὲν ὁ ταῦρος, ἔχει τέλος, ἔστιν ὁ θύσων"· τοῦτο μὲν δὴ οὐ μετὰ πολὺ ἐδήλωσεν οὐκ ἐς τὸν Μῆδον, ἀλλὰ ἐς αὐτὸν ἔχον Φίλιππον.

79. Paus. 8.7.8: Εἰ δὲ τῶν ἐς Γλαῦκον τὸν Σπαρτιάτην ἐποιήσατο ὁ Φίλιππος λόγον καὶ τὸ ἔπος ἐφ᾽ ἑκάστου τῶν ἔργων ἀνεμίμνησκεν αὐτόν, "ἀνδρὸς δ᾽ εὐόρκου γενεὴ μετόπισθεν ἀρείων", οὐκ ἂν οὕτω δίχα λόγου δοκεῖ μοι θεῶν τις Ἀλεξάνδρου τε ὁμοῦ τὸν βίον καὶ ἀκμὴν τὴν Μακεδόνων σβέσαι.

80. Paus. 7.7.1-16.10.

81. Paus. 1.20.7, 9.33.6 (Sulla), 9.27.3-4 (Caligula, Nero). Other examples of divine vengeance as a factor in history: 1.36.3, 2.9.4-5. 2.18.2, 3.4.5-6, 3.10.4-5, 3.12.7, 3.23.5, 4.17.2-6, 4.24.6, 4.26.4, 7.15.6, 7.24.6-7, 7.25.1-4, 9.2.3, 9.25.9-10, 10.11.2, 10.33.2. See Elliger (2005) 188-91, 199-202, Segre (2004) 137-49.

82. Thuc. 1.20.

83. Polyb. 4.2, 12.25-28, 15.36, 20.12.8, Lucian *Hist. Conscr.* 15, 26 (imitation of Thucydides), 42, 57 (Thucydides as ideal).

84. See Lucian *Hist. Conscr.* 47-9, Avenarius (1956) 71-85, Porod (2007). On Pausanias and Thucydides see Hutton (2005a) 219-21, Segre (2004) 45-8, Fischbach (1893); cf. Eide (1992).

85. E.g. Paus. 9.9.1, 8.2.4-5, cf. 1.38.7, 3.13.2, 4.2.3, 8.53.5, 9.16.7. See Arafat (1996) 58-79, Sidebottom (2002).

86. Paus. 4.32.4-6, 8.10.8-9; cf. 1.32.5, 10.23.1-2, cf. Veyne (1988) 95-102.

87. Bowie (1996) 214-16.

7. Describing a City

1. Paus. 10.4.1-2: Στάδια δὲ ἐκ Χαιρωνείας εἴκοσιν ἐς Πανοπέας ἐστὶ πόλιν Φωκέων, εἴγε ὀνομάσαι τις πόλιν καὶ τούτους οἷς γε οὐκ ἀρχεῖα οὐ γυμνάσιόν ἐστιν, οὐ θέατρον οὐκ ἀγορὰν ἔχουσιν, οὐχ ὕδωρ κατερχόμενον ἐς κρήνην, ἀλλὰ ἐν στέγαις κοίλαις κατὰ τὰς καλύβας μάλιστα τὰς ἐν τοῖς ὄρεσιν, ἐνταῦθα οἰκοῦσιν ἐπὶ χαράδρα. ὅμως δὲ ὅροι γε τῆς χώρας εἰσὶν αὐτοῖς ἐς τοὺς ὁμόρους, καὶ ἐς τὸν σύλλογον συνέδρους καὶ οὗτοι πέμπουσι τὸν Φωκικόν. ... Πανοπέων δὲ τὸν ἀρχαῖον θεώμενοι περίβολον ἑπτὰ εἶναι σταδίων μάλιστα εἰκάζομεν· ὑπῆει τε ἐπὼν ἡμᾶς τῶν Ὁμήρου μνήμη ὧν ἐποίησεν ἐς Τιτυόν, καλλίχορον τῶν Πανοπέων ὀνομάσας τὴν πόλιν, καὶ ὡς ἐν τῇ μάχῃ τῇ ἐπὶ τῷ Πατρόκλου νεκρῷ καὶ Σχεδίον τὸν Ἰφίτου βασιλεύοντα Φωκέων καὶ ἀποθανόντα ὑφ᾽ Ἕκτορος κατοικεῖν εἶπεν ἐν τῷ Πανοπεῖ.

2. Paus. 8.33, cf. 8.13.2-3, 9.7.6, 10.32.10, 10.33.1-2, 10.33.8; see Porter (2001).

3. Finley (1977) 305-6, cf. Alcock (1995), Rubinstein (1995), see also Elsner (1994) 251-2.

4. Paus. 10.33.12: Ἀμφικλείας δὲ ἀπωτέρω σταδίοις πεντεκαίδεκά ἐστι Τιθρώνιον ἐν πεδίῳ κειμένη· παρέχεται δὲ οὐδὲν ἐς μνήμην. ἐκ Τιθρωνίου δὲ εἴκοσιν ἐς Δρυμαίαν στάδιοι.

5. Ledon: Paus. 10.33.1. Alcock (1995) esp. 329-31, Hutton (2005a) 127-32.

6. Paus. 8.22.1-9; Williams et al. (1997) 43, see also Williams et al. (2002); cf. Snodgrass (1987) 120-1.

7. Hom. *Il.* 2.511 (Catalogue of Ships), 17.307-11 (the death of Schedios), Hom. *Od.* 11.581.

8. Paus. 10.4.2. Fortifications: see Winter (1971) 146, 172-3, 248, Osborne (1987) 117-18.

9. Paus. 10.4.3.

10. Cf. Hutton (2005b) on Pausanias' 're-hellenising' description of Roman Corinth.

11. Paus. 8.44.7-54.6, Goldmann (1991).

12. Hom. *Il.* 2.607; Hdt. 1.66-8, 9.26-8, 9.56, 9.60-2, 9.70; Thuc. 4.134, 5.32, 5.62, 5.67-78; Xen. *Hell.* 6.5.6-9, 6.5.10-21, 7.5.5-8.

13. Hdt. 1.66, 9.70, Strabo 8.8.2; cf. Pretzler (1999) 108.

14. Paus. 8.45.4. Dugas et al. (1924), Picard (1983).

15. Dugas (1921), Dugas et al. (1924), Østby (1986), Voyatzis (1990), (1997).

16. Ødegård (2005), Ødegård pers. com.

17. Olympia: Paus. 5.14.4, 5.14.10 (5.14.4-15.10: altars), 5.21.1 (5.21.2-24.10: statues of Zeus), 5.25.5 (5.25.2-27.12: dedications), 6.1.1 (6.1.1-18.7: statues of athletes); Athens: 1.1.2-5 (harbours), 1.18.9 (Hadrian's foundations), 1.28.8-11 (lawcourts), 1.31.1-6 (demes), 1.32.1-2 (mountains), 1.35.1-36.2 (islands).

18. E.g. Robert (1909) 330 with Vanderpool (1949) esp. 130, Hutton (2005a) 140-1 (Athenian agora).

19. Bommelaer (2001); see also Habicht (1985) 71-3, Jacquemin (2001).

20. Hutton (2005a) 145-74, Torelli (2001), Osanna (2001).

21. Hutton (2005a) 132-66.

22. Paus. 8.45.4-8.47.3. Ødegård (2005), Ødegård pers. com.

23. Paus. 8.45.4-5.

24. Paus. 8.48.1-8 (agora), 8.49.1. (theatre), 8.49.1-52.6. (Philopoimen). On this passage see also pp. 39-40, 80.

25. Paus. 8.53.6-11: Τεγεάταις δὲ τοῦ Ἀγυιέως τὰ ἀγάλματα τέσσαρά εἰσιν ἀριθμόν, ὑπὸ φυλῆς ἐν ἑκάστης ἱδρυμένον. ... ἔστι δὲ καὶ Δήμητρος ἐν Τεγέᾳ καὶ Κόρης ναός, ἃς ἐπονομάζουσι Καρποφόρους, πλησίον δὲ Ἀφροδίτης καλουμένης Παφίας· ... τούτου δέ ἐστιν οὐ πόρρω Διονύσου τε ἱερὰ δύο καὶ Κόρης βωμὸς καὶ Ἀπόλλωνος ναὸς καὶ ἄγαλμα ἐπίχρυσον. ... παρὰ δὲ τῷ Ἀπόλλωνι ὁ Χειρίσοφος ἕστηκε λίθου πεποιημένος. καλοῦσι δὲ οἱ Τεγεᾶται καὶ ἑστίαν Ἀρκάδων κοινήν· ἐνταῦθά ἐστιν ἄγαλμα Ἡρακλέους. ... τὸ δὲ χωρίον τὸ ὑψηλόν, ἐφ' οὗ καὶ οἱ βωμοὶ Τεγεάταις εἰσὶν οἱ πολλοί, καλεῖται μὲν Διὸς Κλαρίου. ... ἐθεασάμην δὲ καὶ ἄλλα ἐν Τεγέᾳ τοσάδε, Ἀλέου οἰκίαν καὶ Ἐχέμου μνῆμα καὶ ἐπειργασμένην ἐς στήλην τὴν Ἐχέμου πρὸς Ὕλλον μάχην. ... Ἐκ Τεγέας δὲ ἰόντι ἐς τὴν Λακωνικὴν ἔστι μὲν βωμὸς ἐν ἀριστερᾷ τῆς ὁδοῦ Πανός, ἔστι δὲ καὶ Λυκαίου Διός.

26. Cf. Bommelaer (2001).

27. Paus. 8.45.1-3: Τεγεᾶται δὲ ἐπὶ μὲν Τεγεάτου τοῦ Λυκάονος τῇ χώρᾳ φασὶν ἀπ' αὐτοῦ γενέσθαι μόνη τὸ ὄνομα, τοῖς δὲ ἀνθρώποις κατὰ δήμους εἶναι τὰς οἰκήσεις. ... ἐπὶ δὲ Ἀφείδαντος βασιλεύοντος καὶ ἔνατός σφισι δῆμος προσεγένετο Ἀφείδαντες· τῆς δὲ ἐφ' ἡμῶν πόλεως οἰκιστὴς ἐγένετο Ἄλεος. Τεγεάταις δὲ παρὲξ ἢ τὰ Ἀρκάδων κοινά, ἐν οἷς ἔστι μὲν ὁ πρὸς Ἰλίῳ πόλεμος, ἔστι δὲ τὰ Μηδικά τε καὶ ἐν Διπαιεῦσιν ὁ πρὸς Λακεδαιμονίους ἀγών, παρὲξ οὖν τῶν καταλελεγμένων ἰδίᾳ Τεγεάταις ἐστὶν αὐτοῖς

τοσάδε ἐς δόξαν. τὸν γὰρ ἐν Καλυδῶνι ὗν Ἀγκαῖος ὑπέμεινεν ὁ Λυκούργου τρωθείς. ...
Ἡρακλειδῶν δὲ ἐς Πελοπόννησον κατιόντων Ἔχεμος ὁ Ἀερόπου Τεγεάτης ἐμονομάχησεν
ἰδίᾳ πρὸς Ὕλλον, καὶ ἐκράτησε τοῦ Ὕλλου τῇ μάχῃ. Λακεδαιμονίους τε οἱ Τεγεᾶται
πρῶτοι Ἀρκάδων σφίσιν ἐπιστρατεύσαντας ἐνίκησαν καὶ αἰχμαλώτους αἱροῦσιν αὐτῶν
τοὺς πολλούς.

28. Sophokles *Aleaidai, Mysoi, Achaion Syllogos* and a satyr play *Telephos*;
Euripides *Auge, Telephos*. For the versions of the story see Schwenn (1934),
Bauchhenss-Thüriedl (1971) 1-13, Strauß (1994).

29. Paus. 8.45.6-7, cf. Apollod. 3.9.2, Jost & Marcadé (1998) 270-2.

30. Hom. *Il.* 2.607, Hdt. 1.66-8, 7.202, 9.26, 9.35, 9.56, 9.60-2, 9.70.

31. Paus. 8.1.4-5.13.

32. Paus. 8.48.4-5, cf. 3.7.3.

33. Paus. 8.6.1-3.

34. Hdt. 1.66, 9.70.

35. Paus. 8.45.6-7. Pausanias' identification of the scenes is confirmed by the
remains of the sculptures: Sculptures: Dugas et al. (1924) 86-7, 105, Steward
(1977) 5-84, Picard (1983).

36. Paus. 8.47.2-3. Temples as 'exhibition space' for special objects: Casson
(1994) 238-52, Arafat (1995).

37. Paus. 8.46.1-5

38. Hdt. 1.66.

39. Hdt. 1.67.1, Paus. 8.48.5.

40. Paus. 8.48.4-5. Jost (1985) 516-7, Moggi (2005).

41. Hdt. 1.67-8, Paus. 8.54.4.

42. Paus. 8.53.9, cf. 2.18.7, 3.1.4-5, 3.15.3-6, 3.19.7.

43. Auge and Telephos exposed together: Hekataios (*FGrHist* 1) fr. 29; Telephos
suckled by a doe: Apollod. 2.4.7, 3.9.1, perhaps from Euripides' *Auge*: Webster
(1967) 238-41.

44. Paus. 8.47.4 (spring), 8.48.7. (temple; comment on contradictory versions),
8.54.6 (*temenos* of Telephos). See Jost (1998) esp. 230-2.

45. Tegeates: 8.48.6, 8.53.1-4; Apheidas: 8.44.8, 8.48.8, 8.53.6, 8.53.9; Aleos:
8.45.4, 8.53.10.

46. Paus. 8.49.1, 8.53.9, 8.48.1, 8.47.6.

47. See Alcock (2002) 36-98, cf. Lucian *Philops.* 3-4.

48. Thompson & Wycherley (1972) 160-8, Alcock (2002) 51-70; for a possible
example see Pikoulas (1986).

49. Hdt. 9.56, 9.60-2, 9.70; on the importance of the Persian War tradition see
Spawforth (1994).

50. For a detailed discussion see Pretzler (1999).

51. Alcock (1996), Dalfen (1996).

52. Frazer (1898) xxxiii-iv, Habicht (1985) 131-2, Arafat (1996) 38-41; cf. Pliny
NH 34.52.

53. Jost (1985) 147.

54. Paus. 8.53.11 (two temples), 8.54.5.

55. Cf. Goldmann (1991), Lacroix (1994) 92-7.

56. See Lucian *Philops.* esp. 3-4; in *Electrum* Lucian subverts the theme: the
visitor looks for traces of 'famous stories' and the locals refuse to humour him.

57. Jost & Marcadé (1998) 272.

58. Hesiod fr. 165 (Merkelbach-West). Hekataios (*FGrHist* 1) fr. 29 (written
after 490 BC). The transfer to Arkadia may be due to a misinterpretation of
Hesiod's text. See Strauß (1994).

Notes to pages 102-108

59. Paus. 5.14.4-10.

60. E.g. Paus. 2.7.8, 3.20.7, 5.14.4-15.10, 7.20.8, 7.21.6, 8.15.9, 8.39.5, 9.3.5-8, 9.4.3; See Polignac (1995) esp. 60-81, Kowalzig (2005).

61. Paus. 2.14.1-4, 8.15.1-3, see also 3.20.5, 8.25.2-3, 8.29.5, 9.4.3; see Jost (1985) 311-12, 318-19.

62. Elsner (2001a) 18-9, Jacquemin (1991a).

63. Lightfoot (2003), on the use of Ionian Greek see 91-158, Hutton (2005a) 195-211, Elsner (2001b).

64. Paus. 9.39.5-14.

65. E.g. Lucian *Dea Syria* 16, 28: phalloi dedicated by Dionysos, 300 fathoms (*c.* 600 m) high.

66. Lightfoot (2003) 161-74, 218.

67. Note that the description of cities was a standard theme for orators: see Menander Rhetor I.2. p. 353.4-359.10.

8. Considering Works of Art

1. Paus. 1.24.5, 7: Ἐς δὲ τὸν ναὸν ὃν Παρθενῶνα ὀνομάζουσιν, ἐς τοῦτον ἐσιοῦσιν ὁπόσα ἐν τοῖς καλουμένοις ἀετοῖς κεῖται, πάντα ἐς τὴν Ἀθηνᾶς ἔχει γένεσιν, τὰ δὲ ὄπισθεν ἡ Ποσειδῶνος πρὸς Ἀθηνᾶν ἐστιν ἔρις ὑπὲρ τῆς γῆς· αὐτὸ δὲ ἔκ τε ἐλέφαντος τὸ ἄγαλμα καὶ χρυσοῦ πεποίηται. μέσῳ μὲν οὖν ἐπίκειταί οἱ τῷ κράνει Σφιγγὸς εἰκών ..., καθ᾽ ἑκάτερον δὲ τοῦ κράνους γρῦπές εἰσιν ἐπειργασμένοι. ... τὸ δὲ ἄγαλμα τῆς Ἀθηνᾶς ὀρθόν ἐστιν ἐν χιτῶνι ποδήρει καί οἱ κατὰ τὸ στέρνον ἡ κεφαλὴ Μεδούσης ἐλέφαντός ἐστιν ἐμπεποιημένη· καὶ Νίκην τε ὅσον τεσσάρων πηχῶν, ἐν δὲ τῇ χειρὶ δόρυ ἔχει, καί οἱ πρὸς τοῖς ποσὶν ἀσπίς τε κεῖται καὶ πλησίον τοῦ δόρατος δράκων ἐστίν· εἴη δ᾽ ἂν Ἐριχθόνιος οὗτος ὁ δράκων. ἔστι δὲ τῷ βάθρῳ τοῦ ἀγάλματος ἐπειργασμένη Πανδώρας γένεσις.

2. Hopper (1971) 159-68, 182-8, Gaifman (2006) 260-72.

3. Letter to Parliament, quoted in Smith (1916) 334; see St Clair (1967) 221-9.

4. Kreilinger (1997) 476. For Pausanias' impact on art history see pp. 121-5.

5. Arafat (1995); cf. Pliny *NH* 34.37.

6. Full name: A.C.P. de Tubières, Compte de Caylus.

7. Caylus (1752-86) II.105-8.

8. Paus. 10.25-31.12, cf. 1.15.1-3, 1.22.6-7.

9. Paus. 10.25-31, 5.17.5-5.19.10, see also 3.18.9-19.2 (throne of Apollo at Amyklai), 5.11.1-11 (Zeus of Olympia).

10. E.g. Stansbury-O'Donnell (1989) and (1990), based on Paus. 10.25.1-31.12 (Knidian Lesche); Stuart Jones (1894), based on 5.17.5-19.10 (chest of Kypselos), see also Snodgrass (2001).

11. Cf. Paus. 5.17.6, 10.25.3, 10.31.9. He also discussed the Chest of Kypselos with local guides: 5.18.6.

12. Habicht (1985) 131-2.

13. E.g. Dio Chrysostom 12 (*Olympic Discourse*). The élite also had a personal interest in honorary statues: see Dio Chrysostom 32 (*Rhodians*), Favorinus (= Dio Chrysostom 37), Cic. *Att.* 6.1.26. Cf. Blanck (1969), Ma (2006).

14. Elsner (1998), Arafat (1996) 45-75.

15. E.g. Paus. 10.17.12; cf. Arrian *Periplous* 9.1.

16. Lucian *Eikones* 6-7.

17. Ridgway (1984), Gazda (2002), Perry (2005) with Hallett (2005), Trimble & Elsner (2006); cf. Lucian *Zeuxis* 3.

178

18. Paus. 7.26.6: Ἔστι καὶ Ἀπόλλωνος ἱερὸν ἐς τὰ μάλιστα ἀρχαῖον τό τε ἱερὸν αὐτὸ καὶ ὁπόσα ἐν τοῖς ἀετοῖς, ἀρχαῖον δὲ καὶ τοῦ θεοῦ τὸ ξόανον, γυμνός, μεγέθει μέγας· τὸν ποιήσαντα δὲ εἶχεν οὐδεὶς τῶν ἐπιχωρίων εἰπεῖν· ὅστις δὲ ἤδη τὸν Ἡρακλέα τὸν ἐν Σικυῶνι ἐθεάσατο, τεκμαίροιτο ἂν καὶ ἐν Αἰγείρᾳ τὸν Ἀπόλλωνα ἔργον εἶναι τοῦ αὐτοῦ Φλιασίου Λαφάους.

19. Similar arguments: Paus. 2.4.5, 3.19.2, 5.17.2-3, 5.25.5, 7.26.6, 9.11.4; see Elsner (1998), esp. 421-2.

20. Paus. 5.20.2 (literature), 5.16.1, 5.20.9, 6.10.2, 6.24.2, 8.45.5 (architectural orders), 4.33.3 (Attic), 1.42.5, 2.30.1, 5.25.13, 8.53.11, 10.36.5 (Aeginetan), 7.5.5 (both compared to Egyptian).

21. Paus. 2.4.5 (ἀτοπώτερα μέν ἐστιν ἐς τὴν ὄψιν, ἐπιπρέπει δὲ ὅμως τι καὶ ἔνθεον τούτοις), cf. 9.40.8-9 (overview of Daidalos' works).

22. Pollitt (1974) 8-9; see also Ameling (1996) 126-30.

23. Pollitt (1974) 117-297. He presents forty-one special terms to describe the qualities of art. Pausanias uses eleven of these, Dionysios of Halikarnassos and Dio Chrysostom twelve, Plutarch fifteen and Lucian seventeen.

24. Lucian *Hist. Conscr.* 27: Εἰσὶ γάρ τινες, οἳ τὰ μεγάλα μὲν τῶν πεπραγμένων καὶ ἀξιομνημόνευτα παραλείπουσιν ἢ παραθέουσιν, ὑπὸ δὲ ἰδιωτείας καὶ ἀπειροκαλίας καὶ ἀγνοίας τῶν λεκτέων ἢ σιωπητέων τὰ μικρότατα πάνυ λιπαρῶς καὶ φιλοπόνως ἑρμηνεύουσιν ἐμβραδύνοντες, ὥσπερ ἂν εἴ τις τοῦ Διὸς τοῦ ἐν Ὀλυμπίᾳ τὸ μὲν ὅλον κάλλος τοσοῦτο καὶ τοιοῦτο ὂν μὴ βλέποι μηδὲ ἐπαινοίη μηδὲ τοῖς οὐκ εἰδόσιν ἐξηγοῖτο, τοῦ ὑποποδίου δὲ τό τε εὐθυεργὲς καὶ τὸ εὔξεστον θαυμάζοι καὶ τῆς κρηπῖδος τὸ εὔρυθμον, καὶ ταῦτα πάνυ μετὰ πολλῆς φροντίδος διεξιών. Cf. Hutton (2005a) 201, Paus. 5.11.1-11.

25. E.g. Paus. 2.3.5, 8.9.8 (coloured marble), 8.28.1, 10.32.1 (Pentelic marble), 1.44.6 (local stone), 5.20.10, 6.20.11, 10.4.4, 10.25.10 (brick), see also 8.8.7-8, a discussion of the merits of brick walls.

26. E.g. Paus. 5.5.6, 6.21.2, 7.25.9, 7.26.4, 8.30.10, 8.47.1, 9.2.7, 9.4.1, 9.11.6, 9.25.3, 9.27.3, 10.4.4, 10.33.4, 10.35.10 (Pentelic marble); 1.14.7, 1.33.2-3, 1.43.5, 2.2.8, 2.29.1, 2.35.3, 4.31.6, 5.12.6, 8.25.6, 9.20.4 (Parian marble), 1.18.6, 8.24.12 (coloured marble). See Arafat (1996) 50-2, Kreilinger (1997) 478.

27. Arafat (1996) 53-7, Vincent (2003).

28. Paus. 8.46.4. (gold and hippopotamus teeth), 5.12.7 (amber).

29. Paus. 8.17.2, 8.8.7-8.

30. Paus. 5.11.10-11, 5.12.1-3; cf. 4.31.6.

31. E. g. Paus. 3.17.6, 8.14.7, 10.16.1.

32. Paus. 1.24.3 (ὅστις δὲ τὰ σὺν τέχνῃ πεποιημένα ἐπίπροσθε τίθεται τῶν ἐς ἀρχαιότητα ἡκόντων), 10.18.6.

33. Hom. *Il.* 18.478-607; Simon (1995), Heffernan (1993) 9-22, Becker (1995) and 51-77 on other *ekphrases* in the *Iliad*.

34. Goldhill (1994).

35. Reardon (1971) 155-65, Graf (1995), Bartsch (1989) 7-10, Becker (1995) 23-40, Elsner (2002). Note the inclusion of *ekphrasis* in ancient rhetorical handbooks: Hermogenes 2.16-17 (Spengel), Aphthonios 2.46-9 (Spengel), Theon 2.118-20 (Spengel), Nikolaos 3.491-93 (Spengel). *Ekphrasis* in historiography: Lucian *Hist. Conscr.* 51, Walker (1993). In Pausanias: Calame (1990) 231-3, 239-42.

36. Lucian *De Domo* 22-31, Newby (2002). Note Dio 12 (*Olympic Oration*), ostensibly delivered in Olympia and dealing with the statue of Zeus.

37. See especially Josephus *Bellum Iudaicum* 7.26; Procopius *De Aedificiis* organises a historical account around the description of buildings in Constantinople.

38. Bartsch (1989) 36-79, see also Fowler (1991).

39. Esp. Lucian *Zeuxis, Herodotus/Aetion, Calumniae.*

40. Also note Kallistratos, *Ekphraseis* (*Descriptions*), dealing with statues (fourth century AD), and Kebes' *Pinax* (*Painting*) (first century AD).

41. Theon 2.118-19 (Spengel); Graf (1995) 146-7.

42. Schönberger (1995), esp. 167-9, Becker (1995) 41-4, Elsner (2000).

43. Bryson (1994), esp. 269-74. On Philostratos see Anderson (1986) 259-68, Lehmann-Hartleben (1941), Elsner (2004b).

44. See Blümner (1867) 46-52, Le Morvan (1932) 390, more recently Jones (1986) 154. Note that Lucian claimed to have the talent to be an artist: Lucian *Somn.* 2-4.

45. Lucian *Zeuxis* 3-7.

46. He does occasionally hint at the impression that architecture can make on the viewer, e.g. Paus. 1.19.6 (Stadium of Herodes Atticus), 2.27.5. I owe this observation to W. Hutton (pers. comm.).

47. Paus. 10.25.1-31.12.

48. Paus. 10.25.3, 10.26.2.

49. Stansbury-O'Donnell (1989), (1990).

50. Paus. 5.17.5-19.10.

51. Paus. 5.19.7, 5.17.6.

52. Paus. 8.40.1: ἀνδριάς ... τά τε ἄλλα ἀρχαῖος καὶ οὐχ᾽ ἥκιστα ἐπὶ τῷ σχήματι· οὐ διεστᾶσι μὲν πολὺ οἱ πόδες, καθεῖνται δὲ παρὰ πλευρὰν αἱ χεῖρες ἄχρι τῶν γλουτῶν.

53. Paus. 3.18.10; description: 3.18.11-16.

54. Paus. 5.17.5-5.19.10; guides: 5.18.6-8, unusual iconography: 5.19.5, 5.19.7-9; Snodgrass (2001).

55. Paus. 5.19.10.

56. E.g. Paus. 10.28.2, 10.26.2. See Sidebottom (2002) 498. On artists' interpretations of mythical traditions see Hedreen (2001) 3-18.

57. See Pollitt (1974) 60-1; e.g. Cicero, Quintilian, Dionysios of Halikarnassos; see also Barasch (2000) 1-44.

58. Dio Chrysostom 12, esp. 12.46, 12.64-81. Cf. Lucian *Imagines.*

59. Philostr. *Eikones* 1.1 : Ὅστις μὴ ἀσπάζεται τὴν ζωγραφίαν, ἀδικεῖ τὴν ἀλήθειαν, ἀδικεῖ καὶ σοφίαν, ὁπόση ἐς ποιητὰς ἥκει – φορὰ γὰρ ἴση ἀμφοῖν ἐς τὰ τῶν ἡρώων ἔργα καὶ εἴδη – ξυμμετρίαν τε οὐκ ἐπαινεῖ, δι᾽ ἣν καὶ λόγου ἡ τέχνη ἅπτεται.

60. Paus. 1.33.3-6, 5.18.6-8, 10.28.7.

61. Paus. 1.33.3, 2.24.3-4, 3.15.11, 7.20.3-5, 7.23.6, 6.9.1, 8.31.4, 8.41.5-6.

62. Arafat (1996) 71-5.

63. Elsner (1998) 424-7, Arafat (1996) 46-7, Kreilinger (1997) 478-80; cf. Paus. 8.14.7.

64. Paus. 7.22.4; cf. 9.12.4, 2.19.3, 9.24.3, 9.27.1 (aniconic images); see Vincent (2003), Pritchett (1998) 61-95, 295-363, Pritchett (1999) 168-94, Jourdain-Annequin (1998), Arafat (1996) 48-9, 54-6, Donohue (1988).

65. Paus. 2.4.5, 9.40.1-4, cf. 1.27.1, 9.11.4, 9.39.8 (Daidalos), 9.41.1-5 (Hephaistos); cf. books by mythical characters: e.g. 9.27.2. See Arafat (1992) 398-405.

66. Pliny *NH* 34.37, cf. Paus. 1.18.6. Selection: Paus. 1.39.3, 2.2.6, 3.11.1, 6.1.2, 10.9.2; Hutton (2005a) 13-14, Steinhart (2003), Kreilinger (1997), Arafat (1996) 4-8, 24-7, 36-42, 75-9, Habicht (1985) 23-4, Regenbogen (1956) 1090, Frazer (1998) I.xxxiii-xxxvi.

67. Stuart-Jones (1895) xxvi, Bowie (1974) 188, Habicht (1985) 131, Arafat (1996) 36-42, Ameling (1996) 126-30, Kreilinger (1997) 483-6; cf. Pliny *NH* 51-2.

68. Habicht (1985) 134-7.

69. E.g. Paus. 2.2.6-4.5, esp. 2.3.1, 2.3.5. (Corinth), 2.27.6 (Epidauros), 8.9.7-8 (Mantinea).

70. Dio Chrysostom 12.44-5.

71. Dio Chrysostom 12.53, 56-7. Lucian's *Iup. Trag.* esp. 7-11 satirises the idea that gods look like their statues.

72. Paus. 2.24.4, 8.31.4, 8.41.5-6, 8.42.1-7.

9. Pausanias and his Readers

1. Cf. Leake (1830) I.viii.

2. For a list of the most important editions, translations and commentaries see Musti (1982) lxxxi-lxxxiii.

3. E.g. the 1991 edition of Franciscus Iunius' *De Pictura Veterum* (1638). Pausanias is one of Iunius' main sources, yet he is not mentioned in the editors' introduction which includes a discussion of his sources. Iunius (1991) lxiv; cf. Demandt (1986) 306 on Winckelmann.

4. Diller (1956) 94. Colin (1967) 464 notes possible (uncredited) references to Pausanias in Guarino's letters as early as in 1415 and 1416.

5. For a full discussion of the history of the *Periegesis* through the Middle Ages and early Renaissance see Diller (1956) and (1957), cf. Marcotte (1992), Irigoin (2001). There are eighteen preserved manuscript copies, all directly or indirectly based on Niccoli's manuscript. See also Reynolds & Wilson (1974) 137-42.

6. Diller (1957) 172-3, 185.

7. Irwin (1972) 12-24.

8. E.g. Spon (1678), Wheler (1682); note Jacques Carrey's drawings of 1674, Bowie & Thimme (1971); fully illustrated work on Athens: Le Roy (1770); for a description see Spon (1678) II.145-8.

9. See Winckelmann (2006) 71, translation based on Winckelmann (1964) 7-8. He cites Monier (1698), Durand (1725) and Turnbull (1740) as examples.

10. Wickelmann (2006) 75; see also Justi (1956) II, esp. 11-193.

11. Iunius (1991); in fact, *pictura* usually has the more narrow meaning 'painting', but Iunius uses the word for all forms of art which aim to depict or imitate natural subjects. See also Iunius (1987), the *Catalogus Architectorum* of 1694.

12. Pliny *NH* 35, esp. 15-29, 50-158; see Jex-Blake & Sellers (1896).

13. Iunius (1991) lv-lvi, lxiv.

14. Winckelmann, *Gedanken über die Nachahmung der Griechischen Werke in der Malerei und der Bildhauerkunst* (1755), in Holtzhauer (1969) 1-47, Caylus (1752-68); cf. Barasch (1990) 98-102.

15. Caylus (1752-68) I.ii.

16. Winckelmann acknowledges this, see his letter to Bianconi 22 July 1758 (Rehm (1952) 393-6). On the development of the concept of style see Einem (1986) 318.

17. Caylus (1752-68) I.vii-viii.

18. Caylus (1752-68) I.ix, 119-20; II.105, II.108.

19. Note Winckelmann's discussion of this matter, and his suggestion that these vases are Greek (opposing Caylus): Rehm (1952) 395-6 (letter to Bianconi 22 July 1758).

20. Caylus (1752-68) II.105, cf. II.110 where he notes that he read Pausanias in the French translation of Gedoyn (1731-3).

21. Caylus (1752-68) II.109-10.

22. Caylus (1752-68) II.105-17.

23. Caylus (1752-68) II.106, cf. 114.

24. Caylus (1752-68) II.116, V.130.

25. Caylus (1752-68) I.117-19.

26. Caylus (1752-68) II.111-17; most relevant evidence cited: Paus. 1.42.5, 7.5.5.

27. Winckelmann was aware of Caylus' work and stresses his importance as the first to distinguish the styles of ancient peoples. See Uhlig (1988) 16, Rehm (1952) 393-6 (letter to Bianconi 22 July 1758).

28. Lepenies (1986).

29. Borbein (1986) 290, Demant (1986), Irwin (1972) 53-7.

30. Potts (1991) 27-8, Borbein (1986) 290.

31. Häsler (1973).

32. Letter to Hagedorn, 6 February 1756. Rehm (1952) I.208 (n. 130).

33. Häsler (1973) 41; Winckelmann (2006) 338 with 369 n. 347. The edition he used included the Greek text, notes and a Latin translation: Kuhn et al. (1696).

34. Winckelmann (2006) 338 with 369 n. 347; cf. Diller (1955).

35. Winckelmann (2006) 187-91.

36. Borbein (1986) 291.

37. Winckelmann (2006) 299-302.

38. Winckelmann (2006) 241 with Paus. 3.16.1; translation based on Winckelmann (1964) 202-3.

39. Winckelmann (2006) 230 with Paus. 1.26.7.

40. Winckelmann (2006) 187-90, cf. 304. See also Barasch (1990) 119.

41. Winckelmann (2006) 303-16.

42. Winckelmann (2006) 317-45; freedom: e.g. 321-2 (196-146 BC).

43. Pliny *NH* 35, esp. 15-29, 50-158.

44. Cf. Demand (1986).

45. Uhlig (1988) 8-13.

46. Uhlig (1988) 16.

47. Shilleto (1886), Hitzig & Blümner (1896-1910), Frazer (1898).

48. E.g. the location of the Enneakrounos fountain in Athens: Paus. 1.14.1, with Frazer (1898) 112-18, Beard (2001) 224-5; Monuments at the entrance of the sanctuary in Delphi: Paus. 10.9.3-7, Roux (1963), Daux (1936) 73-95, Habicht (1985) 71-3, Olympia: Jacquemin (2001). General observations: Bommelaer (2001).

49. Wilamowitz (1877) 344-78; followed by Kalkmann (1886), Robert (1909), Pasquali (1913). Opposing Wilamowitz: Schöll (1878), Schubart (1883), Brunn (1884), Gurlitt (1890), Frazer (1898) I.lxvii-lxix, lxviii-xcvi; see also Ackermann (1987) 134, Habicht (1985) 165-75.

50. Tozer (1887). Note the success of Harrison & Verrall (1890).

51. Ackermann (1987) 54-9. Frazer (1890).

52. Ackermann (1987) 58-67, Fraser (1990a) 39-49.

53. Ackermann (2002) 29-44; Tyler (1871).

54. Vickery (1973), Fraser (1990b); see also Ackermann (2002) 46-7.

55. Harrison & Verrall (1890) iii.

56. Esp. Harrison (1903), (1912). Her approach was shared by the 'Cambridge Ritualists', e.g. G. Murray (at Oxford) and A.B. Cook. See Ackermann (2002), esp 63-197.

57. Farnell (1896-1909), see Henderson (2001a).

58. Beard (2001) 226-9, Henderson (2001a) 208-12, Beard (1999).

59. Alcock (2001), Snodgrass (1987) 100-31.

60. Henderson (2001a) 209, Beard (2001) 228-9.

61. Ackermann (1987) 127-8.

62. Fraser (1990a) 40-3, cf. Levi (1971) 2-3.

63. Compare the contemporary, more traditional edition with commentary by Hitzig & Blümner (1896-1910).

10. Discovering Greece with Pausanias

1. Angelomatis-Tsougarakis (1990) 9-11, 25-7; for an overview see Eisner (1991), Stoneman (1984) 1-15.

2. Reynolds & Wilson (1974) 130-2.

3. Paton (1951), Weiss (1969) 131-7, Van der Vin (1980) esp. 197-225, Eisner (1991) 37-46.

4. Italian name: Ciriaco d'Ancona or Ciriaco de' Pizzicolli, lived from *c*. 1391 to shortly after 1453. Bodnar (1960) esp. 2-119, Colin (1967), see also Bodnar (2003), Weiss (1969) 138-42, Stoneman (1987) 22-36.

5. Bodnar (2003) x-xii, Weiss (1969) 138-42.

6. Eisner (1991) 47, Miller (1908) 417-25, Bodnar (2003) ix; overview of Cyriac's journeys: Bodnar (1960) 21-68.

7. Wolters (1915) 91-100.

8. Bodnar (2003) xiii. On Cyriac's library and access to ancient texts see Colin (1967) 444-90.

9. See Colin (1967) 464.

10. Babin (1674); Wheeler (1896) 178-9, Paton (1951) 3-19, Augustinos (1994) 49-54, 94-8, Eisner (1991) 56, Stoneman (1987) 56-61.

11. Greek islands: e.g. Boschini (1658), Meursius (1675), Coronelli & Parisotti (1688), Dapper (1688a).

12. Dapper (1688a) and (1688b).

13. Cf. Augustinos (1994) 73.

14. Coronelli (1688), esp. 13-21.

15. Dapper (1688b), *Voorrede*.

16. Dapper (1688b), *Voorrede,* see also p. 8 (*4 verso).

17. Guillet (1676), 1st edn 1675.

18. Guillet (1676) 128-9.

19. Spon (1678) II.100-2, Spon (1679). Cf. Wheeler (1896) 179; see Augustinos (1994) 99-112, Stoneman (1987) 77-80.

20. Spon (1678), Wheler (1682); Stoneman (1987) 61-80.

21. E.g. at Delphi: Spon (1678) II.54-66, cf. I.iv-vi (usefulness of inscriptions).

22. Spon (1678) II.72-3.

23. Stoneman (1987) 144-62.

24. Chandler (1817) (first edition 1775/6), Dodwell (1819), Gell (1817), Gell (1819), Leake (1830).

25. Gell (1817) x-xi. On British travellers to Greece in this period see Angelomatis-Tsougarakis (1990) 1-24.

26. Wagstaff (2001).

27. Leake (1830), (1835); see also Leake (1821), (1846).

28. E.g. Leake (1830) 27-8: comparing notes on the measurements of the temple at Bassai.

29. 'Homeric geography' e.g. Strabo 8.3.1-29 (Elis and Triphylia); Corinth: Strabo 8.6.21-2. See Prontera (1993).

30. E.g. Meyer (1939), Pritchett (1969-89), Pikoulas (1999) with an extensive bibliography of individual studies, Tausend (1999), (2006).

31. Dodwell only believed that he was outside 'Pausanias country': he is discussing Galaxidhi, probably the ancient Oiantheia in Phocis; Paus. 10.38.9.

32. Snodgrass (1987) 100-31.

33. Thompson & Wycherley (1972) 204-7, Wycherley (1959), Daux (1936), Roux (1958), Jost (1973). See also Habicht (1985) 29-31.

34. See Alcock (2002) 3-5.

35. Sutton (2001)

36. The original notes of 1876-7 were preserved and published over a century later: see Lolling (1989); cf. Hinrichsen (1991) 41-4.

37. See Beard (2001) 232-6.

38. E.g. Paus. 1.19.3, 1.22.4, 1.29.16, 1.39.3, 2.1.3, 2.27.3, 3.24.4, 4.14.6, 4.16.6, 4.27.11, 4.34.11, 5.4.2, 5.4.4, 5.11.9, 5.13.6, 5.13.7, 5.17.10, 7.16.8, 7.17.14, 7.24.4, 8.5.2, 8.9.10, 8.48.2, 9.2.6, 9.4.4, 9.8.4, 9.38.1, 10.16.5, 10.17.7, 10.35.5. Cf. Akujärvi (2005) 69-77.

39. Cf. Cic. *De Fin.* 5.1.1-2; Casson (1994) 229-37.

40. Augustinos (1994) 176-8.

41. Cic. *Ad Fam.* 4.5.4: Ex Asia rediens cum ab Aegina Megaram versus navigarem, coepi regiones circumcirca prospicere: post me erat Aegina, ante me Megara, dextra Piraeus, sinistra Corinthus, quae oppida quodam tempore florentissima fuerunt, nunc prostrata et diruta ante oculos iacent.

42. Alcock (1993) 24-32, Touloumakos (1971) 51-5. Herzfeld (1986) 3-23, (1987) 28-64; note Byron, *Childe Harold's Pilgimage* IV.44-6, which refers to Cic. *Ad Fam.* 4.5.4.

43. Porter (2001) 67-75.

44. E.g. Porter (2001), esp. 67, Goldmann (1991) esp. 145-8, Hartog (2001) 143-6, Elsner (1992) esp. 17-20. For a more balanced picture see Konstan (2001b) 40-3.

45. E.g. Polyb. 36.17.5-9, Strabo 8.8.1, Plutarch *De Defectu Oraculorum* esp. 413F-414A. See Alcock (1993) 25-32; see also Pritchett (1999) 195-222.

46. Ruins as memorials: e.g. Paus. 1.38.9, 1.1.5, 2.15.2-3, 2.16.5-7, 3.24.6-7, 4.31.2, 8.35.5-7, 8.44.1-3, 8.53.11, 10.35.2-3; ruins as a sign of loss: 2.9.7, 2.11.1, 2.11.2, 2.25.9, 2.36.2, 3.24.1, 6.22.1-2, 7.25.12, 8.14.4, 8.17.6, 8.24.6, 8.25.3, 8.32.2-3, 9.7.6, 9.29.2. Not even ruins remain: 5.5.5-6, 5.6.2, 8.18.8. See Akujärvi (2005) 76-89, Hartog (2001) 143-6; on attitudes to ruins in general see Woodward (2001).

47. Paus. 7.17.1-4, 8.52.1-5.

48. Paus. 10.4.1-6; cf. pp. 91-3.

49. Paus. 8.33.1: Εἰ δὲ ἡ Μεγάλη πόλις προθυμίᾳ τε τῇ πάσῃ συνοικισθεῖσα ὑπὸ Ἀρκάδων καὶ ἐπὶ μεγίσταις τῶν Ἑλλήνων ἐλπίσιν ἐς αὐτὴν κόσμον τὸν ἅπαντα καὶ εὐδαιμονίαν τὴν ἀρχαίαν ἀφῄρηται καὶ τὰ πολλά ἐστιν αὐτῆς ἐρείπια ἐφ᾽ ἡμῶν, θαῦμα οὐδὲν ἐποιησάμην, εἰδὼς τὸ δαιμόνιον νεώτερα ἀεί τινα ἐθέλον ἐργάζεσθαι, καὶ ὁμοίως τὰ πάντα τά τε ἐχυρὰ καὶ τὰ ἀσθενῆ καὶ τὰ γινόμενά τε καὶ ὁπόσα ἀπόλλυνται μεταβάλλουσαν τὴν τύχην, καὶ ὅπως ἂν αὐτῇ παριστῆται μετὰ ἰσχυρᾶς ἀνάγκης ἄγουσαν.

50. Cf. Hdt. 1.5, Lucian *Charon* 23; on Spon & Wheler in Delphi see also Miller (1972) 149-51.

51. Elsner (2001) 18.

52. Angelomatis-Tsougarakis (1990) 85-95.

53. Cyriac of Ancona (2003) 322-4; but he, too, was not unreservedly sympathetic: cf. Weiss (1969) 140-1.

54. Cyriac of Ancona (2003) 328.

55. E.g. Spon (1678) II.83-4.

56. Angelomatis-Tsougarakis (1990) 13-14.

57. The opening ceremony of the 2004 Olympics was a particularly poignant example: its presentation of Greek history displayed the usual 'Ottoman gap'.

58. Augustinos (1994) 131-73, Herzfeld (1987) 87-94.

59. Augustinos (1994) 287-9, Stoneman (1987) 247-64.

60. Spon (1678) II.48-50.

61. Cf. Herzfeld (1987) esp. 101-22.

62. Paus. 8.45.4-47.3 (Alea), 8.47.4 (stadium), 8.45.1 (tribes of the Gareatai and Manthureis).

63. Paus. 8.23.8.

64. Cf. the 'Pausanias plane tree' in Egio/Aigion which grows by a spring (probably) mentioned in Paus. 7.24.3.

65. Paus. 8.23.4.

Bibliography

Ackerman, R. (1987), *J.G. Frazer: His Life and Work* (Cambridge University Press).

Ackerman, R. (2002), *The Myth and Ritual School: J.G. Frazer and the Cambridge Ritualists*, second edition (Routledge).

Adams, C. (2007), '"Travel Narrows the Mind": Cultural Tourism in Graeco-Roman Egypt', in C. Adams and J. Roy (eds), *Travel, Geography and Culture in Ancient Greece and the Near East* (Routledge), 161-84.

Akujärvi, J. (2005), *Researcher, Traveller, Narrator: Studies in Pausanias' Periegesis*, (Almquist & Wiksell International).

Alcock, S.E. (1993), *Graecia Capta: The Landscapes of Roman Greece* (Cambridge University Press).

Alcock, S.E. (1995), 'Pausanias and the *Polis*: Use and Abuse', in M.H. Hansen (ed.), *Sources for the Ancient Greek City State. Acts of the Copenhagen Polis Centre 2* (Munksgaard), 326-44.

Alcock, S.E. (1996), 'Landscapes of Memory and the Authority of Pausanias', in J. Bingen (ed.), *Pausanias Historien. Entretiens sur l'antiquité classique* XLI (Fondation Hardt), 241-67.

Alcock, S.E. (2001), 'The Peculiar Book IV and the Problem of the Messenian Past', in S.E. Alcock, J.F. Cherry and J. Elsner (eds), *Pausanias: Travel and Memory in Roman Greece* (Oxford University Press), 142-66.

Alcock, S.E. (2002), *Archaeologies of the Greek Past: Landscapes, Monuments, and Memories* (Cambridge University Press).

Alcock, S.E., Cherry, J.F. and Elsner, J. (eds) (2001), *Pausanias: Travel and Memory in Roman Greece* (Oxford University Press).

Allen, T.W. (1921), *The Homeric Catalogue of Ships: Edited with a Commentary* (Clarendon Press).

Aly, W. (1927), 'Die Entdeckung des Westens', *Hermes* 62, 299-341.

Amboglio, D. (1991), 'La periegesi di Pausania e la storiografia greca tradita per citazioni', *Quaderni Urbinati di Cultura Classica* n.s. 39.3, 129-38.

Ameling, W. (1983), *Herodes Atticus* (Georg Olms Verlag).

Ameling, W. (1996), 'Pausanias und die hellenistische Geschichte', in J. Bingen (ed.), *Pausanias Historien. Entretiens sur l'antiquité classique* XLI (Fondation Hardt), 117-60.

Anderson, G. (1984), *Ancient Fiction: The Novel in the Graeco-Roman World.* (Croom Helm: Barnes & Noble).

Anderson, G. (1986), *Philostratus: Biography and Belles Lettres in the Third Century AD* (Croom Helm).

Anderson, G. (1993), *The Second Sophistic* (Routledge).

André, J.-M. and Baslez, M.-F. (1993), *Voyager dans l'antiquité* (Fayard).

Angelomatis-Tsougarakis, H. (1990), *The Eve of the Greek Revival: British Travellers' Perceptions of Early Nineteenth-Century Greece* (Routledge).

Arafat, K.W. (1992), 'Pausanias' Attitude to Antiquities', *ABSA* 87, 387-409.

Bibliography

Arafat, K.W. (1995), 'Pausanias and the Temple of Hera at Olympia', *ABSA* 90, 461-73.

Arafat, K.W. (1996), *Pausanias' Greece: Ancient Artists and Roman Rulers* (Cambridge University Press).

Arafat, K.W. (1999), 'Pausanias the Traveller: Digressions on the Wonders of Nature and of Foreign Lands', *Euphrosyne* 27, 237-48.

Arafat, K.W. (2000), 'The Recalcitrant Mass: Athenaeus and Pausanias' in D. Braund and J. Wilkins (eds), *Athenaeus and his World: Reading Greek Culture in the Roman Empire* (University of Exeter Press), 191-202.

Arenz, A. (2006), *Herakleides Kritikos, Über die Städte in Griechenland: Eine Periegese Griechenlands am Vorabend des Chremonideischen Krieges* (Herbert Utz Verlag).

Auberger, J. (1992), 'Pausanias et les Messéniens: Une histoire d'amour!', *REA* 94, 187-97.

Auberger, J. (1994), 'Les mots de courage chez Pausanias', *RPh* 68, 7-18.

Auberger, J. (2000), 'Pausanias et le livre 4: Une leçon pour l'empire', *Phoenix* 54, 255-81.

Auberger, J. (2001), 'D'un héros à l'autre: Pausanias au pied de l'Ithôme', in D. Knoepfler and M. Piérart (eds), *Éditer, traduire, commenter Pausanias en l'an 2000* (Université de Neuchâtel. Faculté des lettres et sciences humaines), 261-73.

Auberger, J. (2005), 'Commentaire', in M. Casevitz, J. Auberger, *Pausanias: Description de la Grèce. Livre IV. La Messénie* (Budé, Les Belles Lettres), 103-259.

Augustinos, O. (1994), *French Odysseys: Greece in French Travel Literature from the Renaissance to the Romantic Era* (John Hopkins University Press).

Avenarius, G. (1956), *Lukians Schrift zur Geschichtsschreibung* (Hain).

Babin, J. (1674), *Relation de l'état présent de la ville d'Athènes* (Louis Pascal).

Baedeker, K. (1883), *Griechenland: Handbuch für Reisende* (Karl Baedeker).

Bagrow, L. (1945), 'The Origin of Ptolemy's *Geographia*', *Geografiska Annaler* 27, 318-87.

Baillet, M.J. (1926), *Inscriptions grecques et latines des Tombeaux des Rois ou Syringes* (Impr. de l'Institut Français d'Archéologie Orientale).

Barasch, M. (1990), *Modern Theories of Art, Part 1: From Winckelmann to Baudelaire* (New York University Press).

Barasch, M. (2000), *Theories of Art 1: From Plato to Winckelmann* (Routledge).

Bartsch, S. (1989), *Decoding the Ancient Novel* (Princeton University Press).

Bauchhenss-Thüriedl, C. (1971), *Der Mythos von Telephos in der antiken Bildkunst* (Triltsch).

Beard, M. (1999), 'The Invention (and Re-Invention) of "Group D": An Archaeology of the Classical Greek Tripos, 1879-1984', in C. Stray (ed.), *Classics in Nineteenth and Twentieth Century Cambridge: Curriculum, Culture and Community*, PCPS Supplement 24 (Cambridge Philological Society), 95-134.

Beard, M. (2001), '"Pausanias in Petticoats," or *The Blue Jane*', in S.E. Alcock, J.F. Cherry and J. Elsner (eds), *Pausanias: Travel and Memory in Roman Greece* (Oxford University Press), 224-39.

Bearzot, C. (1988), 'La Grecia di Pausania, geografia e cultura nella definizione del concetto di Hellas', in M. Sordi, *Geografia e storiografia nel mondo classico* (Vita e Pensiero).

Bearzot, C. (1992), *Storia e storiografia ellenistica in Pausanias il Periegeta* (Il Cardo).

Bibliography

Bearzot, C. (1995) 'L'epigramma come fonte storica in Pausania' in L. Belloni, G. Milanese and A. Porro (eds), *Studia Classica Iohanni Tarditi oblata*, vol. I (Vita e Pensiero), 695-710.

Becker, A.S. (1995), *The Shield of Achilles and the Poetics of Ekphrasis* (Rowman & Littlefield Publishers).

Behr, C.A. (1968), *Aelius Aristides and the Sacred Tales* (A.M. Hakkert).

Belger, C (1899), 'Schliemann als Interpret des Pausanias', *Berliner Philologische Wochenschrift* 19, 1180-3, 1211-5.

Bender, B. (1999), 'Subverting the Western Gaze: Mapping Alternative Worlds', in P. Ucko and R. Layton (eds), *The Archaeology and Anthropology of Landscape* (Routledge), 31-45.

Bernand, A. and Bernand E. (1960), *Les inscriptions grecques et latines du Colosse de Memnon* (Institut Français d'Archéologie Orientale).

Bernand, E. (1969), *Les inscriptions grecques ou latines de Philae*, vol. 2: *Haut et Bas-Empire* (Éditions du Centre National de la Recherche Scientifique).

Bigwood, J.M. (1989), 'Ctesias' *Indika* and Photius', *Phoenix* 43, 302-16.

Bingen, J. (1996), *Pausanias Historien. Entretiens sur l'antiquité classique* XLI (Fondation Hardt).

Bischoff, E. (1938), 'Perieget' *RE* XIX, 725-42.

Blanck, H. (1969), *Wiederverwendung alter Statuen als Ehrendenkmäler bei Griechen und Römern* ('L'Erma' di Bretschneider).

Blomquist, J. (1979), *The Date and Origin of the Greek Version of Hanno's Periplus* (Gleerop).

Blümner, H. (1867), *Archäologische Studien zu Lucian* (Mälzer).

Bodnar, E.W. (1960), *Cyriacus of Ancona and Athens: Collection Latomus* XLIII (Latomus).

Bodnar, E.W. (2003), 'Introduction', in E.W. Bodnar (ed.), *Cyriac of Ancona (Ciriaco d'Ancona): Later Travels* (Harvard University Press), ix-xxii.

Bol, P.C. (1978), *Grossplastik aus Bronze in Olympia. Olympische Forschungen IX* (Walter de Gruyter).

Bol, R. (1984), *Das Statuenprogramm des Herodes-Atticus-Nymphäums. Olympische Forschungen XV* (Walter de Gruyter).

Bolton, J.D.P (1962), *Aristeas of Proconnesus* (Clarendon Press).

Bommelaer, J.-F. (1999), 'Traces de l'épigraphie Delphique dans le texte de Pausanias', in R.G. Khouri (ed.), *Urkunden und Urkundenformulare im klassischen Altertum und in den orientalischen Kulturen* (Universitätsverlag Winter), 83-93.

Bommelaer, J.-F. (2001), 'Les prodécés de la localisation dans le dixième livre de Pausanias', in D. Knoepfler and M. Piérart (eds), *Éditer, traduire, commenter Pausanias en l'an 2000* (Université de Neuchâtel. Faculté des lettres et sciences humaines), 375-86.

Borbein, A.H. (1986), 'Winckelmann und die klassische Archaeologie', in T.W. Gaehtgens (ed.), *Johann Joachim Winckelmann 1717-1768, Studien zum Achzehnten Jahrhundert 7* (Felix Meiner Verlag), 289-99.

Boschini, M. (1658), *L'Archipelago: Con tutte le Isole, Scogli Secche e Bassi Fondi, con i Mari, Golfi, Seni, Porti, Città, e Castelli; nella Forma, che si vedomo al Tempo Presente. Con una succinta narrativa de i loro nomi, Favole, & Historie, tanto antiche quanto moderne* (Francesco Nicolini).

Bosworth, A.B. (1993), 'Arrian and Rome: The Minor Works', *ARNW* 34.1, 226-75.

Bowersock, G.W. (1969), *Greek Sophists in the Roman Empire* (Clarendon Press).

Bowersock, G.W. (2002), 'Philosophy in the Second Sophistic', in G. Clark and T.

Bibliography

Rajak (eds), *Philosophy and Power in the Graeco-Roman World: Essays in Honour of Miriam Griffin* (Oxford University Press).

Bowie, E.L. (1974), 'Greeks and their Past in the Second Sophistic', in M.I. Finley (ed.), *Studies in Ancient Society* (Routledge & Kegan Paul), 166-209.

Bowie, E.L. (1982), 'The Importance of Sophists', *Yale Classical Studies* 27, 29-59.

Bowie, E.L. (1996), 'Past and Present in Pausanias', in J. Bingen (ed.), *Pausanias Historien. Entretiens sur l'antiquité classique* XLI (Fondation Hardt), 207-30.

Bowie, E.L. (2001), 'Inspiration and aspiration: Date, genre and readership', in S.E. Alcock, J.F. Cherry and J. Elsner (eds), *Pausanias: Travel and Memory in Roman Greece* (Oxford University Press), 21-32.

Bowie, E.L. and Krasser, H. (1997), 'Buntschriftstellerei' *DNP* II, 850-53.

Bowie, T. and Thimme, D. (1971), *The Carrey Drawings of the Parthenon Sculptures* (Indiana University Press).

Braund, D. (1993), 'Piracy under the Principate and the Ideology of Imperial Eradication', in J. Rich and G. Shipley (eds), *War and Society in the Roman World* (Routledge), 195-212.

Braund, D. (1994), *Georgia in Antiquity: A History of Colchis and Transcaucasian Iberia 550 BC-AD 562* (Clarendon Press).

Brodersen, K. (2003), *Terra Cognita: Studien zur römischen Raumerfassung, Spudasmata* 59, second edition (Georg Olms Verlag).

Brunn, H. (1884), 'Pausanias und seine Ankläger', *Jahrbuch für Classische Philologie* 30, 23-30.

Brunt, P.A. (1994), 'The Bubble of the Second Sophistic', *BICS* 39, 25-52.

Bryson, N. (1994), 'Philostratus and the Imaginary Museum', in S. Goldhill and R. Osborne (eds), *Art and Text in Greek Culture* (Cambridge University Press), 255-83.

Bultrighini, U. (1990a), *Pausania e le tradizioni democratiche: Argo e Elide* (Editoriale Programma).

Bultrighini, U. (1990b), 'La Grecia descritta da Pausania: Trattazione diretta e trattazione indiretta', *Rivista di filologia e di istruzione classica* 118, 282-305.

Calame, C. (1990), 'Pausanias le périégète en ethnographe, ou comment d'écrire un culte grec', in M. Adam, M.-J. Borel, C. Calame and M. Kilani (eds), *Le discours anthropologique: Description, narration, savoir* (Méridiens Klincksieck), 227-50.

Cameron, A. (2004), *Greek Mythography in the Roman World* (Oxford University Press).

Camp, J. McK. and Reger, G. (2000), 'Peloponnesus', in R.J.A. Talbert (ed.), *Barrington Atlas of the Greek and Roman World* (Princeton University Press), 58.

Campbell, M.B. (1988), *The Witness and the Other World* (Cornell University Press).

Campbell, M.B. (1991), 'The Object of One's Gaze: Landscape, Writing, and Early Medieval Pilgrimage', in S.D. Westrem (ed.), *Discovering New Worlds: Essays on Medieval Exploration and Imagination* (Garland Publishing), 3-15.

Campbell, M.B. (2002), 'Travel Writing and its Theory', in P. Hulme and T. Youngs (eds), *The Cambridge Companion to Travel Writing* (Cambridge University Press), 261-78.

Carter, L.B. (1986), *The Quiet Athenian* (Oxford University Press).

Carpenter, R. (1966), *Beyond the Pillars of Heracles: The Classical World through the Eyes of its Discoverers* (Delacorte Press).

Bibliography

Cartledge, P. and Spawforth, A. (1989), *Hellenistic and Roman Sparta: A Tale of Two Cities* (Routledge).

Cary, M. and Warmington, E.H. (1963), *The Ancient Explorers*, revised edition (Pelican Books).

Casevitz, M. et al. (1992-) *Pausanias*: Description de la Grèce. 10 vols in progress (Les Belles Lettres/Budé).

Casevitz, M., Jost, M. and Marcadé, J. (1998), *Pausanias*: Description de la Grèce. *Livre VIII. L'Arcadie* (Les Belles Lettres/Budé).

Casson, L. (1989), *The Periplus Maris Erythraei* (Princeton University Press).

Casson, L. (1994), *Travel in the Ancient World* (George Allen & Unwin Ltd).

Cawkwell, G. (2004), 'When, How and Why did Xenophon write the *Anabasis*?', in R. Lane Fox (ed.), *The Long March: Xenophon and the Ten Thousand* (Yale University Press), 47-67.

Caylus, A.C.P. (1752-68), *Recueil d'Antiquités Egyptiennes, Etrusques, Grecques et Romaines* (Desaint & Saillant).

Chamoux, F. (1974), 'Pausanias géographe', in R. Chevallier (ed.), *Mélanges offerts à Roger Dion: Littérature gréco-romaine et géographie historique* (A. & J. Picard), 83-90.

Chamoux (1996), 'La méthode historique de Pausanias', in J. Bingen (ed.), *Pausanias Historien. Entretiens sur l'antiquité classique* XLI (Fondation Hardt), 45-69.

Chamoux, F. (2001), 'Les épigrammes dans Pausanias', in D. Knoepfler and M. Piérart (eds), *Éditer, traduire, commenter Pausanias en l'an 2000* (Université de Neuchâtel. Faculté des lettres et sciences humaines), 79-91.

Chandler, R. (1817), *Travels in Asia Minor, and Greece: or, an Account of a Tour made at the expense of the Society of Dilettanti*, third edition (J. Booker & R. Priestley).

Clarke, K. (1999), *Between Geography and History: Hellenistic Constructions of the Roman World* (Clarendon Press).

Cohen, E. (1992), 'Pilgrimage and Tourism: Convergence and Divergence', in E.A. Morinis (ed.), *Sacred Journeys: The Anthropology of Pilgrimage* (Greenwood Press), 47-61.

Colin, J. (1967), *Cyriaque d'Ancône: Le voyageur, le marchand, l'humaniste* (Maloine Éditeur).

Comfort, H. (1931), 'The Date of Pausanias, Book II', *AJA* 35, 310-14.

Conolly, J. (2001), 'Problems of the Past in Imperial Greek Education', in Y.L. Too (ed.), *Education in Greek and Roman Antiquity* (Brill), 289-316.

Coronelli, V. (1688) *Memorie istoriografiche de Regni della Morea, Negroponte e littorali fin' a Salonichi*, second edition (P.M. Coronelli).

Coronelli V. and Parisotti, G.A. (1688), *Isola de Rodi: Geografica-Storica, Antica, e Moderna, coll' altre adiacenti già possedute da Cavalieri Hospitalieri di S. Giovanni di Gerusalemme. Vol. 1 dell'Archipelago* (Libraria della Geografia sopra il Ponte di Rialto).

Counillon, P. (2004), *Pseudo-Skylax: Le Périple du Pont-Euxin* (De Boccard).

Crapanzano, V. (1986), 'Hermes' Dilemma: the Masking of Subversion in Ethnographic Description', in J. Clifford and G.E. Marcus (eds), *Writing Culture: The Poetics and Politics of Ethnography* (University of California Press), 51-76.

Cunliffe, B. (2002), *The Extraordinary Voyage of Pytheas the Greek* (Walker and Company).

Curty, O. (1995), *Les parentés légendaires entre cités grecques* (Éditions Droz).

Dalfen, J. (1996), 'Dinge, die Pausanias nicht sagt', in R. Faber, B. Seidensticker (eds), *Worte, Bilder, Töne: Studien zur Antike and Antikenrezeption B. Kytzler zu Ehren* (Königshausen & Neumann), 159-77.

Dapper, O. (1688a), *Naukeurige Beschryving der Eilanden in de Archipel der Middelantsche Zee, en ontrent dezelve, gelegen: Waer onder de voornaemste Cyprus, Rhodus, Kandien, Samos, Scio, Negroponte, Lemnos, Paros, Delos, Patmos, en andere, in groten getale, Behelzende Der zelveer benamingen, gelegentheden, fleden, kastelen, gedenkwaerdige aeloude en hedendaeghse geschiednenissen, bestieringen, veroveringen, gewassen, dieren, &c. Verrijkt met zee-en eilant-kaerten, en afbeeldingen van steden, dieren, gewassen, &c.* (Wolfgangh, Waesbergen, Boom, Someren en Goethals).

Dapper, O. (1688b), *Naukeurige Beschryving Van Morea Eertijs Peloponnesus En de Eilanden, Gelegen onder de kusten van Morea en binnenen buiten de Golf van Venetien: Waer onder de Voornaemste Korfu, Cefalonia, Sant Maura, Zanten, en andere in grooten getale. Behelzende derzelver Landschappen, steden, rivieren, poelen, Bergen, gewassen, dieren, &c. Met de kaerten van Morea, Golf van Venetien, en verscheide eilanden: beneffens afbeeldingen van steden en kastelen, als Patrasso, Modon, Koron, Navarino, Napoli di Romania en Malvasia, Korinthen, Misitra, & c.* (Wolfgangh, Waesbergen, Boom, Someren en Goethals).

Daux, G. (1936), *Pausanias à Delphes* (Picard).

Day, J.W. (1980), *The Glory of Athens: The Popular Tradition as Reflected in the Panathenaicus of Aelius Aristides* (Ares).

Deicke, L. (1935), *Questiones Pausanianae* (Schönhütte & Söhne).

Demandt, A. (1986), 'Winckelmann und die Alte Geschichte', in T.W. Gaehtgens (ed.), *Johann Joachim Winckelmann 1717-1768. Studien zum Achzehnten Jahrhundert 7* (Felix Meiner Verlag), 301-13.

Dewald, C. (1987), 'Narrative Surface and Authorial Voice in Herodotus' *Histories*', *Arethusa* 20, 147-70.

Di Napoli, V. (2005), 'The Theatres of Roman Arcadia, Pausanias and the History of the Region', in E. Østby (ed.), *Ancient Arcadia: Papers from the Third International Seminar on Ancient Arcadia, held at the Norwegian Institute at Athens 7-10 May 2002* (Oxbow), 509-20.

Dickie, M.W. (1997), 'Philostratus and Pindar's Eighth Paean', *Bulletin of the American Society of Papyrologists* 34, 11-20.

Dilke, O.A.W. (1985) *Greek and Roman Maps* (Thames and Hudson).

Diller, A. (1952), *The Tradition of the Minor Greek Geographers*, Philological Monographs XIV (American Philological Association).

Diller, A. (1955), 'The Authors Named Pausanias', *TAPA* 86, 268-79.

Diller, A. (1956), 'Pausanias in the Middle Ages', *TAPA* 87, 84-97.

Diller, A. (1957), 'The Manuscripts of Pausanias', *TAPA* 88, 169-88.

Dillon, M. (1997), *Pilgrims and Pilgrimage in Ancient Greece* (Routledge).

Dinsmoor, W.B. (1974), 'The Temple of Poseidon: A Missing Sima and Other Matters', *AJA* 78, 211-38.

Dodwell, E. (1819), *A Classical and Topographical Tour Through Greece, During the Years 1801, 1805 and 1806*, 2 vols (Rodwell and Martin).

Donohue, A.A. (1988), *Xoana and the Origins of Greek Sculpture* (Scholars Press).

Dougherty, C. (2001), *The Raft of Odysseus: The Ethnographic Imagination of Homer's Odyssey* (Oxford University Press).

Dueck, D. (2000), *Strabo of Amasia: A Greek Man of Letters in Augustan Rome* (Routledge).

Dugas, C. (1921), 'Le sanctuaire d'Aléa Athéna à Tegée', *BCH* 45, 335-435.

Bibliography

Dugas, C., Beuchmans, J. and Clemmensen, M. (1924), *Le sanctuaire d'Aléa Athéna à Tegée au IVe siècle* (P. Geuthner).

Durand, D. (1725), *Histoire de la peinture ancienne, extraite de l'Histoire naturelle de Pline, liv. XXXV* (Guillaume Boyer).

Ebeling, H.L. (1892), *Study of the Sources of the Messeniaca of Pausanias* (Murphy).

Ebeling, H.L. (1913), 'Pausanias as an Historian', *CW* 7, 138-50.

Eide, T. (1992), 'Pausanias and Thucydides', *Symbolae Osloenses* 67, 124-37.

Einem, H.v. (1986), 'Winckelmann und die Kunstgeschichte', in T.W. Gaehtgens (ed.), *Johann Joachim Winckelmann 1717-1768. Studien zum Achzehnten Jahrhundert 7* (Felix Meiner Verlag), 315-26.

Eisner, R. (1991), *Travelers to an Antique Land* (University of Michigan Press).

Elliger, W. (1975), *Die Darstellung der Landschaft in der griechischen Dichtung* (Walter de Gruyter).

Ellinger, P. (2005), *La fin des maux: D'un Pausanias à l'autre* (Les Belles Lettres).

Elsner, J. (1992), 'Pausanias: a Greek Pilgrim in the Roman World', *P&P* 135, 5-29.

Elsner, J. (1994), 'From the Pyramids to Pausanias and Piglet: Monuments, Travel and Writing', in S. Goldhill and R. Osborne (eds), *Art and Text in Ancient Greek Culture* (Cambridge University Press), 224-54.

Elsner, J. (1995), *Art and the Roman Viewer: The Transformation of Art from the Pagan World to Christianity* (Cambridge University Press).

Elsner, J. (1997a), 'The Origins of the Icon: Pilgrimage, Religion and Visual Culture in the Roman East as Resistance to the Centre', in S.E. Alcock (ed.), *The Early Roman Empire in the East* (Oxbow), 178-99.

Elsner, J. (1997b), 'Hagiographic Geography: Travel and Allegory in the *Life of Apollonius of Tyana*', *JHS* 117, 22-37.

Elsner, J. (1998), 'Ancient Viewing and Modern Art History', *Metis* 13, 417-37.

Elsner, J. (2000), 'Making Myth Visual: The Horae of Philostratus and the Dance of the Text', *Mitteilungen des DAI (Römische Abteilung)* 107, 253-76.

Elsner, J. (2001a), 'Structuring "Greece": Pausanias' *Periegesis* as a Literary Construct', in S.E. Alcock, J.F. Cherry and J. Elsner (eds), *Pausanias: Travel and Memory in Roman Greece* (Oxford University Press), 3-20.

Elsner, J. (2001b), 'Describing Self in the Language of the Other: Pseudo (?) Lucian at the Temple of Hierapolis', in S. Goldhill (ed.), *Being Greek under Rome* (Cambridge University Press), 123-53.

Elsner, J. (2002), 'Introduction: The genres of Ekphrasis', in J. Elsner (ed.), *The Verbal and the Visual: Cultures of Ekphrasis in Antiquity, Ramus* 31 (n. 1&2), 1-18.

Elsner, J. (2004a), 'Pausanias: A Pilgrim in the Roman World. Postscript 2003', in R. Osborne (ed.), *Studies in Ancient Greek and Roman Society* (Past & Present Publications), 282-5.

Elsner, J. (2004b), 'Seeing and Saying: A Psychoanalytic Account of Ekphrasis', *Helios* 31, 157-85.

Elsner, J. and Rutherford, I. (eds) (2005), *Pilgrimage in Graeco-Roman and Christian Antiquity* (Oxford University Press).

Engels, D. (1990), *Roman Corinth* (University of Chicago Press).

Engels, J. (1999), *Augusteische Oikumenegeographie und Universalhistorie im Werk Strabons von Amaseia* (F. Steiner).

Evans, J. (1968), 'Father of History or Father of Lies: The Reputation of Herodotus', *CJ* 64, 11-17.

Faber, T. (1667) *Claudii Aeliani Varia Historia* (Saumur).

Bibliography

Farnell, L.R. (1896-1909), *The Cults of the Greek States*, 5 vols (Clarendon Press).

Fehling, D. (1988), 'A Guide to Pausanias: Christian Habicht, *Pausanias' Guide to Ancient Greece*', *CR* 38, 18-19.

Finley, M.I. (1977), 'The Ancient City: From Fustel de Coulanges to Max Weber and beyond', *Comparative Studies in Society and History* 19, 305-27; reprinted in M.I. Finley (ed.) (1981), *Economy and Society in Ancient Greece* (Chatto & Windus), 2-23.

Fischbach, O. (1893), 'Die Benutzung des thukydideischen Geschichtswerkes durch den Periegeten Pausanias', *Wiener Studien* 15, 161-91.

Flinterman, J.-J. (1995), *Power,* Paideia, *and Pythagoreanism: Greek Identity, Conceptions of the Relationship between Philosophers and Monarchs and Political Ideas in Philostratus'* Life of Apollonius (Gieben).

Foss, C., Mitchell, S. and Reger, G. (2000), 'Pergamum', in R.J.A. Talbert (ed.), *Barrington Atlas of the Greek and Roman World* (Princeton University Press), 58.

Forte, B. (1972), *Rome and the Romans as the Greeks Saw Them* (American Academy in Rome).

Fowler, D.P. (1991), 'Narrate and Describe: The Problem of Ekphrasis', *JRS* 81, 25-35.

Fraser, R. (1990a), *The Making of the* Golden Bough: *The Origins and Growth of an Argument* (Macmillan).

Fraser, R. (ed.) (1990b) *Sir James Frazer and the Literary Imagination* (Macmillan).

Frazer, J.G. (1890), *The Golden Bough: A Study in Comparative Religion* (Macmillan).

Frazer, J.G. (1898), *Pausanias' Description of Greece*, 6 vols (Macmillan).

Frézouls, E. (1991), 'L'hellénisme dans l'épigraphie de l'Asie Mineure romaine', in S. Saïd (ed.), ΕΛΛΗΝΙΣΜΟΣ: *Quelques jalons pour une histoire de l'identité grecque* (E.J. Brill), 125-47.

Friedländer, P. (1919-21), *Darstellungen aus der Sittengeschichte Roms*, 3 vols (S. Hirzel).

Gaertner, J.F. (2006), 'Die Kultepiklesen und Kultaitia in Pausanias' *Periegesis*', *Hermes* 134, 471-87.

Gaifman, M. (2006), 'Statue, Cult and Reproduction', in J. Trimble and J. Elsner (eds), *Art and Replication: Greece, Rome and Beyond, Art History* 29 (n.2), 258-79.

Gallazzi, C. and Kramer, B. (1998), 'Artemidorus im Zeichensaal: Eine Papyrusrolle mit Text, Landkarte und Skizzenbüchern aus spälhellenistischer Zeit', *Archiv für Papyrusforschung* 44, 189-208.

Galli, M. (2002), *Die Lebenswelt eines Sophisten: Untersuchungen zu den Bauten und Stiftungen des Herodes Atticus* (Philip von Zabern).

Galli, M. (2005), 'Pilgrimage as Elite *Habitus:* Educated Pilgrims in Sacred Landscape During the Second Sophistic' in J. Elsner and I. Rutherford (eds), *Pilgrimage in Graeco-Roman and Christian Antiquity* (Oxford University Press), 251-90.

Gardiner, E.N. (1925), *Olympia: Its History and Remains* (Clarendon Press).

Garnsey, P. and Saller, R. (1987), *The Roman Empire: Economy, Society and Culture* (Duckworth).

Gazda, E.K. (ed.) (2002), *The Ancient Art of Emulation: Studies in Artistic Originality and Tradition from the Present to Classical Antiquity* (University of Michigan Press).

Bibliography

Gedoyn, N. (1731-3), *Pausanias ou Voyage historique, pittoresque et philosophique de la Grèce* (Didot).

Gell, W. (1817), *Itinerary of the Morea: Being a Description of the Routes of that Peninsula* (Rodwell and Martin).

Gell, W. (1819), *The Itinerary of Greece: Containing one hundred routes in Attica, Boeotia, Phocis, Locris and Thessaly* (Rodwell and Martin).

Georgiadou, A. and Larmour, D.H.J. (1998), *Lucian's Science Fiction Novel* True Histories (Brill).

Geus, K. (2002), *Eratosthenes von Kyrene: Studien zur hellenistischen Kultur- und Wissenschaftsgeschichte* (C.H. Beck).

Giesinger, F. (1937), 'Periplous (2)', *RE* XIX, 841-50.

Goldhill, S. (1994), 'The Naïve and the Knowing Eye: Ecphrasis and the Culture of Viewing in the Hellenistic world', in S. Goldhill and R. Osborne (eds), *Art and Text in Greek Culture* (Cambridge University Press), 197-223.

Goldhill, S. (2002), *Who Needs Greek? Contests in the Cultural History of Hellenism* (Cambridge University Press).

Goldmann, S. (1991), 'Topoi des Gedenkens: Pausanias' Reise durch die griechische Gedächnislandschaft', in A. Haverkamp and R. Lachmann (eds), *Gedächniskunst: Raum – Bild – Schrift: Studien zur Mnemotechnik* (Suhrkamp), 145-64.

Gould, J. (1989), *Herodotus* (Weidenfeld & Nicolson).

Graf, F. (1995), 'Ekphrasis: Die Entstehung der Gattung in der Antike', in G. Boehm and H. Pfotenhauer (eds), *Beschreibungskunst – Kunstbeschreibung: Ekphrasis von der Antike bis zur Gegenwart* (Wilhelm Fink Verlag), 143-55.

Guillet de St-George, G. (1676), *Athènes Ancienne et Nouvelle et l'Estat Présent de l'Empire des Turcs Contenant la Vie du Sultan Mahomet IV,* third revised edition (Estienne Michallet).

Gurlitt, W. (1890), *Über Pausanias* (Leuschner & Lubensky).

Gwynn, A. (1929), 'Xenophon and Sophaenetus', *CQ* 23, 38-9.

Habicht, C. (1969), *Die Inschriften des Asklepieions: Altertümer von Pergamon,* vol. 8 part 3 (Walter de Gruyter).

Habicht, C. (1984), 'Pausanias and the Evidence of Inscriptions', *Classical Antiquity* 3, 40-56.

Habicht, C. (1985) *Pausanias' Guide to Ancient Greece* (University of California Press).

Hägg, T. (1983), *The Novel in Antiquity* (University of California Press).

Halfmann, H. (1979), *Die Senatoren aus dem östlichen Teil des Imperium Romanum bis zum Ende des 2. Jh. n. Chr* (Vandenhoeck & Ruprecht).

Halfmann, H. (1986), *Itinera Principum: Geschichte und Typologie der Kaiserreisen im Römischen Reich* (Franz Steiner Verlag).

Hall, E. (1989) *Inventing the Barbarian: Greek Self-definition through Tragedy* (Oxford Clarendon Press).

Hall, J.M. (1997), *Ethnic Identity in Greek Antiquity* (Cambridge University Press).

Hallett, C.H. (2005), 'Emulation versus Replication: Redefining Roman Copying', *JRA* 18, 419-35.

Hanell, K. (1938), 'Phaidryntes', *RE* XIX, 1560.

Harding, P. (1994), *Androtion and his* Atthis (Clarendon Press).

Harrison, J.E. (1903), *Prolegomena to the Study of Greek Religion* (Cambridge University Press).

195

Bibliography

Harrison, J.E. (1912), *Themis: A Study of the Social Origins of Greek Religion* (Cambridge University Press).

Harrison, J.E. and Verrall, M. de G. (1890), *Mythology and Monuments of Athens, Being a Translation of a Portion of the* Attica *of Pausanias by M de G. Verrall, with Introductory Essay and Archaeological Commentary by J.E. Harrison* (Macmillan).

Harrison, S.J. (2000) *Apuleius: a Latin Sophist* (Oxford University Press).

Harrison, T. (2007), 'The Place of Geography in Herodotus' *Histories*', in C. Adams and J. Roy (eds), *Travel, Geography and Culture in Ancient Greece and the Near East* (Routledge), 44-65.

Hartog, F. (1988), *The Mirror of Herodotus: The Representation of the Other in the Writing of History*, translated by J. Lloyd (University of California Press).

Hartog, F. (2001), *Memories of Odysseus: Frontier Tales from Ancient Greece*, translated by J. Lloyd (Edinburgh University Press).

Häsler, B. (1973), 'Winckelmanns Verhältnis zur griechischen Literatur', in B. Häsler (ed.), *Beiträge zu einem neuen Winckelmannbild* (Akademie Verlag Berlin), 39-42.

Heberdey, R. (1894), *Die Reisen des Pausanias in Griechenland* (F. Tempsky & G. Freitag).

Hedreen, G. (2001), *Capturing Troy: The Narrative Functions of Landscape in Archaic and Early Classical Greek Art* (University of Michigan Press).

Heer, J. (1979), *La personnalité de Pausanias* (Les Belles Lettres).

Heffernan, J.A.W. (1993), *The Museum of Words: The Poetics of Ekphrasis from Homer to Ashberry* (University of Chicago Press).

Hejnic, J. (1961), *Pausanias the Periegete and the Archaic History of Arkadia* (Nakladatelství Ceskoslovenské Akademie Ved).

Henderson, J. (2001a), 'Farnell's Cults: The Making and Breaking of Pausanias in Victorian Archaeology and Anthropology', in S.E. Alcock, J.F. Cherry and J. Elsner (eds), *Pausanias: Travel and Memory in Roman Greece* (Oxford University Press), 207-33.

Henderson, J. (2001b), 'From Megalopolis to Cosmopolis: Polybius, or There and Back Again', in S. Goldhill (ed.), *Being Greek under Rome: Cultural Identity, the Second Sophistic and the Development of the Empire* (Cambridge University Press), 29-49.

Herington, C.J. (1964), '*Aristeas of Prokonnesos. By J.D.P. Bolton*' (Review), *Phoenix* 18, 78-82.

Herrmann, H.-V. (1972), *Olympia: Heiligtum und Wettkampfstätte* (Hirmer Verlag)

Herzfeld, M. (1986), *Ours Once More: Folklore, Ideology and the Making of Modern Greece* (Pella).

Herzfeld, M. (1987), *Anthropology Through the Looking-Glass: Critical Ethnography in the Margins of Europe* (Cambridge University Press).

Hiller v. Gärtringen, F. (1927), 'Pausanias' arkadische Königsliste', *Klio* 21, 1-13.

Hinrichsen, A. (1991), *Baedeker's Reisehandbücher 1832-1990*, second edition (Ursula Hinrichsen Verlag).

Hirschfeld, G. (1882), 'Pausanias und die Inschriften von Olympia', *Archäologische Zeitung* 40, 98-130.

Hitzig, H. and Blümner, H. (1896-1910), *Pausaniae Graeciae Descriptio*, 3 vols (Reisland).

Holleaux, M. (1898), 'Apollon Spodios' in *Mélanges Henri Weil* (A. Fontemoing), 193-206.

196

Bibliography

Holleaux, M. (1938), *Études d'épigraphie et d'histoire grecques*, vol. 1 (De Boccard).

Holtzhauer, H. (ed.) (1969), *Winckelmanns Werke in einem Band* (Aufbau Verlag).

Holum, K. (1990), 'Hadrian and St. Helena: Imperial Travel and the Origins of Christian Holy Land Pilgrimage', in R.G. Ousterhout (ed.), *The Blessings of Pilgrimage* (University of Illinois Press), 61-81.

Hopper, R.J. (1971), *The Acropolis* (Weidenfeld & Nicolson).

Horden, P. and Purcell, N. (2000), *The Corrupting Sea: A Study of Mediterranean History* (Blackwell).

Hornblower, J. (1981), *Hieronymus of Cardia* (Oxford University Press).

Hornblower, S. (1990), 'When was Megalopolis founded?', *ABSA* 85, 71-7.

Hunt, E.D. (1984), 'Travel, Tourism and Piety in the Roman Empire: A Context for the Beginnings of Christian Pilgrimage', *EMC* 3, 391-417.

Huntingford, G.W.B. (1980) *The Periplus of the Eythraean Sea* (The Hakluyt Society).

Hutton, W.E. (2005a), *Describing Greece: Landscape and Literature in the* Periegesis *of Pausanias* (Cambridge University Press).

Hutton, W.E. (2005b), 'The Construction of Religious Space in Pausanias', in J. Elsner and I. Rutherford (eds), *Pilgrimage in Graeco-Roman and Christian Antiquity* (Oxford University Press), 291-317.

Imhoof-Blumer, F. and Gardner, P. (1885), 'A Numismatic Commentary on Pausanias: Megarica, Corinthiaca', *JHS* 6, 50-101.

Imhoof-Blumer, F. and Gardner, P. (1886), 'A Numismatic Commentary on Pausanias, Part II: Books III-VIII', *JHS* 7, 57-113.

Imhoof-Blumer, F. and Gardner, P. (1887), 'A Numismatic Commentary on Pausanias, Part III: Books IX, X, 1.1-38.', *JHS* 8, 6-63.

Irigoin, J. (2001), 'Les manuscripts de Pausanias, quarante ans après: Hommage à la mémoire d'Aubrey Diller', in D. Knoepfler and M. Piérart (eds), *Éditer, traduire, commenter Pausanias en l'an 2000* (Université de Neuchâtel. Faculté des lettres et sciences humaines), 9-24.

Irwin, D. (1972), *Winckelmann: Writings on Art* (Phaidon).

Iunius, F. (1987), *A Lexicon of Artists and their Works (Catalogus Architectorum) Translated From the Original Latin of 1694, edited by K. Aldrich, P. Fehl & R. Fehl* (University of California Press).

Iunius, F. (1991), *The Painting of the Ancients (De Pictura veterum) According to the English Translation (1638), edited by K. Aldrich, P. Fehl & R. Fehl* (University of California Press).

Jacob, C. (1980), 'Paysages hantés et jardins merveilleux', *L'Ethnographie* 81-2 (year 102, vol. 76), 35-67.

Jacob, C. (1991), *Géographie et ethnographie en Grèce ancienne* (Armand Colin).

Jacoby, F. (1944), '*Patrios Nomos:* State Burial in Athens and the Public Cemetery in the Kerameikos', *JHS* 64, 37-66.

Jacoby, F. (1949), *Atthis: The Local Chronicles of Ancient Athens* (Clarendon Press).

Jacoby, F. (1955), *Fragmente der griechischen Historiker*, part IIIb, Commentary (Brill).

Jacquemin, A. (1991a), 'Delphes au II siècle: Un lieu de la mémoire grecque', in S. Saïd (ed.), *ΕΛΛΗΝΙΣΜΟΣ: Quelques jalons pour une histoire de l'identité grecque* (E.J. Brill), 217-31.

Jacquemin, A. (1991b), 'Les curiosités naturelles chez Pausanias', *Ktema* 16, 123-30.

Jacquemin, A. (1996), 'Pausanias et les empereurs romains', *Ktema* 21, 29-42.

197

Jacquemin, A. (2001), 'Pausanias, le sanctuaire d'Olympie et les archéologues', in D. Knoepfler and M Piérart (eds), *Éditer, traduire, commenter Pausanias en l'an 2000* (Université de Neuchâtel, Faculté des lettres et sciences humaines), 283-300.

Janni, P. (1984), *La mappa e il periplo: Cartografia antica e spazio odologico* (Bretschneider).

Janni, P. (1998), 'Cartographie et art nautique dans le monde ancien', in P. Arnaud, P. Counillon, *Geographica Historica* (Ausonius), 41-53.

Jex-Blake, K. and Sellers, E. (1896), *The Elder Pliny's Chapters on the History of Art* (Macmillan).

Jones, C.P. (1971), *Plutarch and Rome* (Clarendon Press).

Jones, C.P. (1986), *Culture and Society in Lucian* (Harvard University Press).

Jones, C.P. (1996a), 'The Panhellenion', *Chiron* 26, 29-56.

Jones, C.P. (1996b), 'Review of K.W. Arafat, *Pausanias' Greece*', *EMC* 15, 458-62.

Jones, C.P. (1999), *Kinship Diplomacy in the Ancient World* (Harvard University Press).

Jones, C.P, (2001), 'Pausanias and His Guides', in S.E. Alcock, J.F. Cherry and J. Elsner (eds), *Pausanias: Travel and Memory in Ancient Greece* (Oxford University Press), 33-9.

Jost, M. (1973), 'Pausanias en Mégalopolitide', *REA* 75, 241-67.

Jost, M. (1985), *Sanctuaires et cultes d'Arcadie* (Librairie Philosophique).

Jost, M. (1998), 'Versions locales et versions "panhelléniques" des mythes arcadiens chez Pausanias', in V. Pirenne-Delforge, *Les Panthéons des cités: des origines à la Périégèse de Pausanias* (*Kernos* Suppl. 8) (Centre International d'Étude de la Religion Grecque Antique), 227-40.

Jost, M. (2007), 'Pausanias in Arkadia: an Example of Cultural Tourism', in C. Adams and J. Roy (eds), *Travel, Geography and Culture in Ancient Greece and the Near East* (Routledge), 104-22.

Jost, M. and Marcadé, M. (1998), 'Commentaire', in M. Casevitz, M. Jost and J. Marcadé (eds), *Pausanias:* Description de la Grèce. *Livre VIII. L'Arcadie* (Budé, Les Belles Lettres), 161-293.

Jourdain-Annequin, C. (1998), 'Réprésenter les dieux: Pausanias et le panthéon des cités', in V. Pirenne-Delforge, *Les Panthéons des cités: des origines à la Périégèse de Pausanias* (*Kernos* Suppl. 8) (Centre International d'Étude de la Religion Grecque Antique), 241-61.

Justi, C. (1956), *Winckelmann und seine Zeitgenossen*, 3 vols, fifth edition (Phaidon).

Kalkmann, A. (1886), *Pausanias der Perieget: Untersuchungen über seine Schriftstellerei und seine Quellen* (G. Reimer).

König, J. (2001), 'Favorinus' *Corinthian Oration* in its Corinthian Context', *PCPS* 47, 141-71.

Konstan, D. (2001a), 'The Joys of Pausanias', in S.E. Alcock, J.F. Cherry and J. Elsner (eds), *Pausanias: Travel and Memory in Ancient Greece* (Oxford University Press), 57-60.

Konstan, D. (2001b), '*To Hellênikon Ethnos*: Ethnicity and the Construction of Ancient Greek Identity', in I. Malkin (ed.), *Ancient Perceptions of Greek Ethnicity* (Harvard University Press), 29-50.

Kourinou, E. (2007), 'The Representation of Means of Transport on Reliefs in the Collection of the National Archaeological Museum in Athens', in C. Adams and J. Roy (eds), *Travel, Geography and Culture in Ancient Greece and the Near East* (Routledge), 88-103.

Bibliography

Kowalzig, B. (2005), 'Mapping out *Communitas:* Performances of *Theoria* in their Sacred and Political Context', in J. Elsner and I. Rutherford (eds), *Pilgrimage in Graeco-Roman and Christian Antiquity* (Oxford University Press), 41-72.

Kramer, B. (2001), 'The Earliest Map of Spain (?) and the Geography of Artemidorus of Ephesus on Papyrus', *Mappa Mundi* 53, 115-20.

Kreilinger, U. (1997), 'Die Kunstauswahlkriterien des Pausanias', *Hermes* 125, 470-91.

Kroymann, J. (1943), *Pausanias und Rhianos* (Junker und Dünnhaupt).

Kuhn, J. et al. (1696), *Pausaniae Graeciae descriptio accurata, qua lector ceu manu per eam regionem circumducitur* (Thomas Fritsch).

Lacroix, L. (1994), 'Traditions locales et légendes étiologiques dans la Périégèse de Pausanias', *Journal des Savants* 1994.1, 75-99.

Lafond, Y. (1994), 'Pausanias et les paysages d'Achaïe', *REA* 96, 485-97.

Lafond, Y. (1996), 'Pausanias et l'histoire du Péloponnèse depuis la conquête romaine', in J. Bingen (ed.), *Pausanias Historien. Entretiens sur l'antiquité classique* XLI (Fondation Hardt), 167-98.

Lafond, Y. (2001), 'Lire Pausanias à l'époque des Antonins: Réflexions sur la place de la *Périègèse* dans l'histoire culturelle, religieuse et sociale de la Grèce romaine' in D. Knoepfler and M. Piérart (eds), *Éditer, traduire, commenter Pausanias en l'an 2000* (Université de Neuchâtel. Faculté des lettres et sciences humaines), 387-406.

Lanzillotta, E. (1988), 'Geografia e storia da Ecateo a Tucidide', in M. Sordi (ed.), *Geografia e storiografia nel mondo classico* (Università Cattolica del Sacro Cuore Milano), 19-31.

Le Morvan, A. (1932), 'La description artistique chez Lucien', *Révue des Études Grecques* 45, 280-90.

Le Roy, M. (1770), *Les Ruines des plus beaux Monuments de la Grece: Considéréés du côté de l'histoire et du côté de l'architecture*, second edition (L-F. Delatour).

Leake, M.W. (1821), *The Topography of Athens: With some Remarks on its Antiquities* (John Murray).

Leake, M.W. (1830), *Travels in the Morea* (John Murray).

Leake, M.W. (1835), *Travels in Northern Greece* (J. Rodwell).

Leake, M.W. (1846), *Peloponnesiaca: A Supplement to Travels in the Morea* (J. Rodwell).

Lehmann-Hartleben, K. (1941), 'The *Imagines* of the Elder Philostratus', *Art Bulletin* 23, 16-44.

Lepenies, W. (1986), 'Johann Joachim Winckelmann: Kunst und Naturgeschichte im 18. Jahrhundert', in T.W. Gaehtgens (ed.), *Johann Joachim Winckelmann 1717-1768, Studien zum Achzehnten Jahrhundert 7* (Felix Meiner Verlag), 221-37.

Levi, P. (1971), *Pausanias: Guide to Greece*, 2 vols (Penguin).

Leyerle, B. (1996), 'Landscape as Cartography in Early Christian Pilgrimage Narratives', *Journal of the American Academy of Religion* 64, 119-43.

Liddle, A. (2003), *Arrian: Periplous Ponti Euxini. Edited with Translation and Commentary* (Bristol Classical Press).

Lightfoot, J.L. (2003), *Lucian: On the Syrian Goddess* (Oxford University Press).

Lippold, G. (1939), 'Onatas (1)', *RE* XVIII, 408-11.

Lolling, H.G. (1989), *Reisenotizen aus Griechenland 1878 und 1877: Bearbeitet von B. Heinrich, Eingeleitet von H. Kalcyk* (Dietrich Reimer Verlag).

Ma, J. (2003), 'Peer Polity Interaction in the Hellenistic Age', *P&P* 180, 9-39.

Ma, J. (2006), 'The Two Cultures: Connoisseurship and Civic Honours', in J.

Bibliography

Trimble and J. Elsner (eds), *Art and Replication: Greece, Rome and Beyond, Art History* 29 (n.2), 325-38.

Marasco, G. (1978), *I viaggi nella Grecia antica* (Edizioni dell'Ateneo & Bizarri).

Marcotte, D. (1992), 'La redécouverte de Pausanias à la Renaissance', *Studi italiani di Filologia Classica* 85 (ser. III 10), 872-7.

Marincola, J. (1997), *Authority and Tradition in Ancient Historiography* (Cambridge University Press).

Marinescu-Himu, M. (1975), 'Les sources d'inspiration de Pausanias dans le livre 4 de la Périègèse', in *Actes de la XIIe conférence internationale d'études classiques 'Eirene'*, Clúj-Napoca 2-7 Oct. 1972 (Editura Academiei Republicii Socialiste Romania; A.M. Hakkert), 251-7.

Meadows, A.R. (1995), 'Pausanias and the Historiography of Classical Sparta', *CQ* 89, 91-113.

Meister, K. (1975), *Historische Kritik bei Polybios: Palingenesia* IX (Franz Steiner Verlag).

Mette, H.J. (1952), *Pytheas von Massalia* (Walter de Gruyter & Co).

Meursius, J. (1675), *Creta, Cyprus, Rhodus sive: De Nobilissimarum harum insularum rebus & antiquitatibus. Comentarii postumi, nunc primum editi* (Abrahamus Wolfgangus).

Meyer, E. (1939), *Peloponnesische Wanderungen* (Max Niehaus Verlag).

Meyer, E. (1954), *Pausanias: Beschreibung Griechenlands* (Artemis).

Meyer, E. (1978), 'Messenien', *RE* Suppl. XV, 155-289.

Milani, C. (1988), 'Geografia micenea e geografia del Catalogo delle navi', in. M. Sordi (ed.), *Geografia e storiografia nel mondo classico* (Università Cattolica del Sacro Cuore Milano), 3-18.

Millar, F. (1981), 'The World of the Golden Ass', *JRS* 71, 63-75.

Millar, F. (1992), *The Emperor in the Roman World (31 BC-AD 337)*, second edition (Duckworth).

Miller, H.H. (1972), *Greece Through the Ages: As Seen by Travelers From Herodotus to Byron* (Dent).

Miller, K. (1916), *Itineraria Romana: Römische Reisewege an der Hand der Tabula Peutingeriana* (Strecker und Schröder).

Miller, K. (1962), *Die Peutingersche Tafel: Neudruck der letzten von K. Miller bearbeiteten Auflage* (Brockhaus).

Miller, W. (1908), *The Latins in the Levant: A History of Frankish Greece* (John Murray).

Mitchell, S. (1976), 'Requisitioned Transport in the Roman Empire: a New Inscription From Pisidia', *JRS* 66, 106-31.

Moggi, M. (1993), 'Scittura e riscrittura della storia in Pausania', *Rivista di filologia e di istruzione classica* 121, 396-418.

Moggi, M. (1996), 'L'*excursus* di Pausania sulla Ionia', in J. Bingen (ed.), *Pausanias Historien. Entretiens sur l'antiquité classique* XLI (Fondation Hardt), 79-105.

Moggi, M. (2001), 'Passato remoto, passato recente e contemporaneità in Pausania', in G. Bianchetti et al. (eds), *ΠΟΙΚΙΛΜΑ: Studi in onore di Michele R. Catardella* vol. II (Agorà Edizioni), 903-16.

Moggi, M. (2002), 'Pausanias e Roma: Nota di lettura a VIII 27.1', *Gerion* 20, 435-49.

Moggi, M. (2005), 'Marpessa detta Choira e Ares Gynaikothoinas', in E. Østby (ed.), *Ancient Arcadia: Papers from the Third International Seminar on Ancient*

Bibliography

Arcadia, held at the Norwegian Institute at Athens 7-10 May 2002 (Oxbow), 139-50.

Moggi, M. and Osanna, M. (2003), *Pausania: Guida della Grecia*, vol. VII (Fondazione Lorenzo Valla).

Momigliano, A. (1975), *Alien Wisdom: The Limits of Hellenisation* (Cambridge University Press).

Monier, P. (1698), *Histoire des arts qui ont raport au dessein, divisé en trois livres, où il est traité de son origine, de son progrés, de sa chute, et de son rétablissement: Ouvrage utile au public pour savoir ce qui s'est fait de plus considerable en tous les âges, dans la peinture, la sculture, l'architecture et la gravure; et pour distinguer les bonnes manieres des mauvaises* (Pierre Giffart).

Morgan, J.R. (2007), 'Travel in the Greek Novel: Function and Interpretation', in C. Adams and J. Roy (eds), *Travel, Geography and Culture in Ancient Greece and the Near East* (Routledge), 139-60.

Morinis, E.A. (1992), *Sacred Journeys: The Anthropology of Pilgrimage* (Greenwood Press).

Murray, J. (1884), *Handbook for Travellers in Greece* (J. Murray).

Musti, D. (1982), 'Introduzione generale', in D. Musti and L. Beschi (eds), *Pausania: Guida della Grecia. Libro I: L'Attica* (Fondazione Lorenzo Valla), ix-cx.

Musti, D. (1984), 'L'itinerario di Pausania: Dal viaggio alla storia', *Quaderni Urbinati di Cultura Classica* N.S. 17.2, 7-18.

Musti, D. (1988), 'La struttura del libro di Pausania sulla Boiozia', in A. Beklaris (ed.), Επετηρίς της εταιρείας βοιωτικών μελετών 1.1. A' διεθνές συνέδριο βοιωτικών μελετών (von Zabern), 333-44.

Musti, D. (1996), 'La struttura del discorso storico in Pausania', in J. Bingen (ed.), *Pausanias Historien. Entretiens sur l'antiquité classique* XLI (Fondation Hardt), 9-34.

Musti, D. (2001), 'L'ora di Pausania: Sequenze cronologiche nella *Guida della Grecia* (sull'Anfizionia di Delfi e altri argomenti)', in D. Knoepfler and M. Piérart (eds), *Éditer, traduire, commenter Pausanias en l'an 2000* (Université de Neuchâtel, Faculté des lettres et sciences humaines), 43-78.

Musti, D. et al. (1982-) *Pausania: Guida della Grecia*, 7 vols in progress (Fondazione Lorenzo Valla).

Nenci, G. (1953), 'Il motivo dell' autopsia nella storiografia greca', *Studi Classici e Orientali* 3, 14-46.

Newby, Z. (2002), 'Testing the Boundaries of Ekphrasis: Lucian on the Hall', in J. Elsner (ed.), *The Verbal and the Visual: Cultures of Ekphrasis in Antiquity*, *Ramus* 31 (n. 1&2), 126-35.

Ní Mheallaigh, K. (2008), 'Pseudo-documentarism and the limits of ancient fiction', *AJPhil* 129.

Nicolet, C. (1988), *L'inventaire du monde: Géographie et politique aux origines de l'Empire romain* (Fayard).

Nippel, W. (1996), 'La costruzione dell' altro', in S. Settis (ed.), *I Greci: Storia Cultura Arte Società I: Noi e i Greci* (Einaudi), 165-96.

Nörenberg, H.-W. (1973), 'Untersuchungen zum Schluß der *Periegesis tes Hellados* des Pausanias', *Hermes* 101, 235-52.

Ødegård, K. (2005), 'The Topography of Ancient Tegea: New Discoveries and Old Problems', in E. Østby (ed.), *Ancient Arcadia: Papers from the Third International Seminar on Ancient Arcadia, held at the Norwegian Institute at Athens 7-10 May 2002* (Oxbow), 209-21.

Bibliography

Oikonomides, A.N. and Miller, M.C.J. (1995), *Hanno: Periplus, or, Circumnavigation of Africa*, third edition (Ares Publishers).

Oliver, J.H. (1972), 'The Conversion of the Periegete Pausanias', in *Homenaje a Antonio Tovar* (Editorial Gredos), 319-21.

Osanna, M. (2001), 'Tra monumenti, *agalmata e mirabilia*: organizzazione del percorso urbano di Corinto nella *Periegesi* di Pausania', in D. Knoepfler and M. Piérart (eds), *Éditer, traduire, commenter Pausanias en l'an 2000* (Université de Neuchâtel. Faculté des lettres et sciences humaines), 185-202.

Osborne, R. (1987), *Classical Landscape with Figures* (G. Philip).

Østby, E. (1986), 'The Archaic Temple of Athena Alea at Tegea', *Op. Ath.* 16, 75-102.

Palm, J. (1959), *Rom, Römertum und Imperium in der griechischen Literatur der Kaiserzeit* (C.W.K. Gleerup).

Papachatzis, N.D. (1963-9) *Παυσανίου Ελλάδος Περιήγησις*, 5 vols (Brabeio Akademias Athenon).

Pasquali, G. (1913), 'Die schriftstellerische Form des Pausanias', *Hermes* 48, 161-223.

Paton, J.M. (1951) *Chapters on Mediaeval and Renaissance Visitors to Greek Lands* (American School of Classical Studies at Athens).

Patterson, J.R. (1991), 'Settlement, City and Elite in Samnium and Lycia', in J. Rich and A. Wallace-Hadrill (eds), *City and Country in the Ancient World* (Routledge), 149-68.

Pearson, L. (1960), *The Lost Histories of Alexander the Great* (American Philological Association).

Pearson, L. (1962), 'The Pseudo-History of Messenia and its Authors', *Historia* 11, 397-426.

Peretti, A. (1979), *Il Periplo di Scilace: studio sul primo portolano del Mediterraneo* (Giardini).

Perry, E. (2005), *The Aesthetics of Emulation in the Visual Arts of Ancient Rome* (Cambridge University Press).

Petersen, E. (1909), 'Pausanias der Perieget', *Rh. Mus.* 64 (1909), 481-538.

Pfister, F. (1951), *Die Reisebilder des Herakleides*. Sitzungsberichte der Österreichischen Akademie der Wissenschaften, Philosophisch-Historische Klasse, 227(2) (R.M. Rohrer).

Picard, C. (1983), 'Remarques sur les sculptures monumentales du sanctuaires d'Aléa Athéna à Tégée', *Revue des Études Grecques* 46, 381-422.

Pikoulas, Y.A. (1986), Τεγεατικὰ: Ἔχεμος', *Archaiognosia* 2, 283-6.

Pikoulas, Y.A. (1999), 'The Road-Network of Arkadia', in T.H. Nielsen and J. Roy, *Defining Ancient Arkadia. Acts of the Copenhagen Polis Centre* 6 (Munksgaard), 248-319.

Pikoulas, Y.A. (2001), *Λεξικό των Οικισμών της Πελοποννήσου* (Megali Vivliothiki).

Pikoulas, Y.A. (2007), 'Travelling by Land in Ancient Greece', in C. Adams and J. Roy (eds), *Travel, Geography and Culture in Ancient Greece and the Near East* (Routledge), 78-87.

Pirenne-Delforge, V. (1998a), 'La notion de "panthéon" dans la *Périégèse* de Pausanias', in V. Pirenne-Delforge (ed.), *Les panthéons des cités: Des origines à la* Périégèse *de Pausanias*', *Kernos* suppl. 8 (Centre International d'étude de la Religion Grecque Antique), 129-48.

Pirenne-Delforge, V. (1998b), *Les panthéons des cités: Des origines à la* Périégèse *de Pausanias*', *Kernos* suppl. 8 (Centre International d'étude de la Religion Grecque Antique).

Bibliography

Polignac, F. de (1995), *Cults, Territory, and the Origins of the Greek City-State*, translated by J. Lloyd (University of Chicago Press).

Pollitt, J.J. (1974), *The Ancient View of Greek Art: Criticism, History and Terminology* (Yale University Press).

Porod, R. (2007), 'Von der historischen Wahrheit und dem Ende der Fiktionalität: Überlegungen zu Lukians Schrift Πῶς δεῖ ἱστορίαν συγγράφειν', *Antike und Abendland* 53, 120-40.

Porter, J.I. (2001) 'Ideals and Ruins: Pausanias, Longinus, and the Second Sophistic', in S.E. Alcock, J.F. Cherry and J. Elsner (eds), *Pausanias: Travel and Memory in Roman Greece* (Oxford University Press), 63-92.

Pothecary, S. (1997), 'The Expression "Our Times" in Strabo's *Geography*', *CP* 92, 235-46.

Potts, A. (1994), *Flesh and the Ideal: Winckelmann and the Origins of Art History* (Yale University Press).

Pouilloux, J. (1992) 'L'homme et l'oeuvre', in: M. Casevitz, J. Pouilloux and F. Chamoux (eds), *Pausanias: Description de la Grèce. Tome I. Introduction générale. Livre I. L'Attique* (Les Belles Lettres/Budé), IX-XXIX.

Pretzler, M. (1999) 'Myth and History at Tegea: Local Tradition and Community Identity', in T.H. Nielsen and J. Roy (eds), *Defining Ancient Arkadia. Acts of the Copenhagen Polis Centre* 6 (Munksgaard), 89-128.

Pretzler, M. (2004), 'Turning Travel into Text: Pausanias at Work', *G&R* 51, 199-216.

Pretzler, M. (2005a), 'Pausanias and Oral Tradition', *CQ* 55, 235-49.

Pretzler, M. (2005b), 'Pausanias at Mantinea: Invention and Manipulation of Local History' *PCPS* 51, 21-34.

Pretzler (2005c), 'Comparing Strabo with Pausanias: Greece in Context vs. Greece in Depth', in D. Dueck, H. Lindsay and S. Pothecary (eds), *Strabo's Cultural Geography: The Making of a Kolossurgia* (Cambridge University Press), 144-60.

Pretzler, M. (2007), 'Pausanias' Intellectual Background: the Travelling *Pepaideumenos*', in C. Adams and J. Roy (eds), *Travel, Geography and Culture in Ancient Greece and the Near East* (Routledge), 123-38.

Price, S. (1999), *Religions of the Ancient Greeks* (Cambridge University Press).

Pritchett, W.K. (1969-89), *Studies in Ancient Greek Topography*, 6 vols (University of California Press).

Pritchett, W.K. (1998), *Pausanias Periegetes I* (J.C. Gieben).

Pritchett, W.K. (1999), *Pausanias Periegetes II* (J.C. Gieben).

Prontera, F. (1993), 'Sull'esegesi ellenistica della geografia omerica', in G.W. Most, H. Petersmann and A.M. Ritter (eds), *Philanthropia kai Eusebeia: Festschrift für Albrecht Dihle zum 70. Geburtstag* (Vandenhoek & Ruprecht), 387-97.

Quaß, F. (1993), *Die Honoratiorenschicht in den Städten des griechischen Ostens: Untersuchungen zur politischen und sozialen Entwicklung in hellenistischer und römischer Zeit* (Franz Steiner Verlag).

Reardon, B.P. (1971), *Courants littéraires grecs des IIe et IIIe siècles après J.C.* (Belles Lettres).

Redfield, J. (1985), 'Herodotus the Tourist', *CP* 80, 97-118.

Regenbogen, O. (1956), 'Pausanias', *RE* Suppl. VIII, 1008-97.

Rehm, W. (ed.) (1952), *J.J. Winckelmann: Briefe*, vol. 1 (Walter de Gruyter).

Reynolds, L.D. and Wilson N.G. (1974), *Scribes and Scholars: A Guide to the Transmission of Greek and Latin Literature* (Clarendon Press).

Ridgway, B.S. (1984), *Roman Copies of Greek Sculpture: The Problem of the Originals* (University of Michigan Press).

Bibliography

Robert, C. (1909), *Pausanias als Schriftsteller* (Wiedmann)

Robert, L. (1977), 'Documents d'Asie Mineure', *BCH* 101, 43-132.

Roberts, C.H. and Skeat, T.C. (1983), *The Birth of the Codex* (British Academy, Oxford University Press).

Rocha-Pereira, M.H. (1990), *Pausaniae Graeciae Descriptio* (Bibliotheca Teubneriana).

Rohde, E. (1960), *Der griechische Roman und seine Vorläufer*, fourth edition (Georg Olms).

Romeo, I. (2002), 'The Panhellenion and Ethnic Identity', *Classical Philology* 97, 21-37.

Romm, J.S. (1989), 'Herodotus and Mythic Geography: The Case of the Hyperboreans', *TAPA* 119, 97-117.

Romm, J.S. (1992), *The Edges of the Earth in Ancient Thought: Geography, Exploration, and Fiction* (Princeton University Press).

Rood, T. (1998), *Thucydides: Narrative and Explanation* (Clarendon Press).

Rood, T. (2004), *The Sea! The Sea! The Shout of the Ten Thousand in the Modern Imagination* (Duckworth Overlook).

Roseman, C.H. (1994), *Pytheas of Massalia: On the Ocean. Text, Translation and Commentary* (Ares).

Roux, G. (1958), *Pausanias en Corinthie* (Société d'Édition les Belles Lettres).

Roux, G. (1963), 'Pausanias à l'entrée du sanctuaire Pythique', in J. Pouilloux and G. Roux (eds), *Énigmes à Delphes* (Éditions E. de Boccard), 3-68.

Roy, J. (1968), 'The Sons of Lycaon in Pausanias' Arcadian king-list', *ABSA* 63, 287-92.

Roy, J. (2007), 'Xenophon's *Anabasis* as a Traveller's Memoir', in C. Adams and J. Roy (eds), *Travel, Geography and Culture in Ancient Greece and the Near East* (Routledge), 66-77.

Rubinstein, L. (1995), 'Pausanias as a Source for the Classical Greek *Polis*', in M.H. Hansen and K. Raaflaub (eds), *Studies in the Ancient Greek Polis: Papers from the Copenhagen Polis Centre 2. Historia Einzelschriften* 95 (Franz Steiner), 211-19.

Rutherford, I. (2001), 'Tourism and the Sacred: Pausanias and the Traditions of Greek Pilgrimage', in S.E. Alcock, J.F. Cherry and J. Elsner (eds), *Pausanias: Travel and Memory in Roman Greece* (Oxford University Press), 40-52.

Saïd, S. (1994), 'Lucien ethnographe', in A. Billault (ed.), *Lucien de Samosate* (De Boccard), 149-70.

Saïd, S. (2001), 'The Discourse of Identity in Greek Rhetoric from Isocrates to Aristides', in I. Malkin (ed.), *Ancient Perceptions of Greek Ethnicity* (Harvard University Press), 275-99.

St Clair, W. (1967), *Lord Elgin and the Marbles* (Oxford University Press).

Sandy, G. (1997), *The Greek World of Apuleius: Apuleius and the Second Sophistic* (Brill).

Schlam, C.C. (1992), *The Metamorphoses of Apuleius: On Making an Ass of Oneself* (Duckworth).

Schliemann, H. (1878), *Mycenae: A Narrative of Researches and Discoveries at Mycenae and Tiryns* (John Murray).

Schmitz, T. (1997), *Bildung und Macht: Zur sozialen und politischen Funktion der zweiten Sophistik in der griechischen Welt der Kaiserzeit. Zetemata 97* (C.H. Beck).

Schöll, R. (1878), 'Zur Thukydides-Biographie', *Hermes* 13, 433-51.

Schönberger, O. (1995), 'Die *Bilder* des Philostratos', in G. Boehm and H. Pfotenhauer (eds), *Beschreibungskunst – Kunstbeschreibung: Ekphrasis von der Antike bis zur Gegenwart* (Wilhelm Fink Verlag), 157-73.

Schubart, J.H.C. (1853), 'Über die Handschriften des Pausanias', *Zeitschrift für Altertumswissenschaften* 20, 385-510.

Schubart, J.H.C. (1883), 'Pausanias und seine Ankläger', *Jahrbuch für Classische Philologie* 29, 469-82.

Schwenn, F. (1934), 'Telephos (1)', *RE* 5A, 36-369.

Scullion, S. (2005), '"Pilgrimage" and Greek Religion: Sacred and Secular in the Pagan *Polis*', in J. Elsner and I. Rutherford (eds), *Pilgrimage in Graeco-Roman and Christian Antiquity* (Oxford University Press), 111-30.

Seel, O. (1961), *Antike Entdeckerfahrten: Zwei Reiseberichte* (Artemis).

Segre, M. (1927), 'Pausania come fonte storica', *Historia* (Milan) 1, 202-34.

Segre, M. (2004), *Pausania come fonte storica*, tesi di laurea of 1926/7 (Biblioteca Umberto Segre).

Settis, S. (1968), 'Il ninfeo di Erode Attico a Olimpia e il problema della composizione della Periegesi di Pausania', *ASNP* ser. 2, 37, 1-63.

Shilleto, A.R. (1886), *Pausanias' Description of Greece, Translated with Notes* (Bohn's Classical Library).

Sidebottom, H. (2002), 'Pausanias: Past, Present and Closure', *CQ* 52, 494-9.

Silberman, A. (1993), Arrien, *Périple du Pont-Euxin*. Essai d'interprétation et d'évaluation des données historiques et géographiques', *ANRW* 34.1. 276-311.

Simon, E. (1995), 'Der Schild des Achilleus', in G. Boehm and H. Pfotenhauer (eds), *Beschreibungskunst – Kunstbeschreibung: Ekphrasis von der Antike bis zur Gegenwart* (Wilhelm Fink Verlag), 123-41.

Sivan, H. (1988a), 'Who was Egeria? Piety and Pilgrimage in the Age of Gratian', *Harvard Theological Review* 81, 59-72.

Sivan, H. (1988b), 'Holy Land Pilgrimages and Western Audiences: Some Reflections on Egeria and her Circle', *CQ* 38, 528-35.

Smith, A.H. (1916), 'Lord Elgin and his Collection', *JHS* 36, 163-372.

Snodgrass, A.M. (1987), *An Archaeology of Greece: The Present State and Future Scope of a Discipline* (University of California Press).

Snodgrass, A.M. (2001), 'Pausanias and the Chest of Kypselos', in S.E. Alcock, J.F. Cherry and J. Elsner (eds), *Pausanias: Travel and Memory in Roman Greece* (Oxford University Press), 127-41.

Snodgrass, A.M. (2003), 'Another Early Reader of Pausanias?', *JHS* 123, 187-9.

Sordi, M. (1988), 'Gli interessi geografici e topografici nelle "Elleniche" di Senofonte', in M. Sordi (ed.), *Geografia e storiografia nel mondo classico* (Università Cattolica del Sacro Cuore Milano), 32-40.

Spawforth, A. (1994), 'Symbol of Unity? The Persian-Wars Tradition in the Roman Empire', in S. Hornblower (ed.), *Greek Historiography* (Clarendon Press), 233-47.

Spawforth, A.J. and Walker, S. (1985) 'The World of the Panhellenion: I. Athens and Eleusis', *JRS* 75, 78-104.

Spawforth, A.J. and Walker, S. (1986), 'The World of the Panhellenion: II. Three Dorian Cities', *JRS* 76, 88-105.

Spon, J. (1678), *Voyage d'Italie, de Dalmatie, de Grece, et du Levant: Fait aux années 1675 & 1676*, 3 vols (Antoine Cellier).

Spon, J. (1679), *Réponse à la critique publiée par M. Guillet sur le* Voyage de Grèce *de Jacob Spon. Avec quatre lettres sur le mesme sujet, le Journal d'Angleterre du sieur Vernon et la liste des erreurs commises par M. Guillet dans son* Athènes ancienne et nouvelle (Antoine Celier fils) 1679.

Bibliography

Stadter, P.A. (1980), *Arrian of Nicomedia* (University of North Carolina Press).

Stadter, P.A. (1989), *A Commentary on Plutarch's Pericles* (University of North Carolina Press).

Stansbury-O'Donnell, M. (1989), 'Polygnotos's *Iliupersis*: a New Reconstruction', *AJA* 93, 203-15.

Stansbury-O'Donnell, M. (1990), 'Polygnotos's *Nekyia*: a Reconstruction and Analysis', *AJA* 94, 213-35.

Steinhardt, M. (2002a), 'Tyrannenhaus und Kaiserkult: zu einer angeblich römer-feindlichen Bemerkung bei Pausanias', *Thetis* 9, 95-6.

Steinhardt, M. (2002b), 'Das Unglück der römischen Herrschaft? Zum Verständnis von Pausanias 8.27.1', *Würzburger Jahrbücher für die Altertumswissenschaft* 26, 145-50.

Steinhardt, M. (2003), 'Pausanias und das Philopappos-Monument – ein Fall von *Damnatio Memoriae?*', *Klio* 85, 171-88.

Steward, A.F. (1977), *Skopas of Paros* (Noyes).

Stichtenoth, D. (1959), *Pytheas von Marseille: Über das Weltmeer* (Böhlau Verlag).

Stoneman, R. (1984), *A Literary Companion to Travel in Greece* (Penguin).

Stoneman, R. (1987), *Land of Lost Gods: the Search for Classical Greece* (Hutchinson).

Strauß, M. (1994), 'Telephos', *LIMC* 7.1, 856-7.

Strid, O. (1976), *Über Sprache und Stil des Periegeten Pausanias* (Almquist & Wiksell International).

Stuart-Jones, H. (1894), 'The Chest of Kypselos', *JHS* 14, 30-80.

Stuart Jones, H. (1895), *Select Passages From Ancient Writers Illustrative of the History of Greek Sculpture* (Macmillan).

Stylianou, P.J. (2004), 'One *Anabasis* or Two?', in R. Lane Fox (ed.), *The Long March. Xenophon and the Ten Thousand* (Yale University Press), 68-96.

Sutton, S.B. (2001), 'A Temple Worth Seeing: Pausanias, Travelers, and the Narrative Landscape at Nemea', in S.E. Alcock, J.F. Cherry and J. Elsner (eds), *Pausanias. Travel and Memory in Roman Greece* (Oxford University Press), 175-89.

Swain, S. (1996), *Hellenism and Empire: Language, Classicism, and Power in the Greek World, AD 50-250* (Oxford University Press).

Talbert, R. (2004), 'Cartography and Taste in Peutinger's Map', in R. Talbert and K. Brodersen (eds), *Space in the Roman World: Its Perception and Presentation* (Lit Verlag), 113-41.

Tarrant, H. (1999), 'Dialogue and Orality in a Post-Platonic Age', in E.A. Mackay, *Signs of Orality* (Brill), 181-98.

Tausend, K. (ed.) (1999), *Pheneos und Lousoi: Untersuchungen zu Geschichte und Topographie Nordostarkadiens* (Peter Lang).

Tausend, K. (2006), *Verkehrswege der Argolis: Rekonstruktion und historische Bedeutung* (Franz Steiner Verlag).

Taylor, T. (1794), *The Description of Greece by Pausanias: Translated from the Greek with Notes, in which much of the mythology of Greece is unfolded from a Theory which has been for many Ages unknown*, 3 vols (R. Faulder).

Thompson, H.A. and Wycherley, R.E. (1972), *The Agora of Athens: The History, Shape and Uses of an Ancient City Center* (American School of Classical Studies at Athens).

Tod, M. and Wace, A.J.B. (1906), *Catalogue of the Sparta Museum* (Clarendon Press).

Torelli, M. (2001) 'Pausania a Corinto: Un intellettuale greco del secondo secolo e la propaganda imperiale romana', in D. Knoepfler and M. Piérart (eds), *Éditer, traduire, commenter Pausanias en l'an 2000* (Université de Neuchâtel. Faculté des lettres et sciences humaines), 135-84.

Touloumakos, J. (1971), *Zum Geschichtsbewusstsein der Griechen in der Zeit der römischen Herrschaft* (Habelt).

Tozer, H.F. (1887), 'Two Books on Pausanias', *CR* 1, 101-3.

Tozzi, P. (1963), 'Studi su Ecataeo di Mileto', *Athenaeum* 41, 39-50, 318-26.

Travlos, J. (1971), *Pictorial Dictionary of Ancient Athens* (Thames and Hudson).

Trendelenburg, A. (1911), *Pausanias' Hellenika* (Weidmann).

Trendelenburg, A. (1914), *Pausanias in Olympia* (Weidmann).

Trimble, J. and Elsner, J. (2006), 'Introduction: "If You Need a Statue...", in J. Trimble and J. Elsner (eds), *Art and Replication: Greece, Rome and Beyond*, *Art History* 29 (n.2), 201-12.

Turnbull, G. (1740), *A Treatise on Ancient Painting, containing observations on the Rise, progress, and Decline of That Art amongst the Greeks and Romans. ... The Whole Illustrated and Adorned with Fifty Pieces of Ancient Painting... Lately Done from the Originals with Great Exactness and Elegance* (A Millar).

Tylor, E.B. (1871), *Primitive Culture* (J. Murray).

Tzifopoulos, Y.Z. (1991), *Pausanias as a* Steloskopas: *An Epigraphical Commentary of Pausanias'* Eliakon *A and B* (PhD Diss., Ohio State University).

Tzifopoulos, Y.Z. (1993), 'Mummius' Dedications at Olympia and Pausanias' Attitude to the Romans', *GRBS* 34, 93-100.

Uhlig, L. (1988), *Griechenland als Ideal: Winckelmann und seine Rezeption in Deutschland* (Gunter Narr Verlag).

Urban, R (1979), *Wachstum und Krise des Achäischen Bundes* (Franz Steiner Verlag).

Van der Vin, J.P.A (1980), *Travellers to Greece and Constantinople: Ancient Monuments and Old Traditions in Medieval Travellers' Tales* (Nederlands Historisch-Archaeologisch Instituut te Istanbul).

Vanderpool, E. (1949), 'The Route of Pausanias in the Athenian Agora', *Hesperia* 18, 128-37.

Veyne, P. (1988), *Did the Greeks Believe in Their Myths?*, translated by P. Wissing (University of Chicago Press).

Vickery, J. (1973), *The Literary Impact of the Golden Bough* (Princeton University Press).

Vincent, J.-C. (2003), 'Le *xoanon* chez Pausanias: Littératures et réalités culturelles', *Dialogues d'histoire ancienne* 29, 31-75.

Voyatzis, M.E. (1990), *The Early Sanctuary of Athena Alea at Tegea* (Paul Åströms Förlag).

Voyatzis, M.E. (1997), 'Illuminating the Dark Age: An Examination of the Early Iron Age Pottery From Tegea', *AJA* 101, 349-50.

Wagstaff, J.M. (2001), 'Pausanias and the Topographers: the Case of Colonel Leake', in S.E. Alcock, J.F. Cherry and J. Elsner (eds), *Pausanias: Travel and Memory in Roman Greece* (Oxford University Press), 190-206.

Walbank, F.W. (1962) 'Polemic in Polybius', *JHS* 52, 1-12.

Walker, A.D. (1993), '*Enargeia* and the Spectator in Greek Historiography', *TAPA* 123, 353-77.

Webster, T.B.L. (1967), *The Tragedies of Euripides* (Methuen).

Weiss, R. (1969), *The Renaissance Discovery of Classical Antiquity* (Basil Blackwell).

Westlake, H.D. (1987), 'Diodorus and the Expedition of Cyrus', *Phoenix* 41, 241-54.

Bibliography

Westra, H.J. (1995), 'The Pilgrim Egeria's Concept of Place', *Mittellateinisches Jahrbuch* 30, 93-100.

Wheeler, J.R. (1896), 'Corelli's Maps of Athens', *Harvard Studies in Classical Philology* 7, 177-89.

Wheler, G. (1682), *A Journey Into Greece... in company of Dr. Spon of Lyons. In six books* (William Cademan & Robert Kettlewell).

Whitmarsh, T. (2001a), '"Greece is the World": Exile and Identity in the Second Sophistic', in S. Goldhill (ed.), *Being Greek under Rome* (Cambridge University Press), 269-305.

Whitmarsh, T. (2001b), *Greek Literature and the Roman Empire: The Politics of Imitation* (Oxford University Press).

Whittaker, H. (1991), 'Pausanias and his Use of Inscriptions', *Symbolae Osloenses* 66, 171-86.

Wide, S. (1893), *Lakonische Kulte* (Teubner).

Wilamowitz-Möllendorff, U.v. (1877), 'Die Thukydideslegende', *Hermes* 12, 326-67.

Wilcken, U. (1910), 'Die attische Periegese von Hawara', in *Genethliakon*, Festschrift Carl Robert (Weidmannsche Buchhandlung), 191-225.

Williams, H. et al. (1997), 'Excavations at Ancient Stymphalos, 1996', *EMC* 16, 23-73.

Williams, H. et al. (2002), 'Excavations at Ancient Stymphalos, 1999-2002', *Mouseion* 46, 135-88.

Williamson, G. (2005), 'Mucianus and a Touch of the Miraculous: Pilgrimage and Tourism in Roman Asia Minor', in J. Elsner and I. Rutherford (eds), *Pilgrimage in Graeco-Roman and Christian Antiquity* (Oxford University Press), 219-52.

Wilkinson, J. (1981), *Egeria's Travels* (SPCK).

Winckelmann, J.J. (1964), *Geschichte der Kunst des Altertums: Vollständige Ausgabe herausgegeben von William Senff* (Hermann Böhlaus Nachfolger).

Winckelmann, J.J. (2006), *History of the Art of Antiquity: Introduction by Alex Potts. Translation by Harry Francis Mallgrave* (Getty Research Institute).

Winkler, J.J. (1985), *Auctor and Actor: A Narratological Reading of Apuleius' Golden Ass* (University of California Press).

Winter, F.E. (1971), *Greek Fortifications* (Routledge & Kegan Paul).

Wolters, P. (1915) 'Cyriacus in Mykene und am Tainaron', *Athenische Mitteilungen* 40, 91-105.

Woodward, C. (2001), *In Ruins* (Chatto & Windus).

Woolf, G. (1994), 'Becoming Roman, Staying Greek: Culture, Identity and the Civilising Process in the Roman East', *PCPS* 40, 116-43.

Wycherley, R.E. (1959), 'Pausanias in the Agora of Athens', *GRBS* 2, 21-4.

Wycherley, R.E. (1963), 'Pausanias at Athens, II', *GRBS* 4, 157-75.

Zanker, P. (1995), *Die Maske des Sokrates: Das Bild des Intellektuellen in der antiken Kunst* (C.H. Beck).

Zizza, C. (2006), *Le iscrizioni nella Periegesi di Pausania* (Edizioni ETS).

Index Locorum

Passages that appear in bold are discussed in the main text, all the others are cited in the notes.

Aelian *Varia Historia* 12.61: 27n73
Aphthonios 2.46-9 (Spengel): 110n35
Apollodoros 2.4.7: 99n43, 3.9.1: 99n43, 3.9.2: 97n29
Apuleius
  Apologia 23: 25n50
  Florida 20.9-10: 37n38
  Metamorphoses 1.21-2: 36n25, 11.27-8: 25n50
Aristeides 26.100-1: **33n6**, 36.1: 41n62, 55n55, 47.17: 24n45, 48.12-13: 49n21, 50.63-108: 25n53, 50.102: 24n45
  Sacred Tales 4.4: 35n18
Aristophanes
  Birds 868: 2n3
  Knights 559: 2n3
Arrian
  Anabasis Proem: 51n35
  Periplous 9.1: 108n15
Athenagoras *Leg.* 17: 27n74
Cicero
  Ad Familiares 4.5.4: **143n41**, 143n42
  Ad Atticum 6.1.26: 107n13
  De Finibus 5.1.1-2: 143n39
  De Officiis 3.46: 86n67
Dikaiarchos F. 33 (Wehrli): 37n35
Dio Chrysostom 1.50-6: 55n55, 1.52-3: **62n15**, 7.1-7: 55n55, 12.25: 38n42, 12.44-5: 116n70, 12.46: 114n58, 12.53: 116n71, 12.56-7: 116n71, 12.64-81: 114n58, 18.6-17: 26n57, 33.1: 30n94, 44.6: 25n52
Diodoros 1.96: 37n33, 37n35, 14.19-31: 51n30, 15.66.3-4: 83n50
Favorinus *De Exilio* 10.4: 37n31
Hanno 1: 49n21, 1.8: **49n22**
Herodotos 1.5: 145n50, 1.29-33:

37n35, 1.30: **37n34**, 1.66: 93n13, 98n34, 98n38, 1.66-8: 93n12, 97n30, 1.67.1: 98n39, 1.67-8: 99n41, 1.183.2-3: 54n49, 2.4: 37n33, 2.20-3: 44n3, 2.29.1: 54n49, 2.49-50: 37n33, 2.58: 37n33, 2.64: 37n33, 2.99.1: 54n49, 2.99-144: 37n33, 2.123.1: 54n49, 2.147.1: 54n49, 2.148.5-6: 54n49, 3.139: **33n3**, 4.13-16: 50n28, 4.16.1-2: 54n49, 4.36: 44n3, 4.44: 50n25, 4.76-7: 37n35, 7.145: 84n57, 7.153-63: 84n57, 7.202: 97n30, 9.26: 97n30, 9.26-8: 93n12, 9.35: 97n30, 9.56: 93n12, 97n30, 100n49, 9.60-2: 93n12, 97n30, 100n49, 9.70: 93n12, 93n13, 97n30, 98n34, 100n49, 9.122: 8n26
Hekataios *FGrHist* 1 F.27: 81n36, F.29: 99n43, 102n58
Herakleides 1.8: **63n17**, 1.9: 59n9
Hermogenes 2.16-17 (Spengel): 110n35
Hesiod
  Fr. 165 (Merkelbach-West): 102n58
  Works and Days 618-40: **33n4**
Homer
  Iliad 2.484-760: 6n18, 52n40, 68n34, 2.511: 92n7, 2.570: 57n5, 2.606: 6n19, 2.607: 93n12, 97n30, 2.815-77: 52n40, 17.307-11: 92n7, 18.478-607: 110n33
  Odyssey 1.3: **37n32**, 9.12: 46n7, 9.106-55: 62n13, 9.252-71: 46n9, 11.362-72: 46n8, 11.581: 92n7, 13.96-112: 62n13, 13.194-6: 62n13, 13.236-49: 62n13, 13.256-86: 46n11, 13.291-5: **46-7n11**, 14.199-359: 46n12, 19.172-307: 46n12, 19.203:

General Index

Achaia, 5, 59, 77, 151
Achaia, Roman province, 6, 29
Achaian League, 74, 78, 80, 86, 89
acroliths, 109
Aelian, *Varia Historia*, 27, 27n67
Africa, 67; North Africa, 37-8, 53;
    West Africa, 49
Agamemnon, 55, 73
agora, 17, 91, 95; Athens, 76, 94, 100;
    Messene, 17; Tegea, 40, 93, 95,
    98-9
agriculture, 59, 62-3
Aigeira, 108
Aigina, 59, 143; temple of Aphaia, 125
aitia, 40, 74-5
Aitolia, 6
Akarnania, 6
Aleos, 95-7, 99
Alexander historians, 51-2
Alexander Romance, 52
Alexander the Great, 6, 29, 38, 51-2,
    88
Alkinoos, 44, 46
Alpheios, 62
altars, 95-6, 100, 102
Altertumswissenschaften, 125
amber, 110
Amphiktyony (of Delphi), 6
Amphissa, 147
Amyklai, Throne of Apollo, 41n61,
    107n9, 113
Anacharsis, 37, 56
Anatolia, 51
ancient art, modern approaches,
    120-5, 130
ancient sites, 1, 3, 12-14, 94-5, 120,
    125, 128, 131-2, 133, 135-9, 141-2,
    144-5
animals (fauna), 27n66, 49, 51-2, 59
anthropology, 126-7
Antinoos, 27
antiquarian travel, 131-2, 135-46
Antoninus Pius, 24

Antoninus Pythodorus, 25n55, 27
Aphrodite, 17, 20, 21, 68, 95
Apollo, 17, 95, 108, 113
Apollonios of Tyana, 37, 47
Apuleius, 25, 27n70, 37;
    Metamorphoses, 48
archaeology, 12-14, 93-4, 118, 125-8,
    136, 139; classical, 15, 125, 128-9,
    131
archaic style, 112-13
architects, 121
architecture, 38, 106-7; orders, 107,
    108
archon dates, 84
Ares, 98
Argolid, 4, 69, 70-1, 72, 77, 131-2, 151
Argonauts, 83
Argos, 72, 131, 151
Arimaspians, 50
Aristarchos (guide at Olympia), 36
Aristeas of Prokonnesos, 50
Aristeides, 25, 27n70, 33, 41, 55;
    Praise of Rome, 33; *Sacred Tales*,
    20, 47
Aristomenes, 83
Aristotle, 51
Arkadia, 59, 61-62, 64, 67-8, 72, 74,
    77-8, 93, 96-7, 139, 145, 151;
    Arkadian genealogy 82-3, 97;
    history 77-8, 96-7
Arrian, 55; *Indike*, 52, 55n61;
    Periplous of the Black Sea, 49
art history, 19, 106, 120-5; modern
    (Winckelmann), 123-4; in
    Pausanias, 114-15
art, 105-17; ancient connoisseurship,
    106-9; ancient criticism, 107-9,
    111-12, 113-14, 111; material,
    107, 109-10, 112, 116, 122, 123;
    public art, 106-7, 110, 115-17,
    124, 130, 141; and religion,
    113-16; as source, 114-15; style
    analysis, 107-9, 112-13, 115;

217

Kalydonian boar hunt, 96-8, 101-2
Kaphyai, 150
Kebes, *Pinax*, 111n40
Kenchreai, 57-8
Kerne, 49
Kinaithon, 18-19
Kleitor, 61, 149
kômê, 92
Kroisos, 37
Ktesias of Knidos, 44, 50, 52

Lakedaimon, see Sparta
Lakonia, 72, 74, 77, 84, 95
Lamian War, 76-7
landscape, 53, 54, 128, 153, 154;
    description, 59-63, 67-71; Greek,
    131-2, 136-7, 140-5;
    Mediterranean, 61-2
Latin, 29, 35, 118-19
Leake, William, 135-6, 141
Lebadeia, 42
Lechaion, 57-8
Ledon, 92
Lesche of the Knidians, 41n61, 107,
    112-13
Leto, 92
Leuktra, 77, 84
linear landscape description, 67-71, 90
lists, 27, 60, 67, 68, 70, 84, 87, 91-2,
    97, 107, 110, 112-13, 115
literary tradition, 15, 18, 38, 40, 42,
    54, 92, 97, 100-2, 106, 128, 142,
    152-3
local culture, 53, 152
local customs, 1, 10-11, 53, 74, 81, 92
local informants, 30, 35-6, 40, 69, 79,
    101, 113, 136, 146, 152-3; Egypt,
    34; guides, 107n11, 113; modern,
    135, 146-7
local tradition, 17-18, 18-19, 29-30,
    40-1, 54, 56, 79, 80-2, 91, 93,
    99-102, 114-15, 144, 152
logbooks, 48-9
logoi, 7-8, 10-12, 18, 27, 53, 96, 115; in
    Herodotos, 54
Lokris, Opountian, 5, 6, 8
Longus, 27
looting: modern, 125; Roman, 28, 87,
    107
Lucian, 20, 27, 27n70, 37, 44, 46, 55,
    109, 109n23, 111-12; *Ass*, 48; *De*

Domo, 110; *Dea Syria*, 20, 54,
    55n61, 103; *Eikones*, 108; *How to
    write history*, 54; *Verae Historiae*,
    44; *Zeuxis*, 111-12
Lydia, 21
Lykomidai, 36
Lykosoura, 10

Macedonia, 28, 65, 7-78, 88-9, 124
Magnesia on Sipylos, 21-2, 25, 139
Mantinea, 10, 67, 68-9, 79, 101, 140
maps, 53, 60, 64-7, 69, 137; modern,
    132-4
Marathon, 87
marble, 17, 109, 131
Marcus Aurelius, 24
Mardonios, 98
Mark Antony, 101
market-place, see agora
Marpessa, 98
Maurya, 52
Mediterranean, 6, 33, 47, 49, 55, 64,
    67, 152; landscape, 61-2
Megalopolis, 68, 80, 145
Megara, 4, 58, 77, 143; Megarid, 52,
    59, 64
Megasthenes, 52
Meleager, 97
Melos, 86
Memnon (Statue of Amenhotep III),
    32, 34
memorial landscape, 73, 77, 79-80, 90,
    96-102, 103, 114, 116, 142-5, 152
Mesopotamia, 37, 51
Messene, 17, 80; agora, 17
Messenia, 5, 77; history, 10, 81-2
Messenian Wars, 74, 77, 82-3
military campaigns, 50-2, 63
mimesis, 109
monuments, 17, 20, 30, 53, 59, 76, 79,
    80, 83, 87, 91, 96-104, 115, 131-2,
    135, 139, 141, 143-5, 144, 146, 152
Morea (Peloponnese), 133-4
mountains, 39n48, 60, 67-8, 70, 72
Mummius, 86
Musurus, Marcus, 118-19
Mycenae, 131-2, 139
Myron of Priene, 82-3
Mysians, 102
mythology, 12, 118, 126-7, 141
myths, 19, 20-1, 40, 59, 72, 74, 77-8,

221